SOURCES

Notable Selections in *Sociology*

About the Editors

KURT FINSTERBUSCH received his bachelor's degree in history from Princeton University in 1957 and a bachelor of divinity degree from Grace Theological Seminary in 1960. His Ph.D. in sociology, from Columbia University, was conferred in 1969. He has authored three books: *Understanding Social Impacts* (Sage Publications, 1980); *Social Research for Policy Decisions* (Wadsworth, 1980), with Annabelle Bender Motz; and *Organizational Change as a Development Strategy* (Lynne Rienner Publishers, 1987). He is currently a professor of sociology at the University of Maryland, College Park, and is the academic editor for the Dushkin Publishing Group's *Annual Editions: Sociology.*

JANET S. SCHWARTZ received her bachelor's degree in sociology from City College of New York in 1952, a master's degree in organizational behavior from Cornell University in 1961, and a doctorate in sociology from Cornell University in 1967. From 1967 to 1983, she taught and conducted her research in the sociology departments for Wells College in New York, George Mason University in Virginia, the University of Maryland, and the American University in Washington, D.C. She currently does research and consulting work as an independent sociologist, and her research interests and writings center around the Soviet Union and East European societies, especially on work and organizations, civil-military relations, and social stratification.

SOURCES
Notable Selections
in *Sociology*

Edited by

KURT FINSTERBUSCH

University of Maryland

JANET S. SCHWARTZ

DPG

The Dushkin Publishing Group, Inc.

We dedicate this book to John, Alec, Ned, Joe, David, Neil, Katy, and Adam. We have tried to pass the best part of ourselves onto them, even as profound, important, and fascinating ideas are passed from generation to generation in *Sources: Notable Selections in Sociology.*

Library of Congress Catalog Card Number: 91-77884

Manufactured in the United States of America

First Edition, First Printing

ISBN: 1-56134-055-3

ACKNOWLEDGMENTS

1.1. From Peter L. Berger, *Invitation to Sociology: A Humanistic Perspective* (Anchor Books, 1963). Copyright © 1963 by Peter L. Berger. Reprinted by permission of Doubleday, a division of Bantam Doubleday Dell Publishing Group, Inc.

1.2. From C. Wright Mills, *The Sociological Imagination* (Oxford University Press, 1959). Copyright © 1959 by Oxford University Press, Inc.; renewed 1987 by Yaraslava Mills. Reprinted by permission of Oxford University Press, Inc.

2.1. From Clyde Kluckhohn, *Mirror for Man: The Relation of Anthropology to Modern Life* (McGraw-Hill, 1949). Copyright © 1949 by George E. Taylor. Reprinted by permission.

2.2. From Horace Miner, "Body Ritual Among the Nacirema," *American Anthropologist*, vol. 38, no. 3 (June 1956). Copyright © 1956 by the American Anthropological Association. Reprinted by permission. Not for further reproduction.

Acknowledgments and copyrights are continued at the back of the book on pages 363–365, which constitute an extension of the copyright page.

Preface

*T*he subject matter of sociology is ourselves—people interacting with one another in groups. Sociologists seek to understand in a systematic and scientific way the social behavior of human beings and human arrangements. Sociologists question seemingly familiar and commonplace aspects of our social lives, and offer novel and surprising answers. To study sociology is to explore society in new and dynamic ways.

Sociology is a form of scientific inquiry that gives us the intellectual tools for understanding our world more profoundly. As a discipline, sociology has evolved its own history of ideas and thinkers, research methods, and theories. In this volume, we have put into your hands directly those researchers and writers whose works have enduring value for the study of society.

Sources: Notable Selections in Sociology brings together 44 selections (classic articles, book excerpts, and case studies) that have shaped the study of society and our contemporary understanding of it. We have included the works of distinguished sociological observers, past and present, from Marx and Engels on class to Mills on the sociological imagination to Bernard on the female world and Bell on technology and social change. The selections also reflect the long-standing tradition in sociology of incorporating useful insights from related disciplines. Thus, the volume includes contributions by anthropologists, political scientists, psychologists, ecologists, and economists.

Each selection was chosen because, in our opinion, it has helped shape the sociological inquiry. Each contains essential ideas used in the sociological enterprise, or has served as some kind of a touchstone for other scholars. As a whole, *Sources* is designed to be an accessible, reasonably comprehensive introduction to sociological classics. We have tried to select readings across a broad spectrum, i.e., the ideas, insights, and themes presented in these selections are not necessarily limited to a particular society. Accordingly, they should enable students to analyze the behaviors and institutions of many nations.

Plan of the book These selections are well suited to courses that attempt to convey the richness of the sociological perspective and require more than a superficial grasp of major sociological concepts and theories. The selections are organized topically around the major areas of study within sociology: the selections in Part 1 introduce the sociological perspective; Part 2, the individual and society; Part 3, stratification; Part 4, social institutions; and Part 5, society

i

and social change. Each selection is preceded by a headnote that establishes the relevance of the selection and provides biographical information on the author.

Supplements An *Instructor's Manual with Test Questions* (multiple-choice and essay) is available through the publisher for the instructor using *Sources* in the classroom.

We welcome your comments and observations about the selections in this volume and encourage you to write to us with suggestions for other selections to include or changes to consider. Please send your remarks to us in care of The Dushkin Publishing Group, Sluice Dock, Guilford, CT 06437.

Kurt Finsterbusch

Janet S. Schwartz

Contents

CHAPTER 5 Deviance and Social Control 81

PART FOUR *Social Institutions* 197

PART ONE

Introduction to Sociology

CHAPTER 1 The Sociological Perspective

1.1 PETER L. BERGER

Sociology as an Individual Pastime

What is sociology and what are the defining characteristics of a sociologist? Among the best answers to these questions are those given by Peter L. Berger. Berger (b. 1929) is the director of the Institute for the Study of Economic Culture at Boston University and a prominent contemporary sociologist who is known for his pithy prose. In the following selection from his book *Invitation to Sociology*, Berger explains that sociology involves the passion to deeply understand the everyday social reality around us. The sociologist is a passionate questioner. Sociologists also desire to help people and improve society, but these characteristics are not unique to sociologists. They share these passions with many citizens and many other professions. According to Berger, sociologists are relatively unique in that they seek to understand society not as it is taught in Sunday school (i.e., not the way it should be) but as it actually is. Those who fear or are eager to avoid what Berger calls "shocking discoveries" should best stay away from sociology. *Invitation to Sociology,* first published in 1963, is considered to be one of the best statements on sociology and sociologists.

Key Concept: sociology as the passion to understand

*T*he sociologist . . . is someone concerned with understanding society in a disciplined way. The nature of this discipline is scientific. This means that what the sociologist finds and says about the social phenomena he studies

3

occurs within a certain rather strictly defined frame of reference. One of the main characteristics of this scientific frame of reference is that operations are bound by certain rules of evidence. As a scientist, the sociologist tries to be objective, to control his personal preferences and prejudices, to perceive clearly rather than to judge normatively. This restraint, of course, does not embrace the totality of the sociologist's existence as a human being, but is limited to his operations *qua* sociologist. Nor does the sociologist claim that his frame of reference is the only one within which society can be looked at. For that matter, very few scientists in any field would claim today that one should look at the world only scientifically. The botanist looking at a daffodil has no reason to dispute the right of the poet to look at the same object in a very different manner. There are many ways of playing. The point is not that one denies other people's games but that one is clear about the rules of one's own. The game of the sociologist, then, uses scientific rules. As a result, the sociologist must be clear in his own mind as to the meaning of these rules. That is, he must concern himself with methodological questions. Methodology does not constitute his goal. The latter, let us recall once more, is the attempt to understand society. Methodology helps in reaching this goal. . . . Finally, the interest of the sociologist is primarily theoretical. That is, he is interested in understanding for its own sake. He may be aware of or even concerned with the practical applicability and consequences of his findings, but at that point he leaves the sociological frame of reference as such and moves into realms of values, beliefs and ideas that he shares with other men who are not sociologists. . . .

We would say then that the sociologist (that is, the one we would really like to invite to our game) is a person intensively, endlessly, shamelessly interested in the doings of men. His natural habitat is all the human gathering places of the world, wherever men come together. The sociologist may be interested in many other things. But his consuming interest remains in the world of men, their institutions, their history, their passions. And since he is interested in men, nothing that men do can be altogether tedious for him. He will naturally be interested in the events that engage men's ultimate beliefs, their moments of tragedy and grandeur and ecstasy. But he will also be fascinated by the commonplace, the everyday. He will know reverence, but this reverence will not prevent him from wanting to see and to understand. He may sometimes feel revulsion or contempt. But this also will not deter him from wanting to have his questions answered. The sociologist, in his quest for understanding, moves through the world of men without respect for the usual lines of demarcation. Nobility and degradation, power and obscurity, intelligence and folly—these are equally *interesting* to him, however unequal they may be in his personal values or tastes. Thus his questions may lead him to all possible levels of society, the best and the least known places, the most respected and the most despised. And, if he is a good sociologist, he will find himself in all these places because his own questions have so taken possession of him that he has little choice but to seek for answers. . . .

The sociologist will occupy himself with matters that others regard as too sacred or as too distasteful for dispassionate investigation. He will find rewarding the company of priests or of prostitutes, depending not on his personal preferences but on the questions he happens to be asking at the moment. He will also concern himself with matters that others may find much too boring. He will be interested in the human interaction that goes with warfare or with great intellectual discoveries, but also in the relations between people employed in a restaurant or between a group of little girls playing with their dolls. His main focus of attention is not the ultimate significance of what men do, but the action in itself, as another example of the infinite richness of human conduct. So much for the image of our playmate.

In these journeys through the world of men the sociologist will inevitably encounter other professional Peeping Toms. Sometimes these will resent his presence, feeling that he is poaching on their preserves. In some places the sociologist will meet up with the economist, in others with the political scientist, in yet others with the psychologist or the ethnologist. Yet chances are that the questions that have brought him to these same places are different from the ones that propelled his fellow-trespassers. The sociologist's questions always remain essentially the same: "What are people doing with each other here?" "What are their relationships to each other?" "How are these relationships organized in institutions?" "What are the collective ideas that move men and institutions?" In trying to answer these questions in specific instances, the sociologist will, of course, have to deal with economic or political matters, but he will do so in a way rather different from that of the economist or the political scientist. . . .

The fascination of sociology lies in the fact that its perspective makes us see in a new light the very world in which we have lived all our lives. This also constitutes a transformation of consciousness. Moreover, this transformation is more relevant existentially than that of many other intellectual disciplines, because it is more difficult to segregate in some special compartment of the mind. The astronomer does not live in the remote galaxies, and the nuclear physicist can, outside his laboratory, eat and laugh and marry and vote without thinking about the insides of the atom. The geologist looks at rocks only at appropriate times, and the linguist speaks English with his wife. The sociologist lives in society, on the job and off it. His own life, inevitably, is part of his subject matter. Men being what they are, sociologists too manage to segregate their professional insights from their everyday affairs. But it is a rather difficult feat to perform in good faith.

The sociologist moves in the common world of men, close to what most of them would call real. The categories he employs in his analyses are only refinements of the categories by which other men live—power, class, status, race, ethnicity. As a result, there is a deceptive simplicity and obviousness about some sociological investigations. One reads them, nods at the familiar scene, remarks that one has heard all this before and don't people have better things to do than to waste their time on truisms—until one is suddenly brought up against an insight that radically questions everything one had previously assumed about this familiar scene. This is the point at which one begins to sense the excitement of sociology.

Let us take a specific example. Imagine a sociology class in a Southern college where almost all the students are white Southerners. Imagine a lecture on the subject of the racial system of the South. The lecturer is talking here of matters that have been familiar to his students from the time of their infancy. Indeed, it may be that they are much more familiar with the minutiae of this system than he is. They are quite bored as a result. It seems to them that he is only using more pretentious words to describe what they already know. Thus he may use the term "caste," one commonly used now by American sociologists to describe the Southern racial system. But in explaining the term he shifts to traditional Hindu society, to make it clearer. He then goes on to analyze the magical beliefs inherent in cast tabus, the social dynamics of commensalism and connubium [two types of relationship between two individuals], the economic interests concealed within the system, the way in which religious beliefs relate to the tabus, the effects of the caste system upon the industrial development of the society and vice versa—all in India. But suddenly India is not very far away at all. The lecture then goes back to its Southern theme. The familiar now seems not quite so familiar any more. Questions are raised that are new, perhaps raised angrily, but raised all the same. And at least some of the students have begun to understand that there are functions involved in this business of race that they have not read about in the newspapers (at least not those in their hometowns) and that their parents have not told them—partly, at least, because neither the newspapers nor the parents knew about them.

It can be said that the first wisdom of sociology is this—things are not what they seem. This too is a deceptively simple statement. It ceases to be simple after a while. Social reality turns out to have many layers of meaning. The discovery of each new layer changes the perception of the whole. . . .

People who like to avoid shocking discoveries, who prefer to believe that society is just what they were taught in Sunday School, who like the safety of the rules and the maxims of what Alfred Schutz [educator and author (1899–1959)] has called the "world-taken-for-granted," should stay away from sociology. People who feel no temptation before closed doors, who have no curiosity about human beings, who are content to admire scenery without wondering about the people who live in those houses on the other side of that river, should probably also stay away from sociology. They will find it unpleasant or, at any rate, unrewarding. People who are interested in human beings only if they can change, convert or reform them should also be warned, for they will find sociology much less useful than they hoped. And people whose interest is mainly in their own conceptual constructions will do just as well to turn to the study of little white mice. Sociology will be satisfying, in the long run, only to those who can think of nothing more entrancing than to watch men and to understand things human.

It may now be clear that we have, albeit deliberately, understated the case in the title of this chapter. To be sure, sociology is an individual pastime in the sense that it interests some men and bores others. Some like to observe human beings, others to experiment with mice. The world is big enough to hold all kinds and there is no logical priority for one interest as against another. But the word "pastime" is weak in describing what we mean. Sociology is more like a passion. The sociological perspective is more like a demon that possesses one, that drives one compellingly, again and again, to the questions that are its own. An introduction to sociology is, therefore, an invitation to a very special kind of passion. No passion is without its dangers. The sociologist who sells his wares should make sure that he clearly pronounces a *caveat emptor* quite early in the transaction.

Peter L. Berger

The Sociological Imagination

C. Wright Mills (1916–1962) was a leader of mid-twentieth-century American sociological thought and supported the idea that social scientists should play an active role in society, as opposed to merely observing and reporting on it. Outspoken and radical in his views, Mills was an inspiration to many young sociologists who followed in his footsteps in the 1960s. In the selection from his work reprinted here, Mills discusses what he calls the "sociological imagination." He notes that problems such as divorce and unemployment tend to be perceived as only the problems of individual men and women. However, if half of all marriages end in divorce, as is currently the case in the United States, for example, then divorce should also be considered a social problem, the result of numerous forces outside of the individual and sometimes beyond the control of the individual. Similarly, when unemployment is high, it is necessary to examine social, political, and economic factors that cause loss of employment, rather than to seek a purely personal explanation. According to Mills, whose book *The Sociological Imagination* (Oxford University Press, 1959) helped illuminate the purposes of sociology, it is the task of the sociologist to explain the distinction between the personal and the social and the relationship among the social forces that cause specific problems.

Key Concept: the sociological imagination

Nowadays men often feel that their private lives are a series of traps. They sense that within their everyday worlds, they cannot overcome their troubles, and in this feeling, they are often quite correct: What ordinary men are directly aware of and what they try to do are bounded by the private orbits in which they live; their visions and their powers are limited to close-up scenes of job, family, neighborhood; in other milieux, they move vicariously and remain spectators. And the more aware they become, however vaguely, of ambitions and of threats which transcend their immediate locales, the more trapped they seem to feel.

Underlying this sense of being trapped are seemingly impersonal changes in the very structure of continent-wide societies. The facts of contemporary history are also facts about the success and the failure of individual men and women. When a society is industrialized, a peasant becomes a worker; a feudal lord is liquidated or becomes a businessman. When classes rise or fall, a man is employed or unemployed; when the rate of investment goes up or down, a man takes new heart or goes broke. When wars happen, an insurance salesman becomes a rocket launcher; a store clerk, a radar man; a wife lives alone; a child grows up without a father. Neither the life of an individual nor the history of a society can be understood without understanding both.

Yet men do not usually define the troubles they endure in terms of historical change and institutional contradiction. The well-being they enjoy, they do not usually impute to the big ups and downs of the societies in which they live. Seldom aware of the intricate connection between the patterns of their own lives and the course of world history, ordinary men do not usually know what this connection means for the kinds of men they are becoming and for the kinds of history-making in which they might take part. They do not possess the quality of mind essential to grasp the interplay of man and society, of biography and history, of self and world. They cannot cope with their personal troubles in such ways as to control the structural transformations that usually lie behind them. . . .

It is not only information that they need—in this Age of Fact, information often dominates their attention and overwhelms their capacities to assimilate it. It is not only the skills of reason that they need—although their struggles to acquire these often exhaust their limited moral energy.

What they need, and what they feel they need, is a quality of mind that will help them to use information and to develop reason in order to achieve lucid summations of what is going on in the world and of what may be happening within themselves. It is this quality, I am going to contend, that journalists and scholars, artists and publics, scientists and editors are coming to expect of what may be called the sociological imagination.

The sociological imagination enables its possessor to understand the larger historical scene in terms of its meaning for the inner life and the external career of a variety of individuals. It enables him to take into account how individuals, in the welter of their daily experience, often become falsely conscious of their social positions. Within that welter, the framework of modern society is sought, and within that framework the psychologies of a variety of men and women are formulated. By such means the personal uneasiness of individuals is focused upon explicit troubles and the indifference of publics is transformed into involvement with public issues.

The first fruit of this imagination—and the first lesson of the social science that embodies it—is the idea that the individual can understand his own experience and gauge his own fate only by locating himself within his period, that he can know his own chances in life only by becoming aware of those of all individuals in his circumstances. In many ways it is a terrible lesson; in many ways a magnificent one. We do not know the limits of man's capacities for supreme effort or willing degradation, for agony or glee, for pleasurable brutality or the sweetness of reason. But in our time we have come to know that the limits of 'human nature' are frighteningly broad. We have come to know that every individual lives, from one generation to the next, in some society; that he lives out a biography, and that he lives it out within some historical sequence. By the fact of his living he contributes, however minutely, to the shaping of this society and to the course of its history, even as he is made by society and by its historical push and shove. . . .

No social study that does not come back to the problems of biography, of history and of their intersections within a society has completed its intellectual journey. Whatever the specific problems of the classic social analysts, however limited or however broad the features of social reality they have examined, those who have been imaginatively aware of the promise of their work have consistently asked three sorts of questions:

(1) What is the structure of this particular society as a whole? What are its essential components, and how are they related to one another? How does it differ from other varieties of social order? Within it, what is the meaning of any particular feature for its continuance and for its change?

(2) Where does this society stand in human history? What are the mechanics by which it is changing? What is its place within and its meaning for the development of humanity as a whole? How does any particular feature we are examining affect, and how is it affected by, the historical period in which it moves? And this period—what are its essential features? How does it differ from other periods? What are its characteristic ways of history-making?

(3) What varieties of men and women now prevail in this society and in this period? And what varieties are coming to prevail? In what ways are they selected and formed, liberated and repressed, made sensitive and blunted? What kinds of 'human nature' are revealed in the conduct and character we observe in this society in this period? And what is the meaning for 'human nature' of each and every feature of the society we are examining?

Whether the point of interest is a great power state or a minor literary mood, a family, a prison, a creed—these are the kinds of questions the best social analysts have asked. They are the intellectual pivots of classic studies of man in society—and they are the questions inevitably raised by any mind possessing the sociological imagination. For that imagination is the capacity to shift from one perspective to another—from the political to the psychological; from examination of a single family to comparative assessment of the national budgets of the world; from the theological school to the military establishment; from considerations of an oil industry to studies of contemporary poetry. It is the capacity to range from the most impersonal and remote transformations to the most intimate features of the human self—and to see the relations between the two. Back of its use there is always the urge to know the social and historical meaning of the individual in the society and in the period in which he has his quality and his being. . . .

Perhaps the most fruitful distinction with which the sociological imagination works is between 'the personal troubles of milieu' and 'the public issues of social structure.' This distinction is an essential tool of the sociological imagination and a feature of all classic work in social science.

Troubles occur within the character of the individual and within the range of his immediate relations with others; they have to do with his self and with those limited areas of social life of which he is directly and personally aware. Accordingly, the statement and the resolution of troubles properly lie within the individual as a biographical entity and within the scope of his immediate milieu—the social setting that is directly open to his personal experience and to some extent his willful activity. A trouble is a private matter: values cherished by an individual are felt by him to be threatened.

Issues have to do with matters that transcend these local environments of the individual and the range of his inner life. They have to do with the organization of many such milieux into the institutions of an historical society as a whole, with the ways in which various milieux overlap and interpenetrate to form the larger structure of social and historical life. An issue is a public matter: some value cherished by publics is felt to be threatened. Often there is a debate about what that value really is and about what it is that really threatens it. This debate is often without focus if only because it is the very nature of an issue, unlike even widespread trouble, that it cannot very well be defined in terms of the immediate and everyday environments of ordinary men. An issue, in fact, often involves a crisis in institutional arrangements, and often too it involves what Marxists call 'contradictions' or 'antagonisms.'

In these terms, consider unemployment. When, in a city of 100,000, only one man is unemployed, that is his personal trouble, and for its relief we properly look to the character of the man, his skills, and his immediate opportunities. But when in a nation of 50 million employees, 15 million men are unemployed, that is an issue, and we may not hope to find its solution within the range of opportunities open to any one individual. The very structure of opportunities has collapsed. Both the correct statement of the problem and the range of possible solutions require us to consider the economic and political institutions of the society, and not merely the personal situation and character of a scatter of individuals.

Consider war. The personal problem of war, when it occurs, may be how to survive it or how to die in it with honor; how to make money out of it; how to climb into the higher safety of the military apparatus; or how to contribute to the war's termination. In short, according to one's values, to find a set of milieux and within it to survive the war or make one's death in it meaningful. But the structural issues of war have to do with its causes; with what types of men it throws up into command; with its effects upon economic and political, family and religious institutions, with the unorganized irresponsibility of a world of nation-states.

Consider marriage. Inside a marriage a man and a woman may experience personal troubles, but when the divorce rate during the first four years of marriage is 250 out of every 1,000 attempts, this is an indication of a structural issue having to do with the institutions of marriage and the family and other institutions that bear upon them.

Or consider the metropolis—the horrible, beautiful, ugly, magnificent sprawl of the great city. For many upper-class people, the personal solution to 'the problem of the city' is to have an apartment with private garage under it in the heart of the city, and forty miles out, a house by Henry Hill, garden by Garrett Eckbo, on a hundred acres of private land. In these two controlled environments—with a small staff at each end and a private helicopter connection—most people could solve many of the problems of personal milieux caused by the facts of the city. But all this, however splendid, does not solve the public issues that the structural fact of the city poses. What should be done with this wonderful monstrosity? Break it all up into scattered units, combining residence and work? Refurbish it as it stands? Or, after evacuation, dynamite it and build new cities according to new plans in new places? What should those plans be? And who is to decide and to accomplish whatever choice is made? These are structural issues; to confront them and to solve them requires us to consider political and economic issues that affect innumerable milieux.

In so far as an economy is so arranged that slumps occur, the problem of unemployment becomes incapable of personal solution. In so far as war is inherent in the nation-state system and in the uneven industrialization of the world, the ordinary individual in his restricted milieu will be powerless—with or without psychiatric aid—to solve the troubles this system or lack of system imposes upon him. In so far as the family as an institution turns women into darling little slaves and men into their chief providers and unweaned dependents, the problem of a satisfactory marriage remains incapable of purely private solution. In so far as the overdeveloped megalopolis and the overdeveloped automobile are built-in features of the overdeveloped society, the issues of urban living will not be solved by personal ingenuity and private wealth.

What we experience in various and specific milieux, I have noted, is often caused by structural changes. Accordingly, to understand the changes of many personal milieux we are required to look beyond them. And the number and variety of such structural changes increase as the institutions within which we live become more embracing and more intricately connected with one another. To be aware of the idea of social structure and to use it with sensibility is to be capable of tracing such linkages among a great variety of milieux. To be able to do that is to possess the sociological imagination.

PART TWO

The Individual and Society

CHAPTER 2 Culture

2.1 CLYDE KLUCKHOHN

The Meaning of Culture

Culture is a key concept in sociology and basic to understanding all social behavior. For sociologists, *culture* does not mean good manners, fine wine, or the behavior of individuals who are perceived as cultured. Rather, *culture* refers to the total way of life commonly followed by the members of a society. It includes values, beliefs, customs, technology, religion, and the roles people play. In the following selection, anthropologist Clyde Kluckhohn explains how knowledge of a society's culture can lead to an understanding of human behavior. He points out that culture is learned and that each society transmits informally and formally the required rules that regulate behavior in small and large ways.

Culture explains why people act so differently, and, in what is considered to be one of the best explanations of culture, Kluckhohn adeptly uses these differences to teach the significance of culture. Kluckhohn (1905–1960) was a long-time professor of anthropology at Harvard University and was best known for his demographic studies of the Navaho Indian. Widely respected as a cultural anthropologist, he brought to his studies of cultural patterns rich psychological insights and a systematic method of analyzing values, religion, and ritual.

Key Concept: culture defined as the total way of life of a society's people

Why do the Chinese dislike milk and milk products? Why would the Japanese die willingly in a Banzai charge that seemed senseless to Americans? Why do some nations trace descent through the father, others through the

15

mother, still others through both parents? Not because different peoples have different instincts, not because they were destined by God or Fate to different habits, not because the weather is different in China and Japan and the United States. Sometimes shrewd common sense has an answer that is close to that of the anthropologist: "because they were brought up that way." By "culture" anthropology means the total life way of a people, the social legacy the individual acquires from his group. Or culture can be regarded as that part of the environment that is the creation of man. . . .

One of the interesting things about human beings is that they try to understand themselves and their own behavior. While this has been partic-ularly true of Europeans in recent times, there is no group which has not developed a scheme or schemes to explain man's actions. To the insistent human query "why?" the most exciting illumination anthropology has to offer is that of the concept of culture. Its explanatory importance is comparable to categories such as evolution in biology, gravity in physics, disease in medicine. A good deal of human behavior can be understood, and indeed predicted, if we know a people's design for living. Many acts are neither accidental nor due to personal peculiarities nor caused by supernatural forces nor simply mysterious. Even those of us who pride ourselves on our individualism follow most of the time a pattern not of our own making. We brush our teeth on arising. We put on pants—not a loincloth or a grass skirt. We eat three meals a day—not four or five or two. We sleep in a bed—not in a hammock or on a sheep pelt. I do not have to know the individual and his life history to be able to predict these and countless other regularities, including many in the thinking process, of all Americans who are not incarcerated in jails or hospitals for the insane.

To the American woman a system of plural wives seem "instinctively" abhorrent. She cannot understand how any woman can fail to be jealous and uncomfortable if she must share her husband with other women. She feels it "unnatural" to accept such a situation. On the other hand, a Koryak woman of Siberia, for example, would find it hard to understand how a woman could be so selfish and so undesirous of feminine companionship in the home as to wish to restrict her husband to one mate.

Some years ago I met in New York City a young man who did not speak a word of English and was obviously bewildered by American ways. By "blood" he was as American as you or I, for his parents had gone from Indiana to China as missionaries. Orphaned in infancy, he was reared by a Chinese family in a remote village. All who met him found him more Chinese than American. The facts of his blue eyes and light hair were less impressive than a Chinese style of gait, Chinese arm and hand movements, Chinese facial expression, and Chinese modes of thought. The biological heritage was American, but the cultural training had been Chinese. He returned to China.

Another example of another kind: I once knew a trader's wife in Arizona who took a somewhat devilish interest in producing a cultural reaction. Guests who came her way were often served delicious sandwiches filled with a meat that seemed to be neither chicken nor tuna fish yet was reminiscent of both. To queries she gave no reply until each had eaten his fill. She then explained that what they had eaten was not chicken, not tuna fish, but the rich, white flesh of freshly killed rattlesnakes. The response was instantaneous—vomiting, often violent vomiting. A biological process is caught in a cultural web. . . .

Culture arises out of human nature, and its forms are restricted both by man's biology and by natural laws. It is equally true that culture channels biological processes—vomiting, weeping, fainting, sneezing, the daily habits of food intake and waste elimination. When a man eats, he is reacting to an internal "drive," namely, hunger contractions consequent upon the lowering of blood sugar, but his precise reaction to these internal stimuli cannot be predicted by physiological knowledge alone. Whether a healthy adult feels hungry twice, three times, or four times a day and the hours at which this feeling recurs is a question of culture. *What* he eats is of course limited by availability, but is also partly regulated by culture. It is a biological fact that some types of berries are poisonous; it is a cultural fact that, a few generations ago, most Americans considered tomatoes to be poisonous and refused to eat them. Such selective, discriminative use of the environment is characteristically cultural. In a still more general sense, too, the process of eating is channeled by culture. Whether a man eats to live, lives to eat, or merely eats and lives is only in part an individual matter, for there are also cultural trends. Emotions are physiological events. Certain situations will evoke fear in people from any culture. But sensations of pleasure, anger, and lust may be stimulated by cultural cues that would leave unmoved someone who has been reared in a different social tradition.

Except in the case of newborn babies and of individuals born with clear-cut structural or functional abnormalities we can observe innate endowments only as modified by cultural training. In a hospital in New Mexico where Zuñi Indian, Navaho Indian, and white American babies are born, it is possible to classify the newly arrived infants as unusually active, average, and quiet. Some babies from each "racial" group will fall into each category, though a higher proportion of the white babies will fall into the unusually active class. But if a Navaho baby, a Zuñi baby, and a white baby—all classified as unusually active at birth—are again observed at the age of two years, the Zuñi baby will no longer seem given to quick and restless activity—*as compared with the white child*—though he may seem so as compared with the other Zuñis of the same age. The Navaho child is likely to fall in between as contrasted with the Zuñi and the white, though he will probably still seem more active than the average Navaho youngster. . . .

Culture is a *way* of thinking, feeling, believing. It is the group's knowledge stored up (in memories of men; in books and objects) for future use. We study the products of this "mental" activity: the overt behavior, the speech and gestures and activities of people, and the tangible results of these things such as tools, houses, cornfields, and what not. . . .

Since culture is an abstraction, it is important not to confuse culture with society. A "society" refers to a group of people who interact more with each other than they do with other individuals—who cooperate with each other for the attainment of certain ends. You can see and indeed count the individuals who make up a society. A "culture" refers to the distinctive ways of life of such a group of people. Not all social events are culturally patterned. New types of circumstances arise for which no cultural solutions have as yet been devised.

A culture constitutes a storehouse of the pooled learning of the group. A rabbit starts life with some innate responses. He can learn from his own experience and perhaps from observing other rabbits. A human infant is born with fewer instincts and greater plasticity. His main task is to learn the answers that persons he will never see, persons long dead, have worked out. Once he has learned the formulas supplied by the culture of his group, most of his behavior becomes almost as automatic and unthinking as if it were instinctive. There is a tremendous amount of intelligence behind the making of a radio, but not much is required to learn to turn it on.

The members of all human societies face some of the same unavoidable dilemmas, posed by biology and other facts of the human situation. This is why the basic categories of all cultures are so similar. Human culture without language is unthinkable. No culture fails to provide for aesthetic expression and aesthetic delight. Every culture supplies standardized orientations toward the deeper problems, such as death. Every culture is designed to perpetuate the group and its solidarity, to meet the demands of individuals for an orderly way of life and for satisfaction of biological needs.

However, the variations on these basic themes are numberless. Some languages are built up out of twenty basic sounds, others out of forty. Nose plugs were considered beautiful by predynastic Egyptians but are not by the modern French. Puberty is a biological fact. But one culture ignores it, another prescribes informal instructions about sex but no ceremony, a third has impressive rites for girls only, a fourth for boys and girls. In this culture, the first menstruation is welcomed as a happy, natural event; in that culture the atmosphere is full of dread and supernatural threat. Each culture dissects nature according to its own system of categories. . . .

Every culture must deal with the sexual instinct. Some, however, seek to deny all sexual expression before marriage, whereas a Polynesian adolescent who was not promiscuous would be distinctly abnormal. Some cultures enforce lifelong monogamy, others, like our own, tolerate serial monogamy; in still other cultures, two or more women may be joined to one man or several men to a single woman. Homosexuality has been a permitted pattern in the Greco-Roman world, in parts of Islam, and in various primitive tribes. Large portions of the population of Tibet, and of Christendom at some places and periods, have practiced complete celibacy. To us marriage is first and foremost an arrangement between two individuals. In many more societies marriage is merely one facet of a complicated set of reciprocities, economic and otherwise, between two families or clans.

The essence of the cultural process is selectivity. The selection is only exceptionally conscious and rational. Cultures are like Topsy. They just grew. Once, however, a way of handling a situation becomes institutionalized, there is ordinarily great resistance to change or deviation. When we speak of "our sacred beliefs," we mean of course that they are beyond criticism and that the person who suggests modification or abandonment must be punished. No person is emotionally indifferent to his culture. Certain cultural premises may become totally out of accord with a new factual situation. Leaders may recognize this and reject the old ways in theory. Yet their emotional loyalty continues in the face of reason because of the intimate conditionings of early childhood.

A culture is learned by individuals as the result of belonging to some particular group, and it constitutes that part of learned behavior which is shared with others. It is our social legacy, as contrasted with our organic heredity. It is one of the important factors which permits us to live together in an organized society, giving us ready-made solutions to our problems, helping us to predict the behavior of others, and permitting others to know what to expect of us.

Culture regulates our lives at every turn. From the moment we are born until we die there is, whether we are conscious of it or not, constant pressure upon us to follow certain types of behavior that other men have created for us. Some paths we follow willingly, others we follow because we know no other way, still others we deviate from or go back to most unwillingly. Mothers of small children know how unnaturally most of this comes to us—how little regard we have, until we are "culturalized," for the "proper" place, time and manner for certain acts such as eating, excreting, sleeping, getting dirty, and making loud noises. But by more or less adhering to a system of related designs for carrying out all the acts of living, a group of men and women feel themselves linked together by a powerful chain of sentiments. [American anthropologist] Ruth Benedict gave an almost complete definition of the concept when she said, "Culture is that which binds men together."

It is true any culture is a set of techniques for adjusting both to the external environment and to other men. However, cultures create problems as well as solve them. If the lore of a people states that frogs are dangerous creatures, or that it is not safe to go about at night because of witches or ghosts, threats are posed which do not arise out of the inexorable facts of the external world. Cultures produce needs as well as provide a means of fulfilling them. There exists for every group culturally defined, acquired drives that may be more powerful in ordinary daily life than the biologically inborn drives. Many Americans, for example, will work harder for "success" than they will for sexual satisfaction.

Most groups elaborate certain aspects of their culture far beyond maximum utility or survival value. In other words, not all culture promotes physical survival. At times, indeed, it does exactly the opposite. Aspects of culture which once were adaptive may persist long after they have ceased to be useful. An analysis of any culture will disclose many features which cannot possibly be construed as adaptations to the total environment in which the group now finds itself. However, it is altogether likely that these apparently useless features represent survivals, with modifications through time, of cultural forms which were adaptive in one or another previous situation.

Any cultural practice must be functional or it will disappear before long. That is, it must somehow contribute to the survival of the society or to the adjustment of the individual. However, many cultural functions are not manifest but latent. A cowboy will walk three miles to catch a horse which he then rides one mile to the store. From the point of view of manifest function this is positively irrational. But the act has the latent function of maintaining the cowboy's prestige in the terms of his own subculture. One can instance the buttons on the sleeve of a man's coat, our absurd English spelling, the use of capital letters, and a host of other apparently nonfunctional customs. They serve mainly the latent function of assisting individuals to maintain their security by preserving continuity with the past and by making certain sectors of life familiar and predictable.

Every culture is a precipitate of history. In more than one sense history is a sieve. Each culture embraces those aspects of the past which, usually in altered form and with altered meanings, live on in the present. Discoveries and inventions, both material and ideological, are constantly being made available to a group through its historical contacts with other peoples or being created by its own members. However, only those that fit the total immediate situation in meeting the group's needs for survival or in promoting the psychological adjustment of individuals will become part of the culture. The process of culture building may be regarded as an addition to man's innate biological capacities, an addition providing instruments which enlarge, or may even substitute for, biological functions, and to a degree, compensating for biological limitations—as in ensuring that death does not always result in the loss of humanity of what the deceased has learned.

Culture is like a map. Just as a map isn't the territory but an abstract representation of a particular area, so also a culture is an abstract description of trends toward uniformity in the words, deeds, and artifacts of a human group. If a map is accurate and you can read it, you won't get lost; if you know a culture, you will know your way around in the life of a society. . . .

Every group's way of life, then, is a structure—not a haphazard collection of all the different physically possible and functionally effective patterns of belief and action. A culture is an interdependent system based upon linked premises and categories whose influence is greater, rather than less, because they are seldom put in words. Some degree of internal coherence which is felt rather than rationally constructed seems to be demanded by most of the participants in any culture. As [philosopher Alfred North] Whitehead has remarked, "Human life is driven forward by its dim apprehension of notions too general for its existing language."

In sum, the distinctive way of life that is handed down as the social heritage of a people does more than supply a set of skills for making a living and a set of blueprints for human relations. Each different way of life makes its own assumptions about the ends and purposes of human existence, about what human beings have a right to expect from each other and the gods, about what constitutes a fulfillment or frustration. Some of these assumptions are made explicit in the lore of the folk; others are tacit premises which the observer must infer by finding consistent trends in word and deed.

2.2 HORACE MINER

Body Ritual Among the Nacirema

For decades, leading Western anthropologists have focused their cultural research on so-called primitive societies, journeying to foreign lands to study new and exotic societies and cultures. Horace Miner (b. 1912), who is professor emeritus of sociology and anthropology at the University of Michigan, devoted his research to the social structure of preindustrial cities and the urbanization and modernization of peasants. In the following selection Miner holds a mirror to the exotic people of Nacirema. He systematically examines their cultural patterns—their preoccupation with cleanliness, how they handle their physical and mental health, the various aspects of their economic behavior, and so on. The rituals of the Nacirema, elegantly depicted by Miner, give shape to a culture that at first could appear quite foreign to most Americans; however, on closer examination, there is something familiar sounding to all this! This selection from Minor, first published in *American Anthropologist* in June 1956, is an enlightening and popular account of how an anthropologist looks at one society's culture.

Key Concept: the diversity of human behavior and how it can be studied

*T*he anthropologist has become so familiar with the diversity of ways in which different peoples behave in similar situations that he is not apt to be surprised by even the most exotic customs. In fact, if all of the logically possible combinations of behavior have not been found somewhere in the world, he is apt to suspect that they must be present in some yet undescribed tribe. This point has, in fact, been expressed with respect to clan organization by Murdock (1949:71). In this light, the magical beliefs and practices of the Nacirema present such unusual aspects that it seems desirable to describe them as an example of the extremes to which human behavior can go.

Professor Linton first brought the ritual of the Nacirema to the attention of anthropologists twenty years ago (1936:326), but the culture of this people is still very poorly understood. They are a North American group living in the territory between the Canadian Cree, the Yaqui and Tarahumare of Mexico, and the Carib and Arawak of the Antilles. Little is known of their origin, though tradition states that they came from the east. According to Nacirema mythology, their nation was originated by a culture hero, Notgnishaw, who is otherwise known for two great feats of strength—the throwing of a piece of wampum across the river Pa-To-Mac and the chopping down of a cherry tree in which the Spirit of Truth resided.

Nacirema culture is characterized by a highly developed market economy which has evolved in a rich natural habitat. While much of the people's time is devoted to economic pursuits, a large part of the fruits of these labors and a considerable portion of the day are spent in ritual activity. The focus of this activity is the human body, the appearance and health of which loom as a dominant concern in the ethos of the people. While such a concern is certainly not unusual, its ceremonial aspects and associated philosophy are unique.

The fundamental belief underlying the whole system appears to be that the human body is ugly and that its natural tendency is to debility and disease. Incarcerated in such a body, man's only hope is to avert these characteristics through the use of the powerful influences of ritual and ceremony. Every household has one or more shrines devoted to this purpose. The more powerful individuals in the society have several shrines in their houses and, in fact, the opulence of a house is often referred to in terms of the number of such ritual centers it possesses. Most houses are of wattle and daub construction [woven rods and twigs plastered with clay], but the shrine rooms of the more wealthy are walled with stone. Poorer families imitate the rich by applying pottery plaques to their shrine walls.

While each family has at least one such shrine, the rituals associated with it are not family ceremonies but are private and secret. The rites are normally only discussed with children, and then only during the period when they are being initiated into these mysteries. I was able, however, to establish sufficient rapport with the natives to examine these shrines and to have the rituals described to me.

The focal point of the shrine is a box or chest which is built into the wall. In this chest are kept the many charms and magical potions without which no native believes he could live. These preparations are secured from a variety of specialized practitioners. The most powerful of these are the medicine men, whose assistance must be rewarded with substantial gifts. However, the medicine men do not provide the curative potions for their clients, but decide what the ingredients should be and then write them down in an ancient and secret language. This writing is understood only by the medicine men and by the herbalists who, for another gift, provide the required charm.

The charm is not disposed of after it has served its purpose, but is placed in the charm-box of the household shrine. As these magical materials are specific for certain ills, and the real or imagined maladies of the people are many, the charm-box is usually full to overflowing. The magical packets are so numerous that people forget what their purposes were and fear to use them again. While the natives are very vague on this point, we can only assume that the idea in retaining all the old magical materials is that their presence in the charm-box, before which the body rituals are conducted, will in some way protect the worshipper.

Beneath the charm-box is a small font. Each day every member of the family, in succession, enters the shrine room, bows his head before the charm-box, mingles different sorts of holy water in the font, and proceeds with a brief rite of ablution. The holy waters are secured from the Water Temple of the community, where the priests conduct elaborate ceremonies to make the liquid ritually pure.

In the hierarchy of magical practitioners, and below the medicine men in prestige, are specialists whose designation is best translated "holy-mouth-men." The Nacirema have an almost pathological horror and fascination with the mouth, the condition of which is believed to have a supernatural influence on all social relationships. Were it not for the rituals of the mouth, they believe that their teeth would fall out, their gums bleed, their jaws shrink, their friends desert them, and their lovers reject them. . . .

[T]he people seek out a holy-mouth-man once or twice a year. These practitioners have an impressive set of paraphernalia, consisting of a variety of augers, awls, probes, and prods. The use of these objects in the exorcism of the evils of the mouth involves almost unbelievable ritual torture of the client. The holy-mouth-man opens the client's mouth and, using the above mentioned tools, enlarges any holes which decay may have created in the teeth. Magical materials are put into these holes. . . .

It is to be hoped that, when a thorough study of the Nacirema is made, there will be a careful inquiry into the personality structure of these people. One has but to watch the gleam in the eye of a holy-mouth-man, as he jabs an awl into an exposed nerve, to suspect that a certain amount of sadism is involved. If this can be established, a very interesting pattern emerges, for most of the population shows definite masochistic tendencies. It was to these that Professor Linton referred in discussing a distinctive part of the daily body ritual which is performed only by men. This part of the rite involves scraping and lacerating the surface of the face with a sharp instrument. Special women's rites are performed only four times during each lunar month, but what they lack in frequency is made up in barbarity. As part of this ceremony, women bake their heads in small ovens for about an hour. The theoretically interesting point is that what seems to be a preponderantly masochistic people have developed sadistic specialists.

The medicine men have an imposing temple, or *latipso*, in every community of any size. The more elaborate ceremonies required to treat very sick patients can only be performed at this temple. These ceremonies involve not only the thaumaturge but a permanent group of vestal maidens who move sedately about the temple chambers in distinctive costume and headdress.

The *latipso* ceremonies are so harsh that it is phenomenal that a fair proportion of the really sick natives who enter the temple ever recover. Small children whose indoctrination is still incomplete have been known to resist attempts to take them to the temple because "that is where you go to die." Despite this fact, sick adults are not only willing but eager to undergo the protracted ritual purification, if they can afford to do so. No matter how ill the supplicant or how grave the emergency, the guardians of many temples will not admit a client if he cannot give a rich gift to the custodian. Even after one has gained admission and survived the ceremonies, the guardians will not permit the neophyte to leave until he makes still another gift.

The supplicant entering the temple is first stripped of all his or her clothes. In every-day life the Nacirema avoids exposure of his body and its natural functions. Bathing and excretory acts are performed only in the secrecy of the household shrine, where they are ritualized as part of the body-rites. Psychological shock results from the fact that body secrecy is suddenly lost upon entry into the *latipso*. A man, whose own wife has never seen him in an excretory act, suddenly finds himself naked and assisted by a vestal maiden while he performs his natural functions into a sacred vessel. This sort of ceremonial treatment is necessitated by the fact that the excreta are used by a diviner to ascertain the course and nature of the client's sickness. Female clients, on the other hand, find their naked bodies are subjected to the scrutiny, manipulation and prodding of the medicine men.

Few supplicants in the temple are well enough to do anything but lie on their hard beds. The daily ceremonies, like the rites of the holy-mouth-men, involve discomfort and torture. With ritual precision, the vestals awaken their miserable charges each dawn and roll them about on their beds of pain while performing ablutions, in the formal movements of which the maidens are highly trained. At other times they insert magic wands in the supplicant's mouth or force him to eat substances which are supposed to be healing. From time to time the medicine men come to their clients and jab magically treated needles into their flesh. The fact that these temple ceremonies may not cure, and may even kill the neophyte, in no way decreases the people's faith in the medicine men.

There remains one other kind of practitioner, known as a "listener." This witch-doctor has the power to exorcise the devils that lodge in the heads of people who have been bewitched. The Nacirema believe that parents bewitch their own children. Mothers are particularly suspected of putting a curse on children while teaching them the secret body rituals. The counter-magic of the witch-doctor is unusual in its lack of ritual. The patient simply tells the "listener" all his troubles and fears, beginning with the earliest difficulties he can remember. The memory displayed by the Nacirema in these exorcism sessions is truly remarkable. It is not uncommon for the patient to bemoan the rejection he felt upon being weaned as a babe, and a few individuals even see their troubles going back to the traumatic effects of their own birth.

In conclusion, mention must be made of certain practices which have their base in native esthetics but which depend upon the pervasive aversion to the natural body and its functions. There are ritual fasts to make fat people thin and ceremonial feasts to make thin people fat. Still other rites are used to make women's breasts large if they are small, and smaller if they are large. General dissatisfaction with breast shape is symbolized in the fact that the ideal form is virtually outside the range of human variation. A few women afflicted with almost inhuman hypermammary development are so idolized that they make a handsome living by simply going from village to village and permitting the natives to stare at them for a fee.

Reference has already been made to the fact that excretory functions are ritualized, routinized, and relegated to secrecy. Natural reproductive functions are similarly distorted. Intercourse is taboo as a topic and scheduled as an act. Efforts are made to avoid pregnancy by the use of magical materials or by limiting intercourse to certain phases of the moon. Conception is actually very infrequent. When pregnant, women dress so as to hide their condition. Parturition takes place in secret, without friends or relatives to assist, and the majority of women do not nurse their infants.

Our review of the ritual life of the Nacirema has certainly shown them to be a magic-ridden people. It is hard to understand how they have managed to exist so long under the burdens which they have imposed upon themselves. But even such exotic customs as these take on real meaning when they are viewed with the insight provided by Malinowski when he wrote (1948:70):

> Looking from far and above, from our high places of safety in the developed civilization, it is easy to see all the crudity and irrelevance of magic. But without its power and guidance early man could not have mastered his practical difficulties as he has done, nor could man have advanced to the higher stages of civilization.

REFERENCES

Linton, Ralph. 1936. *The Study of Man*. New York, D. Appleton-Century Co.
Malinowski, Bronislaw. 1948. *Magic, Science, and Religion*. Glencoe, The Free Press.
Murdock, George P. 1949. *Social Structure*. New York, The Macmillan Co.

The Mountain People

Anthropologists who study the culture of people in less-developed societies invariably find social organizations and institutions that are responsible for the survival and continuity of the group. In the following excerpt, Colin M. Turnbull describes the Ik tribe of Northern Uganda, who appear to lack a social organization and who, for various reasons, have failed to develop a minimum of institutional arrangements that would enable them to develop a humanity and provide continuity for the group.

Many positive aspects of relatively integrated societies are taken for granted and overlooked by their members. The unique case of the Ik—a minimally organized, integrated, and functioning society—reveals, by contrast, the value of relatively integrated societies, such as those in North America. Turnbull, however, argues that the industrial world is in considerable danger of suffering some of the evils of excessive individualism that the Ik suffer.

Turnbull (b. 1924) is an anthropologist who has intensively studied several tribes in Africa and whose interests lie in exploring deteriorating human interpersonal and intergroup relationships. A former consultant to the U.S. State Department, his best-known publications include *The Forest People* (Simon & Schuster, 1961) and *The Mountain People* (Simon & Schuster, 1972).

Key Concept: survival by diligent attention to one's own needs while ignoring the needs of others

*I*n what follows, there will be much to shock, and the reader will be tempted to say, "how primitive, how savage, how disgusting," and, above all, "how inhuman." The first judgments are typical of the kind of ethno- and egocentricism from which we can never quite escape. But "how inhuman" is of a different order and supposes that there are certain values inherent in humanity itself, from which the people described here seem to depart in a most drastic manner. In living the experience, however, and perhaps in reading it, one finds that it is oneself one is looking at and questioning; it is a voyage in quest of the basic human and a discovery of his potential for inhumanity, a potential that lies within us all.

Just before World War II the Ik tribe had been encouraged to settle in northern Uganda, in the mountainous northeast corner bordering on Kenya to the east and Sudan to the north. Until then they had roamed in nomadic bands, as hunters and gatherers, through a vast region in all three countries. The Kidepo Valley below Mount Morungole was their major hunting territory. After they were confined to a part of their former area, Kidepo was made a national park and they were forbidden to hunt or gather there.

The concept of family in a nomadic society is a broad one; what really counts most in everyday life is community of residence, and those who live close to each other are likely to see each other as effectively related, whether there is any kinship bond or not. Full brothers, on the other hand, who live in different parts of the camp may have little concern for each other.

It is not possible, then, to think of the family as a simple, basic unit. A child is brought up to regard any adult living in the same camp as a parent, and age-mate as a brother or sister. The Ik had this essentially social attitude toward kinship, and it readily lent itself to the rapid and disastrous changes that took place following the restriction of their movement and hunting activities. The family simply ceased to exist.

It is a mistake to think of small-scale societies as "primitive" or "simple." Hunters and gatherers, most of all, appear simple and straightforward in terms of their social organization, yet that is far from true. If we can learn about the nature of society from a study of small-scale societies, we can also learn about human relationships. The smaller the society, the less emphasis there is on the formal system and the more there is on interpersonal and intergroup relations. Security is seen in terms of these relationships, and so is survival. The result, which appears so deceptively simple, is that hunters frequently display those characteristics that we find so admirable in man: kindness, generosity, consideration, affection, honesty, hospitality, compassion, charity. For them, in their tiny, close-knit society, these are necessities for survival. In our society anyone possessing even half these qualities would find it hard to survive, yet we think these virtues are inherent in man. I took it for granted that the Ik would possess these same qualities. But they were as unfriendly, uncharitable, inhospitable and generally mean as any people can be. For those positive qualities we value so highly are no longer functional for them; even more than in our own society they spell ruin and disaster. It seems that, far from being basic human qualities, they are luxuries we can afford in times of plenty or are mere mechanisms for survival and security. Given the situation in which the Ik found themselves, man has no time for such luxuries, and a much more basic man appears, using more basic survival tactics. . . .

Atum ["the senior of all the Ik on Morungole"] was waiting for me. He said that he had told all the Ik that Iciebam [friend of the Ik] had arrived to live with them and that I had given the workers a "holiday" so they could greet me. They were waiting in the villages. They were very hungry, he added, and many were dying. That was probably one of the few true statements he ever made, and I never even considered believing it. . . .

After [touring the Ik villages] Atum said we should start back and called over his shoulder to his village. A muffled sound came from within, and he said, "That's my wife, she is very sick—and hungry." I offered to go and see her, but he shook his head. Back at the Land Rover I gave Atum some food and some aspirin, not knowing what else to give him to help his wife. . . .

While the Ik were working, their heads kept turning as though they were expecting something to happen. Every now and again one would stand up and peer into the distance and then take off into the bush for an hour or so. On one such occasion, after the person had been gone two hours, the others started drifting off. By then I knew them better; I looked for a wisp of smoke and followed it to where the road team was cooking a goat. Smoke was a giveaway, though, so they economized on cooking and ate most food nearly raw. It is a curious hangover from what must once have been a moral code that Ik will offer food if surprised in the act of eating, though they now go to enormous pains not to be so surprised.

I was always up before dawn, but by the time I got up to the villages they were always deserted. One morning I followed the little *oror* [gulley] up from *oror a pirre'i* [Ravine of Pirre] while it was still quite dark, and I met Lomeja on his way down. He took me on my first illicit hunt in Kidepo. He told me that if he got anything he would share it with me and with anyone else who managed to join us but that he certainly would not take anything back to his family. "Each one of them is out seeing what he can get for himself, and do you think they will bring any back for me?"

Lomeja was one of the very few Ik who seemed glad to volunteer information. Unlike many of the others, he did not get up and leave as I approached. Apart from him, I spent most of my time, those days, with Losike, the potter. She told me that Nangoli, the old lady in the adjoining compound, and her husband, Amuarkuar, were rather peculiar. They helped each other get food and water, and they brought it back to their compound to eat together.

I still do not know how much real hunger there was at that time, for most of the younger people seemed fairly well fed, and the few skinny old people seemed healthy and active. But my laboriously extracted genealogies showed that there were quite a number of old people still alive and allegedly in these villages, though they were never to be seen. Then Atum's wife died.

Atum told me nothing about it but kept up his demands for food and medicine. After a while the beady-eyed Lomongin told me that Atum was selling the medicine I was giving him for his wife. I was not unduly surprised and merely remarked that that was too bad for his wife. "Oh no," said Lomongin, "she has been dead for weeks." . . .

Kauar [one of the Ik workers] always played and joked with the children when they came back from foraging. He used to volunteer to make the two-day walk into Kaabong and the even more tiring two-day climb back to get mail for me or to buy a few things for others. He always asked if he had made the trip more quickly than the last time.

Then one day Kauar went to Kaabong and did not come back. He was found on the last peak of the trail, cold and dead. Those who found him took the things he had been carrying and pushed his body into the bush. I still see his open, laughing face, see him giving precious tidbits to the children, comforting some child who was crying, and watching me read the letters he carried so lovingly for me. And I still think of him probably running up that viciously steep mountainside so he could break his time record and falling dead in his pathetic prime because he was starving. . . .

Anyone falling down was good for a laugh, but I never saw anyone actually trip anyone else. The adults were content to let things happen and then enjoy them; it was probably conservation of energy. The children, however, sought their pleasures with vigor. The best game of all, at this time, was teasing poor little Adupa. She was not so little—in fact she should have been an adult, for she was nearly 13 years old—but Adupa was a little mad. Or you might say she was the only sane one, depending on your point of view. Adupa did not jump on other people's play houses, and she lavished enormous care on hers and would curl up inside it. That made it all the more jump-on-able. The other children beat her viciously.

Children are not allowed to sleep in the house after they are "put out," which is at about three years old, four at the latest. From then on they sleep in the open courtyard, taking what shelter they can against the stockade. They may ask for permission to sit in the doorway of their parents' house but may not lie down or sleep there. "The same thing applies to old people," said Atum, "if they can't build a house of their own and, of course, *if* their children let them stay in their compounds."

I saw a few old people, most of whom had taken over abandoned huts. For the first time I realized that there really was starvation and saw why I had never known it before: it was confined to the aged. Down in Giriko's village the old ritual priest, Lolim, confidentially told me that he was sheltering an old man who had been refused shelter by his son. But Lolim did not have enough food for himself, let alone his guest; could I . . . I liked old Lolim, so, not believing that Lolim had a visitor at all, I brought him a double ration that evening. There was a rustling in the back of the hut, and Lolim helped ancient Lomeraniang to the entrance. They shook with delight at the sight of the food.

When the two old men had finished eating, I left; I found a hungry-looking and disapproving little crowd clustered outside. They muttered to each other about wasting food. From then on I brought food daily, but in a very short time Lomeraniang was dead, and his son refused to come down from the village above to bury him. Lolim scratched a hole and covered the body with a pile of stones he carried himself, one by one.

Hunger was indeed more severe than I knew, and, after the old people, the children were the next to go. It was all quite impersonal—even to me, in most cases, since I had been immunized by the Ik themselves against sorrow on their behalf. But Adupa was an exception. Her madness was such that she did not know just how vicious humans could be. Even worse, she thought that parents were for loving, for giving as well as receiving. Her parents were not given to fantasies. When she came for shelter, they drove her out; and when she came because she was hungry, they laughed the Icien laugh, as if she had made them happy.

Adupa's reactions became slower and slower. When she managed to find food—fruit peels, skins, bits of bone, half-eaten berries—she held it in her hand and looked at it with wonder and delight. Her playmates caught on quickly; they put tidbits in her way and watched her simple drawn little face wrinkle in a smile. Then as she raised her hand to her mouth, they set on her with cries of excitement, fun and laughter, beating her savagely over the head. But that is not how she died. I took to feeding her, which is probably the cruelest thing I could have done, a gross selfishness on my part to try to salve my own rapidly disappearing conscience. I had to protect her, physically, as I fed her. But the others would beat her anyway, and Adupa cried, not because of the pain in her body but because of the pain she felt at the great, vast, empty wasteland where love should have been.

It was *that* that killed her. She demanded that her parents love her. Finally they took her in, and Adupa was happy and stopped crying. She stopped crying forever because her parents went away and closed the door tight behind them, so tight that weak little Adupa could never have moved it.

The Ik seem to tell us that the family is not such a fundamental unit as we usually suppose, that it is not essential to social life. In the crisis of survival facing the Ik, the family was one of the first institutions to go, and the Ik as a society have survived.

The other quality of life that we hold to be necessary for survival—love— the Ik dismiss as idiotic and highly dangerous. But we need to see more of the Ik before their absolute lovelessness becomes truly apparent.

In this curious society there is one common value to which all Ik hold tenaciously. It is *ngag*, "food." That is the one standard by which they measure right and wrong, goodness and badness. The very word for "good" is defined in terms of food. "Goodness" is "the possession of food," or the "*individual* possession of food." If you try to discover their concept of a "good man," you get the truly Icien answer: one who has a full stomach.

We should not be surprised, then, when the mother throws her child out at three years old. At that age a series of *rites de passage* begins. In this environment a child has no chance of survival on his own until he is about 13, so children form age bands. The junior band consists of children between three and seven, the senior of eight- to twelve-year-olds. Within the band each child seeks another close to him in age for defense against the older children. These friendships are temporary, however, and inevitably there comes a time when each turns on the one that up to then had been the closest to him; that is the *rite de passage*, the destruction of that fragile bond called friendship. When this has happened three or four times, the child is ready for the world.

The weakest are soon thinned out, and the strongest survive to achieve leadership of the band. Such a leader is eventually driven out, turned against by his fellow band members. Then the process starts all over again; he joins the senior age band as its most junior member.

The final *rite de passage* is into adulthood, at the age of 12 or 13. By then the candidate has learned the wisdom of acting on his own, for his own good, while acknowledging that on occasion it is profitable to associate temporarily with others. . . .

There seemed to be increasingly little among the Ik that could by any stretch of the imagination be called social life, let alone social organization. The family does not hold itself together; economic interest is centered on as many stomachs as there are people; and cooperation is merely a device for furthering an interest that is consciously selfish. We often do the same thing in our so-called "altruistic" practices, but we tell ourselves it is for the good of others. The

Ik have dispensed with the myth of altruism. Though they have no centralized leadership or means of physical coercion, they do hold together with remarkable tenacity.

In our world, where the family has also lost much of its value as a social unit and where religious belief no longer binds us into communities, we maintain order only through coercive power that is ready to uphold a rigid law and through an equally rigid penal system. The Ik, however, have learned to do without coercion, either spiritual or physical. It seems that they have come to a recognition of what they accept as man's basic selfishness, of his natural determination to survive as an individual before all else. This they consider to be man's basic right, and they allow others to pursue that right without recrimination. . . .

[The oldest and greatest Icien ritual priest] Lolim became ill and had to be protected while eating the food I gave him. Then the children began openly ridiculing him and teasing him, dancing in front of him and kneeling down so that he would trip over them. His grandson used to creep up behind him and with a pair of hard sticks drum a lively tattoo on the old man's bald head.

I fed him whenever I could, but often he did not want more than a bite. Once I found him rolled up in his protective ball, crying. He had had nothing to eat for four days and no water for two. He had asked his children, who all told him not to come near them.

The next day I saw him leaving Atum's village, where his son Longoli lived. Longoli swore that he had been giving his father food and was looking after him. Lolim was not shuffling away; it was almost a run, the run of a drunken man, staggering from side to side. I called to him, but he made no reply, just a kind of long, continuous and horrible moan. He had been to Longoli to beg him to let him into his compound because he knew he was going to die in a few hours, Longoli calmly told me afterward. Obviously Longoli could not do a thing like that: a man of Lolim's importance would have called for an enormous funeral feast. So he refused. Lolim begged Longoli then to open up Nangoli's *asak* for him so that he could die in *her* compound. But Longoli drove him out, and he died alone. . . .

If there was such a thing as an Icien morality, I had not yet perceived it, though traces of a moral past remained. But it still remained a possibility, as did the existence of an unspoken, unmanifest belief that might yet reveal itself and provide a basis for the reintegration of society. I was somewhat encouraged in this hope by the unexpected flight of old Nangoli, widow of Amuarkuar.

When Nangoli returned and found her husband dead, she did an odd thing: she grieved. She tore down what was left of their home, uprooted the stockade, tore up whatever was growing in her little field. Then she fled with a few belongings.

Some weeks later I heard that she and her children had gone over to the Sudan and built a village there. This migration was so unusual that I decided to see whether this runaway village was different.

Lojieri led the way, and Atum came along. One long day's trek got us there. Lojieri pulled part of the brush fence aside, and we went in and wandered around. He and Atum looked inside all the huts, and Lojieri helped himself to tobacco from one and water from another. Surprises were coming thick and fast. That households should be left open and untended with such wealth inside . . . That there should have been such wealth, for as well as tobacco and jars of water there were baskets of food, and meat was drying on racks. There were half a dozen or so compounds, but they were separated from each other only by a short line of sticks and brush. It was a village, and these were homes, the first and last I was to see.

The dusk had already fallen, and Nangoli came in with her children and grandchildren. They had heard us and came in with warm welcomes. There was no hunger here, and in a very short time each kitchen hearth had a pot of food cooking. Then we sat around the central fire and talked until late, and it was another universe.

There was no talk of "how much better it is here than there"; talk revolved around what had happened on the hunt that day. Loron was lying on the ground in front of the fire as his mother made gentle fun of him. His wife, Kinimei, whom I had never seen even speak to him at Pirre, put a bowl of fresh-cooked berries and fruit in front of him. It was all like a nightmare rather than a fantasy, for it made the reality of Pirre seem all the more frightening. . . .

[Back at Pirre, t]he days of drought wore on into weeks and months and, like everyone else, I became rather bored with sickness and death. I survived rather as did the young adults, by diligent attention to my own needs while ignoring those of others.

More and more it was only the young who could go far from the village as hunger became starvation. Famine relief had been initiated down at Kasile, and those fit enough to make the trip set off. When they came back, the contrast between them and the others was that between life and death. Villages were villages of the dead and dying, and there was little difference between the two. People crawled rather than walked. After a few feet some would lie down to rest, but they could not be sure of ever being able to sit up again, so they mostly stayed upright until they reached their destination. They were going nowhere, these semianimate bags of skin and bone; they just wanted to be with others, and they stopped whenever they met. Perhaps it was the most important demonstration of sociality I ever saw among the Ik. Once they met, they neither spoke nor did anything together.

Early one morning, before dawn, the village moved. In the midst of a hive of activity were the aged and crippled, soon to be abandoned, in danger of being trampled but seemingly unaware of it. Lolim's widow, Lo'ono, whom I had never seen before, also had been abandoned and had tried to make her way down the mountainside. But she was totally blind and had tripped and rolled to the bottom of the *oror a pirre'i;* there she lay on her back, her legs and arms thrashing feebly, while a little crowd laughed.

At this time a colleague was with me. He kept the others away while I ran to get medicine and food and water, for Lo'ono was obviously near dead from hunger and thirst as well as from the fall. We treated her and fed her and asked her to come back with us. But she asked us to point her in the direction of her son's new village. I said I did not think she would get much of a welcome there, and she replied that she knew it but wanted to be near him when she died. So we gave her more food, put her stick in her hand and pointed her the right way. She suddenly cried. She was crying, she said, because we had reminded her that there had been a time when people had helped each other, when people had been kind and good. Still crying, she set off.

The Ik up to this point had been tolerant of my activities, but all this was too much. They said that what we were doing was wrong. Food and medicine were for the living, not the dead. I thought of Lo'ono. And I thought of other old people who had joined in the merriment when they had been teased or had a precious morsel of food taken from their mouths. They knew that it was silly of them to expect to go on living, and, having watched others, they knew that the spectacle really was quite funny. So they joined in the laughter. Perhaps if we had left Lo'ono, she would have died laughing. But we prolonged her misery for no more than a few brief days. Even worse, we reminded her of when things had been different, of days when children had cared for parents and parents for children. She was already dead, and we made her unhappy as well. At the time I was sure we were right, doing the only "human" thing. In a way we *were*—we were making life more comfortable for ourselves. But now I wonder if the Ik way was not right, if I too should not have laughed as Lo'ono flapped about, then left her to die. . . .

And now that all the old are dead, what is left? Every Ik who is old today was thrown out at three and has survived, and in consequence has thrown his own children out and knows that they will not help him in his old age any more than he helped his parents. The system has turned one full cycle and is now self-perpetuating; it has eradicated what we know as "humanity" and has turned the world into a chilly void where man does not seem to care even for himself, but survives. Yet into this hideous world Nangoli and her family quietly returned because they could not bear to be alone.

For the moment abandoning the very old and the very young, the Ik as a whole must be searched for one last lingering trace of humanity. They appear to have disposed of virtually all the qualities that we normally think of as differentiating us from other primates, yet they survive without seeming to be greatly different from ourselves in terms of behavior. Their behavior is more extreme, for we do not start throwing our children out until kindergarten. We have shifted responsibility from family to state, the Ik have shifted it to the individual.

It has been claimed that human beings are capable of love and, indeed, are dependent upon it for survival and sanity. The Ik offer us an opportunity for testing this cherished notion that love is essential to survival. If it is, the Ik should have it.

Love in human relationships implies mutuality, a willingness to sacrifice the self that springs from a consciousness of identity. This seems to bring us back to the Ik, for it implies that love is self-oriented, that even the supreme sacrifice of one's life is no more than selfishness, for the victim feels amply rewarded by the pleasure he feels in making the sacrifice. The Ik, however, do not value emotion above survival, and they are without love. . . .

When the rains failed for the second year running, I knew that the Ik as a society were almost certainly finished and that the monster they had created in its place, that passionless, feelingless association of individuals, would spread like a fungus, contaminating all it touched. When I left, I too had been contaminated. . . .

I departed with a kind of forced gaiety, feeling that I should be glad to be gone but having forgotten how to be glad. I certainly was not thinking of returning within a year, but I did. The following spring I heard that rain had come at last and that the fields of the Ik had never looked so prosperous, nor the country so green and fertile. A few months away had refreshed me, and I wondered if my conclusions had not been excessively pessimistic. So early that summer, I set off to be present for the first harvests in three years.

I was not surprised too much when two days after my arrival and installation at the police post I found Logwara, the blind man, lying on the roadside bleeding, while a hundred yards up other Ik were squabbling over the body of a hyena. Logwara had tried to get there ahead of the others to grab the meat and had been trampled on.

First I looked at the villages. The lush outer covering concealed an inner decay. All the villages were like this to some extent, except for Lokelea's. There the tomatoes and pumpkins were so carefully pruned and cleaned, so that the fruits were larger and healthier. In what had been my own compound the shade trees had been cut down for firewood, and the lovely hanging nests of the weaver birds were gone.

The fields were even more desolate. Every field without exception had yielded in abundance, and it was a new sensation to have vision cut off by thick crops. But every crop was rotting from sheer neglect.

The Ik said that they had no need to bother guarding the fields. There was so much food they could never eat it all, so why not let the birds and baboons take some? The Ik had full bellies; they were good. The *di* at Atum's village was much the same as usual, people sitting or lying about. People were still stealing from each other's fields, and nobody thought of saving for the future.

It was obvious that nothing had really changed due to the sudden glut of food except that interpersonal relationships had deteriorated still further and that Icien individualism had heightened beyond what I thought even Ik to be capable of.

The Ik had faced a conscious choice between being humans and being parasites and had chosen the latter. When they saw their fields come alive, they were confronted with a problem. If they reaped the harvest, they would have to store grain for eating and planting, and every Ik knew that trying to store anything was a waste of time. Further, if they made their fields look too promising, the government would stop famine relief. So the Ik let their fields rot and continued to draw famine relief.

The Ik were not starving any longer; the old and infirm had all died the previous year, and the younger survivors were doing quite well. But the famine relief was administered in a way that was little short of criminal. As before, only the young and well were able to get down from Pirre to collect the relief; they were given relief for those who could not come and told to take it back. But they never did—they ate it themselves.

The facts are there, though those that can be read here form but a fraction of what one person was able to gather in under two years. There can be no mistaking the direction in which those facts point, and that is the most important thing of all, for it may affect the rest of mankind as it has affected the Ik. The Ik have "progressed," one might say, since the change that has come to them came with the advent of civilization to Africa. They have made of a world that was alive a world that is dead—a cold, dispassionate world that is without ugliness because it is without beauty, without hate because it is without love, and without any realization of truth even, because it simply is. And the symptoms of change in our own society indicate that we are heading in the same direction.

Those values we cherish so highly may indeed be basic to human society but not to humanity, and that means that the Ik show that society itself is not indispensable for man's survival and that man is capable of associating for purposes of survival without being social. The Ik have replaced human society with a mere survival system that does not take human emotion into account. . . .

Such interaction as there is within this system is one of mutual exploitation. That is how it already is with the Ik. In our own world the mainstays of a society based on a truly social sense of mutuality are breaking down, indicating that perhaps society as we know it has outworn its usefulness and that by clinging to an outworn system we are bringing about our own destruction. Family, economy, government and religion, the basic categories of social activity and behavior, no longer create any sense of social unity involving a shared and mutual responsibility among all members of our society. At best they enable the individual to survive as an individual. It is the world of the individual, as is the world of the Ik. . . .

The Ik teach us that our much vaunted human values are not inherent in humanity at all but are associated only with a particular form of survival called society and that all, even society itself, are luxuries that can be dispensed with. That does not make them any less wonderful, and if man has any greatness, it is surely in his ability to maintain these values, even shortening an already pitifully short life rather than sacrifice his humanity. But that too involves choice, and the Ik teach us that man can lose the will to make it. That is the point at which there is an end to truth, to goodness and to beauty, an end to the struggle for their achievement, which gives life to the individual and strength and meaning to society. The Ik have relinquished all luxury in the name of individual survival, and they live on as a people without life, without passion, beyond humanity. We pursue those trivial, idiotic technological encumbrances, and all the time we are losing our potential for social rather than individual survival, for hating as well as loving, losing perhaps our last chance to enjoy life with all the passion that is our nature.

CHAPTER 3 Socialization and Personality Development

3.1 GEORGE HERBERT MEAD

The Development of the Self in Social Interaction

Unless they are socialized, people lack language, culture, abstract thought, and a concept of the self. How does this socialization take place and allow the human animal to attain complexity of thought, motivations, and actions? George Herbert Mead provided a truly brilliant answer to this question in the 1920s.

Mead (1863–1931) was a sociologist and social philosopher at the University of Chicago in the 1920s. Together with his colleagues Charles H. Cooley, W. I. Thomas, and others, he developed the field of symbolic interactionism, which holds that social interactions develop through symbols, language, signs, and gestures. He helped change the way we think about ourselves and about the way we develop through interaction with relatives and the larger society.

In the following excerpt, Mead discusses his theory on the development of the self through social interaction. He elaborates on the process of socialization and the concepts of role-taking, the significant other, and the generalized other.

Key Concept: the self

*I*n our statement of the development of intelligence we have already suggested that the language process is essential for the development of the self.

The self has a character which is different from that of the physiological organism proper. The self is something which has a development; it is not initially there, at birth, but arises in the process of social experience and activity, that is, develops in the given individual as a result of his relations to that process as a whole and to other individuals within that process. . . .

The individual experiences himself as such, not directly, but only indirectly, from the particular standpoints of other individual members of the same social group, or from the generalized standpoint of the social group as a whole to which he belongs. For he enters his own experience as a self or individual, not directly or immediately, not by becoming a subject to himself, but only in so far as he first becomes an object to himself just as other individuals are objects to him or in his experience; and he becomes an object to himself only by taking the attitudes of other individuals toward himself within a social environment or context of experience and behavior in which both he and they are involved. . . .

The self, as that which can be an object to itself, is essentially a social structure, and it arises in social experience. After a self has arisen, it in a certain sense provides for itself its social experiences, and so we can conceive of an absolutely solitary self. But it is impossible to conceive of a self arising outside of social experience. When it has arisen we can think of a person in solitary confinement for the rest of his life, but who still has himself as a companion, and is able to think and to converse with himself as he had communicated with others. That process to which I have just referred, of responding to one's self as another responds to it, taking part in one's own conversation with others, being aware of what one is saying and using that awareness of what one is saying to determine what one is going to say thereafter—that is a process with which we are all familiar. We are continually following up our own address to other persons by an understanding of what we are saying, and using that understanding in the direction of our continued speech. We are finding out what we are going to say, what we are going to do, by saying and doing, and in the process we are continually controlling the process itself. In the conversation of gestures what we say calls out a certain response in another and that in turn changes our own action, so that we shift from what we started to do because of the reply the other makes. The conversation of gestures is the beginning of communication. The individual comes to carry on a conversation of gestures with himself. He says something, and that calls out a certain reply in himself which makes him change what he was going to say. One starts to say something, we will presume an unpleasant something, but when he starts to say it he realizes it is cruel. The effect on himself of what he is saying checks him; there is here a conversation of gestures between the individual and himself. We mean by significant speech that the action is one that affects the individual himself, and that the effect upon the individual himself is part of the intelligent carrying-out of the conversation with others. Now we, so to speak, amputate that social phase and dispense with it for the time being, so that one is talking to one's self as one would talk to another person. . . .

We find in children . . . imaginary companions which a good many children produce in their own experience. They organize in this way the responses which they call out in other persons and call out also in themselves. Of course, this playing with an imaginary companion is only a peculiarly interesting phase of ordinary play. Play in this sense, especially the stage which precedes the organized games, is a play at something. A child plays at being a mother, at being a teacher, at being a policeman; that is, it is taking different rôles, as we say. We have something that suggests this in what we call the play of animals: a cat will play with her kittens, and dogs play with each other. Two dogs playing with each other will attack and defend, in a process which if carried through would amount to an actual fight. There is a combination of responses which checks the depth of the bite. But we do not have in such a situation the dogs taking a definite rôle in the sense that a child deliberately takes the rôle of another. This tendency on the part of the children is what we are working with in the kindergarten where the rôles which the children assume are made the basis for training. When a child does assume a rôle he has in himself the stimuli which call out that particular response or group of responses. He may, of course, run away when he is chased, as the dog does, or he may turn around and strike back just as the dog does in his play. But that is not the same as playing at something. Children get together to "play Indian." This means that the child has a certain set of stimuli which call out in itself the responses that they would call out in others, and which answer to an Indian. In the play period the child utilizes his own responses to these stimuli which he makes use of in building a self. The response which he has a tendency to make to these stimuli organizes them. He plays that he is, for instance, offering himself something, and he buys it; he gives a letter to himself and takes it away; he addresses himself as a parent, as a teacher; he arrests himself as a policeman. He has a set of stimuli which call out in himself the sort of responses they call out in others. He takes this group of responses and organizes them into a certain whole. Such is the simplest form of being another to one's self. It involves a temporal situation. The child says something in one character and responds in another character, and then his responding in another character is a stimulus to himself in the first character, and so the conversation goes on. A certain organized structure arises in him and in his other which replies to it, and these carry on the conversation of gestures between themselves.

If we contrast play with the situation in an organized game, we note the essential difference that the child who plays in a game must be ready to take the attitude of everyone else involved in that game, and that these different rôles must have a definite relationship to each other. Taking a very simple game such as hide-and-seek, everyone with the exception of the one who is hiding is a person who is hunting. A child does not require more than the person who is hunted and the one who is hunting. If a child is playing in the first sense he just goes on playing, but there is no basic organization gained. In that early stage he passes from one rôle to another just as a whim takes him. But in a game where a number of individuals are involved, then the child taking one rôle must be ready to take the rôle of everyone else. If he gets in a baseball nine he must have the responses of each position involved in his own position. He must know what everyone else is going to do in order to carry out his own play. He has to take all of these rôles. They do not all have to be present in consciousness at the same time, but at some moments he has to have three or four individuals present in his own attitude, such as the one who is going to throw the ball, the one who is going to catch it, and so on. These responses must be, in some degree, present in his own make-up. In the game, then, there is a set of responses of such others so organized that the attitude of one calls out the appropriate attitudes of the other.

This organization is put in the form of the rules of the game. Children take a great interest in rules. They make rules on the spot in order to help themselves out of difficulties. Part of the enjoyment of the game is to get these rules. Now, the rules are the set of responses which a particular attitude calls out. You can demand a certain response in others if you take a certain attitude. These responses are all in yourself as well. There you get an organized set of such responses as that to which I have referred, which is something more elaborate than the rôles found in play. Here there is just a set of responses that follow on each other indefinitely. At such a stage we speak of a child as not yet having a fully developed self. The child responds in a fairly intelligent fashion to the immediate stimuli that come to him, but they are not organized. He does not organize his life as we would like to have him do, namely, as a whole. There is just a set of responses to the type of play. The child reacts to a certain stimulus, and the reaction is in himself that is called out in others, but he is not a whole self. In his game he has to have an organization of these rôles; otherwise he cannot play the game. The game represents the passage in the life of the child from taking the rôle of others in play to the organized part that is essential to self-consciousness in the full sense of the term. . . .

The organized community or social group which gives to the individual his unity of self may be called "the generalized other." The attitude of the generalized other is the attitude of the whole community. Thus, for example, in the case of such a social group as a ball team, the team is the generalized other in so far as it enters—as an organized process or social activity—into the experience of any one of the individual members of it. . . .

It is in the form of the generalized other that the social process influences the behavior of the individuals involved in it and carrying it on, i.e., that the community exercises control over the conduct of its individual members; for it is in this form that the social process or community enters as a determining factor into the individual's thinking. In abstract thought the individual takes the attitude of the generalized other toward himself, without reference to its expression in any particular other individuals; and in concrete thought he takes that attitude in so far as it is expressed in the attitudes toward his behavior of those other individuals with whom he is involved in the given social situation or act. But only by taking the attitude of the generalized other toward himself, in one or another of these ways, can he think at all; for only thus can thinking—or the internalized conversation of gestures which constitutes thinking—occur. And only through the taking by individuals of the attitude or attitudes of the generalized other toward themselves is the existence of a universe of discourse, as that system of common or social meanings which thinking presupposes at its context, rendered possible. . . .

What goes to make up the organized self is the organization of the attitudes which are common to the group. A person is a personality because he belongs to a community, because he takes over the institutions of that community into his own conduct. He takes its language as a medium by which he gets his personality, and then through a process of taking the different rôles that all the others furnish he comes to get the attitude of the members of the community. Such, in a certain sense, is the structure of a man's personality. There are certain common responses which each individual has toward certain common things, and in so far as those common responses are awakened in the individual when he is affecting other persons he arouses his own self. The structure, then, on which the self is built is this response which is common to all, for one has to be a member of a community to be a self. Such responses are abstract attitudes, but they constitute just what we term a man's character. They give him what we term his principles, the acknowledged attitudes of all members of the community toward what are the values of that community. He is putting himself in the place of the generalized other, which represents the organized responses of all the members of the group. It is that which guides conduct controlled by principles, and a person who has such an organized group of responses is a man whom we say has character, in the moral sense. . . .

There is one other matter which I wish briefly to refer to now. The only way in which we can react against the disapproval of the entire community is by setting up a higher sort of community which in a certain sense out-votes the one we find. A person may reach a point of going against the whole world about him; he may stand out by himself over against it. But to do that he has to speak with the voice of reason to himself. He has to comprehend the voices of the past and of the future. That is the only way in which the self can get a voice which is more than the voice of the community. As a rule we assume that this general voice of the community is identical with the larger community of the past and the future; we assume that an organized custom represents what we call morality. The things one cannot do are those which everybody would condemn. If we take the attitude of the community over against our own responses, that is a true statement, but we must not forget this other capacity, that of replying to the community and insisting on the gesture of the community changing. We can reform the order of things; we can insist on making the community standards better standards. We are not simply bound by the community. We are engaged in a conversation in which what we say is listened to by the community and its response is one which is affected by what we have to say. This is especially true in critical situations. A man rises up and defends himself for what he does; he has his "day in court"; he can present his views. He can perhaps change the attitude of the community toward himself. The process of conversation is one in which the individual has not only the right but the duty of talking to the community of which he is a part, and bringing about those changes which take place through the interaction of individuals. That is the way, of course, in which society gets ahead, by just such interactions as those in which some person thinks a thing out. We are continually changing our social system in some respects, and we are able to do that intelligently because we can think.

Erik Erikson's Eight Ages of Man: One Man in His Time Plays Many Psychosocial Parts

Sigmund Freud changed the world's understanding of human nature by demonstrating the importance and richness of the unconscious in human behavior and personality. He argued that many of the crucial experiences in the development of the unconscious and of personality occur in early childhood, meaning that pathologies in adults could be traced back to their early years. Later psychoanalysts concluded that Freud overemphasized the extent to which personality is formed in early childhood. Erik Erikson, a pupil of Freud, was a leader in revising Freudian theory to explain how personalities develop during adulthood. Erikson theorized that the early years are indeed important but not decisive. The process of socialization and development continues throughout the life cycle of the individual.

David Elkind (b. 1931) is a child development psychologist and a professor in and chair of the Department of Child Study at Tufts University in Medford, Massachusetts. He has written a superb summary of Erikson's work, which appears in the following selection. He discusses Erikson's eight stages of development, beginning with the first year of an infant's life and continuing to old age. The last stage can be either one of integrity or despair, depending on one's life experiences. The importance of Erikson's work, as viewed by Elkind, is that he advanced psychoanalytical theory beyond Freud without minimizing the historic achievements of Freud.

Key Concept: stages of development

*A*t a recent faculty reception I happened to join a small group in which a young mother was talking about her "identity crisis." She and her husband, she said, had decided not to have any more children and she was depressed at the thought of being past the child-bearing stage. It was as if, she continued, she had been robbed of some part of herself and now needed to find a new function to replace the old one.

When I remarked that her story sounded like a case history from a book by Erik Erikson, she replied, "Who's Erikson?" It is a reflection on the intellectual modesty and literary decorum of Erik H. Erikson, psychoanalyst and professor of developmental psychology at Harvard, that so few of the many people who today talk about the "identity crisis" know anything of the man who pointed out its pervasiveness as a problem in contemporary society two decades ago.

Erikson has, however, contributed more to social science than his delineation of identity problems in modern man. His descriptions of the stages of the life cycle, for example, have advanced psychoanalytic theory to the point where it can now describe the development of the healthy personality on its own terms and not merely as the opposite of a sick one. Likewise, Erikson's emphasis upon the problems unique to adolescents and adults living in today's society has helped to rectify the one-sided emphasis on childhood as the beginning and end of personality development.

Finally, in his biographical studies, such as "Young Man Luther" and "Gandhi's Truth" (which . . . won a National Book Award in philosophy and religion), Erikson emphasizes the inherent strengths of the human personality by showing how individuals can use their neurotic symptoms and conflicts for creative and constructive social purposes while healing themselves in the process. . . .

It is with the psychosocial development of the ego that Erikson's observations and theoretical constructions are primarily concerned. Erikson has thus been able to introduce innovations into psychoanalytic theory without either rejecting or ignoring Freud's monumental contribution. [see box] . . .

Erikson set forth the implications of his clinical observations in "Childhood and Society." In that book, the summation and integration of 15 years of research, he made three major contributions to the study of the human ego. He posited (1) that, side by side with the stages of psychosexual development described by Freud (the oral, anal, phallic, genital, Oedipal and pubertal), were psychosocial stages of ego development, in which the individual had to establish new basic orientations to himself and his social world; (2) that personality development continued throughout the whole life cycle; and (3) that each stage had a positive *as well* as a negative component.

Much about these contributions—and about Erikson's way of thinking—can be understood by looking at his scheme of life stages. Erikson identifies eight stages in the human life cycle, in each of which a new dimension of "social interaction" becomes possible—that is, a new dimension in a person's interaction with himself, and with his social environment.

David Elkind

TRUST VS. MISTRUST

The first stage corresponds to the oral stage in classical psychoanalytic theory and usually extends through the first year of life. In Erikson's view, the new dimension of social interaction that emerges during this period involves basic

Freud's "Ages of Man"

Erik Erikson's definition of the "eight ages of man" is a work of synthesis and insight by a psychoanalytically trained and worldly mind. Sigmund Freud's description of human phases stems from his epic psychological discoveries and centers almost exclusively on the early years of life. A brief summary of the phases posited by Freud:

Oral stage—roughly the first year of life, the period during which the mouth region provides the greatest sensual satisfaction. Some derivative behavioral traits which may be seen at this time are *incorporativeness* (first six months of life) and *aggressiveness* (second six months of life).

Anal stage—roughly the second and third years of life. During this period the site of greatest sensual pleasures shifts to the anal and urethral areas. Derivative behavioral traits are *retentiveness* and *expulsiveness*.

Phallic stage—roughly the third and fourth years of life. The site of greatest sensual pleasure during this stage is the genital region. Behavior traits derived from this period include *intrusiveness* (male) and *receptiveness* (female).

Oedipal stage—roughly the fourth and fifth years of life. At this stage the young person takes the parent of the opposite sex as the object or provider of sensual satisfaction and regards the same-sexed parent as a rival. (The "family romance.") Behavior traits originating in this period are *seductiveness* and *competitiveness*.

Latency stage—roughly the years from age 6 to 11. The child resolves the Oedipus conflict by identifying with the parent of the [same] sex and by so doing satisfies sensual needs vicariously. Behavior traits developed during this period include *conscience* (or the internalization of parental moral and ethical demands).

Puberty stage—roughly 11 to 14. During this period there is an integration and subordination of oral, anal and phallic sensuality to an overriding and unitary genital *sexuality*. The genital sexuality of puberty has another young person of the opposite sex as its object, and discharge (at least for boys) as its aim. Derivative behavior traits (associated with the control and regulation of genital sexuality) are *intellectualization* and *estheticism*.

—D.E.

trust at the one extreme, and *mistrust* at the other. The degree to which the child comes to trust the world, other people and himself depends to a considerable extent upon the quality of the care that he receives. The infant whose needs are met when they arise, whose discomforts are quickly removed, who is cuddled, fondled, played with and talked to, develops a sense of the world as a safe place to be and of people as helpful and dependable. When, however, the care is inconsistent, inadequate and rejecting, it fosters a basic mistrust, an attitude of fear and suspicion on the part of the infant toward the world in general and people in particular that will carry through to later stages of development.

It should be said at this point that the problem of basic trust-versus-mistrust (as is true for all the later dimensions) is not resolved once and for all during the first year of life; it arises again at each successive stage of development. There is both hope and danger in this. The child who enters school with a sense of mistrust may come to trust a particular teacher who has taken the trouble to make herself trustworthy; with this second chance, he overcomes his early mistrust. On the other hand, the child who comes through infancy with a vital sense of trust can still have his sense of mistrust activated at a later stage if, say, his parents are divorced and separated under acrimonious circumstances.

This point was brought home to me in a very direct way by a 4-year-old patient I saw in a court clinic. He was being seen at the court clinic because his adoptive parents, who had had him for six months, now wanted to give him back to the agency. They claimed that he was cold and unloving, took things and could not be trusted. He was indeed a cold and apathetic boy, but with good reason. About a year after his illegitimate birth, he was taken away from his mother, who had a drinking problem, and was shunted back and forth among several foster homes. Initially he had tried to relate to the persons in the foster homes, but the relationships never had a chance to develop because he was moved at just the wrong times. In the end he gave up trying to reach out to others, because the inevitable separations hurt too much.

Like the burned child who dreads the flame, this emotionally burned child shunned the pain of emotional involvement. He had trusted his mother, but now he trusted no one. Only years of devoted care and patience could now undo the damage that had been done to this child's sense of trust.

AUTONOMY VS. DOUBT

Stage Two spans the second and third years of life, the period which Freudian theory calls the anal stage. Erikson sees here the emergence of *autonomy*. This autonomy dimension builds upon the child's new motor and mental abilities. At this stage the child can not only walk but also climb, open and close, drop, push and pull, hold and let go. The child takes pride in these new accomplishments and wants to do everything himself, whether it be pulling the wrapper off a piece of candy, selecting the vitamin out of the bottle or flushing the toilet. If parents recognize the young child's need to do what he is capable of doing at his own pace and in his own time, then he develops a sense that he is able to control his muscles, his impulses, himself and, not insignificantly, his environment—the sense of autonomy.

When, however, his caretakers are impatient and do for him what he is capable of doing himself, they reinforce a sense of shame and doubt. To be sure, every parent has rushed a child at times and children are hardy enough to endure such lapses. It is only when caretaking is consistently overprotective and criticism of "accidents" (whether these be wetting, soiling, spilling or breaking things) is harsh and unthinking that the child develops an excessive sense of shame with respect to other people and an excessive sense of doubt about own abilities to control his world and himself.

If the child leaves this stage with less autonomy than shame or doubt, he will be handicapped in his attempts to achieve autonomy in adolescence and adulthood. Contrariwise, the child who moves through this stage with his sense of autonomy buoyantly outbalancing his feelings of shame and doubt is well prepared to be autonomous at later phases in the life cycle. Again, however, the balance of autonomy to shame and doubt set up during this period can be changed in either positive or negative directions by later events.

It might be well to note, in addition, that too much autonomy can be as harmful as too little. I have in mind a patient of 7 who had a heart condition. He had learned very quickly how terrified his parents were of any signs in him of cardiac difficulty. With the psychological acuity given to children, he soon ruled the household. The family could not go shopping, or for a drive, or on a holiday if he did not approve. On those rare occasions when the parents had had enough and defied him, he would get angry and his purple hue and gagging would frighten them into submission.

Actually, this boy was frightened of this power (as all children would be) and was really eager to give it up. When the parents and the boy came to realize this, and to recognize that a little shame and doubt were a healthy counterpoise to an inflated sense of autonomy, the three of them could once again assume their normal roles.

INITIATIVE VS. GUILT

In this stage (the genital stage of classical psychoanalysis) the child, age 4 to 5, is pretty much master of his body and can ride a tricycle, run, cut and hit. He can thus initiate motor activities of various sorts on his own and no longer merely responds to or imitates the actions of other children. The same holds true for his language and fantasy activities. Accordingly, Erikson argues that the social dimension that appears at this stage has *initiative* at one of its poles and *guilt* at the other.

Whether the child will leave this stage with his sense of initiative far outbalancing his sense of guilt depends to a considerable extent upon how parents respond to his self-initiated activities. Children who are given much freedom and opportunity to initiate motor play such as running, bike riding, sliding, skating, tussling and wrestling have their sense of initiative reinforced. Initiative is also reinforced when parents answer their children's questions (intellectual initiative) and do not deride or inhibit fantasy or play activity. On the other hand, if the child is made to feel that his motor activity is bad, that his questions are a nuisance and that his play is silly and stupid, then he may develop a sense of guilt over self-initiated activities in general that will persist through later life stages.

INDUSTRY VS. INFERIORITY

Stage Four is the age period from 6 to 11, the elementary school years (described by classical psychoanalysis as the *latency phase*). It is a time during which the child's love for the parent of the opposite sex and rivalry with the same-sexed parent (elements in the so-called family romance) are quiescent. It is also a period during which the child becomes capable of deductive reasoning, and of playing and learning by rules. It is not until this period, for example, that children can really play marbles, checkers and other "take turn" games that require obedience to rules. Erikson argues that the psychosocial dimension that emerges during this period has a sense of *industry* at one extreme and a sense of *inferiority* at the other.

The term industry nicely captures a dominant theme of this period during which the concern with how things are made, how they work and what they do predominates. It is the Robinson Crusoe age in the sense that the enthusiasm and minute detail with which Crusoe describes his activities appeals to the child's own budding sense of industry. When children are encouraged in their efforts to make, do, or build practical things (whether it be to construct creepy crawlers, tree houses, or airplane models—or to cook, bake or sew), are allowed to finish their products, and are praised and rewarded for the results, then the sense of industry is enhanced. But parents who see their children's efforts at making and doing as "mischief," and as simply "making a mess," help to encourage in children a sense of inferiority.

During these elementary-school years, however, the child's world includes more than the home. Now social institutions other than the family come to play a central role in the developmental crisis of the individual. (Here Erikson introduced still another advance in psychoanalytic theory, which heretofore concerned itself only with the effects of the parents' behavior upon the child's development.)

A child's school experiences affect his industry-inferiority balance. The child, for example, with an I.Q. of 80 to 90 has a particularly traumatic school experience, even when his sense of industry is rewarded and encouraged at home. He is "too bright" to be in special classes, but "too slow" to compete with children of average ability. Consequently he experiences constant failures in his academic efforts that reinforce a sense of inferiority.

On the other hand, the child who had his sense of industry derogated at home can have it revitalized at school through the offices of a sensitive and committed teacher. Whether the child develops a sense of industry or inferiority, therefore, no longer depends solely on the caretaking efforts of the parents but on the actions and offices of other adults as well.

IDENTITY VS. ROLE CONFUSION

When the child moves into adolescence (Stage Five—roughly the ages 12–18), he encounters, according to traditional psychoanalytic theory, a reawakening of the family-romance problem of early childhood. His means of resolving the problem is to seek and find a romantic partner of his own generation. While Erikson does not deny this aspect of adolescence, he points out that there are other problems as well. The adolescent matures mentally as well as physiologically and, in addition to the new feelings, sensations and desires he experiences as a result of changes in his body, he develops a multitude of new ways of looking at and thinking about the world. Among other things, those in adolescence can now think about other people's thinking and wonder about what other people think of them. They can also conceive of ideal families, religions and societies which they then compare with the imperfect families, religions and societies of their own experience. Finally, adolescents become capable of constructing theories and philosophies designed to bring all the varied and conflicting aspects of society into a working, harmonious and peaceful whole. The adolescent, in a word, is an impatient idealist who believes that it is as easy to realize an ideal as it is to imagine it.

Erikson believes that the new interpersonal dimension which emerges during this period has to do with a sense of *ego identity* at the positive end and a sense of *role confusion* at the negative end. That is to say, given the adolescent's newfound integrative abilities, his task is to bring together all of the things he has learned about himself as a son, student, athlete, friend, Scout, newspaper boy, and so on, and integrate these different images of himself into a whole that makes sense and that shows continuity with the past while preparing for the future. To the extent that the young person succeeds in this endeavor, he arrives at a sense of psychosocial identity, a sense of who he is, where he has been and where he is going.

In contrast to the earlier stages, where parents play a more or less direct role in the determination of the result of the developmental crises, the influence of parents during this stage is much more indirect. If the young person reaches adolescence with, thanks to his parents, a vital sense of trust, autonomy, initiative and industry, then his chances of arriving at a meaningful sense of ego identity are much enhanced. The reverse, of course, holds true for the young person who enters adolescence with considerable mistrust, shame, doubt, guilt, and inferiority. Preparation for a successful adolescence, and the attainment of an integrated psychosocial identity must, therefore, begin in the cradle.

Over and above what the individual brings with him from his childhood, the attainment of a sense of personal identity depends upon the social milieu in which he or she grows up. For example, in a society where women are to some extent second-class citizens, it may be harder for females to arrive at a sense of psychosocial identity. Likewise at times, such as the present, when rapid social and technological change breaks down many traditional values, it may be more difficult for young people to find continuity between what they learned and experienced as children and what they learn and experience as adolescents. At such times young people often seek causes that give their lives meaning and direction. The activism of the current generation of young people may well stem, in part at least, from this search.

When the young person cannot attain a sense of personal identity, either because of an unfortunate childhood or difficult social circumstances, he shows a certain amount of *role confusion*—a sense of not knowing what he is, where he belongs or whom he belongs to. Such confusion is a frequent symptom in delinquent young people. Promiscuous adolescent girls, for example, often seem to have a fragmented sense of ego identity. Some young people seek a "negative identity," an identity opposite to the one prescribed for them by their family and friends. Having an identity as a "delinquent," or as a "hippie," or even as an "acid head," may sometimes be preferable to having no identity at all.

In some cases young people do not seek a negative identity so much as they have it thrust upon them. I remember another court case in which the defendant was an attractive 16-year-old girl who had been found "tricking it" in a trailer located just outside the grounds of an Air Force base. From about the age of 12, her mother had encouraged her to dress seductively and to go out with boys. When she returned from dates, her sexually frustrated mother demanded a kiss-by-kiss, caress-by-caress description of the evening's activities. After the mother had vicariously satisfied her sexual needs, she proceeded to call her daughter a "whore" and a "dirty tramp." As the girl told me, "Hell, I have the name, so I might as well play the role."

Failure to establish a clear sense of personal identity at adolescence does not guarantee perpetual failure. And the person who attains a working sense of ego identity in adolescence will of necessity encounter challenges and threats to that identity as he moves through life. Erikson, perhaps more than any other personality theorist, has emphasized that life is constant change and that confronting problems at one stage in life is not a guarantee against the reappearance of these problems at later stages, or against the finding of new solutions to them.

INTIMACY VS. ISOLATION

Stage Six in the life cycle is young adulthood; roughly the period of courtship and early family life that extends from late adolescence till early middle age. For this stage, and the stages described hereafter, classical psychoanalysis has nothing new or major to say. For Erikson, however, the previous attainment of a sense of personal identity and the engagement in productive work that marks this period give rise to a new interpersonal dimension of *intimacy* at the one extreme and *isolation* at the other.

When Erikson speaks of intimacy he means much more than love-making alone; he means the ability to share with and care about another person without fear of losing oneself in the process. In the case of intimacy, as in the case of identity, success or failure no longer depends directly upon the parents but only indirectly as they have contributed to the individual's success or failure at the earlier stages. Here, too, as in the case of identity, social conditions may help or hinder the establishment of a sense of intimacy. Likewise, intimacy need not involve sexuality; it includes the relationship between friends. Soldiers who have served together under the most dangerous circumstances often develop a sense of commitment to one another that exemplifies intimacy in its broadest sense. If a sense of intimacy is not established with friends or a marriage partner, the result, in Erikson's view, is a sense of isolation—of being alone without anyone to share with or care for.

GENERATIVITY VS. SELF-ABSORPTION

This stage—middle age—brings with it what Erikson speaks of as either *generativity* or *self-absorption*, and stagnation. What Erikson means by generativity is that the person begins to be concerned with others beyond his immediate family, with future generations and the nature of the society and world in which those generations will live. Generativity does not reside only in parents; it can be found in any individual who actively concerns himself with the welfare of young people and with making the world a better place for them to live and to work.

Those who fail to establish a sense of generativity fall into a state of self-absorption in which their personal needs and comforts are of predominant concern. A fictional case of self-absorption is Dickens's Scrooge in "A Christmas Carol." In his one-sided concern with money and in his disregard for the interests and welfare of his young employee, Bob Cratchit, Scrooge exemplifies the self-absorbed, embittered (the two often go together) old man. Dickens also illustrated, however, what Erikson points out: namely, that unhappy solutions to life's crises are not irreversible. Scrooge, at the end of the tale, manifested both a sense of generativity and of intimacy which he had not experienced before.

INTEGRITY VS. DESPAIR

Stage Eight in the Eriksonian scheme corresponds roughly to the period when the individual's major efforts are nearing completion and when there is time for reflection—and for the enjoyment of grandchildren, if any. The psychosocial dimension that comes into prominence now has *integrity* on one hand and *despair* on the other.

The sense of integrity arises from the individual's ability to look back on his life with satisfaction. At the other extreme is the individual who looks back upon his life as a series of missed opportunities and missed directions; now in the twilight years he realizes that it is too late to start again. For such a person the inevitable result is a sense of despair at what might have been.

These, then, are the major stages in the life cycle as described by Erikson. Their presentation, for one thing, frees the clinician to treat adult emotional problems as failures (in part at least) to solve genuinely adult personality crises and not, as heretofore, as mere residuals of infantile frustrations and conflicts. This view of personality growth, moreover, takes some of the onus off parents and takes account of the role which society and the person himself play in the formation of an individual personality. Finally, Erikson has offered hope for us all by demonstrating that each phase of growth has its strengths as well as its weaknesses and that failures at one stage of development can be rectified by successes at later stages.

3.3 LENORE J. WEITZMAN, DEBORAH EIFLER, ELIZABETH HOKADA, AND CATHERINE ROSS

Sex-Role Socialization in Picture Books for Preschool Children

To a large extent we become what we have been taught by example, instruction, and through give and take. It is interesting to examine some of the materials that helped socialize us to find out what values and behavior patterns these materials teach or reinforce. The selection that follows analyzes the picture books to which young people born between 1966 and 1970 were exposed, in order to examine the values and ideas that these books promulgated.

Lenore J. Weitzman is a professor in the Department of Sociology at Harvard University, whose research interests include the sociology of law, sex roles, the family, family law, the process of legal change, divorce law reform, and the social effects of divorce. In the following article, originally published to wide attention in 1972, Weitzman and her colleagues report on a study in which they found that books that won distinguished awards were mainly about males and that male characters outnumbered females eleven to one. Furthermore, these books portray boys in positive terms and girls in largely negative terms. Boys are seen as active and adventurous; girls are seen as passive and immobile. Boys seek exciting pursuits and independence; girls are shy and dependent. The discussion by Weitzman et al. on these inequities and how they affect the development of a child's self-image and future expectations is enlightening.

Key Concept: sex roles

INTRODUCTION

Sex-role socialization constitutes one of the most important learning experiences for the young child. By the time the child enters kindergarten, he or she is able to make sex-role distinctions and express sex-role preferences. Boys already identify with masculine roles, and girls with feminine roles (Brown 1956). They also learn the appropriate behavior for both boys and girls and men and women. Hartley (1960) reports that, by the time they are four, children realize that the primary feminine role is housekeeping, while the primary masculine role is wage earning.

In addition to learning sex-role identification and sex-role expectations, boys and girls are socialized to accept society's definition of the relative worth of each of the sexes and to assume the personality characteristics that are "typical" of members of each sex. With regard to relative status, they learn that boys are more highly valued than girls. And, with regard to personality differences, they learn that boys are active and achieving while girls are passive and emotional. Eight-year-old boys describe girls as clean, neat, quiet, gentle, and fearful, while they describe adult women as unintelligent, ineffective, unadventurous, nasty, and exploitative (Hartley 1959). Indeed, Maccoby finds that, although girls begin life as better achievers than boys, they gradually fall behind as they become socialized (Maccoby 1966).

In this paper we wish to concentrate on one aspect of sex-role socialization: the socialization of preschool children through picture books. Picture books play an important role in early sex-role socialization because they are a vehicle for the presentation of societal values to the young child. Through books, children learn about the world outside of their immediate environment: they learn about what other boys and girls do, say, and feel; they learn about what is right and wrong; and they learn what is expected of children their age. In addition, books provide children with role models—images of what they can and should be like when they grow up.

Children's books reflect cultural values and are an important instrument for persuading children to accept those values. They also contain role prescriptions which encourage the child to conform to acceptable standards of behavior. The Child Study Association (1969), aware of the socialization potential of books, states that a book's emotional and intellectual impact on a young reader must be considered. Therefore it recommends that children's books present positive ethical values. . . .

STUDY DESIGN

Our study focuses on picture books for the preschool child. These books are often read over and over again at a time when children are in the process of developing their own sexual identities. Picture books are read to children when they are most impressionable, before other socialization influences (such as school, teachers, and peers) become more important at later stages in the child's development.

We have chosen to examine how sex roles are treated in those children's books identified as the "very best": the winners of the Caldecott Medal. The Caldecott Medal is given by the Children's Service Committee of the American

Library Association for the most distinguished picture book of the year. The medal is the most coveted prize for preschool books. Books on the list of winners (and runners-up) are ordered by practically all children's libraries in the United States. . . .

Although we have computed a statistical analysis of all the Caldecott winners from the inception of the award in 1938, we have concentrated our intensive analysis on the winners and runners-up for the past five years. Most of the examples cited in this paper are taken from the 18 books in this latter category. . . .

In order to assure ourselves of the representativeness of our study, we have also examined three other groups of children's books: the Newbery Award winners, the Little Golden Books, and the "prescribed behavior" or etiquette books.

The Newbery Award is given by the American Library Association for the best book for school-age children. . . .

The Little Golden Books we have sampled are the best sellers in children's books, since we have taken only those Little Golden Books that sold over three million copies. These books sell for 39 cents in grocery stores, Woolworth's, Grant's, and toy and game stores. Consequently, they reach a more broadly based audience than do the more expensive Caldecott winners.

The last type of book we studied is what we call the "prescribed behavior" or etiquette book. Whereas other books only imply sex-role prescriptions, these books are explicit about the proper behavior for boys and girls. They also portray adult models and advise children on future roles and occupations.

If we may anticipate our later findings, we would like to note here that the findings from the latter three samples strongly parallel those from the Caldecott sample. Although the remainder of this paper will be devoted primarily to the Caldecott sample, we will use some of the other books for illustrative purposes.

THE INVISIBLE FEMALE

It would be impossible to discuss the image of females in children's books without first noting that, in fact, women are simply invisible. We found that females were underrepresented in the titles, central roles, pictures, and stories of every sample of books we examined. Most children's books are about boys, men, and male animals, and most deal exclusively with male adventures. Most pictures show men—singly or in groups. Even when women can be found in the books, they often play insignificant roles, remaining both inconspicuous and nameless.

A tabulation of the distribution of illustrations in the picture books is probably the single best indicator of the importance of men and women in these books. Because women comprise 51% of our population, if there were no bias in these books they should be presented in roughly half of the pictures. However, in our sample of 18 Caldecott winners and runners-up in the past five years we found 261 pictures of males compared with 23 pictures of females. This is a ratio of 11 pictures of males for every one picture of a female. If we include animals with obvious identities, the bias is even greater. The ratio of male to female animals is 95:1.

Turning to the titles of the Caldecott Medal winners since the award's inception in 1938, we find that the ratio of titles featuring males to those featuring females is 8:3. Despite the presence of the popular *Cinderella, Snow White, Hansel and Gretel,* and *Little Red Riding Hood* in the sample of Golden Books that have sold more than three million copies, we find close to a 3:1 male/ female ratio in this sample. The 49 books that have received the Newbery Award since 1922 depict more than three males to every one female. . . .

When there are female characters, they are usually insignificant or inconspicuous. The one girl in *Goggles* (Keats 1969) is shown playing quietly in a corner. The wife in *The Sun and the Moon* (Dayrell 1968) helps by carrying wood but never speaks. There are two women in *The Fool of the World* (Ronsome 1968): the mother, who packs lunch for her sons and waves goodby, and the princess whose hand in marriage is the object of the Fool's adventures. The princess is shown only twice: once peering out of the window of the castle, and the second time in the wedding scene in which the reader must strain to find her. She does not have anything to say throughout the adventure, and of course she is not consulted in the choice of her husband; on the last page, however, the narrator assures us that she soon "loved him to distraction." Loving, watching, and helping are among the few activities allowed to women in picture books. . . .

Although there is much variation in plot among the picture books, a significant majority includes some form of male adventure. . . . The male central characters engage in many exciting and heroic adventures which emphasize their cleverness.

In our sample of the Caldecott winners and runners-up in the last five years, we found only two of the 18 books were stories about girls. In one of these stories, *Sam, Bangs, and Moonshine* (Ness 1967), the girl has a boy's name. In the second, *The Emperor and the Kite* (Yolen 1967), the heroine is a foreign princess.

Each of these girls does engage in an adventure. Sam's adventure takes place in her daydreams, while the adventure of the princess Djeow Seow occurs when her father's kingdom is seized by evil men. Like the male central characters who engage in rescues, Djeow Seow manages to save her father, but she accomplishes this task only by being so tiny and inconspicuous that the evil men do not notice her. Although Djeow Seow is one of the two women central characters, the message conveyed to readers seems to be that a girl can only triumph by playing the traditional feminine role. Women who succeed are those who are unobtrusive and work quietly behind the scenes. Women who succeed are little and inconspicuous—as are most women in picture books. Even heroines remain "invisible" females.

THE ACTIVITIES OF BOYS AND GIRLS

We can summarize our first findings about differences in the activities of boys and girls by noting that in the world of picture books boys are active and girls are passive. Not only are boys presented in more exciting and adventure-some roles, but they engage in more varied pursuits and demand more independence. . . .

In contrast, most of the girls in the picture books are passive and immobile. Some of them are restricted by their clothing—skirts and dresses are soiled easily and prohibit more adventuresome activities. In *The Fool of the World and the Flying Ship* (Ronsome 1968), the hero, the Fool, is dressed in a sensible manner, one which does not inhibit his movement in the tasks he has to accomplish. The princess, however, for whom all the exploits are waged, remains no more than her long gown allows her to be: a prize, an unrealistic passive creature symbolizing the reward for male adventuresomeness.

A second difference between the activities of boys and girls is that the girls are more often found indoors. This places another limitation on the activities and potential adventures of girls. . . . While boys play in the real world outdoors, girls sit and watch them—cut off from that world by the window, porch, or fence around their homes. This distinction parallels Erik Erikson's (1964) conception of the masculine outer space and the feminine inner space.

Our third observation deals with the service activities performed by the girls who remain at home. Even the youngest girls in the stories play traditional feminine roles, directed toward pleasing and helping their brothers and fathers. Obadiah's sisters cook in the kitchen as he sits at the table sipping hot chocolate after his adventures. In *The Emperor and the Kite* (Yolen 1967), the emperor's daughters bring food to the emperor's table, but their brothers rule the kingdom.

While girls serve, boys lead, Drummer Hoff, although only a boy, plays the crucial role in the final firing of the cannon. Lupin, the Indian boy in *The Angry Moon* (Sleator 1970), directs the escape from the moon god. He leads Lapowinsa, a girl exactly his size and age, every step of the way. Even at the end of the story, after the danger of the Angry Moon is past, Lupin goes down the ladder first "so that he could catch Lapowinsa if she should slip."

Training for a dependent passive role may inhibit a girl's chance for intellectual or creative success. It is likely that the excessive dependency encouraged in girls contributes to the decline in their achievement which becomes apparent as they grow older. Maccoby (1966, p. 35) has found that "For both sexes, there is a tendency for more passive-dependent children to perform poorly on a variety of intellectual tasks, and for independent children to excel."

The rescues featured in many stories require independence and self-confidence. Once again, this is almost exclusively a male activity. Little boys rescue girls or helpless animals. . . .

Finally, we want to note the sense of camaraderie that is encouraged among boys through their adventures. For example, *The Fool of the World* depends upon the help and talents of his male companions. In *Goggles* (Keats 1969), the two male companions together outwit a gang of older boys. . . .

In contrast, one rarely sees only girls working or playing together. Although in reality women spend much of their time with other women, picture books imply that women cannot exist without men. The role of most of the girls is defined primarily in relation to that of the boys and men in their lives. It is interesting to note that Sam turns to a boy, not a girl, to accomplish all of the activity of her fantasies. Her dreams would have no reality without Thomas. . . .

Little girls are often pictured as pretty dolls who are not meant to do anything but be admired and bring pleasure. Their constant smile teaches that women are meant to please, to make others smile, and be happy. This image may reflect parental values. In a study of the attitudes of middle-class fathers toward their children, Aberle and Naegele (1960, pp. 188–98) report that the parent satisfaction with their daughters seemed to focus on their daughters being nice, sweet, pretty, affectionate, and well liked.

If we follow the little boy and little girl as they grow up, we can watch the development of the proper service role in the little woman. We are shown that the girl grows big enough to water the rosebush, stir the cake batter, set the table, play nurse, and help the doctor (who is, of course, a boy), pick fruit from the trees, take milk from the refrigerator, prepare a baby's formula, and feed her baby brother. Conveniently enough for their future husbands, girls in storybooks learn to wash, iron, hang up clothes to dry, cook, and set the table. Of course, when the boy grows up, he engages in more active pursuits: he catches butterflies, mows the lawn, marches in the parade, visits the zoo to feed the elephants, and hammers wood at the workbench. . . .

The rigidity of sex-role stereotypes is not harmful only to little girls. Little boys may feel equally constrained by the necessity to be fearless, brave, and clever at all times. While girls are allowed a great deal of emotional expression, a boy who cries or expresses fear is unacceptable. Just as the only girls who are heroines in picture books have boys' names or are foreign princesses, the only boys who cry in picture books are animals—frogs and toads and donkeys. . . .

ROLE MODELS: ADULT MEN AND WOMEN

Adult role models provide another crucial component of sex-role socialization. By observing adult men and women, boys and girls learn what will be expected of them when they grow older. They are likely to identify with adults of the same sex, and desire to be like them. Thus, role models not only present children with future images of themselves but they also influence a child's aspirations and goals.

We found the image of the adult woman to be stereotyped and limited. Once again, the females are passive while the males are active. Men predominate in the outside activities while more of the women are inside. In the house, the women perform almost exclusively service functions, taking care of the men and children in their families. When men lead, women follow. When men rescue others, women are the rescued.

In most of the stories, the sole adult woman is identified only as a mother or a wife. . . .

The remaining three roles that women play are also exclusively feminine roles: one is a fairy, the second a fairy godmother, and the third an underwater maiden. The fairy godmother is the only adult female who plays an active leadership role. The one nonstereotyped woman is clearly not a "normal" woman—she is a mythical creature.

In contrast to the limited range in women's roles, the roles that men play are varied and interesting. They are storekeepers, housebuilders, kings, spiders, storytellers, gods, monks, fighters, fishermen, policemen, soldiers, adventurers, fathers, cooks, preachers, judges, and farmers.

Perhaps our most significant finding was that *not one* woman in the Caldecott sample had a job or profession. In a country where 40% of the women are in the labor force, and close to 30 million women work, it is absurd to find that women in picture books remain only mothers and wives (U.S. Department of Labor 1969). In fact, 90% of the women in this country will be in the labor force at some time in their lives.

Motherhood is presented in picture books as a full-time, lifetime job, although for most women it is in reality a part-time 10-year commitment. . . .

The way in which the motherhood role is presented in children's books is also unrealistic. She is almost always confined to the house, although she is usually too well dressed for housework. Her duties are not portrayed as difficult or challenging—she is shown as a housebound servant who cares for her husband and children. She washes dishes, cooks, vacuums, yells at the children, cleans up, does the laundry, and takes care of babies. . . .

The picture books do not present a realistic picture of what real mothers do. Real mothers drive cars, read books, vote, take children on trips, balance checkbooks, engage in volunteer activities, ring doorbells canvassing, raise money for charity, work in the garden, fix things in the house, are active in local politics, belong to the League of Women Voters and the PTA, etc.

Nor do these picture books provide a realistic image of fathers and husbands. Fathers never help in the mundane duties of child care. Nor do husbands share the dishwashing, cooking, cleaning, or shopping. From these stereotyped images in picture books, little boys may learn to expect their wives to do all the housework and to cater to their needs. These unreal expectations of marriage will inevitably bring disappointment and discontent to both the male and the female partners. . . .

[W]hen Daddy comes home he not only plays in a more exciting way with the children but he provides their contact with the outside world. While Mommies are restrictive, and "shout if you play near the street," Daddies take you on trips in cars, buses, and trains; Daddies take you to the circus, park, and zoo; buy you ice cream; and teach you to swim. Daddies also understand you better because they "know you're big enough and brave enough to do lots of things that mommies think are much too hard for you." Mothers, however, are useful for taking care of you when you are sick, cleaning up after you, and telling you what to do. Mommies do smile, hug, comfort, and nurture, but they also scold and instruct in a not altogether pleasant manner. They tell you to be quiet, and to "Sit still and eat!" Ironically, this negative image of the nagging mother may be a result of an exclusive devotion to motherhood. As Alice Rossi has observed: "If a woman's adult efforts are concentrated exclusively on her children, she is likely more to stifle than broaden her children's perspective and preparation for adult life. . . . In myriad ways the mother binds the child to her, dampening his initiative, resenting his growing independence in adolescence, creating a subtle dependence which makes it difficult for the child to achieve full adult stature" (1964, p. 113).

In addition to having a negative effect on children, this preoccupation with motherhood may also be harmful to the mother herself. Pauline Bart (1970, p. 72) has reported extreme depression among middle-aged women who have been overinvolved with and have overidentified with their children. . . .

We already observed that little girls are encouraged to succeed by looking pretty and serving others. It should therefore not be surprising to find that the women are concentrated in glamorous and service occupations. The most prestigious feminine occupations are those in which a girl can succeed only if she is physically attractive. The glamour occupations of model and movie star are the two most highly rewarded among the female choices. Since few women can ever achieve high status in these glamorous professions, the real message in these books is that women's true function lies in service. Service occupations, such as nurse, secretary, housewife, mother, and stewardess, reinforce the traditional patterns to feminine success.

Although some of the male occupations also require physical attractiveness (actor) and service (bus driver), there is a much greater range of variation in the other skills they require: baseball players need athletic ability, policemen are supposed to be strong and brave, pilots and doctors need brains, astronauts need mechanical skills and great energy, clowns must be clever and funny, and presidents need political acumen.

If we compare the status level of the male and female occupations, it is apparent that men fill the most prestigious and highly paid positions. They are the doctors, pilots, astronauts, and presidents. Even when men and women are engaged in occupations in the same field, it is the men who hold the positions which demand the most skill and leadership. While men are doctors, women are nurses; while men are pilots, women are stewardesses. Only one of the women is engaged in a professional occupation: the teacher. It is important to note, however, that the authors carefully specified that she was a *nursery school teacher*. . . .

CONCLUSION

Preschool children invest their intellects and imaginations in picture books at a time when they are forming their self-images and future expectations. Our study has suggested that the girls and women depicted in these books are a dull and stereotyped lot. We have noted that little girls receive attention and praise for their attractiveness, while boys are admired for their achievements and cleverness. Most of the women in picture books have status by virtue of their relationships to specific men—they are the wives of the kings, judges, adventurers, and explorers, but they themselves are not the rulers, judges, adventurers, and explorers.

Through picture books, girls are taught to have low aspirations because there are so few opportunities portrayed as available to them. The world of picture books never tells little girls that as women they might find fulfillment outside of their homes or through intellectual pursuits. Women are excluded from the world of sports, politics, and science. Their future occupational world is presented as consisting primarily of glamour and service. Ironically, many of these books are written by prize-winning female authors whose own lives are probably unlike those they advertise.

REFERENCES

Aberle, David F., and Kasper D. Naegele. 1960. "Middle-Class Fathers' Occupational Role and Attitudes towards Children." In *A Modern Introduction to the Family*, edited by Norman W. Bell and Ezra F. Vogel. New York: Free Press.

Bart, Pauline. 1970. "Portney's Mother's Complaint." *Trans-Action* (November/December).

Brown, Daniel G. 1956. "Sex Role Preference in Young Children." *Psychological Monograph* 70, no. 14.

Child Study Association. 1969. *List of Recommended Books*. New York: Child Study Association.

Dayrell, Elphinstone. 1968. *Why the Sun and the Moon Live in the Sky*. Boston: Houghton-Mifflin.

Erikson, Erik H. 1964. "Inner and Outer Space: Reflections on Womanhood." *The Woman in America*, edited by Robert Jay Lifton. Boston: Houghton-Mifflin.

Hartley, Ruth E. 1959. "Sex-Role Pressures and the Socialization of the Male Child." *Psychological Reports* 5:457-68.

_____. 1960. "Children's Concepts of Males and Female Roles." *Merrill-Palmer Quarterly* 6:83-91.

Keats, Jack Ezra. 1969. *Goggles!* Toronto: Macmillan.

Maccoby, Eleanor E. 1966. "Sex Differences in Intellectual Functioning." In *The Development of Sex Differences*. Stanford, Calif.: Stanford University Press.

Ness, Evaline. 1967. *Sam, Bangs, and Moonshine*. New York: Holt, Rinehart & Winston.

Ronsome, Arthur. 1968. *The Fool of the World and the Flying Ship*. New York: Farrar, Straus & Giroux.

Rossi, Alice. 1964. "Equality between the Sexes." *The Woman in America*, edited by Robert Jay Lifton. Boston: Houghton-Mifflin.

Sleator, William. 1970. *The Angry Moon*. Boston: Little, Brown.

U.S. Department of Labor. 1969. *1969 Handbook on Women Workers*. Washington, D.C.: Government Printing Office.

Yolen, Jane. 1967. *The Emperor and the Kite*. Cleveland: World.

3.4 J. ALLEN WILLIAMS, JR., JOETTA A. VERNON, MARTHA C. WILLIAMS, AND KAREN MALECHA

Sex Role Socialization in Picture Books: An Update

In the mid-1980s J. Allen Williams, Jr., and his colleagues replicated the research of Lenore J. Weitzman and her colleagues on sex-role socialization in picture books for preschool children that was reported on in 1972 (see chapter 3, selection 3.3). Their main findings are presented in the following reading. This parallel study enables the reader to learn what has changed and what has not changed during the critical period of the women's movement, at least with respect to gender expectations and gender stereotyping. Williams and his colleagues find that the number of women in picture books has increased significantly, but the characteristics of women have changed very little. Generally women continue to be depicted as passive and nurturant, while a majority of males are shown as independent, active, and frequently quite creative. Williams et al. make some rather illuminating commentary on the social desirability of increasing women's visibility versus expanding their role-playing capacities.

Williams (b. 1936) is a professor of sociology at the University of Lincoln, Nebraska, and he serves on the editorial board of the *Journal of Marriage and the Family.* His research interests include family, environmental sociology, and race and ethnic relations.

Key Concept: sex roles

The current study updates previous research on the way gender is presented in picture books to preschool-age children by replicating and extending the classic study by Weitzman et al. . . .

Based upon the findings from Weitzman et al., and similar studies which followed . . ., efforts arose to promote change. . . .

The present research addresses the question of how effective such efforts have been since the pioneering study by Weitzman et al. fifteen years ago. Have

TABLE 1

61

Comparisons of Gender Visibility

*J. Allen
Williams, Jr.,
et al.*

	1967–71[a]	1972–79	1980–85	p[b]
Human single-gender illustrations				
Total number	188	339	178	
Percent female	11.7	31.6	37.1	.001
Male/female ratio	7.5	2.2	1.7	
Humans illustrated				
Total number	685	1,315	1,041	
Percent female	19.1	32.9	42.2	.001
Male/female ratio	4.2	2.0	1.4	
Nonhuman single-gender illustrations				
Total number	96	39	59	
Percent female	1.0	30.8	15.3	.001
Male/female ratio	95.0	2.3	5.6	
Nonhumans illustrated				
Total number	196	156	168	
Percent female	7.1	23.7	28.6	.001
Male/female ratio	13.0	3.2	2.5	
Books				
Total number	18	29	24	
Percent with no female characters	33.3	27.6	12.5	NS
Percent with female central characters	11.1	24.1	33.3	.094

[a]From Weitzman et al. (1972). Computations for the total numbers of human and nonhuman characters were done by the authors of the present study.

[b]The *p* refers to statistical probabilities using a one-tailed test, determined through the significance of difference between proportions or Fisher's exact test where *N* is small, $Np + 9p < 9$. The significance of difference test is between proportions from Weitzman et al. and the books from 1980–85.

females become visible, significant, independent? Does Jane unabashedly aspire to a career? Does Dick now speak of his tender feelings without embarrassment? . . .

The current investigation examines the 53 Caldecott winners and runners-up for the years since the original study, with particular attention to the 24 Caldecotts of the 1980s. . . .

A QUESTION OF VISIBILITY

. . . Table 1 provides measures of male and female visibility for the time periods covered by the two studies.

Following the procedure used by Weitzman et al., human single-gender illustrations are those containing only males or only females. As can be seen, whereas those showing only females made up 11.7 percent of the total among the 1967–71 Caldecotts, the percentage increased to 31.6 in the following years from 1972 through 1979 and 37.1 percent in the 1980s. The difference of 25.4 percent between the percent female in the original study and in the first half of the 1980s is statistically significant and in an equalitarian direction.

In addition to using each picture as a unit (all male, all female, both), we examined the total number of times human males and females were depicted. Using this procedure, we counted 685 humans, of which 19.1 percent are female in the books originally studied by Weitzman et al. For the intervening years, 1972–79, we found a shift toward parity with 32.9 percent female. The numbers for 1980–85 are yet closer to equality with 42.2 percent of the human characters being female. The difference of 23.1 percent between the original study and the books of the 1980s is statistically significant.

Doubtlessly the finding of only 1.0 percent female among single-gender illustrations (95:1 male/female ratio) reported by Weitzman et al. for nonhuman animals was an exceptional deviation from the norm even fifteen to twenty years ago. The nonhuman counts are based on fewer books and fewer illustrations, and thus smaller numbers. There are five books with nonhuman characters in the set examined in the first study, four in the following years up to 1980, and six among the books of the 1980s. Nevertheless, the figures do show a significant proportional increase in females depicted in single-gender illustrations and in the total counts of all anthropomorphized nonhumans. . . .

The central character's gender is an especially important factor in visibility since by definition the story revolves around this individual. In the books from 1967–71, only 2 of 18 have females in a central role. Seven of the 29 winners and honor books (24.1 percent) during the rest of the 1970s have female main characters. The Caldecott books for 1980 through 1985 include 8 with females as central characters (one-third), 13 have males in a central role, 1 could not be identified, and in 2 the central figure has no gender. Thus, there has been a shift toward parity between the time period examined by Weitzman et al. and the most recent set of award winners.

LOCATION: INDOORS/OUTDOORS

Weitzman et al. commented, "While boys play in the real world outdoors, girls sit and watch them. . . . For the Caldecotts of the 1980s, we found 31 of 141 boys (22.0 percent) and 65 of 204 girls (31.9 percent) shown indoors. Though a majority of both genders are shown outdoors, boys are nonetheless significantly less likely to be depicted indoors ($p < .03$). This, of course, is consistent with the traditional notion that a girl should be passive and immobile, that her place is with her mother in the home.

Adult females have a larger percentage pictured indoors in the books examined by Weitzman et al., 40 percent of the females compared to 31 percent of the adult males. Current study data show 21.8 percent (124 of 568) of the males and 26.0 percent (74 of 285) of females indoors ($p < .09$). Thus, there is the suggestion that adult females continue to have a higher percentage shown indoors, but both groups have tended to move outside with females making the greater change.

ROLE MODELS

While visibility and location are important, the way gender is represented may be even more so. And, as mentioned, all of the early studies found evidence of stereotyped attitudes and behavior being portrayed by storybook characters. Children in the books provide messages about how young people should or should not think and behave as children while the adults may serve as role models for the future, shaping aspirations and goals through anticipatory socialization.

As can be seen from the data presented in Table 2, no behavioral profile stands out for the females. Nearly half are judged to be active and around one-third are nurturant, passive, and perform services for others, but, apart from this, they do not seem to have much character, one way or the other. A large majority of the males are independent, persistent, and active and one-third are explorative and creative as well.

Considering male/female differences, it can be seen that females are more often shown as dependent, submissive, nurturant, and passive and more likely to serve others whereas males are more likely to be independent, competitive, persistent, creative, and active. All differences are in the predicted direction of conforming to traditional stereotypes of males and females in American culture. . . .

CONCLUSIONS

. . . From the findings in the present study it seems fair to say that females are no longer invisible. Males continue to hold something of a visibility edge, but, especially among humans, the male-to-female ratios, both by a count of individual pictures and the total number of characters depicted, have moved closer to parity. Males and females are about equally likely to be included in a book, and about one-third of central characters are females in the recent books. Individual books vary considerably, but a child exposed to all of the Caldecott winners and honor books over the past six years will encounter nearly as many females as males, certainly many more than in the past.

Although a male/female difference remains, females appear to have begun to move outside the home, but not into the labor market. With respect to role portrayal and characterization, females do not appear to be so much stereotyped as simply colorless. No behavior was shared by a majority of the females,

TABLE 2

*Behavior of Central Characters and Most Important Characters of the
Opposite Sex, 1980–85*

	Female (N = 17)	Male (N = 18)	Probability[a]
Dependent	5	1	.08
Independent	4	12	.02
Cooperative	5	3	NS
Competitive	0	5	.03
Directive	2	4	NS
Submissive	5	0	.02
Persistent	5	12	.02
Explorative	2	6	NS
Creative	1	6	.05
Imitative	0	1	NS
Nurturant	6	2	.10
Aggressive	1	4	NS
Emotional	3	3	NS
Active	8	16	.01
Passive	6	1	.04
Rescue	3	3	NS
Service	7	1	.02
Camaraderie with same-sex peers	0	0	NS
Traditional role	17	17	NS
Nontraditional role	0	1	NS

[a]Statistical probabilities based on a one-tailed test, determined using Fisher's exact test, NS refers to p not significant, $p > .10$.

while nearly all males were portrayed as independent, persistent, and active. Furthermore, differences in the way males and females are presented is entirely consistent with traditional culture. In our view, however, the most telling finding is the near unanimity in conformity to traditional gender roles. Not only does Jane express no career goals, but there is no adult female model to provide any ambition. One woman in the entire 1980s collection of 24 books has an occupation outside the home, and she works as a waitress at the Blue Tile Diner. . . . How can we expect Dick to express tender emotions without shame when only two adult males in this collection of books have anything resembling tender emotions and one of them is a mouse?

CHAPTER 4 Social Roles

4.1 PETER L. BERGER

Sociological Perspective—
Society in Man

One of the most elementary concepts in sociology is that of role. It is borrowed from the language of the theater and captures the simple fact that people behave most of the time in accordance with the dictates of society's script for the roles that they play. In the following excerpt, Peter L. Berger, who introduced sociology in chapter 1, selection 1.1, elaborates on the concept of role and shows how important it is for understanding social phenomena.

Although the basic insight that we "play" social roles is relatively obvious, Berger explains several surprising aspects of roles. First, roles not only prescribe certain actions but also the emotions and attitudes that belong to these actions. We learn not only what to do but also what to feel. Second, in the process of learning a role, one takes on the identity of that role and is identified by others with that role. Finally, role theory contradicts the view that the self is relatively fixed and consistent. Rather, the self is relatively fluid and is continuously created and re-created in each role or social situation. This last point of theory particularly contradicts standard sociological views of the self. Berger, however, supports role-playing as a natural, unconscious aspect of socialization and role theory as an accurate way to evaluate human behavior.

Berger (b. 1929) is the director of the Institute for the Study of Economic Culture at Boston University. He supports what he calls "methodological atheism," which argues for explanations of society and social life that are based on scientific study.

Key Concept: role theory

*R*ole theory has been almost entirely an American intellectual development. Some of its germinal insights go back to William James, while its direct parents are two other American thinkers, Charles Cooley and George Herbert Mead. It cannot be our purpose here to give a historical introduction to this quite fascinating portion of intellectual history. Rather than try this even in outline, we shall start more systematically by beginning our consideration of the import of role theory with [a] look at [sociologist William Isaac] Thomas' concept of the definition of the situation.

The reader will recall Thomas' understanding of the social situation as a sort of reality agreed upon *ad hoc* by those who participate in it, or, more exactly, those who do the defining of the situation. From the viewpoint of the individual participant this means that each situation he enters confronts him with specific expectations and demands of him specific responses to these expectations. . . . [P]owerful pressures exist in just about any social situation to ensure that the proper responses are indeed forthcoming. Society can exist by virtue of the fact that most of the time most people's definitions of the most important situations at least coincide approximately. The motives of the publisher and the writers of these lines may be rather different, but the ways the two define the situation in which this book is being produced are sufficiently similar for the joint venture to be possible. In similar fashion there may be quite divergent interests present in a classroom of students, some of them having little connection with the educational activity that is supposedly going on, but in most cases these interests (say, that one student came to study the subject being taught, while another simply registers for every course taken by a certain redhead he is pursuing) can coexist in the situation without destroying it. In other words, there is a certain amount of leeway in the extent to which response must meet expectation for a situation to remain sociologically viable. Of course, if the definitions of the situation are too widely discrepant, some form of social conflict or disorganization will inevitably result—say, if some students interpret the classroom meeting as a party, or if an author has no intention of producing a book but is using his contract with one publisher to put pressure on another.

While an average individual meets up with very different expectations in different areas of his life in society, the situations that produce these expectations fall into certain clusters. A student may take two courses from two different professors in two different departments, with considerable variations in the expectations met with in the two situations (say, as between formality or informality in the relations between professor and students). Nevertheless, the situations will be sufficiently similar to each other and to other classroom situations previously experienced to enable the student to carry into both situations essentially the same overall response. In other words, in both cases, with but a few modifications, he will be able to *play the role* of student. A role, then, may be defined as a typified response to a typified expectation. Society has predefined the fundamental typology. To use the language of the theater, from which the concept of role is derived, we can say that society provides the script for all the *dramatis personae*. The individual actors, therefore, need but slip into the roles already assigned to them before the curtain goes up. As long as they play their roles as provided for in this script, the social play can proceed as planned.

The role provides the pattern according to which the individual is to act in the particular situation. Roles, in society as in the theater, will vary in the exactness with which they lay down instructions for the actor. Taking occupational roles for an instance, a fairly minimal pattern goes into the role of garbage collector, while physicians or clergymen or officers have to acquire all kinds of distinctive mannerisms, speech and motor habits, such as military bearing, sanctimonious diction or bedside cheer. It would, however, be missing an essential aspect of the role if one regarded it merely as a regulatory pattern for externally visible actions. One feels more ardent by kissing, more humble by kneeling and more angry by shaking one's fist. That is, the kiss not only expresses ardor but manufactures it. Roles carry with them both certain actions and the emotions and attitudes that belong to these actions. The professor putting on an act that pretends to wisdom comes to feel wise. The preacher finds himself believing what he preaches. The soldier discovers martial stirrings in his breast as he puts on his uniform. In each case, while the emotion or attitude may have been present before the role was taken on, the latter inevitably strengthens what was there before. In many instances there is every reason to suppose that nothing at all anteceded the playing of the role in the actor's consciousness. In other words, one becomes wise by being appointed a professor, believing by engaging in activities that presuppose belief, and ready for battle by marching in formation.

Let us take an example. A man recently commissioned as an officer, especially if he came up through the ranks, will at first be at least slightly embarrassed by the salutes he now receives from the enlisted men he meets on his way. Probably he will respond to them in a friendly, almost apologetic manner. The new insignia on his uniform are at that point still something that he has merely put on, almost like a disguise. Indeed, the new officer may even tell himself and others that underneath he is still the same person, that he simply has new responsibilities (among which . . . is the duty to accept the salutes of enlisted men). This attitude is not likely to last very long. In order to carry out his new role of officer, our man must maintain a certain bearing. This bearing has quite definite implications. Despite all the double-talk in this area that is customary in so-called democratic armies, such as the American one, one of the fundamental implications is that an officer is a superior somebody, entitled to obedience and respect on the basis of this superiority. Every military salute given by an inferior in rank is an act of obeisance, received as a matter of course by the one who returns it. Thus, with every salute given and accepted (along, of course, with a hundred other ceremonial acts that enhance his new status) our man is fortified in his new bearing—and in its, as it were, ontological presuppositions. He not only acts like an officer, he feels like one. Gone are the embarrassment, the apologetic attitude, the I'm-just-another-guy-really grin. If on some occasion an enlisted man should fail to salute with the appropriate amount of enthusiasm or even commit the unthinkable act of failing to salute at all, our officer is not merely going to punish a violation of military regulations. He will be driven with every fiber of his being to redress an offence against the appointed order of his cosmos.

It is important to stress in this illustration that only very rarely is such a process deliberate or based on reflection. Our man has not sat down and figured out all the things that ought to go into his new role, including the things that he ought to feel and believe. The strength of the process comes precisely from its unconscious, unreflecting character. He has become an officer almost as effortlessly as he grew into a person with blue eyes, brown hair and a height of six feet. . . .

Every role in society has attached to it a certain identity. . . . [S]ome of these identities are trivial and temporary ones, as in some occupations that demand little modification in the being of their practitioners. It is not difficult to change from garbage collector to night watchman. It is considerably more difficult to change from clergyman to officer. It is very, very difficult to change from Negro to white. And it is almost impossible to change from man to woman. These differences in the ease of role changing ought not to blind us to the fact that even identities that we consider to be our essential selves have been socially assigned. Just as there are racial roles to be acquired and identified with, so there are sexual roles. To say "I am a man" is just as much a proclamation of role as to say "I am a colonel in the U.S. Army." We are well aware of the fact that one is born a male, while not even the most humorless martinet imagines himself to have been born with a golden eagle sitting on his umbilical cord. But to be biologically male is a far cry from the specific, socially defined (and, of course, socially relative) role that goes with the statement "I am a man." A male child does not have to learn to have an erection. But he must learn to be aggressive, to have ambitions, to compete with others, and to be suspicious of too much gentleness in himself. The male role in our society, however, requires all these things that one must learn, as does a male identity. To have an erection is not enough—if it were, regiments of psychotherapists would be out of work.

This significance of role theory could be summarized by saying that, in a sociological perspective, identity is socially bestowed, socially sustained and socially transformed. The example of the man in process of becoming an officer may suffice to illustrate the way in which identities are bestowed in adult life. However, even roles that are much more fundamentally part of what psychologists would call our personality than those associated with a particular adult activity are bestowed in very similar manner through a social process. This has been demonstrated over and over again in studies of so-called socialization—the process by which a child learns to be a participant member of society.

Probably the most penetrating theoretical account of this process is the one given by Mead, in which the genesis of the self is interpreted as being one and the same event as the discovery of society. The child finds out who he is as he learns what society is. He learns to play roles properly belonging to him by learning, as Mead puts it, "to take the role of the other"—which, incidentally, is the crucial sociopsychological function of play, in which children masquerade with a variety of social roles and in doing so discover the significance of those being assigned to them. All this learning occurs, and can only occur, in interaction with other human beings, be it the parents or whoever else raises the child. The child first takes on roles *vis-à-vis* what Mead calls his "significant others," that is, those persons who deal with him intimately and whose attitudes are decisive for the formation of his conception of himself. Later, the child learns that the roles he plays are not only relevant to this intimate circle.

but relate to the expectations directed toward him by society at large. This higher level of abstraction in the social response Mead calls the discovery of the "generalized other." That is, not only the child's mother expects him to be good, clean and truthful, society in general does so as well. Only when this general conception of society emerges is the child capable of forming a clear conception of himself. "Self" and "society," in the child's experience, are the two sides of the same coin.

In other words, identity is not something "given," but is bestowed in acts of social recognition. We become that as which we are addressed. The same idea is expressed in Cooley's well-known description of the self as a reflection in a looking glass. This does not mean, of course, that there are not certain characteristics an individual is born with, that are carried by his genetic heritage regardless of the social environment in which the latter will have to unfold itself. Our knowledge of man's biology does not as yet allow us a very clear picture of the extent to which this may be true. We do know, however, that the room for social formation within those genetic limits is very large indeed. Even with the biological questions left largely unsettled, we can say that to be human is to be recognized as human, just as to be a certain kind of man is to be recognized as such. The child deprived of human affection and attention becomes dehumanized. The child who is given respect comes to respect himself. A little boy considered to be a *schlemiel* [or a bungler] becomes one, just as a grown-up treated as an awe-inspiring young god of war begins to think of himself and act as is appropriate to such a figure—and, indeed, merges his identity with the one he is presented with in these expectations.

Identities are socially bestowed. They must also be socially sustained, and fairly steadily so. One cannot be human all by oneself and, apparently, one cannot hold on to any particular identity all by oneself. The self-image of the officer as an officer can be maintained only in a social context in which others are willing to recognize him in this identity. If this recognition is suddenly withdrawn, it usually does not take very long before the self-image collapses. . . .

Role theory, when pursued to its logical conclusions, does far more than provide us with a convenient shorthand for the description of various social activities. It gives us a sociological anthropology, that is, a view of man based on his existence in society. This view tells us that man plays dramatic parts in the grand play of society, and that, speaking sociologically, he *is* the masks that he must wear to do so. The human person also appears now in a dramatic context, true to its theatrical etymology (*persona*, the technical term given to the actors' masks in classical theater). The person is perceived as a repertoire of roles, each one properly equipped with a certain identity. The range of an individual person can be measured by the number of roles he is capable of playing. The person's biography now appears to us as an uninterrupted sequence of stage performances, played to different audiences, sometimes involving drastic changes of costume, always demanding that the actor *be* what he is playing.

Such a sociological view of personality is far more radical in its challenge to the way that we commonly think of ourselves than most psychological theories. It challenges radically one of the fondest presuppositions about the self—its continuity. Looked at sociologically, the self is no longer a solid, given entity that moves from one situation to another. It is rather a process, continuously created and re-created in each social situation that one enters, held together by the slender thread of memory. . . . Nor is it possible within this framework of understanding to take refuge in the unconscious as containing the "real" contents of the self, because the presumed unconscious self is just as subject to social production as is the so-called conscious one. . . . In other words, man is not *also* a social being, but he is social in every aspect of his being that is open to empirical investigation. Still speaking sociologically then, if one wants to ask who an individual "really" is in this kaleidoscope of roles and identities, one can answer only by enumerating the situations in which he is one thing and those in which he is another.

Now, it is clear that such transformations cannot occur *ad infinitum* and that some are easier than others. An individual becomes so habituated to certain identities that, even when his social situation changes, he has difficulty keeping up with the expectations newly directed toward him. The difficulties that healthy and previously highly active individuals have when they are forced to retire from their occupation show this very clearly. The transformability of the self depends not *only* on its social context, but also on the degree of its habituation to previous identities and perhaps also on certain genetically given traits. While these modifications in our model are necessary to avoid a radicalization of our position, they do not detract appreciably from the discontinuity of the self as revealed by sociological analysis. . . .

One might obtain the impression from all of this that there is really no essential difference between most people and those afflicted with what psychiatry calls "multiple personality." If someone wanted to harp on the word "essential" here, the sociologist might agree with the statement. The actual difference, however, is that for "normal" people (that is, those so recognized by their society) there are strong pressures toward consistency in the various roles they play and the identities that go with these roles. These pressures are both external and internal. Externally the others with whom one must play one's social games, and on whose recognition one's own parts depend, demand that one present at least a relatively consistent picture to the world. A certain degree of role discrepancy may be permitted, but if certain tolerance limits are passed society will withdraw its recognition of the individual in question, defining him as a moral or psychological aberration. . . .

There are also internal pressures toward consistency, possibly based on very profound psychological needs to perceive oneself as a totality. Even the contemporary urban masquerader, who plays mutually irreconcilable roles in different areas of his life, may feel internal tensions though he can successfully control external ones by carefully segregating his several *mises en scène* [environments or settings] from each other. To avoid such anxieties people commonly segregate their consciousness as well as their conduct. By this we do not mean that they "repress" their discrepant identities into some "unconscious," for within our model we have every reason to be suspicious of such concepts. We rather mean that they focus their attention only on that particular identity that, so to speak, they require at the moment. Other identities are forgotten for the duration of this particular act. The way in which socially disapproved sexual acts or morally questionable acts of any kind are segregated in consciousness may serve to illustrate this process. The man who engages in, say, homosexual masochism has a carefully constructed identity set aside for just these occasions. When any given occasion is over, he checks that identity again at the gate, so to speak, and returns home as affectionate father, responsible husband, perhaps even ardent lover of his wife. In the same way, the judge who sentences a man to death segregates the identity in which he does this from the rest of his consciousness, in which he is a kindly, tolerant and sensitive human being. The Nazi concentration-camp commander who writes sentimental letters to his children is but an extreme case of something that occurs in society all the time.

It would be a complete misunderstanding of what has just been said if the reader now thought that we are presenting a picture of society in which everybody schemes, plots and deliberately puts on disguises to fool his fellow men. On the contrary, role-playing and identity-building processes are generally unreflected and unplanned, almost automatic. The psychological needs for consistency of self-image just mentioned ensure this. Deliberate deception requires a degree of psychological self-control that few people are capable of. That is why insincerity is rather a rare phenomenon. Most people are sincere, because this is the easiest course to take psychologically.

The Presentation of Self in Everyday Life

During any one day we engage in a variety of social interactions of variable duration, sometimes long, other times fleeting. In each of these interactions we perform specific social roles, such as mother, friend, customer, student, and so on.

Prominent sociologist Erving Goffman (1922–1982) studied and defined rules that govern social behavior and social interaction. One theory he developed is called the "dramaturgical" approach, in which social behavior is viewed as a staged performance and each actor intentionally conveys specific impressions to the others. This approach is explored in Goffman's most famous book *The Presentation of Self in Everyday Life* (Anchor Books, 1959), from which the following selection is taken. In it, Goffman provides various examples that demonstrate how one tries to control the conduct of others by influencing "the definition of the situation" through the staging of one's behavior according to how one wants to be treated and valued.

Goffman's analysis might raise some perplexing questions about the authenticity of most human behavior. He seems to say that people are always acting or staging their behavior, which suggests that their actions are not authentic expressions of the self but are carefully planned maneuvers designed to create the desired perceptions in others. This interpretation, however, is too simple. Goffman argues that by staging a specific behavior one claims or owns this behavior and demands treatment accordingly.

Key Concept: presentation of self

When an individual enters the presence of others, they commonly seek to acquire information about him or to bring into play information about him already possessed. They will be interested in his general socioeconomic status, his conception of self, his attitude toward them, his competence, his trustworthiness, etc. Although some of this information seems to be sought almost as an end in itself, there are usually quite practical reasons for acquiring it.

Information about the individual helps to define the situation, enabling others to know in advance what he will expect of them and what they may expect of him. Informed in these ways, the others will know how best to act in order to call forth a desired response from him.

For those present, many sources of information become accessible and many carriers (or "sign-vehicles") become available for conveying this information. If unacquainted with the individual, observers can glean clues from his conduct and appearance which allow them to apply their previous experience with individuals roughly similar to the one before them or, more important, to apply untested stereotypes to him. They can also assume from past experience that only individuals of a particular kind are likely to be found in a given social setting. They can rely on what the individual says about himself or on documentary evidence he provides as to who and what he is. If they know, or know of, the individual by virtue of experience prior to the interaction, they can rely on assumptions as to the persistence and generality of psychological traits as a means of predicting his present and future behavior.

However, during the period in which the individual is in the immediate presence of the others, few events may occur which directly provide the others with the conclusive information they will need if they are to direct wisely their own activity. Many crucial facts lie beyond the time and place of interaction or lie concealed within it. For example, the "true" or "real" attitudes, beliefs, and emotions of the individual can be ascertained only indirectly, through his avowals or through what appears to be involuntary expressive behavior. . . . They will be forced to accept some events as conventional or natural signs of something not directly available to the senses. In Ichheiser's terms,[1] the individual will have to act so that he intentionally or unintentionally *expresses* himself, and the others will in turn have to be *impressed* in some way by him.

The expressiveness of the individual (and therefore his capacity to give impressions) appears to involve two radically different kinds of sign activity: the expression that he *gives*, and the expression that he *gives off*. The first involves verbal symbols or their substitutes which he uses admittedly and solely to convey the information that he and the others are known to attach to these symbols. This is communication in the traditional and narrow sense. The second involves a wide range of action that others can treat as symptomatic of the actor, the expectation being that the action was performed for reasons other than the information conveyed in this way. As we shall have to see, this distinction has an only initial validity. The individual does of course intentionally convey misinformation by means of both of these types of communication, the first involving deceit, the second feigning.

Taking communication in both its narrow and broad sense, one finds that when the individual is in the immediate presence of others, his activity will have a promissory character. The others are likely to find that they must accept the individual on faith, offering him a just return while he is present before them in exchange for something whose true value will not be established until after he has left their presence. (Of course, the others also live by inference in their dealings with the physical world, but it is only in the world of social interaction that the objects about which they make inferences will purposely facilitate and hinder this inferential process.) The security that they justifiably feel in making inferences about the individual will vary, of course, depending on such factors as the amount of information they already possess about him, but no amount of such past evidence can entirely obviate the necessity of acting on the basis of inferences. . . .

Let us now turn from the others to the point of view of the individual who presents himself before them. He may wish them to think highly of him, or to think that he thinks highly of them, or to perceive how in fact he feels toward them, or to obtain no clear-cut impression; he may wish to ensure sufficient harmony so that the interaction can be sustained, or to defraud, get rid of, confuse, mislead, antagonize, or insult them. Regardless of the particular objective which the individual has in mind and of his motive for having this objective, it will be in his interests to control the conduct of the others, especially their responsive treatment of him. This control is achieved largely by influencing the definition of the situation which the others come to formulate, and he can influence this definition by expressing himself in such a way as to give them the kind of impression that will lead them to act voluntarily in accordance with his own plan. Thus, when an individual appears in the presence of others, there will usually be some reason for him to mobilize his activity so that it will convey an impression to others which it is in his interests to convey. Since a girl's dormitory mates will glean evidence of her popularity from the calls she receives on the phone, we can suspect that some girls will arrange for calls to be made, and Willard Waller's finding can be anticipated:

> It has been reported by many observers that a girl who is called to the telephone in the dormitories will often allow herself to be called several times, in order to give all the other girls ample opportunity to hear her paged.[2]

Of the two kinds of communication—expressions given and expressions given off—this report will be primarily concerned with the latter, with the more theatrical and contextual kind, the nonverbal, presumably unintentional kind, whether this communication be purposely engineered or not. As an example of what we must try to examine, I would like to cite at length a novelistic incident in which Preedy, a vacationing Englishman, makes his first appearance on the beach of his summer hotel in Spain:

> But in any case he took care to avoid catching anyone's eye. First of all, he had to make it clear to those potential companions of his holiday that they were of no concern to him whatsoever. He stared through them, round them, over them—eyes lost in space. The beach might have been empty. If by chance a ball was thrown his way, he looked surprised; then let a smile of amusement lighten his face (Kindly Preedy), looked around dazed to see that there *were* people on the beach, tossed it back with a smile to himself and not a smile *at* the people, and then resumed carelessly his nonchalant survey of space.
>
> But it was time to institute a little parade, the parade of the Ideal Preedy. By devious handlings he gave any who wanted to look a chance to see the title of his book—a Spanish translation of Homer, classic thus, but not daring, cosmopolitan too—and then gathered together his beachwrap and bag into a neat sand-resistant pile (Methodical and Sensible Preedy), rose slowly to stretch at ease his

huge frame (Big-Cat Preedy), and tossed aside his sandals (Carefree Preedy, after all).

The marriage of Preedy and the sea! There were alternative rituals. The first involved the stroll that turns into a run and a dive straight into the water, thereafter smoothing into a strong splashless crawl towards the horizon. But of course not really to the horizon. Quite suddenly he would turn on to his back and thrash great white splashes with his legs, somehow thus showing that he could have swum further had he wanted to, and then would stand up a quarter out of water for all to see who it was.

The alternative course was simpler, it avoided the cold-water shock and it avoided the risk of appearing too high-spirited. The point was to appear to be so used to the sea, the Mediterranean, and this particular beach, that one might as well be in the sea as out of it. It involved a slow stroll down and into the edge of the water—not even noticing his toes were wet, land and water all the same to *him!*—with his eyes up at the sky gravely surveying portents, invisible to others, of the weather (Local Fisherman Preedy).[3]

The novelist means us to see that Preedy is improperly concerned with the extensive impressions he feels his sheer bodily action is giving off to those around him. We can malign Preedy further by assuming that he has acted merely in order to give a particular impression, that this is a false impression, and that the others present receive either no impression at all, or, worse still, the impression that Preedy is affectedly trying to cause them to receive this particular impression. But the important point for us here is that the kind of impression Preedy thinks he is making is in fact the kind of impression that others correctly and incorrectly glean from someone in their midst.

I have said that when an individual appears before others his actions will influence the definition of the situation which they come to have. Sometimes the individual will act in a thoroughly calculating manner, expressing himself in a given way solely in order to give the kind of impression to others that is likely to evoke from them a specific response he is concerned to obtain. Sometimes the individual will be calculating in his activity but be relatively unaware that this is the case. Sometimes he will intentionally and consciously express himself in a particular way, but chiefly because the tradition of his group or social status require this kind of expression and not because of any particular response (other than vague acceptance or approval) that is likely to be evoked from those impressed by the expression. Sometimes the traditions of an individual's role will lead him to give a well-designed impression of a particular kind and yet he may be neither consciously nor unconsciously disposed to create such an impression. The others, in their turn, may be suitably impressed by the individual's efforts to convey something, or may misunderstand the situation and come to conclusions that are warranted neither by the individual's intent nor by the facts. In any case, insofar as the others act *as if* the individual had conveyed a particular impression, we may take a functional or pragmatic view and say that the individual has "effectively" projected a given definition of the situation and "effectively" fostered the understanding that a given state of affairs obtains.

There is one aspect of the others' response that bears special comment here. Knowing that the individual is likely to present himself in a light that is favorable to him, the others may divide what they witness into two parts: a part that is relatively easy for the individual to manipulate at will, being chiefly his verbal assertions, and a part in regard to which he seems to have little concern or control, being chiefly derived from the expressions he gives off. The others may then use what are considered to be the ungovernable aspects of his expressive behavior as a check upon the validity of what is conveyed by the governable aspects. In this a fundamental asymmetry is demonstrated in the communication process, the individual presumably being aware of only one stream of his communication, the witnesses of this stream and one other. For example, in Shetland Isle one crofter's [or farmer's] wife, in serving native dishes to a visitor from the mainland of Britain, would listen with a polite smile to his polite claims of liking what he was eating; at the same time she would take note of the rapidity with which the visitor lifted his fork or spoon to his mouth, the eagerness with which he passed food into his mouth, and the gusto expressed in chewing the food, using these signs as a check on the stated feelings of the eater. . . .

Now given the fact that others are likely to check up on the more controllable aspects of behavior by means of the less controllable, one can expect that sometimes the individual will try to exploit this very possibility, guiding the impression he makes through behavior felt to be reliably informing. For example, in gaining admission to a tight social circle, the participant observer may not only wear an accepting look while listening to an informant, but may also be careful to wear the same look when observing the informant talking to others; observers of the observer will then not as easily discover where he actually stands. . . .

This kind of control upon the part of the individual reinstates the symmetry of the communication process, and sets the stage for a kind of information game—a potentially infinite cycle of concealment, discovery, false revelation, and rediscovery. It should be added that since the others are likely to be relatively unsuspicious of the presumably unguided aspect of the individual's conduct, he can gain much by controlling it. The others of course may sense that the individual is manipulating the presumably spontaneous aspects of his behavior, and seek in this very act of manipulation some shading of conduct that the individual has not managed to control. This again provides a check upon the individual's behavior, this time his presumably uncalculated behavior, thus re-establishing the asymmetry of the communication process. . . .

When we allow that the individual projects a definition of the situation when he appears before others, we must also see that the others, however passive their role may seem to be, will themselves effectively project a definition of the situation by virtue of their response to the individual and by virtue of any lines of action they initiate to him. Ordinarily the definitions of the situation projected by the several different participants are sufficiently attuned to one another so that open contradiction will not occur. I do not mean that there will be the kind of consensus that arises when each individual present candidly expresses what he really feels and honestly agrees with the expressed feeling of the others present. This kind of harmony is an optimistic ideal and in any case not necessary for the smooth working of society. Rather, each participant is expected to suppress his immediate heartfelt feelings, conveying a view of the situation which he feels the others will be able to find at least temporarily acceptable. The maintenance of this surface of agreement, this veneer of consensus, is facilitated by each participant concealing [his] wants behind statements while asserting values to which everyone present feels obliged to give lip service. Further, there is usually a kind of division of definitional labor. Each participant is allowed to establish the tentative official ruling regarding matters which are vital to him but not immediately important to others, e.g., the rationalizations and justifications by which he accounts for his past activity. In exchange for this courtesy he remains silent or non-committal on matters important to others but not immediately important to him. We have then a kind of interactional *modus vivendi* [manner of living]. Together, the participants contribute to a single over-all definition of the situation which involves not so much a real argument as to what exists but rather a real agreement as to whose claims concerning what issues will be temporarily honored. Real agreement will also exist concerning the desirability of avoiding an open conflict of definitions of the situation. I will refer to this level of agreement as a "working consensus." It is to be understood that the working consensus established in one interaction setting will be quite different in content from the working consensus established in a different type of setting. Thus, between two friends at lunch, a reciprocal show of affection, respect, and concern for the other is maintained. In service occupations, on the other hand, the specialist often maintains an image of disinterested involvement in the problem of the client, while the client responds with a show of respect for the competence and integrity of the specialist. Regardless of such differences in content, however, the general form of these working arrangements is the same.

In noting the tendency for a participant to accept the definitional claims made by the others present, we can appreciate the crucial importance of the information that the individual *initially* possesses or acquires concerning his fellow participants, for it is on the basis of this initial information that the individual starts to define the situation and starts to build up lines of responsive action. The individual's initial projection commits him to what he is proposing to be and requires him to drop all pretenses of being other things. As the interaction among the participants progresses, additions and modifications in this initial informational state will of course occur, but it is essential that these later developments be related without contradiction to, and even built up from, the initial positions taken by the several participants. It would seem that an individual can more easily make a choice as to what line of treatment to demand from and extend to the others present at the beginning of an encounter than he can alter the line of treatment that is being pursued once the interaction is underway.

In everyday life, of course, there is a clear understanding that first impressions are important. Thus, the work adjustment of those in service occupations will often hinge upon a capacity to seize and hold the initiative in the service relations, a capacity that will require subtle aggressiveness on the part of the server when he is of lower socioeconomic status than his client. W. F. Whyte suggests the waitress as an example:

> The first point that stands out is that the waitress who bears up under pressure does not simply respond to her customers. She acts with some skill to control her behavior. The first question to ask when we look at the customer relationship is, "Does the waitress get the jump on the customer, or does the customer get the jump on the waitress?" The skilled waitress realizes the crucial nature of this question. . . .
>
> The skilled waitress tackles the customer with confidence and without hesitation. For example, she may find that a new customer has seated himself before she could clear off the dirty dishes and change the cloth. He is now leaning on the table studying the menu. She greets him, says, "May I change the cover, please?" and, without waiting for an answer, takes his menu away from him so that he moves back from the table, and she goes about her work. The relationship is handled politely but firmly, and there is never any question as to who is in charge.[4]

When the interaction that is initiated by "first impressions" is itself merely the initial interaction in an extended series of interactions involving the same participants, we speak of "getting off on the right foot" and feel that it is crucial that we do so. Thus, one learns that some teachers take the following view:

> You can't ever let them get the upper hand on you or you're through. So I start out tough. The first day I get a new class in, I let them know who's boss. . . . You've got to start off tough, then you can ease up as you go along. If you start out easy-going, when you try to be tough, they'll just look at you and laugh.[5]

Similarly, attendants in mental institutions may feel that if the new patient is sharply put in his place the first day on the ward and made to see who is boss, much future difficulty will be prevented.

Given the fact that the individual effectively projects a definition of the situation when he enters the presence of others, we can assume that events may occur within the interaction which contradict, discredit, or otherwise throw doubt upon this projection. When these disruptive events occur, the interaction itself may come to a confused and embarrassed halt. Some of the assumptions upon which the responses of the participants had been predicated become untenable, and the participants find themselves lodged in an interaction for which the situation has been wrongly defined and is now no longer defined. At such moments the individual whose presentation has been discredited may feel ashamed while the others present may feel hostile, and all the participants may come to feel ill at ease, nonplussed, out of countenance, embarrassed, experiencing the kind of anomy that is generated when the minute social system of face-to-face interaction breaks down.

In stressing the fact that the initial definition of the situation projected by an individual tends to provide a plan for the cooperative activity that follows—

in stressing this action point of view—we must not overlook the crucial fact that any projected definition of the situation also has a distinctive moral character. It is this moral character of projections that will chiefly concern us in this report. Society is organized on the principle that any individual who possesses certain social characteristics has a moral right to expect that others will value and treat him in an appropriate way. Connected with this principle is a second, namely that an individual who implicitly or explicitly signifies that he has certain social characteristics ought in fact to be what he claims he is. In consequence, when an individual projects a definition of the situation and thereby makes an implicit or explicit claim to be a person of a particular kind, he automatically exerts a moral demand upon the others, obliging them to value and treat him in the manner that persons of his kind have a right to expect. He also implicitly forgoes all claims to be things he does not appear to be and hence forgoes the treatment that would be appropriate for such individuals. The others find, then, that the individual has informed them as to what is and as to what they *ought* to see as the "is."

One cannot judge the importance of definitional disruptions by the frequency with which they occur, for apparently they would occur more frequently were not constant precautions taken. We find that preventive practices are constantly employed to avoid these embarrassments and that corrective practices are constantly employed to compensate for discrediting occurrences that have not been successfully avoided. When the individual employs these strategies and tactics to protect his own projections, we may refer to them as "defensive practices"; when a participant employs them to save the definition of the situation projected by another, we speak of "protective practices" or "tact." Together, defensive and protective practices comprise the techniques employed to safeguard the impression fostered by an individual during his presence before others. It should be added that while we may be ready to see that no fostered impression would survive if defensive practices were not employed, we are less ready perhaps to see that few impressions could survive if those who received the impression did not exert tact in their reception of it.

In addition to the fact that precautions are taken to prevent disruption of projected definitions, we may also note that an intense interest in these disruptions comes to play a significant role in the social life of the group. Practical jokes and social games are played in which embarrassments which are to be taken unseriously are purposely engineered. Fantasies are created in which devastating exposures occur. Anecdotes from the past—real, embroidered, or fictitious—are told and retold, detailing disruptions which occurred, almost occurred, or occurred and were admirably resolved. There seems to be no grouping which does not have a ready supply of these games, reveries, and cautionary tales, to be used as a source of humor, a catharsis for anxieties, and a sanction for inducing individuals to be modest in their claims and reasonable in their projected expectations. . . . Journalists tell of times when an all-too-meaningful misprint occurred, and the paper's assumption of objectivity or decorum was humorously discredited. Public servants tell of times a client ridiculously misunderstood form instructions, giving answers which implied an unanticipated and bizarre definition of the situation.[6] . . .

To summarize, then, I assume that when an individual appears before others he will have many motives for trying to control the impression they receive of the situation.

NOTES

1. Gustav Ichheiser, "Misunderstandings in Human Relations," Supplement to *The American Journal of Sociology*, 55 (September 1949): 6–7.
2. Willard Waller, "The Rating and Dating Complex," *American Sociological Review*, 2: 730.
3. William Sansom, *A Contest of Ladies* (London: Hogarth, 1956), pp. 230–32.
4. W. F. Whyte, "When Workers and Customers Meet," Chap. VII, *Industry and Society*, ed. W. F. Whyte (New York: McGraw-Hill, 1946), pp. 132–33.
5. Teacher interview quoted by Howard S. Becker, "Social Class Variations in the Teacher-Pupil Relationship" *Journal of Educational Sociology*, 25: 459.
6. Peter Blau, *Dynamics of Bureaucracy: A Study of Interpersonal Relationships in Two Government Agencies*, 2nd ed. (Chicago: University of Chicago Press, 1963).

CHAPTER 5 Deviance and Social Control

5.1 ROBERT K. MERTON

Social Structure and Anomie

Sociologists often find new and provocative ways of looking at everyday phenomena, such as crime. The nineteenth-century French sociologist Émile Durkheim thought that some crime actually serves a useful purpose in society— it provokes outrage, he claimed, which strengthens citizens' commitment to the values being violated. Prominent twentieth-century sociologist Robert K. Merton also provides a unique way of looking at crime, or more generally, deviance. He starts with the simple idea that deviance involves breaking social norms. Then he distinguishes between deviants who break the norms governing goals and deviants who break the norms governing means. As he elaborates on his theory, he makes deviance out to be quite normal.

In the following selection, Merton illustrates his theory by locating deviant behavior in the combination of American culture and social structure. He argues that there is a gap between the goals valued by American culture and America's social structure, which does not provide many citizens with socially approved means of attaining these goals. In Merton's scheme, only the conformist accepts the cultural goals and the socially approved means to success. Merton does not imply that the conformist invariably achieves the cultural goals—only that the attempt is made within the prescribed norms.

Merton (b. 1910) is an adjunct professor at Rockefeller University and a professor emeritus at Columbia University. He is a well-known defender of sociology as a science, and he emphasizes the interrelationship between social theory and empirical research. This selection is taken from *Social Theory and Social Structure* (Free Press, 1968).

Key Concept: anomie and opportunity structures

*T*he framework set out in this essay is designed to provide one systematic approach to the analysis of social and cultural sources of deviant behavior. Our primary aim is to discover how some *social structures exert a definite pressure upon certain persons in the society to engage in nonconforming rather than conforming conduct.* If we can locate groups peculiarly subject to such pressures, we should expect to find fairly high rates of deviant behavior in these groups, not because the human beings comprising them are compounded of distinctive biological tendencies but because they are responding normally to the social situation in which they find themselves. Our perspective is sociological. We look at variations in the *rates* of deviant behavior, not at its incidence. Should our quest be at all successful, some forms of deviant behavior will be found to be as psychologically normal as conformist behavior, and the equation of deviation and psychological abnormality will be put in question.

PATTERNS OF CULTURAL GOALS AND INSTITUTIONAL NORMS

Among the several elements of social and cultural structures, two are of immediate importance. These are analytically separable although they merge in concrete situations. The first consists of culturally defined goals, purposes and interests, held out as legitimate objectives for all or for diversely located members of the society. The goals are more or less integrated—the degree is a question of empirical fact—and roughly ordered in some hierarchy of value. Involving various degrees of sentiment and significance, the prevailing goals comprise a frame of aspirational reference. They are the things "worth striving for." They are a basic, though not the exclusive, component of what [cultural anthropologist Ralph] Linton has called "designs for group living." And though some, not all, of these cultural goals are directly related to the biological drives of man, they are not determined by them.

A second element of the cultural structure defines, regulates and controls the acceptable modes of reaching out for these goals. Every social group invariably couples its cultural objectives with regulations, rooted in the mores or institutions, of allowable procedures for moving toward these objectives. These regulatory norms are not necessarily identical with technical or efficiency norms. Many procedures which from the standpoint of particular individuals would be most efficient in securing desired values—the exercise of force, fraud, power—are ruled out of the institutional area of permitted conduct. At times, the disallowed procedures include some which would be efficient for the group itself—*e.g.*, historic taboos on vivisection, on medical experimentation, on the sociological analysis of "sacred" norms—since the criterion of acceptability is not technical efficiency but value-laden sentiments (supported by most members of the group or by those able to promote these sentiments through the composite use of power and propaganda). In all instances, the choice of expedients for striving toward cultural goals is limited by institutionalized norms. . . .

Contemporary American culture appears to approximate the polar type in which great emphasis upon certain success-goals occurs without equivalent emphasis upon institutional means. It would of course be fanciful to assert that accumulated wealth stands alone as a symbol of success just as it would be fanciful to deny that Americans assign it a place high in their scale of values. In some large measure, money has been consecrated as a value in itself, over and above its expenditure for articles of consumption or its use for the enhancement of power. "Money" is peculiarly well adapted to become a symbol of prestige. As [German sociologist Georg] Simmel emphasized, money is highly abstract and impersonal. However acquired, fraudulently or institutionally, it can be used to purchase the same goods and services. The anonymity of an urban society, in conjunction with these peculiarities of money, permits wealth, the sources of which may be unknown to the community in which the plutocrat lives or, if known, to become purified in the course of time, to serve as a symbol of high status. Moreover, in the American Dream there is no final stopping point. The measure of "monetary success" is conveniently indefinite and relative. At each income level, as H. F. Clark found, Americans want just about twenty-five per cent more (but of course this "just a bit more" continues to operate once it is obtained). In this flux of shifting standards, there is no stable resting point, or rather, it is the point which manages always to be "just ahead." An observer of a community in which annual salaries in six figures are not uncommon, reports the anguished words of one victim of the American Dream: "In this town, I'm snubbed socially because I only get a thousand a week. That hurts." . . .

Thus the culture enjoins the acceptance of three cultural axioms: First, all should strive for the same lofty goals since these are open to all; second, present seeming failure is but a way-station to ultimate success; and third, genuine failure consists only in the lessening or withdrawal of ambition. . . .

In sociological paraphrase, these axioms represent, first, the deflection of criticism of the social structure onto one's self among those so situated in the society that they do not have full and equal access to opportunity; second, the preservation of a structure of social power by having individuals in the lower social strata identify themselves, not with their compeers, but with those at the top (whom they will ultimately join); and third, providing pressures for conformity with the cultural dictates of unslackened ambition by the threat of less than full membership in the society for those who fail to conform.

It is in these terms and through these processes that contemporary American culture continues to be characterized by a heavy emphasis on wealth as a basic symbol of success, without a corresponding emphasis upon the legitimate avenues on which to march toward this goal. How do individuals living in this cultural context respond? And how do our observations bear upon the doctrine that deviant behavior typically derives from biological impulses breaking through the restraints imposed by culture? What, in short, are the consequences for the behavior of people variously situated in a social structure of a culture in which the emphasis on dominant success-goals has become increasingly separated from an equivalent emphasis on institutionalized procedures for seeking these goals?

TYPES OF INDIVIDUAL ADAPTATION

Turning from these culture patterns, we now examine types of adaptation by individuals within the culture-bearing society. Though our focus is still the cultural and social genesis of varying rates and types of deviant behavior, our perspective shifts from the plane of patterns of cultural values to the plane of types of adaptation to these values among those occupying different positions in the social structure.

We here consider five types of adaptation, as these are schematically set out in the following table, where (+) signifies "acceptance," (−) signifies "rejection," and (±) signifies "rejection of prevailing values and substitution of new values."

A TYPOLOGY OF MODES OF INDIVIDUAL ADAPTATION

Modes of adaptation	*Culture Goals*	*Institutionalized Means*
I. Conformity	+	+
II. Innovation	+	−
III. Ritualism	−	+
IV. Retreatism	−	−
V. Rebellion	±	±

Examination of how the social structure operates to exert pressure upon individuals for one or another of these alternative modes of behavior must be prefaced by the observation that people may shift from one alternative to another as they engage in different spheres of social activities. These categories refer to role behavior in specific types of situations, not to personality. They are types of more or less enduring response, not types of personality organization. To consider these types of adaptation in several spheres of conduct would introduce a complexity unmanageable within the confines of this chapter. For this reason, we shall be primarily concerned with economic activity in the broad sense of "the production, exchange, distribution and consumption of goods and services" in our competitive society, where wealth has taken on a highly symbolic cast.

I. CONFORMITY

To the extent that a society is stable, adaptation type I—conformity to both cultural goals and institutionalized means—is the most common and widely diffused. Were this not so, the stability and continuity of the society could not be maintained. The mesh of expectancies constituting every social order is sustained by the modal behavior of its members representing conformity to the established, though perhaps secularly changing, culture patterns. It is, in fact, only because behavior is typically oriented toward the basic values of the society that we may speak of a human aggregate as comprising a society. Unless there is a deposit of values shared by interacting individuals, there exist social relations, if the disorderly interactions may be so called, but no society. . . .

II. INNOVATION

Great cultural emphasis upon the success-goal invites this mode of adaptation through the use of institutionally proscribed but often effective means of attaining at least the simulacrum of success—wealth and power. This response occurs when the individual has assimilated the cultural emphasis upon the goal without equally internalizing the institutional norms governing ways and means for its attainment.

From the standpoint of psychology, great emotional investment in an objective may be expected to produce a readiness to take risks, and this attitude may be adopted by people in all social strata. From the standpoint of sociology, the question arises, which features of our social structure predispose toward this type of adaptation, thus producing greater frequencies of deviant behavior in one social stratum than in another?

On the top economic levels, the pressure toward innovation not infrequently erases the distinction between business-like strivings this side of the mores and sharp practices beyond the mores. As [economist Thorstein] Veblen observed, "It is not easy in any given case—indeed it is at times impossible until the courts have spoken—to say whether it is an instance of praiseworthy salesmanship or a penitentiary offense." The history of the great American fortunes is threaded with strains toward institutionally dubious innovation as is attested by many tributes to the robber barons. The reluctant admiration often expressed privately, and not seldom publicly, of these "shrewd, smart and successful" men is a product of a cultural structure in which the sacrosanct goal virtually consecrates the means. . . .

Living in the age in which the American robber barons flourished, [Ambrose] Bierce could not easily fail to observe what became later known as "white-collar crime." Nevertheless, he was aware that not all of these large and dramatic departures from institutional norms in the top economic strata are known, and possibly fewer deviations among the lesser middle classes come to light. [Edwin H.] Sutherland has repeatedly documented the prevalence of "white-collar criminality" among business men. He notes, further, that many of these crimes were not prosecuted because they were not detected or, if detected, because of "the status of the business man, the trend away from punishment, and the relatively unorganized resentment of the public against white-collar criminals." A study of some 1,700 prevalently middle-class individuals found that "off the record crimes" were common among wholly "respectable" members of society. Ninety-nine per cent of those questioned confessed to having committed one or more of 49 offenses under the penal law of the State of New York, each of these offenses being sufficiently serious to draw a maximum sentence of not less than one year. The mean number of offenses in adult years—this excludes all offenses committed before the age of sixteen—was 18 for men and 11 for women. Fully 64% of the men and 29% of the women acknowledged their guilt on one or more counts of felony which, under the laws of New York is ground for depriving them of all rights of citizenship. One keynote of these findings is expressed by a minister, referring to false statements he made about a commodity he sold, "I tried truth first, but it's not always successful." On the basis of these results, the authors modestly conclude that "the number of acts legally constituting crimes are far in excess of those officially reported. Unlawful behavior, far from being an abnormal social or psychological manifestation, is in truth a very common phenomenon."

But whatever the differential rates of deviant behavior in the several social strata, and we know from many sources that the official crime statistics uniformly showing higher rates in the lower strata are far from complete or reliable, it appears from our analysis that the greatest pressures toward deviation are exerted upon the lower strata. Cases in point permit us to detect the sociological mechanisms involved in producing these pressures. Several researchers have shown that specialized areas of vice and crime constitute a "normal" response to a situation where the cultural emphasis upon pecuniary success has been absorbed, but where there is little access to conventional and legitimate means for becoming successful. The occupational opportunities of people in these areas are largely confined to manual labor and the lesser white-collar jobs. Given the American stigmatization of manual labor *which has been found to hold rather uniformly in all social classes*, and the absence of realistic opportunities for advancement beyond this level, the result is a marked tendency toward deviant behavior. The status of unskilled labor and the consequent low income cannot readily compete *in terms of established standards of worth* with the promises of power and high income from organized vice, rackets and crime.

For our purposes, these situations exhibit two salient features. First, incentives for success are provided by the established values of the culture *and* second, the avenues available for moving toward this goal are largely limited by the class structure to those of deviant behavior. It is the *combination* of the cultural emphasis and the social structure which produces intense pressure for deviation. Recourse to legitimate channels for "getting in the money" is limited by a class structure which is not fully open at each level to men of good capacity. Despite our persisting open-class-ideology, advance toward the success-goal is relatively rare and notably difficult for those armed with little formal education and few economic resources. The dominant pressure leads toward the gradual attenuation of legitimate, but by and large ineffectual, strivings and the increasing use of illegitimate, but more or less effective, expedients.

Of those located in the lower reaches of the social structure, the culture makes incompatible demands. On the one hand, they are asked to orient their conduct toward the prospect of large wealth—"Every man a king," said Marden and Carnegie and Long—and on the other, they are largely denied effective opportunities to do so institutionally. The consequence of this structural inconsistency is a high rate of deviant behavior. The equilibrium between culturally designated ends and means becomes highly unstable with progressive emphasis on attaining the prestige-laden ends by any means whatsoever. Within this context, Al Capone represents the triumph of amoral intelligence over morally prescribed "failure," when the channels of vertical mobility are closed or narrowed *in a society which places a high premium on economic affluence and social ascent for* all *its members.*

This last qualification is of central importance. It implies that other aspects of the social structure, besides the extreme emphasis on pecuniary success, must be considered if we are to understand the social sources of deviant behavior. A high frequency of deviant behavior is not generated merely by lack of opportunity or by this exaggerated pecuniary emphasis. A comparatively rigidified class structure, a caste order, may limit opportunities far beyond the point which obtains in American society today. It is only when a system of cultural values extols, virtually above all else, certain *common* success-goals *for the population at large* while the social structure rigorously restricts or completely closes access to approved modes of reaching these goals *for a considerable part of the same population*, that deviant behavior ensues on a large scale. Otherwise said, our egalitarian ideology denies by implication the existence of noncompeting individuals and groups in the pursuit of pecuniary success. Instead, the same body of success-symbols is held to apply for all. Goals are held to transcend class lines, not to be bounded by them, yet the actual social organization is such that there exist class differentials in accessibility of the goals. In this setting, a cardinal American virtue, "ambition," promotes a cardinal American vice, "deviant behavior."

This theoretical analysis may help explain the varying correlations between crime and poverty. "Poverty" is not an isolated variable which operates in precisely the same fashion wherever found; it is only one in a complex of identifiably interdependent social and cultural variables. Poverty as such and consequent limitation of opportunity are not enough to produce a conspicuously high rate of criminal behavior. Even the notorious "poverty in the midst of plenty" will not necessarily lead to this result. But when poverty and associated disadvantages in competing for the culture values approved for *all* members of the society are linked with a cultural emphasis on pecuniary success as a dominant goal, high rates of criminal behavior are the normal outcome. Thus, crude (and not necessarily reliable) crime statistics suggest that poverty is less highly correlated with crime in southeastern Europe than in the United States. The economic life-chances of the poor in these European areas would seem to be even less promising than in this country, so that neither poverty nor its association with limited opportunity is sufficient to account for the varying correlations. However, when we consider the full configuration— poverty, limited opportunity and the assignment of cultural goals—there appears some basis for explaining the higher correlation between poverty and crime in our society than in others where rigidified class structure is coupled with *differential class symbols of success. . . .*

In societies such as our own, then, the great cultural emphasis on pecuniary success for all and a social structure which unduly limits practical recourse to approved means for many set up a tension toward innovative practices which depart from institutional norms. But this form of adaptation presupposes that individuals have been imperfectly socialized so that they abandon institutional means while retaining the success-aspiration. Among those who have fully internalized the institutional values, however, a comparable situation is more likely to lead to an alternative response in which the goal is abandoned but conformity to the mores persists. This type of response calls for further examination.

III. RITUALISM

The ritualistic type of adaptation can be readily identified. It involves the abandoning or scaling down of the lofty cultural goals of great pecuniary success and rapid social mobility to the point where one's aspirations can be satisfied. But though one rejects the cultural obligation to attempt "to get ahead in the world," though one draws in one's horizons, one continues to abide almost compulsively by institutional norms.

It is something of a terminological quibble to ask whether this represents genuinely deviant behavior. Since the adaptation is, in effect, an internal decision and since the overt behavior is institutionally permitted, though not culturally preferred, it is not generally considered to represent a social problem. Intimates of individuals making this adaptation may pass judgment in terms of prevailing cultural emphases and may "feel sorry for them," they may, in the individual case, feel that "old Jonesy is certainly in a rut." Whether this is described as deviant behavior or no, it clearly represents a departure from the cultural model in which men are obliged to strive actively, preferably through institutionalized procedures, to move onward and upward in the social hierarchy.

We should expect this type of adaptation to be fairly frequent in a society which makes one's social status largely dependent upon one's achievements. For, as has so often been observed, this ceaseless competitive struggle produces acute status anxiety. One device for allaying these anxieties is to lower one's level of aspiration—permanently. Fear produces inaction, or more accurately, routinized action.

The syndrome of the social ritualist is both familiar and instructive. His implicit life-philosophy finds expression in a series of cultural clichés: "I'm not sticking *my* neck out," "I'm playing safe," "I'm satisfied with what I've got," "Don't aim high and you won't be disappointed." The theme threaded through these attitudes is that high ambitions invite frustration and danger whereas lower aspirations produce satisfaction and security. It is a response to a situation which appears threatening and excites distrust. It is the attitude implicit among workers who carefully regulate their output to a constant quota in an industrial organization where they have occasion to fear that they will "be noticed" by managerial personnel and "something will happen" if their output rises and falls. It is the perspective of the frightened employee, the zealously conformist bureaucrat in the teller's cage of the private banking enterprise or in the front office of the public works enterprise. It is, in short, the mode of adaptation of individually seeking *a private* escape from the dangers and frustrations which seem to them inherent in the competition for major cultural goals by abandoning these goals and clinging all the more closely to the safe routines and the institutional norms.

If we should expect *lower-class* Americans to exhibit Adaptation II— "innovation"— to the frustrations enjoined by the prevailing emphasis on large cultural goals and the fact of small social opportunities, we should expect *lower-middle-class* Americans to be heavily represented among those making Adaptation III, "ritualism." For it is in the lower middle class that parents typically exert continuous pressure upon children to abide by the moral mandates of the society, and where the social climb upward is less likely to meet with success than among the upper middle class. The strong disciplining for conformity with mores reduces the likelihood of Adaptation II and promotes the likelihood of Adaptation III. The severe training leads many to carry a heavy burden of anxiety. The socialization patterns of the lower middle class thus promote the very character structure most predisposed toward ritualism, and it is in this stratum, accordingly, that the adaptive pattern III should most often occur. . . .

IV. RETREATISM

. . . In this category fall some of the adaptive activities of psychotics, autists, pariahs, outcasts, vagrants, vagabonds, tramps, chronic drunkards and drug addicts. They have relinquished culturally prescribed goals and their behavior does not accord with institutional norms. This is not to say that in some cases the source of their mode of adaptation is not the very social structure which they have in effect repudiated nor that their very existence within an area does not constitute a problem for members of the society.

From the standpoint of its sources in the social structure, this mode of adaptation is most likely to occur when *both* the culture goals and the institutional practices have been thoroughly assimilated by the individual and imbued with affect and high value, but accessible institutional avenues are not productive of success. There results a twofold conflict: the interiorized moral obligation for adopting institutional means conflicts with pressures to resort to illicit means (which may attain the goal) and the individual is shut off from means which are both legitimate and effective. The competitive order is maintained but the frustrated and handicapped individual who cannot cope with this order drops out. Defeatism, quietism and resignation are manifested in escape mechanisms which ultimately lead him to "escape" from the requirements of the society. It is thus an expedient which arises from continued failure to near the goal by legitimate measures and from an inability to use the illegitimate route because of internalized prohibitions, *this process occurring while the supreme value of the success-goal has not yet been renounced*. The conflict is resolved by abandoning *both* precipitating elements, the goals and the means. The escape is complete, the conflict is eliminated and the individual is asocialized. . . .

This fourth mode of adaptation, then, is that of the socially disinherited who if they have none of the rewards held out by society also have few of the frustrations attendant upon continuing to seek these rewards. It is, moreover, a privatized rather than a collective mode of adaptation. Although people exhibiting this deviant behavior may gravitate toward centers where they come into contact with other deviants and although they may come to share in the subculture of these deviant groups, their adaptations are largely private and isolated rather than unified under the aegis of a new cultural code. The type of collective adaptation remains to be considered.

V. REBELLION

This adaptation leads men outside the environing social structure to envisage and seek to bring into being a new, that is to say, a greatly modified social structure. It presupposes alienation from reigning goals and standards. These come to be regarded as purely arbitrary. And the arbitrary is precisely that which can neither exact allegiance nor possess legitimacy, for it might as well be otherwise. In our society, organized movements for rebellion apparently aim to introduce a social structure in which the cultural standards of success would be sharply modified and provision would be made for a closer correspondence between merit, effort and reward. . . .

When the institutional system is regarded as the barrier to the satisfaction of legitimized goals, the stage is set for rebellion as an adaptive response. To pass into organized political action, allegiance must not only be withdrawn from the prevailing social structure but must be transferred to new groups possessed of a new myth. The dual function of the myth is to locate the source of large-scale frustrations in the social structure and to portray an alternative structure which would not, presumably, give rise to frustration of the deserving. It is a charter for action. . . .

THE STRAIN TOWARD ANOMIE

The social structure we have examined produces a strain toward anomie and deviant behavior. The pressure of such a social order is upon outdoing one's competitors. So long as the sentiments supporting this competitive system are distributed throughout the entire range of activities and are not confined to the final result of "success," the choice of means will remain largely within the ambit of institutional control. When, however, the cultural emphasis shifts from the satisfactions deriving from competition itself to almost exclusive concern with the outcome, the resultant stress makes for the breakdown of the regulatory structure. With this attenuation of institutional controls, there occurs an approximation to the situation erroneously held by the utilitarian philosophers to be typical of society, a situation in which calculations of personal advantage and fear of punishment are the only regulating agencies.

This strain toward anomie does not operate evenly throughout the society. Some effort has been made in the present analysis to suggest the strata most vulnerable to the pressures for deviant behavior and to set forth some of the mechanisms operating to produce those pressures. For purposes of simplifying the problem, monetary success was taken as the major cultural goal, although there are, of course, alternative goals in the repository of common values. The realms of intellectual and artistic achievement, for example, provide alternative career patterns which may not entail large pecuniary rewards. To the extent that the cultural structure attaches prestige to these alternatives and the social structure permits access to them, the system is somewhat stabilized. Potential deviants may still conform in terms of these auxiliary sets of values.

But the central tendencies toward anomie remain, and it is to these that the analytical scheme here set forth calls particular attention.

5.2 EDWIN H. SUTHERLAND AND DONALD R. CRESSEY

Learning to Be Deviant

In the following selection, criminologists Edwin H. Sutherland and Donald R. Cressey state that criminal behavior should be explained within the same framework as other human behavior: Criminal behavior is learned through interaction with others. The learning takes place in intimate personal groups and is specific and direct, but many skills and understandings are also picked up indirectly. According to the principle of differential association a person becomes delinquent because definitions favorable to law violations are in excess of unfavorable definitions. Stated simply, the number of deviant friends is greater than the number of law-abiding friends. An interesting deduction from this theory is that most middle-class young people would have a very difficult time becoming successful street criminals. The authors would argue that they lack the contact with criminals that is essential to learning the trade.

Sutherland (1883–1950) first developed the differential-association theory of crime causation in 1939. Starting with the theory that crime is a learned behavior, he formulated the nine correlates contained in the following selection. Sutherland's theory has been very influential in the development of sociological theories of deviant behavior.

Cressey (1919–1987), a social psychologist as well as a criminologist, was a member of the California Council on Criminal Justice. His interests in the sociology of delinquency, crime, criminal justice, and corrections are evident in his numerous publications, including *Criminal Organization: Its Elementary Forms* (Harper & Row, 1972).

Key Concept: differential association

The following statement refers to the process by which a particular person comes to engage in criminal behavior.

1. *Criminal behavior is learned.* Negatively, this means that criminal behavior is not inherited, as such; also, the person who is not already trained in crime does not invent criminal behavior, just as a person does not make mechanical inventions unless he has had training in mechanics.

2. *Criminal behavior is learned in interaction with other persons in a process of communication.* This communication is verbal in many respects but includes also "the communication of gestures."

3. *The principal part of the learning of criminal behavior occurs within intimate personal groups.* Negatively, this means that the impersonal agencies of communication, such as movies and newspapers, play a relatively unimportant part in the genesis of criminal behavior.

4. *When criminal behavior is learned, the learning includes (a) techniques of committing the crime, which are sometimes very complicated, sometimes very simple; (b) the specific direction of motives, drives, rationalizations, and attitudes.*

5. *The specific direction of motives and drives is learned from definitions of the legal codes as favorable or unfavorable.* In some societies an individual is surrounded by persons who invariably define the legal codes as rules to be observed, while in others he is surrounded by persons whose definitions are favorable to the violation of the legal codes. In our American society these definitions are almost always mixed, with the consequence that we have culture conflict in relation to the legal codes.

6. *A person becomes delinquent because of an excess of definitions favorable to violation of law over definitions unfavorable to violation of law.* This is the principle of differential association. It refers to both criminal and anti-criminal associations and has to do with counteracting forces. When persons become criminal, they do so because of contacts with criminal patterns and also because of isolation from anti-criminal patterns. Any person inevitably assimilates the surrounding culture unless other patterns are in conflict; a Southerner does not pronounce "r" because other Southerners do not pronounce "r." Negatively, this proposition of differential association means that associations which are neutral so far as crime is concerned have little or no effect on the genesis of criminal behavior. Much of the experience of a person is neutral in this sense, e.g., learning to brush one's teeth. This behavior has no negative or positive effect on criminal behavior except as it may be related to associations which are concerned with the legal codes. This neutral behavior is important especially as an occupier of the time of a child so that he is not in contact with criminal behavior during the time he is so engaged in the neutral behavior.

7. *Differential associations may vary in frequency, duration, priority, and intensity.* This means that associations with criminal behavior and also associations with anti-criminal behavior vary in those respects. "Frequency" and "duration" as modalities of associations are obvious and need no explanation. "Priority" is assumed to be important in the sense that lawful behavior developed in early childhood may persist throughout life, and also that delinquent behavior developed in early childhood may persist throughout life. This tendency, however, has not been adequately demonstrated, and priority seems to be important principally through its selective influence. "Intensity" is not precisely defined but it has to do with such things as the prestige of the source of a criminal or anti-criminal pattern and with emotional reactions related to the associations. In a precise description of the criminal behavior of a person these modalities would be stated in quantitative form and a mathemati-

cal ratio be reached. A formula in this sense has not been developed, and the development of such a formula would be extremely difficult.

8. *The process of learning criminal behavior by association with criminal and anti-criminal patterns involves all of the mechanisms that are involved in any other learning.* Negatively, this means that the learning of criminal behavior is not restricted to the process of imitation. A person who is seduced, for instance, learns criminal behavior by association, but this process would not ordinarily be described as imitation.

9. *While criminal behavior is an expression of general needs and values, it is not explained by those general needs and values since noncriminal behavior is an expression of the same needs and values.* Thieves generally steal in order to secure money, but likewise honest laborers work in order to secure money. The attempts by many scholars to explain criminal behavior by general drives and values, such as the happiness principle, striving for social status, the money motive, or frustration, have been and must continue to be futile since they explain lawful behavior as completely as they explain criminal behavior. They are similar to respiration, which is necessary for any behavior but which does not differentiate criminal from noncriminal behavior.

It is not necessary, at this level of explanation, to explain why a person has the associations which he has; this certainly involves a complex of many things. In an area where the delinquency rate is high, a boy who is sociable, gregarious, active, and athletic is very likely to come in contact with the other boys in the neighborhood, learn delinquent behavior from them, and become a gangster; in the same neighborhood the psychopathic boy who is isolated, introverted, and inert may remain at home, not become acquainted with the other boys in the neighborhood, and not become delinquent. In another situation, the sociable, athletic, aggressive boy may become a member of a scout troop and not become involved in delinquent behavior. The person's associations are determined in a general context of social organization. A child is ordinarily reared in a family; the place of residence of the family is determined largely by family income; and the delinquency rate is in many respects related to the rental value of the houses. Many other aspects of social organization affect the kinds of associations a person has.

The preceding explanation of criminal behavior purports to explain the criminal and noncriminal behavior of individual persons. As indicated earlier, it is possible to state sociological theories of criminal behavior which explain the criminality of a community, nation, or other group. The problem, when thus stated, is to account for variations in crime rates and involves a comparison of the crime rates of various groups or the crime rates of a particular group at different times. The explanation of a crime rate must be consistent with the explanation of the criminal behavior of the person, since the crime rate is a summary statement of the number of persons in the group who commit crimes and the frequency with which they commit crimes. One of the best explanations of crime rates from this point of view is that a high crime rate is due to social disorganization. The term "social disorganization" is not entirely satisfactory and it seems preferable to substitute for it the term "differential social organization." The postulate on which this theory is based, regardless of the name, is that crime is rooted in the social organization and is an expression of that social organization. A group may be organized for criminal behavior or organized against criminal behavior. Most communities are organized both for criminal and anti-criminal behavior and in that sense the crime rate is an expression of the differential group organization. Differential group organization as an explanation of variations in crime rates is consistent with the differential association theory of the processes by which persons become criminals.

*Edwin H.
Sutherland and
Donald R.
Cressey*

Some Conditions of Obedience and Disobedience to Authority

In the aftermath of World War II, civilized people around the world recoiled when they learned the full extent of Nazi Germany's policy of torturing and killing millions of innocent people. Most of the people who participated in the rounding up, transporting, guarding, and killing of the victims of this policy did not want to be instruments of death and torture, but they obeyed the orders of those in authority.

Many social scientists attributed this kind of behavior to the structured obedience of subjects in an authoritarian society. There was the assumption that this phenomenon was unique to authoritarian societies, and that it was something that could not happen in a free and democratic society—America, for example. In totalitarian states, people do what they are told to do, no questions asked, or they suffer terrible consequences. Force, and fear of it, explains their obedient behavior.

But the research of experimental social psychologist Stanley Milgram in the 1960s showed that people in democratic countries will also inflict great pain on others in obedience to authority. In the following article, Milgram describes his now-famous and controversial series of experiments in which he tested a cross section of American men to determine the extent to which they would administer various levels of electric shock to another person when ordered to do so by what is perceived as a legitimate authority.

Milgram (1933–1984) was a professor of psychology at Yale University for many years and also taught at City University of New York. He is especially well-known for his investigations into obedience and group norms. His work sparked much controversy and even protest when it was first published, but *Obedience to Authority: An Experimental View* (Harper & Row, 1975) is considered by many sociologists and psychologists to have revealed a provocative truth.

Key Concept: obedience to authority

*T*he situation in which one agent commands another to hurt a third turns up time and again as a significant theme in human relations. . . . We describe an experimental program, recently concluded at Yale University, in which a particular expression of this conflict is studied by experimental means.

In its most general form the problem may be defined thus: if X tells Y to hurt Z, under what conditions will Y carry out the command of X and under what conditions will he refuse. In the more limited form possible in laboratory research, the question becomes: if an experimenter tells a subject to hurt another person, under what conditions will the subject go along with this instruction, and under what conditions will he refuse to obey. The laboratory problem is not so much a dilution of the general statement as one concrete expression of the many particular forms this question may assume.

One aim of the research was to study behavior in a strong situation of deep consequence to the participants, for the psychological forces operative in powerful and lifelike forms of the conflict may not be brought into play under diluted conditions. . . .

TERMINOLOGY

If Y follows the command of X we shall say that he has obeyed X; if he fails to carry out the command of X, we shall say that he has disobeyed X. The terms to *obey* and to *disobey*, as used here, refer to the subject's overt action only, and carry no implication for the motive or experiential states accompanying the action. . . .

A subject who complies with the entire series of experimental commands will be termed an *obedient* subject; one who at any point in the command series defies the experimenter will be called a *disobedient* or *defiant* subject. As used in this report, the terms refer only to the subject's performance in the experiment, and do not necessarily imply a general personality disposition to submit to or reject authority.

SUBJECT POPULATION

The subjects used in all experimental conditions were male adults, residing in the greater New Haven and Bridgeport [Connecticut] areas, aged 20 to 50 years, and engaged in a wide variety of occupations. Each experimental condition described in this report employed 40 fresh subjects and was carefully balanced for age and occupational types. The occupational composition for each experiment was: workers, skilled and unskilled: 40 per cent; white collar, sales, business: 40 per cent; professionals: 20 per cent. The occupations were intersected with three age categories (subjects in 20s, 30s, and 40s, assigned to each condition in the proportions of 20, 40, and 40 per cent respectively).

THE GENERAL LABORATORY PROCEDURE

The focus of the study concerns the amount of electric shock a subject is willing to administer to another person when ordered by an experimenter to give the 'victim' increasingly more severe punishment. The act of administering shock is set in the context of a learning experiment, ostensibly designed to study the effect of punishment on memory. Aside from the experimenter, one naïve subject and one accomplice perform in each session. On arrival each subject is paid $4.50. After a general talk by the experimenter, telling how little scientists know about the effect of punishment on memory, subjects are informed that one member of the pair will serve as teacher and one as learner. A rigged drawing is held so that the naïve subject is always the teacher, and the accomplice becomes the learner. The learner is taken to an adjacent room and strapped into an 'electric chair'.

The naïve subject is told that it is his task to teach the learner a list of paired associates, to test him on the list, and to administer punishment whenever the learner errs in the test. Punishment takes the form of electric shock, delivered to the learner by means of a shock generator controlled by the naïve subject. The teacher is instructed to increase the intensity of electric shock one step on the generator on each error. The learner, according to plan, provides many wrong answers, so that before long the naïve subject must give him the strongest shock on the generator. Increases in shock level are met by increasingly insistent demands from the learner that the experiment be stopped because of the growing discomfort to him. However, in clear terms the experimenter orders the teacher to continue with the procedure in disregard of the learner's protests. *Thus, the naïve subject must resolve a conflict between two mutually incompatible demands from the social field. He may continue to follow the orders of the experimenter and shock the learner with increasing severity, or he may refuse to follow the orders of the experimenter and heed the learner's pleas. The experimenter's authority operates not in a free field, but against ever-mounting countervailing pressures from the person being punished.*

A few technical points need to be considered before the findings of the study are described. For the purpose of delivering shock, a simulated shock generator is used, with 30 clearly marked voltage levels that range from 15 to 450 volts (and each activated by one of 30 individual lever switches set in a horizontal line). The naïve subject is given a sample shock of 45 volts to convince him of the authenticity of the instrument. The generator bears verbal designations that range from 'Slight Shock' to 'Danger: Severe Shock'.

The responses of the victim are standardized on tape, and each protest is coordinated to a particular voltage level on the shock generator. Starting with 75 volts the learner begins to grunt and moan. At 150 volts he demands to be let out of the experiment. At 180 volts he cries out that he can no longer stand the pain. At 300 volts he refuses to provide any more answers to the memory test, insisting that he is no longer a participant in the experiment and must be freed. In response to this last tactic, the experimenter instructs the naïve subject to treat the absence of an answer as equivalent to a wrong answer, and to follow the usual shock procedure. The experimenter reinforces his demand with the statement: 'You have no other choice, you must go on!' (This imperative is used whenever the naïve subject tries to break off the experiment.) If the subject refuses to give the next higher level of shock, the experiment is considered at an end. A quantitative value is assigned to the subject's performance based on the maximum intensity shock he administered before breaking off. Thus any subject's score may range from zero (for a subject unwilling to administer the first shock level) to 30 (for a subject who proceeds to the highest voltage level on the board). For any particular subject and for any particular experimental condition the degree to which participants have followed the experimenter's orders may be specified with a numerical value, corresponding to the metric on the shock generator. . . .

IMMEDIACY OF THE VICTIM

This series consisted of four experimental conditions. In each condition the victim was brought 'psychologically' closer to the subject giving him shocks.

In the first condition (Remote Feedback) the victim was placed in another room and could not be heard or seen by the subject, except that, at 300 volts, he pounded on the wall in protest. After 315 volts he no longer answered or was heard from.

The second condition (Voice Feedback) was identical to the first except that voice protests were introduced. As in the first condition the victim was placed in an adjacent room, but his complaints could be heard clearly through a door left slightly ajar, and through the walls of the laboratory.

The third experimental condition (Proximity) was similar to the second, except that the victim was now placed in the same room as the subject, and 1 1/2 feet from him. Thus he was visible as well as audible, and voice cues were provided.

The fourth, and final, condition of this series (Touch-Proximity) was identical to the third, with this exception: the victim received a shock only when his hand rested on a shockplate. At the 150-volt level the victim again demanded to be let free and, in this condition, refused to place his hand on the shockplate. The experimenter ordered the naïve subject to force the victim's hand onto the plate. Thus obedience in this condition required that the subject have physical contact with the victim in order to give him punishment beyond the 150-volt level.

Forty adult subjects were studied in each condition. The data revealed that obedience was significantly reduced as the victim was rendered more immediate to the subject. The mean maximum shock for the conditions is shown in *Figure 1*.

Expressed in terms of the proportion of obedient to defiant subjects, the findings are that 34 per cent of the subjects defied the experimenter in the Remote condition, 37.5 per cent in Voice Feedback, 60 per cent in Proximity, and 70 per cent in Touch-Proximity.

How are we to account for this effect? A first conjecture might be that as the victim was brought closer the subject became more aware of the intensity of his suffering and regulated his behavior accordingly. This makes sense, but our evidence does not support the interpretation. There are no consistent differences in the attributed level of pain across the four conditions (i.e. the amount of pain experienced by the victim as estimated by the subject and expressed on a 14-point scale). But it is easy to speculate about alternative mechanisms:

Empathic cues. In the Remote and to a lesser extent the Voice Feedback condition, the victim's suffering possesses an abstract, remote quality for the subject. He is aware, but only in a conceptual sense, that his actions cause pain to another person; the fact is apprehended, but not felt. The phenomenon is common enough. The bombardier can reasonably suppose that his weapons will inflict suffering and death, yet this knowledge is divested of affect, and does not move him to a felt, emotional response to the suffering resulting from his actions. . . .

Denial and narrowing of the cognitive field. The Remote condition allows a narrowing of the cognitive field so that the victim is put out of mind. The subject no longer considers the act of depressing a lever relevant to moral judgement, for it is no longer associated with the victim's suffering. When the victim is close it is more difficult to exclude him phenomenologically. . . . The mechanism of denial can no longer be brought into play. One subject in the Remote condition said:

FIGURE 1 *Mean Maxima in Proximity Series*

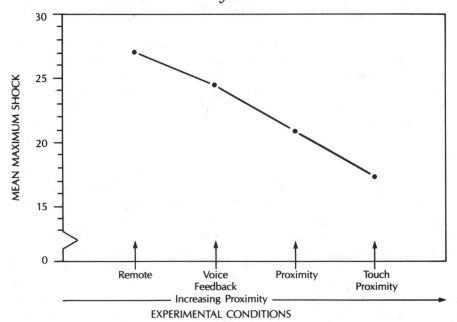

'It's funny how you really begin to forget that there's a guy out there, even though you can hear him. For a long time I just concentrated on pressing the switches and reading the words.'

Reciprocal fields. If in the Proximity condition the subject is in an improved position to observe the victim, the reverse is also true. The actions of the subject now come under proximal scrutiny by the victim. Possibly, it is easier to harm a person when he is unable to observe our actions than when he can see what we are doing. His surveillance of the action directed against him may give rise to shame, or guilt, which may then serve to curtail the action. . . .

Phenomenal unity of act. In the Remote conditions it is more difficult for the subject to gain a sense of *relatedness* between his own actions and the consequences of these actions for the victim. There is a physical and spatial separation of the act and its consequences. The subject depresses a lever in one room, and protests and cries are heard from another. The two events are in correlation, yet they lack a compelling phenomenological unity. . . .

Incipient group formation. Placing the victim in another room not only takes him further from the subject, but the subject and the experimenter are drawn relatively closer. There is incipient group formation between the experimenter and the subject, from which the victim is excluded. The wall between the victim and the others deprives him of an intimacy which the experimenter and subject feel. In the Remote condition, the victim is truly an outsider, who stands alone, physically and psychologically.

When the victim is placed close to the subject, it becomes easier to form an alliance with him against the experimenter. Subjects no longer have to face the experimenter alone. They have an ally who is close at hand and eager to collaborate in a revolt against the experimenter. Thus, the changing set of spatial relations leads to a potentially shifting set of alliances over the several experimental conditions.

Acquired behavior dispositions. It is commonly observed that laboratory mice will rarely fight with their litter mates. . . . [T]he organism learns that it is safer to be aggressive toward others at a distance, and precarious to be so when the parties are within arm's reach. Through a pattern of rewards and punishments, he acquires a disposition to avoid aggression at close quarters, a disposition which does not extend to harming others at a distance. And this may account for experimental findings in the remote and proximal experiments. . . .

CLOSENESS OF AUTHORITY

If the spatial relationship of the subject and victim is relevant to the degree of obedience, would not the relationship of subject to experimenter also play a part?

There are reasons to feel that, on arrival, the subject is oriented primarily to the experimenter rather than to the victim. He has come to the laboratory to fit into the structure that the experimenter—not the victim—would provide. He has come less to understand his behavior than to *reveal* that behavior to a competent scientist, and he is willing to display himself as the scientist's purposes require. Most subjects seem quite concerned about the appearance they are making before the experimenter, and one could argue that this preoccupation in a relatively new and strange setting makes the subject somewhat insensitive to the triadic nature of the social situation. . . .

In a series of experiments we varied the physical closeness and degree of surveillance of the experimenter. In one condition the experimenter sat just a few feet away from the subject. In a second condition, after giving initial instructions the experimenter left the laboratory and gave his orders by telephone; in still a third condition the experimenter was never seen, providing instructions by means of a tape recording activated when the subjects entered the laboratory.

Obedience dropped sharply as the experimenter was physically removed from the laboratory. The number of obedient subjects in the first condition (Experimenter Present) was almost three times as great as in the second, where the experimenter gave his orders by telephone. Twenty-six subjects were fully obedient in the first condition, and only 9 in the second. . . . Subjects seemed able to take a far stronger stand against the experimenter when they did not have to encounter him face to face, and the experimenter's power over the subject was severely curtailed.

Moreover, when the experimenter was absent, subjects displayed an interesting form of behavior that had not occurred under his surveillance. Though continuing with the experiment, several subjects administered lower shocks than were required and never informed the experimenter of their deviation from the correct procedure. . . . Indeed, in telephone conversations some subjects specifically assured the experimenter that they were raising the shock level according to instruction, whereas in fact they were repeatedly using the lowest shock on the board. This form of behavior is particularly interesting: although these subjects acted in a way that clearly undermined the avowed purposes of the experiment, they found it easier to handle the conflict in this manner than to precipitate an open break with authority. . . .

Experiments in this series show that the physical *presence* of an authority is an important force contributing to the subject's obedience or defiance. Taken together with the first experimental series on the proximity of the victim, it would appear that something akin to fields of force, diminishing in effectiveness with increasing psychological distance from their source, have a controlling effect on the subject's performance. As the victim is brought closer, the subject finds it harder to administer shocks to him. When the victim's position is held constant relative to the subject, and the authority is made more remote, the subject finds it easier to break off the experiment. This effect is substantial in both cases, but manipulation of the experimenter's position yielded the more powerful results. Obedience to destructive commands is highly dependent on the proximal relations between authority and subject.

TENSIONS

The description of final scores does not fully convey the character of the subjects' performance, and it would be useful to interrupt our reporting of quantitative relationships to remark on the subjects' general reaction to the situation.

One might suppose that a subject would simply break off or continue as his conscience and temperament dictated. Yet this is very far from what happened. There were powerful reactions of tension and emotional strain in a substantial proportion of the participants. Persons were observed to sweat, tremble, stutter, bite their lips, and groan as they found themselves increasingly implicated in the experimental conflict. Some sense of the subjects' mood can be gotten from a transcript of their remarks at break-off point. Here are the remarks of two defiant subjects:

Is he banging? . . . Is he hurt out there? Well, I don't want to be responsible for anything that happens to him. No, I can't go on with it. I don't know whether he's all right or not. I mean he may have a heart condition or something; I wouldn't feel right doing it. He's banging for help. He's evidently in trouble or he wouldn't bang . . . I don't see any sense to this—to knocking him out or something. I just can't see it.

(*Subject refuses to administer shocks*)   [*Subject 0108*]

The man is banging. He wants to get out . . . I'm sorry. If the man wants to get out I'd just as soon stop . . . I don't want to administer any more [extremely excited] . . . I will gladly refund the check, but I will not harm this man . . . I'm sorry, I will not give him any more if he obviously wants to get out. There is no money in the world that will make me hurt another individual. [*Subject 010X*]

And here is a transcript from an obedient subject. He began the experiment calmly, but became increasingly tense as the experiment proceeded. After administering the 150-volt shock, he began to address the experimenter in agitated tones:

150 volts delivered. You want me to keep going?
165 volts delivered. That guy is hollering in there. There's a lot of them here. He's liable to have heart condition. You want me to go?
180 volts delivered. He can't stand it! I'm not going to kill that man in there! You hear him hollering? He's hollering. He can't stand it. What if something happens to him? . . . I'm not going to get that man sick in there. He's hollering in there. You know what I mean? I mean I refuse to take responsibility. He's getting hurt in there. He's in there hollering. Too many left here. Geez, if he gets them wrong. There's too many of them left. I mean who is going to take responsibility if anything happens to that gentleman?
[*The experimenter accepts responsibility.*] All right.
195 volts delivered. You see he's hollering. Hear that. Gee, I don't know. [*The experimenter says: 'The experiment requires that you go on.'*]—I know it does sir, but I mean—hugh—he don't know what he's in for. He's up to 195 volts.
210 volts delivered
225 volts delivered
240 volts delivered. Aw, no. You mean I've got to keep going up with the scale? No sir. I'm not going to kill that man! I'm not going to give him 450 volts! [*The experimenter says: 'The experiment requires that you go on.'*]—I know it does, but that man is hollering in there, sir. . . .

Despite his numerous, agitated objections, which were constant accompaniments to his actions, the subject unfailingly obeyed the experimenter, proceeding to the highest shock level on the generator. He displayed a curious dissociation between word and action. Although at the verbal level he had resolved not to go on, his actions were fully in accord with the experimenter's commands. This subject did not want to shock the victim, and he found it an extremely disagreeable task, but he was unable to invent a response that would free him from *E*'s authority. Many subjects cannot find the specific verbal formula that would enable them to reject the role assigned to them by the experimenter. Perhaps our culture does not provide adequate models for disobedience. . . .

BACKGROUND AUTHORITY

In psychophysics, animal learning, and other branches of psychology, the fact that measures are obtained at one institution rather than another is irrelevant to the interpretation of the findings, so long as the technical facilities for measurement are adequate and the operations are carried out with competence.

But it cannot be assumed that this holds true for the present study. The effectiveness of the experimenter's commands may depend in an important way on the larger institutional context in which they are issued. The experiments described thus far were conducted at Yale University, an organization which most subjects regarded with respect and sometimes awe. In postexperimental interviews several participants remarked that the locale and sponsorship of the study gave them confidence in the integrity, competence, and benign purposes of the personnel; many indicated that they would not have shocked the learner if the experiments had been done elsewhere.

This issue of background authority seemed to us important for an interpretation of the results that had been obtained thus far; moreover it is highly relevant to any comprehensive theory of human obedience. Consider, for example, how closely our compliance with the imperatives of others is tied to particular institutions and locales in our day-to-day activities. On request, we expose our throats to a man with a razor blade in the barber shop, but would not do so in a shoe store; in the latter setting we willingly follow the clerk's request to stand in our stockinged feet, but resist the command in a bank. In the laboratory of a great university, subjects may comply with a set of commands that would be resisted if given elsewhere. *One must always question the relationship of obedience to a person's sense of the context in which he is operating.*

To explore the problem we moved our apparatus to an office building in industrial Bridgeport and replicated experimental conditions, without any visible tie to the university.

Bridgeport subjects were invited to the experiment through a mail circular similar to the one used in the Yale study, with appropriate changes in letterhead, etc. As in the earlier study, subjects were paid $4.50 for coming to the laboratory. The same age and occupational distributions used at Yale, and the identical personnel, were employed.

The purpose in relocating in Bridgeport was to assure a complete dissociation from Yale, and in this regard we were fully successful. On the surface, the study appeared to be conducted by RESEARCH ASSOCIATES OF BRIDGEPORT, an organization of unknown character (the title had been concocted exclusively for use in this study).

The experiments were conducted in a three-room office suite in a somewhat run-down commercial building located in the downtown shopping area. The laboratory was sparsely furnished, though clean, and marginally respectable in appearance. When subjects inquired about professional affiliations, they were informed only that we were a private firm conducting research for industry. . . .

There was no noticeable reduction in tension for the Bridgeport subjects. And the subjects' estimation of the amount of pain felt by the victim was slightly, though not significantly, higher than in the Yale study.

A failure to obtain complete obedience in Bridgeport would indicate that the extreme compliance found in New Haven subjects was tied closely to the background authority of Yale University; if a large proportion of the subjects remained fully obedient, very different conclusions would be called for.

As it turned out, the level of obedience in Bridgeport, although somewhat reduced, was not significantly lower than that obtained at Yale. A large proportion of the Bridgeport subjects were fully obedient to the experimenter's commands (48 per cent of the Bridgeport subjects delivered the maximum shock *vs.* 65 per cent in the corresponding condition at Yale). . . .

LEVELS OF OBEDIENCE AND DEFIANCE

One general finding that merits attention is the high level of obedience manifested in the experimental situation. Subjects often expressed deep disapproval of shocking a man in the face of his objections, and others denounced it as senseless and stupid. Yet many subjects complied even while they protested. The proportion of obedient subjects greatly exceeded the expectations of the experimenter and his colleagues. At the outset, we had conjectured that subjects would not, in general, go above the level of 'Strong Shock'. In practice, many subjects were willing to administer the most extreme shocks available when commanded by the experimenter. For some subjects the experiment provides an occasion for aggressive release. And for others it demonstrates the extent to which obedient dispositions are deeply ingrained, and are engaged irrespective of their consequences for others. Yet this is not the whole story. Somehow, the subject becomes implicated in a situation from which he cannot disengage himself. . . .

Many people, not knowing much about the experiment, claim that subjects who go to the end of the board are sadistic. Nothing could be more foolish as an overall characterization of these persons. It is like saying that a person thrown into a swift-flowing stream is necessarily a fast swimmer, or that he has great stamina because he moves so rapidly relative to the bank. The context of action must always be considered. The individual, upon entering the laboratory, becomes integrated into a situation that carries its own momentum. The subject's problem then is how to become disengaged from a situation which is moving in an altogether ugly direction.

The fact that disengagement is so difficult testifies to the potency of the forces that keep the subject at the control board. Are these forces to be conceptualized as individual motives and expressed in the language of personality dynamics, or are they to be seen as the effects of social structure and pressures arising from the situational field?

A full understanding of the subject's action will, I feel, require that both perspectives be adopted. The person brings to the laboratory enduring dispositions toward authority and aggression, and at the same time he becomes enmeshed in a social structure that is no less an objective fact of the case. . . .

POSTSCRIPT

Almost a thousand adults were individually studied in the obedience research, and there were many specific conclusions regarding the variables that control obedience and disobedience to authority. Some of these have been discussed briefly in the preceding sections, and more detailed reports will be released subsequently.

There are now some other generalizations I should like to make, which do not derive in any strictly logical fashion from the experiments as carried out, but which, I feel, ought to be made. They are formulations of an intuitive sort that have been forced on me by observation of many subjects responding to the pressures of authority. The assertions represent a painful alteration in my own thinking; and since they were acquired only under the repeated impact of direct observation, I have no illusion that they will be generally accepted by persons who have not had the same experience.

With numbing regularity good people were seen to knuckle under the demands of authority and perform actions that were callous and severe. Men who are in everyday life responsible and decent were seduced by the trappings of authority, by the control of their perceptions, and by the uncritical acceptance of the experimenter's definition of the situation, into performing harsh acts.

What is the limit of such obedience? At many points we attempted to establish a boundary. Cries from the victim were inserted; not good enough. The victim claimed heart trouble; subjects still shocked him on command. The victim pleaded that he be let free, and his answers no longer registered on the signal box; subjects continued to shock him. At the outset we had not conceived that such drastic procedures would be needed to generate disobedience, and each step was added only as the ineffectiveness of the earlier techniques became clear. The final effort to establish a limit was the Touch-Proximity condition. But the very first subject in this condition subdued the victim on command, and proceeded to the highest shock level. A quarter of the subjects in this condition performed similarly.

The results, as seen and felt in the laboratory, are to this author disturbing. They raise the possibility that human nature, or—more specifically—the kind of character produced in American democratic society, cannot be counted on to insulate its citizens from brutality and inhumane treatment at the direction of malevolent authority. A substantial proportion of people do what they are told to do, irrespective of the content of the act and without limitations of conscience, so long as they perceive that the command comes from a legitimate authority. If in this study an anonymous experimenter could successfully command adults to subdue a fifty-year-old man, and force on him painful electric shocks against his protests, one can only wonder what government, with its vastly greater authority and prestige, can command of its subjects. There is, of course, the extremely important question of whether malevolent political institutions could or would arise in American society. The present research contributes nothing to this issue.

Thinking About Crime

The process of socialization is a highly effective instrument of social control. It ensures that the majority of citizens will normally conform to the social norms without pressure from law enforcers. Nevertheless, it does not prevent a significant number of people from not conforming, and thus, other means of social control have to be utilized. The nature and type of social control have varied significantly over time, depending on how deviance was perceived in society. For example, in the early 1900s, biological theories explained criminal behavior as inborn and, therefore, not much influenced by rehabilitation programs. In contrast, in the 1960s, crime was increasingly seen as resulting from abysmal social conditions. If these could be corrected, then fewer people would resort to crime. The War on Poverty and Head Start were two of the measures taken in the 1960s and 1970s to improve the socioeconomic conditions of the American people. The secondary consequences of these programs were to reduce crime and deviance.

James Q. Wilson (b. 1931), a prolific and provocative criminologist and political scientist, is the James Collins Professor of Management and Public Policy at the University of California, Los Angeles, where he has been teaching since 1985. He has studied and advised on issues in crime and law enforcement for nearly 25 years, and he has served on a number of commissions concerned with public policy. In his book *Thinking About Crime* (Basic Books, 1975), from which the following selection is taken, Wilson challenges various accepted theories of crime and prevention. Wilson notes that the programs that were implemented in the 1960s and 1970s to reduce poverty and poor socio-economic conditions have done little to reduce crime. On the contrary, crime has increased. He makes his case for why this is so and what should be done.

Key Concept: the economic theory of crime

I argue for a sober view of man and his institutions that would permit reasonable things to be accomplished, foolish things abandoned, and utopian things forgotten. A sober view of man requires a modest definition of progress. A 20 percent reduction in robbery would still leave us with the highest robbery rate of almost any Western nation but would prevent about sixty thousand robberies. A small gain for society, a large one for the would-be victims. Yet a 20 percent reduction is unlikely if we concentrate our efforts on dealing with the causes of crime or even if we concentrate on improving police efficiency. Were we to devote those resources to a strategy that is well within our abilities—namely, to incapacitating a larger fraction of the convicted serious robbers—then not only is a 20 percent reduction possible, but even larger ones are conceivable.

Most serious crime is committed by repeaters. What we do with first offenders is probably far less important than what we do with habitual offenders. A genuine first offender (and not merely a habitual offender caught for the first time) is in all likelihood a young person who, in the majority of cases, will stop stealing when he gets older. This is not to say we should forgive first offenses, for that would be to license the offense and erode the moral judgments that must underlie any society's attitude toward crime. The gravity of the offense must be appropriately impressed on the first offender, but the effort to devise ways of reeducating or uplifting him in order to insure that he does not steal again is likely to be wasted—both because we do not know how to reeducate or uplift and because most young delinquents seem to reeducate themselves no matter what society does.

After tracing the history of nearly ten thousand Philadelphia boys born in 1945, Marvin Wolfgang and his colleagues at the University of Pennsylvania found that over one-third were picked up by the police for something more serious than a traffic offense, but that 46 percent of these delinquents had no further police contact after their first offense. Though a third started on crime, nearly half seemed to stop spontaneously—a good thing, because the criminal justice system in that city, already sorely taxed, would in all likelihood have collapsed. Out of the ten thousand boys, however, there were six hundred twenty-seven—only 6 percent—who committed five or more offenses before they were eighteen. Yet these few chronic offenders accounted for *over half* of these recorded delinquencies and about *two-thirds* of all the violent crimes committed by the entire cohort.

Only a tiny fraction of all serious crimes lead immediately to an arrest, and only a slightly larger fraction are ultimately "cleared" by an arrest, but this does not mean that the police function is meaningless. Because most serious crime is committed by repeaters, most criminals eventually get arrested. The Wolfgang findings and other studies suggest that the chances of a persistent burglar or robber living out his life, or even going a year, with no arrest are quite small. Yet a large proportion of repeat offenders suffer little or no loss of freedom. Whether or not one believes that such penalties, if inflicted, would act as a deterrent, it is obvious that they could serve to incapacitate these offenders and thus, for the period of the incapacitation, prevent them from committing additional crimes.

We have a limited (and declining) supply of detention facilities, and many of those that exist are decrepit, unsafe, and overcrowded. But as important as expanding the supply and improving the decency of the facilities is the need to think seriously about how we wish to allocate those spaces that exist. At present, that allocation is hit or miss. A 1966 survey of over fifteen juvenile correctional institutions revealed that about 30 percent of the inmates were young persons who had been committed for conduct that would not have been judged criminal were it committed by adults. They were runaways, "stubborn children," or chronic truants—problem children, to be sure, but scarcely major threats to society. Using scarce detention space for them when in Los Angeles over 90 percent of burglars with a major prior record receive no state prison sentence seems, to put it mildly, anomalous.

Shlomo and Reuel Shinnar have estimated the effect on crime rates in New York State of a judicial policy other than that followed during the last decade or so. Given the present level of police efficiency and making some assumptions about how many crimes each offender commits per year, they conclude that the rate of serious crime would be only *one-third* what it is today if every person convicted of a serious offense were imprisoned for three years. This reduction would be less if it turned out (as seems unlikely) that most serious crime is committed by first time offenders, and it would be much greater if the proportion of crimes resulting in an arrest and conviction were increased (as also seems unlikely). The reduction, it should be noted, would be solely the result of incapacitation, making no allowance for such additional reductions as might result from enhanced deterrence or rehabilitation.

The Shinnar estimates are based on uncertain data and involve assumptions that can be challenged. But even assuming they are overly optimistic by a factor of two, a sizable reduction in crime would still ensue. In other countries such a policy of greater incapacitation is in fact followed. A robber arrested in England, for example, is more than three times as likely as one arrested in New York to go to prison. That difference in sentencing does not account for all the difference between English and American crime rates, but it may well account for a substantial fraction of it.

That these gains are possible does not mean that society should adopt such a policy. One would first want to know the costs, in additional prison space and judicial resources, of greater use of incapacitation. One would want to debate the propriety and humanity of a mandatory three-year term; perhaps, in order to accommodate differences in the character of criminals and their crimes, one would want to have a range of sentences from, say, one to five years. One would want to know what is likely to happen to the process of charging and pleading if every person arrested for a serious crime faced a mandatory minimum sentence, however mild. These and other difficult and important questions must first be confronted. But the central fact is that *these are reasonable questions* around which facts can be gathered and intelligent arguments mustered. To discuss them requires us to make few optimistic assumptions about the malleability of human nature, the skills of officials who operate complex institutions, or the capacity of society to improve the fundamental aspects of familial and communal life.

Persons who criticize an emphasis on changing the police and courts to cope with crime are fond of saying that such measures cannot work so long as unemployment and poverty exist. We must acknowledge that we have not done very well at inducting young persons, especially but not only blacks, into the work force. Teenage unemployment rates continue to exceed 20 percent; though the rate of growth in the youthful component of the population has slowed, their unemployment shows little sign of abating. To a degree, anticrime policies may be frustrated by the failure of employment policies, but it would be equally correct to say that so long as the criminal justice system does not impede crime, efforts to reduce unemployment will not work. If legitimate opportunities for work are unavailable, many young persons will turn to crime; but if criminal opportunities are profitable, many young persons will not take those legitimate jobs that exist. The benefits of work and the costs of crime must be increased simultaneously; to increase one but not the other makes sense only if one assumes that young people are irrational.

One rejoinder to this view is the argument that if legitimate jobs are made absolutely more attractive than stealing, stealing will decline even without any increase in penalties for it. That may be true provided there is no practical limit on the amount that can be paid in wages. Since the average "take" from a burglary or mugging is quite small, it would seem easy to make the income from a job exceed the income from crime. But this neglects the advantages of a criminal income: One works at crime at one's convenience, enjoys the esteem of colleagues who think a "straight" job is stupid and skill at stealing is commendable, looks forward to the occasional "big score" that may make further work unnecessary for weeks, and relishes the risk and adventure associated with theft. The money value of all these benefits—that is, what one who is not shocked by crime would want in cash to forego crime—is hard to estimate, but is almost certainly far larger than what either public or private employers could offer to unskilled or semiskilled young workers. The only alternative for society is to so increase the risks of theft that its value is depreciated below what society can afford to pay in legal wages, and then take whatever steps are necessary to insure that those legal wages are available.

Another rejoinder to the "attack poverty" approach to crime is this: The desire to reduce crime is the worst possible reason for reducing poverty. Most poor persons are not criminals; many are either retired or have regular jobs and lead conventional family lives. The elderly, the working poor, and the willing-to-work poor could benefit greatly from economic conditions and government programs that enhance their incomes without there being the slightest reduction in crime—indeed, if the experience of the 1960s is any guide, there might well be, through no fault of most beneficiaries, an increase in crime. Reducing poverty and breaking up the ghettoes are desirable policies in their own right, whatever their effects on crime. It is the duty of government to devise other measures to cope with crime, not only to permit antipoverty programs to succeed without unfair competition from criminal opportunities, but also to insure that such programs do not inadvertently shift the costs of progress, in terms of higher crime rates, onto innocent parties, not the least of whom are the poor themselves.

One cannot press this economic reasoning too far. Some persons will commit crimes whatever the risks; indeed, for some, the greater the risk the greater the thrill, while others—the alcoholic wife beater, for example—are only dimly aware that there are any risks. But more important than the insensitivity of certain criminal activities to changes in risks and benefits is the impropriety of casting the crime problem wholly in terms of a utilitarian calculus. The most serious offenses are crimes not simply because society finds them inconvenient, but because it regards them with moral horror. To steal, to rape, to rob, to assault—these acts are destructive of the very possibility of society and affronts to the humanity of their victims. It is my experience that parents do not instruct their children to be law abiding merely by pointing to the risks of being caught, but by explaining that these acts are wrong whether or not one is caught. I conjecture that those parents who simply warn their offspring about the risks of crime produce a disproportionate number of young persons willing to take those risks.

Even the deterrent capacity of the criminal justice system depends in no small part on its ability to evoke sentiments of shame in the accused. If all it evoked were a sense of being unlucky, crime rates would be even higher. James Fitzjames Stephens makes the point by analogy. To what extent, he asks, would a man be deterred from theft by the knowledge that by committing it he was exposing himself to one chance in fifty of catching a serious but not fatal illness—say, a bad fever? Rather little, we would imagine—indeed, all of us regularly take risks as great or greater than that; when we drive after drinking, when we smoke cigarettes, when we go hunting in the woods. The criminal sanction, Stephens concludes, "operates not only on the fears of criminals, but upon the habitual sentiments of those who are not criminals. [A] great part of the general detestation of crime . . . arises from the fact that the commission of offenses is associated . . . with the solemn and deliberate infliction of punishment wherever crime is proved."

Much is made today of the fact that the criminal justice system "stigmatizes" those caught up in it, and thus unfairly marks such persons and perhaps even furthers their criminal careers by having "labeled" them as criminals. Whether the labeling process operates in this way is as yet unproved, but it would indeed be unfortunate if society treated a convicted offender in such a way that he had no reasonable alternative but to make crime a career. To prevent this, society ought to insure that one can "pay one's debt" without suffering permanent loss of civil rights, the continuing and pointless indignity of parole supervision, and frustration in being unable to find a job. But doing these things is very different from eliminating the "stigma" from crime. To destigmatize crime would be to lift from it the weight of moral judgment and to make crime simply a particular occupation or avocation which society has chosen to reward less (or perhaps more!) than other pursuits. If there is not stigma attached to an activity, then society has no business making it a crime. Indeed, before the invention of the prison in the late eighteenth and early nineteenth centuries, the stigma attached to criminals was the major deterrent to and principal form of protection from criminal activity. The purpose of the criminal justice system is not to expose would-be criminals to a lottery in which they either win or lose, but to expose them in addition and more importantly to the solemn condemnation of the community should they yield to temptation. . . .

One wonders whether the stigma properly associated with crime retains much deterrent or educative value. My strong inclination is to resist explanations for rising crime that are based on the alleged moral breakdown of society, the community, or the family. I resist in part because most of the families and communities I know have not broken down, and in part because, had they broken down, I cannot imagine any collective action we could take consistent with our civil liberties that would restore a moral consensus, and yet the facts are hard to ignore. Take the family: Over one-third of all black children and one in fourteen of all white children live in single-parent families. Over two million children live in single-parent (usually father absent) households, almost *double* the number of ten years ago. In 1950, 18 percent of black families were female-headed; in 1969 the proportion had risen to 27 percent; by 1973 it exceeded 35 percent. The average income for a single-parent family with children under six years of age was, in 1970, only $3,100, well below the official "poverty line."

Studies done in the late 1950s and the early 1960s showed that children from broken homes were more likely than others to become delinquent. In New York State, 58 percent of the variation in pupil achievement in three hundred schools could be predicted by but three variables—broken homes, overcrowded housing, and parental educational level. Family disorganization, writes Urie Bronfenbrenner, has been shown in thousands of studies to be an "omnipresent overriding factor" in behavior disorders and social pathology. And that disorganization is increasing.

These facts may explain some elements of the rising crime rate that cannot be attributed to the increased number of young persons, high teenage unemployment, or changed judicial policies. The age of persons arrested has been declining for more than fifteen years and the median age of convicted defendants (in jurisdictions for which data are available) has been declining for the last six years. Apparently, the age at which persons begin to commit serious crime has been falling. For some young people, thus, whatever forces weaken their resistance to criminal activity have been increasing in magnitude, and these forces may well include the continued disorganization of the family and the continued deterioration of the social structure of inner city communities.

One wants to be objective, if not optimistic. Perhaps single-parent families today are less disorganized or have a different significance than such families in the past. Perhaps the relationship between family structure and social pathology will change. After all, there now seem to be good grounds for believing that, at least on the East Coast, the heroin epidemic of the 1960s has run its course; though there are still thousands of addicts, the rate of formation of new addicts has slowed and the rate of heroin use by older addicts has dropped. Perhaps other aspects of the relationship among family, personality, and crime will change. Perhaps.

No one can say how much of crime results from its increased profitability and how much from its decreased shamefulness. But one or both factors must be at work, for population changes alone simply cannot account for the increases. Crime in our cities has increased far faster than the number of young people, or poor people, or black people, or just plain people who live in those cities. In short, objective conditions alone, whether demographic or economic, cannot account for the crime increases, though they no doubt contributed to it. Subjective forces—ideas, attitudes, values—played a great part, though in ways hard to define and impossible to measure. An assessment of the effect of these changes on crime would provide a partial understanding of changes in the moral structure of our society.

But to understand is not to change. If few of the demographic factors contributing to crime are subject to planned change, virtually none of the subjective ones are. Though intellectually rewarding, from a practical point of view it is a mistake to think about crime in terms of its "causes" and then to search for ways to alleviate those causes. We must think instead of what it is feasible for a government or a community to do, and then try to discover, by experimentation and observation, which of those things will produce, at acceptable costs, desirable changes in the level of criminal victimization.

There are, we now know, certain things we can change in accordance with our intentions, and certain ones we cannot. We cannot alter the number of juveniles who first experiment with minor crimes. We cannot lower the recidivism rate, though within reason we should keep trying. We are not yet certain whether we can increase significantly the police apprehension rate. We may be able to change the teenage unemployment rate, though we have learned by painful trial and error that doing this is much more difficult than once supposed. We can probably reduce the time it takes to bring an arrested person to trial, even though we have as yet made few serious efforts to do so. We can certainly reduce the arbitrary and socially irrational exercise of prosecutorial discretion over whom to charge and whom to release, and we can most definitely stop pretending that judges know, any better than the rest of us, how to provide "individualized justice." We can confine a larger proportion of the serious and repeat offenders and fewer of the common drunks and truant children. We know that confining criminals prevents them from harming society, and we have grounds for suspecting that some would-be criminals can be deterred by the confinement of others.

Above all, we can try to learn more about what works, and in the process abandon our ideological preconceptions about what *ought* to work. Nearly ten years ago I wrote that the billions of dollars the federal government was then preparing to spend on crime control would be wasted, and indeed might even make matters worse if they were merely pumped into the existing criminal justice system. They were, and they have. In the next ten years I hope we can learn to experiment rather than simply spend, to test our theories rather than fund our fears. This is advice, not simply or even primarily to government—for governments are run by men and women who are under irresistible pressures to pretend they know more than they do—but to my colleagues: academics, theoreticians, writers, advisers. We may feel ourselves under pressure to pretend we know things, but we are also under a positive obligation to admit what we do not know and to avoid cant and sloganizing. The government agency, the Law Enforcement Assistance Administration, that has futilely spent those billions was created in consequence of an act passed by Congress on the advice of a presidential commission staffed by academics, myself included.

It is easy and popular to criticize yesterday's empty hopes and mistaken beliefs, especially if they seemed supportive of law enforcement. It is harder, and certainly most unpopular, to criticize today's pieties and pretensions, especially if they are uttered in the name of progress and humanity. But if we were wrong in thinking that more money spent on the police would bring down crime rates, we are equally wrong in supposing that closing our prisons, emptying our jails, and supporting "community-based" programs will do any better. Indeed, there is some evidence that these steps will make matters worse, and we ignore it at our peril.

Since the days of the crime commission we have learned a great deal, more than we are prepared to admit. Perhaps we fear to admit it because of a newfound modesty about the foundations of our knowledge, but perhaps also because the implications of that knowledge suggest an unflattering view of man. Intellectuals, although they often dislike the common person as an individual, do not wish to be caught saying uncomplimentary things about humankind. Nevertheless, some persons will shun crime even if we do nothing to deter them, while others will seek it out even if we do everything to reform them. Wicked people exist. Nothing avails except to set them apart from innocent people. And many people neither wicked nor innocent, but watchful, dissembling, and calculating of their opportunities, ponder our reaction to wickedness as a cue to what they might profitably do. We have trifled with the wicked, made sport of the innocent, and encouraged the calculators. Justice suffers, and so do we all.

CHAPTER 6 Social Organization

6.1 CHARLES HORTON COOLEY

Primary Groups

Charles Horton Cooley (1864–1929) was a sociologist and social psychologist who developed the school of social behaviorism during his teaching career at the University of Michigan. In his studies of society, he integrated socio-psychological and structural phenomena, as reflected in his three major publications: *Human Nature and Social Order* (1902), *Social Organization* (1909), and *Social Process* (1918).

In the following excerpt from *Social Organization,* Cooley discusses primary groups and shows that they are "fundamental in forming the social nature and ideals of the individual." The foremost primary group in all societies (pre-industrial or modern) is the family, with play groups and friendship groups also being important in the formative years. Relationships in such groups are face-to-face, emotional, enduring, and involve the whole person. Primary groups are the major source for the socialization of children, and they teach children their basic skills, such as language, walking, the values they cherish, the customs that guide their lives, and even their initial sense of themselves.

Key Concept: primary group and secondary group

By primary groups I mean those characterized by intimate face-to-face association and coöperation. They are primary in several senses, but chiefly in that they are fundamental in forming the social nature and ideals of the individual. The result of intimate association, psychologically, is a certain fusion of individualities in a common whole, so that one's very self, for many purposes at least, is the common life and purpose of the group. Perhaps the simplest way of describing this wholeness is by saying that it is a "we"; it involves the sort of sympathy and mutual identification for which "we" is the natural expression. One lives in the feeling of the whole and finds the chief aims of his will in that feeling.

It is not to be supposed that the unity of the primary group is one of mere harmony and love. It is always a differentiated and usually a competitive unity, admitting of self-assertion and various appropriative passions; but these passions are socialized by sympathy, and come, or tend to come, under the discipline of a common spirit. The individual will be ambitious, but the chief object of his ambition will be some desired place in the thought of the others, and he will feel allegiance to common standards of service and fair play. So the boy will dispute with his fellows a place on the team, but above such disputes will place the common glory of his class and school.

The most important spheres of this intimate association and coöperation—though by no means the only ones—are the family, the play-group of children, and the neighborhood or community group of elders. These are practically universal, belonging to all times and all stages of development; and are accordingly a chief basis of what is universal in human nature and human ideals. The best comparative studies of the family, such as those of Westermarck[1] or Howard,[2] show it to us as not only a universal institution, but as more alike the world over than the exaggeration of exceptional customs by an earlier school had led us to suppose. Nor can any one doubt the general prevalence of play-groups among children or of informal assemblies of various kinds among their elders. Such association is clearly the nursery of human nature in the world about us, and there is no apparent reason to suppose that the case has anywhere or at any time been essentially different.

As regards play, I might, were it not a matter of common observation, multiply illustrations of the universality and spontaneity of the group discussion and coöperation to which it gives rise. The general fact is that children, especially boys after about their twelfth year, live in fellowships in which their sympathy, ambition and honor are engaged even more, often, than they are in the family. Most of us can recall examples of the endurance by boys of injustice and even cruelty, rather than appeal from their fellows to parents or teachers—as, for instance, in the hazing so prevalent at schools, and so difficult, for this very reason, to suppress. And how elaborate the discussion, how cogent the public opinion, how hot the ambitions in these fellowships.

Nor is this facility of juvenile association, as is sometimes supposed, a trait peculiar to English and American boys; since experience among our immigrant population seems to show that the offspring of the more restrictive civilizations of the continent of Europe form self-governing play-groups with almost equal readiness. Thus Miss Jane Addams, after pointing out that the "gang" is almost universal, speaks of the interminable discussion which every detail of the gang's activity receives, remarking that "in these social folkmotes, so to speak, the young citizen learns to act upon his own determination."[3]

Of the neighborhood group it may be said, in general, that from the time men formed permanent settlements upon the land, down, at least, to the rise of modern industrial cities, it has played a main part of the primary, heart-to-heart life of the people. Among our Teutonic forefathers the village community was apparently the chief sphere of sympathy and mutual aid for the commons all through the "dark" and middle ages, and for many purposes it remains so in rural districts at the present day. In some countries we still find it with all its ancient vitality, notably in Russia, where the mir, or self-governing village group, is the main theatre of life, along with the family, for perhaps fifty millions of peasants.

In our own life the intimacy of the neighborhood has been broken up by the growth of an intricate mesh of wider contacts which leaves us strangers to people who live in the same house. And even in the country the same principle is at work, though less obviously, diminishing our economic and spiritual community with our neighbors. How far this change is a healthy development, and how far a disease, is perhaps still uncertain.

Besides these almost universal kinds of primary association, there are many others whose form depends upon the particular state of civilization; the only essential thing, as I have said, being a certain intimacy and fusion of personalities. In our own society, being little bound by place, people easily form clubs, fraternal societies and the like, based on congeniality, which may give rise to real intimacy. Many such relations are formed at school and college, and among men and women brought together in the first instance by their occupations—as workmen in the same trade, or the like. Where there is a little common interest and activity, kindness grows like weeds by the roadside.

But the fact that the family and neighborhood groups are ascendant in the open and plastic time of childhood makes them even now incomparably more influential than all the rest.

Primary groups are primary in the sense that they give the individual his earliest and completest experience of social unity, and also in the sense that they do not change in the same degree as more elaborate relations, but form a comparatively permanent source out of which the latter are ever springing. Of course they are not independent of the larger society, but to some extent reflect its spirit; as the German family and the German school bear somewhat distinctly the print of German militarism. But this, after all, is like the tide setting back into creeks, and does not commonly go very far. Among the German, and still more among the Russian, peasantry are found habits of free coöperation and discussion almost uninfluenced by the character of the state; and it is a familiar and well-supported view that the village commune, self-governing as regards local affairs and habituated to discussion, is a very widespread institution in settled communities, and the continuator of a similar autonomy previously existing in the clan. "It is man who makes monarchies and establishes republics, but the commune seems to come directly from the hand of God."[4]

In our own cities the crowded tenements and the general economic and social confusion have sorely wounded the family and the neighborhood, but it is remarkable, in view of these conditions, what vitality they show; and there is nothing upon which the conscience of the time is more determined than upon restoring them to health.

These groups, then, are springs of life, not only for the individual but for social institutions. They are only in part moulded by special traditions, and, in larger degree, express a universal nature. The religion or government of other civilizations may seem alien to us, but the children or the family group wear the common life, and with them we can always make ourselves at home.

Charles Horton Cooley

NOTES

1. *The History of Human Marriage.*
2. *A History of Matrimonial Institutions.*
3. *Newer Ideals of Peace,* 177.
4. De Tocqueville, *Democracy in America,* vol. i, chap. 5.

Bureaucratic Structure and Personality

Many bureaucracies are highly efficient organizations. Without them modern society might come to a standstill. Why, then, are there so many complaints and horror stories about people's experiences with bureaucracies? Robert K. Merton provides some answers in the following selection.

A bureaucracy is an organization based on hierarchy, an extensive division of labor, formal rules and regulations, impersonality, personnel replaceability, and continuity through staff turnover. These useful qualities may also make bureaucracies dysfunctional, according to Merton. He points out a number of possible problems of bureaucracies, including overconformity, vested interests, and the single-minded concern with means to the detriment of ends. He also raises questions about the effects of working in a bureaucratic organization on the individual and whether or not bureaucracies intentionally recruit and retain personalities that highly value stability and routine and are unusually submissive.

Merton (b. 1910) is a widely known, well-respected sociological theorist. In his work he emphasizes the interrelationship between social theory and empirical research. He is an adjunct professor at Rockefeller University, a professor emeritus at Columbia University, and a resident scholar at the Russell Sage Foundation.

Key Concept: dysfunctions of bureaucracy

A formal, rationally organized social structure involves clearly defined patterns of activity in which, ideally, every series of actions is functionally related to the purposes of the organization.[1] In such an organization there is integrated a series of offices, of hierarchized statuses, in which inhere a number of obligations and privileges closely defined by limited and specific rules. Each of these offices contains an area of imputed competence and responsibility. Authority, the power of control which derives from an acknowledged status, inheres in the office and not in the particular person who performs the official role. Official action ordinarily occurs within the framework of preexisting rules of the organization. The system of prescribed relations between the various offices involves a considerable degree of formality and clearly defined social distance between the occupants of these positions. Formality is manifested by means of a more or less complicated social ritual which symbolizes and supports the pecking order of the various offices. Such formality, which is integrated with the distribution of authority within the system, serves to minimize friction by largely restricting (official) contact to modes which are previously defined by the rules of the organization. Ready calculability of others' behavior and a stable set of mutual expectations is thus built up. Moreover, formality facilitates the interaction of the occupants of offices despite their (possibly hostile) private attitudes toward one another. In this way, the subordinate is protected from the arbitrary action of his superior, since the actions of both are constrained by a mutually recognized set of rules. Specific procedural devices foster objectivity and restrain the "quick passage of impulse into action."[2]

THE STRUCTURE OF BUREAUCRACY

The ideal type of such formal organization is bureaucracy and, in many respects, the classical analysis of bureaucracy is that by Max Weber.[3] As Weber indicates, bureaucracy involves a clear-cut division of integrated activities which are regarded as duties inherent in the office. A system of differentiated controls and sanctions is stated in the regulations. The assignment of roles occurs on the basis of technical qualifications which are ascertained through formalized, impersonal procedures (*e.g.*, examinations). Within the structure of hierarchically arranged authority, the activities of "trained and salaried experts" are governed by general, abstract, and clearly defined rules which preclude the necessity for the issuance of specific instructions for each specific case. The generality of the rules requires the constant use of *categorization*, whereby individual problems and cases are classified on the basis of designated criteria and are treated accordingly. The pure type of bureaucratic official is appointed, either by a superior or through the exercise of impersonal competition; he is not elected. A measure of flexibility in the bureaucracy is attained by electing higher functionaries who presumably express the will of the electorate (*e.g.*, a body of citizens or a board of directors). The election of higher officials is designed to affect the purposes of the organization, but the technical procedures for attaining these ends are carried out by continuing bureaucratic personnel.[4]

Most bureaucratic offices involve the expectation of life-long tenure, in the absence of disturbing factors which may decrease the size of the organization. Bureaucracy maximizes vocational security.[5] The function of security of tenure, pensions, incremental salaries and regularized procedures for promotion is to ensure the devoted performance of official duties, without regard for extraneous pressures.[6] The chief merit of bureaucracy is its technical efficiency, with a premium placed on precision, speed, expert control, continuity, discretion, and optimal returns on input. The structure is one which approaches the complete elimination of personalized relationships and nonrational considerations (hostility, anxiety, affectual involvements, etc.).

With increasing bureaucratization, it becomes plain to all who would see that man is to a very important degree controlled by his social relations to the instruments of production. This can no longer seem only a tenet of Marxism, but a stubborn fact to be acknowledged by all, quite apart from their ideological persuasion. Bureaucratization makes readily visible what was previously dim and obscure. More and more people discover that to work, they must be employed. For to work, one must have tools and equipment. And the tools and equipment are increasingly available only in bureaucracies, private or public. Consequently, one must be employed by the bureaucracies in order to have access to tools in order to work in order to live. It is in this sense that bureaucratization entails separation of individuals from the instruments of production, as in modern capitalistic enterprise or in state communistic enterprise (of the midcentury variety), just as in the post-feudal army, bureaucratization entailed complete separation from the instruments of destruction. Typically, the worker no longer owns his tools nor the soldier, his weapons. And in this special sense, more and more people become workers, either blue collar or white collar or stiff shirt. So develops, for example, the new type of scientific worker, as the scientist is "separated" from his technical equipment—after all, the physicist does not ordinarily own his cyclotron. To work at his research, he must be employed by a bureaucracy with laboratory resources.

Bureaucracy is administration which almost completely avoids public discussion of its techniques, although there may occur public discussion of its policies.[7] This secrecy is confined neither to public nor to private bureaucracies. It is held to be necessary to keep valuable information from private economic competitors or from foreign and potentially hostile political groups. And though it is not often so called, espionage among competitors is perhaps as common, if not as intricately organized, in systems of private economic enterprise as in systems of national states. Cost figures, lists of clients, new technical processes, plans for production—all these are typically regarded as essential secrets of private economic bureaucracies which might be revealed if the bases of all decision and policies had to be publicly defended.

THE DYSFUNCTIONS OF BUREAUCRACY

In these bold outlines, the positive attainments and functions of bureaucratic organization are emphasized and the internal stresses and strains of such structures are almost wholly neglected. The community at large, however, evidently emphasizes the imperfections of bureaucracy, as is suggested by the fact that the "horrid hybrid," bureaucrat, has become an epithet, a *Schimpfwort*.

The transition to a study of the negative aspects of bureaucracy is afforded by the application of [Thorstein] Veblen's concept of "trained incapacity," [John] Dewey's notion of "occupational psychosis" or [Daniel] Warnotte's view of "professional deformation." Trained incapacity refers to that state of affairs in which one's abilities function as inadequacies or blind spots. Actions based upon training and skills which have been successfully applied in the past may result in inappropriate responses *under changed conditions.* An inadequate flexibility in the application of skills, will, in a changing milieu, result in more or less serious maladjustments. Thus, to adopt a barnyard illustration used in this connection by [Kenneth] Burke, chickens may be readily conditioned to interpret the sound of a bell as a signal for food. The same bell may now be used to summon the trained chickens to their doom as they are assembled to suffer decapitation. In general, one adopts measures in keeping with one's past training and, under new conditions which are not recognized as *significantly* different, the very soundness of this training may lead to the adoption of the wrong procedures. Again, in Burke's almost echolalic phrase, "people may be unfitted by being fit in an unfit fitness"; their training may become an incapacity.

Dewey's concept of occupational psychosis rests upon much the same observations. As a result of their day to day routines, people develop special preferences, antipathies, discriminations and emphases. (The term psychosis is used by Dewey to denote a "pronounced character of the mind.") These psychoses develop through demands put upon the individual by the particular organization of his occupational role.

The concepts of both Veblen and Dewey refer to a fundamental ambivalence. Any action can be considered in terms of what it attains or what it fails to attain. "A way of seeing is also a way of not seeing—a focus upon object *A* involves a neglect of object *B.*" In his discussion, Weber is almost exclusively concerned with what the bureaucratic structure attains: precision, reliability, efficiency. This same structure may be examined from another perspective provided by the ambivalence. What are the limitations of the organizations designed to attain these goals?

For reasons which we have already noted, the bureaucratic structure exerts a constant pressure upon the official to be "methodical, prudent, disciplined." If the bureaucracy is to operate successfully, it must attain a high degree of reliability of behavior, an unusual degree of conformity with prescribed patterns of action. Hence, the fundamental importance of discipline which may be as highly developed in a religious or economic bureaucracy as in the army. Discipline can be effective only if the ideal patterns are buttressed by strong sentiments which entail devotion to one's duties, a keen sense of the limitation of one's authority and competence, and methodical performance of routine activities. The efficacy of social structure depends ultimately upon infusing group participants with appropriate attitudes and sentiments. As we shall see, there are definite arrangements in the bureaucracy for inculcating and reinforcing these sentiments.

At the moment, it suffices to observe that in order to ensure discipline (the necessary reliability of response), these sentiments are often more intense than is technically necessary. There is a margin of safety, so to speak, in the pressure exerted by these sentiments upon the bureaucrat to conform to his patterned obligations, in much the same sense that added allowances (precautionary overestimations) are made by the engineer in designing the supports for a bridge. But this very emphasis leads to a transference of the sentiments from the *aims* of the organization onto the particular details of behavior required by the rules. Adherence to the rules, originally conceived as a means, becomes transformed into an end-in-itself; there occurs the familiar process of *displacement of goals* whereby "an instrumental value becomes a terminal value." Discipline, readily interpreted as conformance with regulations, whatever the situation, is seen not as a measure designed for specific purposes but becomes an immediate value in the life-organization of the bureaucrat. This emphasis, resulting from the displacement of the original goals, develops into rigidities and an inability to adjust readily. Formalism, even ritualism, ensues with an unchallenged insistence upon punctilious adherence to formalized procedures. This may be exaggerated to the point where primary concern with conformity to the rules interferes with the achievement of the purposes of the organization, in which case we have the familiar phenomenon of the technicism or red tape of the official. An extreme product of this process of displacement of goals is the bureaucratic virtuoso, who never forgets a single rule binding his action and hence is unable to assist many of his clients. A case in point, where strict recognition of the limits of authority and literal adherence to rules produced this result, is the pathetic plight of Bernt Balchen, Admiral Byrd's pilot in the flight over the South Pole.

> According to a ruling of the department of labor Bernt Balchen . . . cannot receive his citizenship papers. Balchen, a native of Norway, declared his intention in 1927. It is held that he has failed to meet the condition of five years' continuous residence in the United States. The Byrd antarctic voyage took him out of the country, although he was on a ship carrying the American flag, was an invaluable member of the American expedition, and in a region to which there is an American claim because of the exploration and occupation of it by Americans, this region being Little America.
>
> The bureau of naturalization explains that it cannot proceed on the assumption that Little America is American soil. That would be *trespass on international questions* where it has no sanction. So far as the bureau is concerned, Balchen was out of the country and *technically* has not complied with the law of naturalization.[8]

STRUCTURAL SOURCES OF OVERCONFORMITY

Such inadequacies in orientation which involve trained incapacity clearly derive from structural sources. The process may be briefly recapitulated. (1) An effective bureaucracy demands reliability of response and strict devotion to regulations. (2) Such devotion to the rules leads to their transformation into absolutes; they are no longer conceived as relative to a set of purposes. (3) This interferes with ready adaptation under special conditions not clearly envisaged by those who drew up the general rules. (4) Thus, the very elements which conduce toward efficiency in general produce inefficiency in specific instances. Full realization of the inadequacy is seldom attained by members of the group who have not divorced themselves from the meanings which the rules have for them. These rules in time become symbolic in cast, rather than strictly utilitarian.

Thus far, we have treated the ingrained sentiments making for rigorous discipline simply as data, as given. However, definite features of the bureaucratic structure may be seen to conduce to these sentiments. The bureaucrat's official life is planned for him in terms of a graded career, through the organizational devices of promotion by seniority, pensions, incremental salaries, *etc.*, all of which are designed to provide incentives for disciplined action and conformity to the official regulations. The official is tacitly expected to and largely does adapt his thoughts, feelings and actions to the prospect of this career. But *these very devices* which increase the probability of conformance also lead to an over-concern with strict adherence to regulations which induces timidity, conservatism, and technicism. Displacement of sentiments from goals onto means is fostered by the tremendous symbolic significance of the means (rules).

Another feature of the bureaucratic structure tends to produce much the same result. Functionaries have the sense of a common destiny for all those who work together. They share the same interests, especially since there is relatively little competition in so far as promotion is in terms of seniority. In-group aggression is thus minimized and this arrangement is therefore conceived to be positively functional for the bureaucracy. However, the *esprit de corps* and informal social organization which typically develops in such situations often leads the personnel to defend their entrenched interests rather than to assist their clientele and elected higher officials. As President Lowell [1846–1943; was president of Harvard University] reports, if the bureaucrats believe that their status is not adequately recognized by an incoming elected official, detailed information will be withheld from him, leading him to errors for which he is held responsible. Or, if he seeks to dominate fully, and thus violates the sentiment of self-integrity of the bureaucrats, he may have documents brought to him in such numbers that he cannot manage to sign them all, let alone read them. This illustrates the defensive informal organization which tends to arise whenever there is an apparent threat to the integrity of the group.

It would be much too facile and partly erroneous to attribute such resistance by bureaucrats simply to vested interests. Vested interests oppose any new order which either eliminates or at least makes uncertain their differential advantage deriving from the current arrangements. This is undoubtedly involved in part in bureaucratic resistance to change but another process is perhaps more significant. As we have seen, bureaucratic officials affectively identify themselves with their way of life. They have a pride of craft which leads them to resist change in established routines; at least, those changes which are felt to be imposed by others. This nonlogical pride of craft is a familiar pattern found even, to judge from [Edwin H.] Sutherland's *Profes-*

sional Thief, among pickpockets who, despite the risk, delight in mastering the prestige-bearing feat of "beating a left breech" (picking the left front trousers pocket).

In a stimulating paper, [E. C.] Hughes has applied the concepts of "secular" and "sacred" to various types of division of labor; "the sacredness" of caste and *Stände* [status] prerogatives contrasts sharply with the increasing secularism of occupational differentiation in our society. However, as our discussion suggests, there may ensue, in particular vocations and in particular types of organization, the *process of sanctification* (viewed as the counterpart of the process of secularization). This is to say that through sentiment-formation, emotional dependence upon bureaucratic symbols and status, and affective involvement in spheres of competence and authority, there develop prerogatives involving attitudes of moral legitimacy which are established as values in their own right, and are no longer viewed as merely technical means for expediting administration. One may note a tendency for certain bureaucratic norms, originally introduced for technical reasons, to become rigidified and sacred, although, as [Emile] Durkheim would say, they are *laïque en apparence* [secular in appearance]. Durkheim has touched on this general process in his description of the attitudes and values which persist in the organic solidarity of a highly differentiated society.

NOTES

1. For a development of the concept of "rational organization," see Karl Mannheim, *Mensch und Gesellschaft im Zeitalter des Umbaus* (Leiden: A. W. Sijthoff, 1935), esp. 28 ff.
2. H. D. Lasswell, *Politics* (New York: McGraw-Hill, 1936), 120–21.
3. Max Weber, *Wirtschaft und Gesellschaft* (Tübingen: J. C. B. Mohr, 1922), Pt. III, chap. 6; 650–678. For a brief summary of Weber's discussion, see Talcott Parsons, *The Structure of Social Action,* esp. 506 ff. For a description, which is not a caricature, of the bureaucrat as a personality type, see C. Rabany, "Les types sociaux: le fonctionnaire," *Revue générale d'administration,* 1907, 88, 5–28.
4. Karl Mannheim, *Ideology and Utopia* (New York: Harcourt, Brace, 1936), 18n., 105 ff. See also Ramsay Muir, *Peers and Bureaucrats* (London: Constable, 1910), 12–13.
5. E. G. Cahen-Salvador suggests that the personnel of bureaucracies is largely constituted by those who value security above all else. See his "La situation matérielle et morale des fonctionnaires," *Revue politique et parlementaire* (1926), 319.
6. H. J. Laski, "Bureaucracy," *Encyclopedia of the Social Sciences.* This article is written primarily from the standpoint of the political scientist rather than that of the sociologist.
7. Weber, *op. cit.,* 671.
8. Quoted from the *Chicago Tribune* (June 24, 1931, p. 10) by Thurman Arnold, *The Symbols of Government* (New Haven: Yale University Press, 1935), 201–2. (My italics.)

PART THREE

Stratification

CHAPTER 7 Social Inequality

7.1 KARL MARX AND FRIEDRICH ENGELS

On Class

In no society are all people equal. All societies are stratified. The major dimensions of stratification systems are wealth, power, and status, and usually they are strongly related to each other. The powerful are usually wealthy and highly esteemed and vice versa. Locating the factors that account for social inequalities in social systems, not in the nature of human beings, was the analytical approach that characterized the work of many early sociologists, including the German philosopher Karl Marx (1818–1883). Marx was a revolutionary thinker and writer, and his works formed the basis of European socialism in the late nineteenth century. Together with his collaborator Friedrich Engels (1820–1895), who later served as the leading authority on Marx and his philosophies, he published the *Manifest der Kommunistischen Partei* (1848), or what is commonly known as *The Communist Manifesto*. For Marx and Engels, this work was as much a theory of history and social change and an economic analysis of social stratification as it was a call to arms.

In the following excerpt, Marx and Engels describe one type of power as the critical dimension for understanding all stratification systems: the ownership and control of the means of production. In their view, most other inequalities derive from this one. The owners of the land in agricultural societies and the owners of the factories and businesses in industrial societies control, exploit, and oppress the landless and the wage workers. In fact, all human history, according to Marx and Engels, has been a struggle between the haves and the have-nots. Those who have power are determined to keep it (hence the class struggle), and those who control the economy (in a capitalist society they are the bourgeoisie) control all the other institutions in society.

Sociologists continue to find Marx and Engels's perspective profoundly useful.

Key Concept: class and class warfare

BOURGEOIS AND PROLETARIANS[1]

The history of all hitherto existing society is the history of class struggles.

Freeman and slave, patrician and plebeian, lord and serf, guild-master and journeyman, in a word, oppressor and oppressed stood in constant opposition to one another, carried on an uninterrupted, now hidden, now open fight, a fight that each time ended, either in a revolutionary reconstitution of society at large, or in the common ruin of the contending classes.

In the earlier epochs of history, we find almost everywhere a complicated arrangement of society into various orders, a manifold gradation of social rank. In ancient Rome we have patricians, knights, plebeians, slaves; in the Middle Ages, feudal lords, vassals, guild-masters, journeymen, apprentices, serfs; in almost all of these classes, again, subordinate gradations.

The modern bourgeois society that has sprouted from the from the ruins of feudal society has not done away with class antagonisms. It has but established new classes, new conditions of oppression, new forms of struggle in place of the old ones.

Our epoch, the epoch of the bourgeoisie, possesses, however, this distinctive feature: It has simplified the class antagonisms. Society as a whole is more and more splitting up into two great hostile camps, into two great classes directly facing each other—bourgeoisie and proletariat.

From the serfs of the Middle Ages sprang the chartered burghers of the earliest towns. From these burgesses the first elements of the bourgeoisie were developed.

The discovery of America, the rounding of the Cape, opened up fresh ground for the rising bourgeoisie. The East-Indian and Chinese markets, the colonisation of America, trade with the colonies, the increase in the means of exchange and in commodities generally, gave to commerce, to navigation, to industry, an impulse never before known, and thereby, to the revolutionary element in the tottering feudal society, a rapid development.

The feudal system of industry, in which industrial production was monopolised by closed guilds, now no longer sufficed for the growing wants of the new markets. The manufacturing system took its place. The guild-masters were pushed aside by the manufacturing middle class; division of labour between the different corporate guilds vanished in the face of division of labor in each single workshop.

Meantime the markets kept ever growing, the demand ever rising. Even manufacture no longer sufficed. Thereupon, steam and machinery revolutionised industrial production. The place of manufacture was taken by the giant, modern industry, the place of the industrial middle class by industrial millionaires, the leaders of whole industrial armies, the modern bourgeois.

Modern industry has established the world market, for which the discovery of America paved the way. This market has given an immense development to commerce, to navigation, to communication by land. This development has, in its turn, reacted on the extension of industry; and in proportion as industry, commerce, navigation, railways extended, in the same proportion the bourgeoisie developed, increased its capital, and pushed into the background every class handed down from the Middle Ages.

We see, therefore, how the modern bourgeoisie is itself the product of a long course of development, of a series of revolutions in the modes of production and of exchange.

Each step in the development of the bourgeoisie was accompanied by a corresponding political advance of that class. An oppressed class under the sway of the feudal nobility, an armed and self-governing association in the mediaeval commune; here independent urban republic (as in Italy and Germany), there taxable "third estate" of the monarchy (as in France); afterwards, in the period of manufacture proper, serving either the semi-feudal or the absolute monarchy as a counterpoise against the nobility, and, in fact, cornerstone of the great monarchies in general—the bourgeoisie has at last, since the establishment of modern industry and of the world market, conquered for itself, in the modern representative state, exclusive political sway. The executive of the modern state is but a committee for managing the common affairs of the whole bourgeoisie.

The bourgeoisie, historically, has played a most revolutionary part.

The bourgeoisie, wherever it has got the upper hand, has put an end to all feudal, patriarchal, idyllic relations. It has pitilessly torn asunder the motley feudal ties that bound man to his "natural superiors," and has left no other nexus between man and man than naked self-interest, than callous "cash payment." It has drowned the most heavenly ecstasies of religious fervour, of chivalrous enthusiasm, of philistine sentimentalism, in the icy water of egotistical calculation. It has resolved personal worth into exchange value, and in place of the numberless indefeasible chartered freedoms, has set up that single, unconscionable freedom—Free Trade. In one word, for exploitation, veiled by religious and political illusions, it has substituted naked, shameless, direct brutal exploitation.

The bourgeoisie has stripped of its halo every occupation hitherto honoured and looked up to with reverent awe. It has converted the physician, the lawyer, the priest, the poet, the man of science, into its paid wage labourers.

The bourgeoisie has torn away from the family its sentimental veil, and has reduced the family relation to a mere money relation.

The bourgeoisie has disclosed how it came to pass that the brutal display of vigour in the Middle Ages, which reactionaries so much admire, found its fitting complement in the most slothful indolence. It has been the first to show what man's activity can bring about. It has accomplished wonders far surpassing Egyptian pyramids, Roman aqueducts, and Gothic cathedrals; it has conducted expeditions that put in the shade all former exoduses of nations and crusades.

The bourgeoisie cannot exist without constantly revolutionising the instruments of production, and thereby the relations of production, and with them the whole relations of society. Conservation of the old modes of production in unaltered form, was, on the contrary, the first condition of existence for all earlier industrial classes. Constant revolutionising of production, uninterrupted disturbance of all social conditions, everlasting uncertainty and agitation distinguish the bourgeois epoch from all earlier ones. All fixed, fast frozen relations, with their train of ancient and venerable prejudices and opinions, are swept away, all new-formed ones become antiquated before they can ossify. All that is solid melts into air, all that is holy is profaned, and man is at last compelled to face with sober senses his real conditions of life and his relations with his kind.

The need of a constantly expanding market for its products chases the bourgeoisie over the whole surface of the globe. It must nestle everywhere, settle everywhere, establish connections everywhere.

The bourgeoisie has through its exploitation of the world market given a cosmopolitan character to production and consumption in every country. To the great chagrin of reactionaries, it has drawn from under the feet of industry the national ground on which it stood. All old-established national industries have been destroyed or are daily being destroyed. They are dislodged by new industries, whose introduction becomes a life and death question for all civilised nations, by industries that no longer work up indigenous raw material, but raw material drawn from the remotest zones; industries whose products are consumed, not only at home, but in every quarter of the globe. In place of the old wants, satisfied by the production of the country, we find new wants, requiring for their satisfaction the products of distant lands and climes. In place of the old local and national seclusion and self-sufficiency, we have intercourse in every direction, universal inter-dependence of nations. And as in material, so also in intellectual production. The intellectual creations of individual nations become common property. National one-sidedness and narrow-mindedness become more and more impossible, and from the numerous national and local literatures there arises a world literature.

The bourgeoisie, by the rapid improvement of all instruments of production, by the immensely facilitated means of communication, draws all, even the most barbarian, nations into civilisation. The cheap prices of its commodities are the heavy artillery with which it batters down all Chinese walls, with which it forces the barbarians' intensely obstinate hatred of foreigners to capitulate. It compels all nations, on pain of extinction, to adopt the bourgeois mode of production; it compels them to introduce what it calls civilisation into their midst, *i.e.*, to become bourgeois themselves. In one word, it creates a world after its own image.

The bourgeois has subjected the country to the rule of the towns. It has created enormous cities, has greatly increased the urban population as compared with the rural, and has thus rescued a considerable part of the population from the idiocy of rural life. Just as it has made the country dependent on the towns, so it has made barbarian and semi-barbarian countries dependent on the civilised ones, nations of peasants on nations of bourgeois, the East on the West.

The bourgeoisie keeps more and more doing away with the scattered state of the population, of the means of production, and of property. It has agglomerated population, centralised means of production, and has concentrated property in a few hands. The necessary consequence of this was political centralisation. Independent, or but loosely connected provinces, with separate interests, laws, governments and systems of taxation, became lumped together into one nation, with one government, one code of laws, one national class interest, one frontier and one customs tariff.

The bourgeoisie, during its rule of scarce one hundred years, has created more massive and more colossal productive forces than have all preceding generations together. Subjection of nature's forces to man, machinery, application of chemistry to industry and agriculture, steam navigation, railways, electric telegraphs, clearing of whole continents for cultivation, canalisation of rivers, whole populations conjured out of the ground—what earlier century had even a presentiment that such productive forces slumbered in the lap of social labour?

We see then: the means of production and of exchange, on whose foundation the bourgeoisie built itself up, were generated in feudal society. At a certain stage in the development of these means of production and of exchange, the conditions under which feudal society produced and exchanged, the feudal organisation of agriculture and manufacturing industry, in one word, the feudal relations of property became no longer compatible with the already developed productive forces; they became so many fetters. They had to be burst asunder; they were burst asunder.

Into their place stepped free competition, accompanied by a social and political constitution adapted to it, and by the economic and political sway of the bourgeois class.

A similar movement is going on before our own eyes. Modern bourgeois society with its relations of production, of exchange and of property, a society that has conjured up such gigantic means of production and of exchange, is like the sorcerer who is no longer able to control the powers of the nether world whom he has called up by his spells. For many a decade past the history of industry and commerce is but the history of the revolt of modern productive forces against modern conditions of production, against the property relations that are the conditions for the existence of the bourgeoisie and of its rule. It is enough to mention the commercial crises that by their periodical return put the existence of the entire bourgeois society on its trial, each time more threateningly. In these crises a great part not only of the existing products, but also of the previously created productive forces, are periodically destroyed. In these crises there breaks out an epidemic that, in all earlier epochs, would have seemed an absurdity—the epidemic of over-production. Society suddenly finds itself put back into a state of momentary barbarism; it appears as if a famine, a universal war of devastation had cut off the supply of every means of subsistence; industry and commerce seem to be destroyed. And why? Because there is too much civilisation, too much means of subsistence, too much industry, too much commerce. The productive forces at the disposal of society no longer tend to further the development of the conditions of bourgeois property; on the contrary, they have become too powerful for these conditions, by which they are fettered, and so soon as they overcome these fetters, they bring disorder into the whole of bourgeois society, endanger the existence of bourgeois property. The conditions of bourgeois society are too narrow to comprise the wealth created by them. And how does the bourgeoisie get over these crises? On the one hand, by enforced destruction of a mass of productive forces; on the other, by the conquest of new markets, and by the more thorough exploitation of the old ones. That is to say, by paving the way for more extensive and more destructive crises, and by diminishing the means whereby crises are prevented.

The weapons with which the bourgeoisie felled feudalism to the ground are now turned against the bourgeoisie itself.

But not only has the bourgeoisie forged the weapons that bring death to itself; it has also called into existence the men who are to wield those weapons— the modern working class—the proletarians.

In proportion as the bourgeoisie, *i.e.*, capital, is developed, in the same proportion is the proletariat, the modern working class, developed—a class of labourers, who live only so long as they find work, and who find work only so long as their labour increases capital. These labourers, who must sell themselves piecemeal, are a commodity, like every other article of commerce, and are consequently exposed to all the vicissitudes of competition, to all the fluctuations of the market.

Owing to the extensive use of machinery and to division of labour, the work of the proletarians has lost all individual character, and, consequently, all charm for the workman. He becomes an appendage of the machine, and it is only the most simple, most monotonous, and most easily acquired knack, that is required of him. Hence, the cost of production of a workman is restricted, almost entirely, to the means of subsistence that he requires for his maintenance, and for the propagation of his race. But the price of a commodity, and therefore also of labour, is equal to its cost of production. In proportion, therefore, as the repulsiveness of the work increases, the wage decreases. Nay more, in proportion as the use of machinery and division of labour increases, in the same proportion the burden of toil also increases, whether by prolongation of the working hours, by increase of the work exacted in a given time, or by increased speed of the machinery, etc.

Modern industry has converted the little workshop of the patriarchal master into the great factory of the industrial capitalist. Masses of labourers, crowded into the factory, are organised like soldiers. As privates of the industrial army they are placed under the command of a perfect hierarchy of officers and sergeants. Not only are they slaves of the bourgeois class, and of the bourgeois state; they are daily and hourly enslaved by the machine, by the overlooker, and, above all, by the individual bourgeois manufacturer himself. The more openly this despotism proclaims gain to be its end and aim, the more petty, the more hateful and the more embittering it is.

The less the skill and exertion of strength implied in manual labour, in other words, the more modern industry becomes developed, the more is the labour of men superseded by that of women. Differences of age and sex have no longer any distinctive social validity for the working class. All are instruments of labour, more or less expensive to use, according to their age and sex.

No sooner is the exploitation of the labourer by the manufacturer, so far at an end, that he receives his wages in cash, than he is set upon by the other portions of the bourgeoisie, the landlord, the shopkeeper, the pawnbroker, etc.

The lower strata of the middle class—the small tradespeople, shopkeepers, and retired tradesmen generally, the handicraftsmen and peasants—all these sink gradually into the proletariat, partly because their diminutive capital does not suffice for the scale on which modern industry is carried on, and is swamped in the competition with the large capitalists, partly because their specialised skill is rendered worthless by new methods of production. Thus the proletariat is recruited from all classes of the population.

The proletariat goes through various stages of development. With its birth begins its struggle with the bourgeoisie. At first the contest is carried on by individual labourers, then by the work people of a factory, then by the operatives of one trade, in one locality, against the individual bourgeois who directly exploits them. They direct their attacks not against the bourgeois conditions of production, but against the instruments of production themselves; they destroy imported wares that compete with their labour, they smash to pieces machinery, they set factories ablaze, they seek to restore by force the vanished status of the workman of the Middle Ages.

At this stage the labourers still form an incoherent mass scattered over the whole country, and broken up by their mutual competition. If anywhere they unite to form more compact bodies, this is not yet the consequence of their own active union, but of the union of the bourgeoisie, which class, in order to attain its own political ends, is compelled to set the whole proletariat in motion, and is moreover yet, for a time, able to do so. At this stage, therefore, the proletarians do not fight their enemies, but the enemies of their enemies, the remnants of absolute monarchy, the landowners, the non-industrial bourgeois, the petty bourgeoisie. Thus the whole historical movement is concentrated in the hands of the bourgeoisie; every victory so obtained is a victory for the bourgeoisie.

But with the development of industry the proletariat not only increases in number; it becomes concentrated in greater masses, its strength grows, and it feels that strength more. The various interests and conditions of life within the ranks of the proletariat are more and more equalised, in proportion as machinery obliterates all distinctions of labour, and nearly everywhere reduces wages to the same low level. The growing competition among the bourgeois, and the resulting commercial crises, make the wages of the workers ever more fluctuating. The unceasing improvement of machinery, ever more rapidly developing, makes their livelihood more and more precarious; the collisions between individual workmen and individual bourgeois take more and more the character of collisions between two classes. Thereupon the workers begin to form combinations (trades unions) against the bourgeois; they club together in order to keep up the rate of wages; they found permanent associations in order to make provisions beforehand for these occasional revolts. Here and there the contest breaks out into riots.

Now and then the workers are victorious, but only for a time. The real fruit of their battles lies, not in the immediate result, but in the ever expanding union of the workers. This union is helped on by the improved means of communication that are created by modern industry, and that place the workers of different localities in contact with one another. It was just this contact that was needed to centralise the numerous local struggles, all of the same character, into one national struggle between classes. But every class struggle is a political struggle. And that union, to attain which the burghers of the Middle Ages, with their miserable highways, required centuries, the modern proletarians, thanks to railways, achieve in a few years.

This organisation of the proletarians into a class, and consequently into a political party, is continually being upset again by the competition between the workers themselves. But it ever rises up again, stronger, firmer, mightier. It compels legislative recognition of particular interests of the workers, by taking advantage of the divisions among the bourgeoisie itself. Thus the ten-hours' bill in England was carried.

Altogether, collisions between the classes of the old society further in many ways the course of development of the proletariat. The bourgeoisie finds itself involved in a constant battle. At first with the aristocracy; later on, with those portions of the bourgeoisie itself, whose interests have become antagonistic to the progress of industry; at all times with the bourgeoisie of foreign countries. In all these battles it sees itself compelled to appeal to the proletariat, to ask for its help, and thus, to drag it into the political arena. The bourgeoisie itself, therefore, supplies the proletariat with its own elements of political and general education, in other words, it furnishes the proletariat with weapons for fighting the bourgeoisie.

Further, as we have already seen, entire sections of the ruling classes are, by the advance of industry, precipitated into the proletariat, or are at least threatened in their conditions of existence. These also supply the proletariat with fresh elements of enlightenment and progress.

Finally, in times when the class struggle nears the decisive hour, the process of dissolution going on within the ruling class, in fact within the whole range of old society, assumes such a violent, glaring character, that a small section of the ruling class cuts itself adrift, and joins the revolutionary class, the class that holds the future in its hands. Just as, therefore, at an earlier period, a section of the nobility went over to the bourgeoisie, so now a portion of the bourgeoisie goes over to the proletariat, and in particular, a portion of the bourgeois ideologists, who have raised themselves to the level of comprehending theoretically the historical movement as a whole.

Of all the classes that stand face to face with the bourgeoisie today, the proletariat alone is a really revolutionary class. The other classes decay and finally disappear in the face of modern industry; the proletariat is its special and essential product. The lower middle class, the small manufacturer, the shopkeeper, the artisan, the peasant, all these fight against the bourgeoisie, to save from extinction their existence as fractions of the middle class. They are therefore not revolutionary, but conservative. Nay more, they are reactionary, for they try to roll back the wheel of history. If by chance they are revolutionary, they are so only in view of their impending transfer into the proletariat; they thus defend not their present, but their future interests; they desert their own standpoint to place themselves at that of the proletariat.

The "dangerous class," the social scum, that passively rotting mass thrown off by the lowest layers of old society, may, here and there, be swept into the movement by a proletarian revolution; its conditions of life, however, prepare it far more for the part of a bribed tool of reactionary intrigue.

In the conditions of the proletariat, those of old society at large are already virtually swamped. The proletarian is without property; his relation to his wife and children has no longer anything in common with the bourgeois family relations: modern industrial labour, modern subjection to capital, the same in England as in France, in America as in Germany, has stripped him of every trace of national character. Law, morality, religion, are to him so many bourgeois prejudices, behind which lurk in ambush just as many bourgeois interests.

All the preceding classes that got the upper hand, sought to fortify their already acquired status by subjecting society at large to their conditions of appropriation. The proletarians cannot become masters of the productive forces of society, except by abolishing their own previous mode of appropriation, and thereby also every other previous mode of appropriation. They have nothing of their own to secure and to fortify: their mission is to destroy all previous securities for, and insurances of, individual property.

All previous historical movements were movements of minorities, or in the interest of minorities. The proletarian movement is the self-conscious, independent movement of the immense majority, in the interest of the immense majority. The proletariat, the lowest stratum of our present society, cannot stir, cannot raise itself up, without the whole superincumbent strata of official society being sprung into the air.

Though not in substance, yet in form, the struggle of the proletariat with the bourgeoisie is at first a national struggle. The proletariat of each country must, of course, first of all settle matters with its own bourgeoisie.

In depicting the most general phases of the development of the proletariat, we traced the more or less veiled civil war, raging within existing society, up to the point where that war breaks out into open revolution, and where the violent overthrow of the bourgeoisie lays the foundation for the ways of the proletariat.

Hitherto, every form of society has been based, as we have already seen, on the antagonism of oppressing and oppressed classes. But in order to oppress a class, certain conditions must be assured to it under which it can, at least, continue its slavish existence. The serf, in the period of serfdom, raised himself to membership in the commune, just as the petty bourgeois, under the yoke of feudal absolutism, managed to develop into a bourgeois. The modern labourer, on the contrary, instead of rising with the progress of industry, sinks deeper and deeper below the conditions of existence of his own class. He becomes a pauper, and pauperism develops more rapidly than population and wealth. And here it becomes evident, that the bourgeoisie is unfit any longer to be the ruling class in society, and to impose its conditions of existence upon society as an over-riding law. It is unfit to rule because it is incompetent to assure an existence to its slave within his slavery, because it cannot help letting him sink into such a state, that it has to feed him, instead of being fed by him. Society can no longer live under this bourgeoisie, in other words, its existence is no longer compatible with society.

The essential condition for the existence and for the sway of the bourgeois class, is the formation and augmentation of capital; the condition for capital is wage labour. Wage labour rests exclusively on competition between the labourers. The advance of industry, whose involuntary promoter is the bourgeoisie, replaces the isolation of the labourers, due to competition, by their revolutionary combination, due to association. The development of modern industry, therefore, cuts from under its feet the very foundation on which the bourgeoisie produces and appropriates products. What the bourgeoisie therefore produces, above all, are its own grave-diggers. Its fall and the victory of the proletariat are equally inevitable.

NOTE

1. By bourgeoisie is meant the class of modern capitalists, owners of the means of social production and employers of wage labour. By proletariat, the class of modern wage labourers who, having no means of production of their own, are reduced to selling their labour power in order to live. [*Note by F. Engels to the English edition of 1888.*]

7.2 KINGSLEY DAVIS AND WILBERT E. MOORE

Some Principles of Stratification

Kingsley Davis (b. 1908) is a professor emeritus of sociology at the Hoover Institute, Stanford University, and a member of the Behavioral Science Division of the National Research Council. His research mainly focused on comparing population structures, urbanization, and marriage and family among different countries, and especially on the causes and consequences of population change. Wilbert E. Moore (1914–1987) was a professor of sociology and law at the University of Denver. His interests included the measurement of social change. Both men were students of Talcott Parsons, a prominent U.S. sociologist of the 1950s.

In their functional theory of stratification, discussed in the following selection, Davis and Moore argue that income inequalities are good for the effective functioning of societies and that certain positions in a society are more important for the well-being and survival of society than others. In order to ensure that the more competent members of society seek the more important positions and that they are willing to undergo long and arduous training, it is necessary for those positions to provide sufficient rewards in the form of wealth, status, honor, and power. Accordingly, doctors earn more than garbage collectors.

This notion that social stratification is functional has been subject to considerable criticism. Some sociologists have argued that Davis and Moore have provided an ideology in support of social inequality and not an explanation for the functional necessity of social stratification. Others question the functional necessity of wealth, honor, and power for professional athletes, movie stars, and musical performers. Still others suggest that the expenditure of resources to train for the highly rewarded positions tends to preserve the privileges of those who already have the resources. Thus, not only does the system exclude the have-nots, but it also limits the pool of the available talent, restricts competition, and favors the well-off.

Key Concept: the functions of stratification

*I*n a previous paper some concepts for handling the phenomena of social inequality were presented. In the present paper a further step in stratification theory is undertaken—an attempt to show the relationship between stratification and the rest of the social order. Starting from the proposition that no society is "classless," or unstratified, an effort is made to explain, in functional terms, the universal necessity which calls forth stratification in any social system. Next, an attempt is made to explain the roughly uniform distribution of prestige as between the major types of positions in every society. Since, however, there occur between one society and another great differences in the degree and kind of stratification, some attention is also given to the varieties of social inequality and the variable factors that give rise to them.

Clearly, the present task requires two different lines of analysis—one to understand the universal, the other to understand the variable features of stratification. Naturally each line of inquiry aids the other and is indispensable, and in the treatment that follows the two will be interwoven, although, because of space limitations, the emphasis will be on the universals.

Throughout, it will be necessary to keep in mind one thing—namely, that the discussion relates to the system of positions, not to the individuals occupying those positions. It is one thing to ask why different positions carry different degrees of prestige, and quite another to ask how certain individuals get into those positions. Although, as the argument will try to show, both questions are related, it is essential to keep them separate in our thinking. Most of the literature on stratification has tried to answer the second question (particularly with regard to the ease or difficulty of mobility between strata) without tackling the first. The first question, however, is logically prior and, in the case of any particular individual or group, factually prior.

THE FUNCTIONAL NECESSITY OF STRATIFICATION

Curiously, however, the main functional necessity explaining the universal presence of stratification is precisely the requirement faced by any society of placing and motivating individuals in the social structure. As a functioning mechanism a society must somehow distribute its members in social positions and induce them to perform the duties of these positions. It must thus concern itself with motivation at two different levels: to instill in the proper individuals the desire to fill certain positions, and, once in these positions, the desire to perform the duties attached to them. Even though the social order may be relatively static in form, there is a continuous process of metabolism as new individuals are born into it, shift with age, and die off. Their absorption into the positional system must somehow be arranged and motivated. This is true whether the system is competitive or non-competitive. A competitive system gives greater importance to the motivation to achieve positions, whereas a non-competitive system gives perhaps greater importance to the motivation to perform the duties of the positions; but in any system both types of motivation are required.

If the duties associated with the various positions were all equally pleasant to the human organism, all equally important to societal survival, and all equally in need of the same ability or talent, it would make no difference who got into which positions, and the problem of social placement would be greatly reduced. But actually it does make a great deal of difference who gets into which positions, not only because some positions are inherently more agreeable than others, but also because some require special talents or training and some are functionally more important than others. Also, it is essential that the duties of the positions be performed with the diligence that their importance requires. Inevitably, then, a society must have, first, some kind of rewards that it can use as inducements, and, second, some way of distributing these rewards differentially according to positions. The rewards and their distribution become a part of the social order, and thus give rise to stratification.

One may ask what kind of rewards a society has at its disposal in distributing its personnel and securing essential services. It has, first of all, the things that contribute to sustenance and comfort. It has, second, the things that contribute to humor and diversion. And it has, finally, the things that contribute to self-respect and ego expansion. The last, because of the peculiarly social character of the self, is largely a function of the opinion of others, but it nonetheless ranks in importance with the first two. In any social system all three kinds of rewards must be dispensed differentially according to positions.

In a sense the rewards are "built into" the position. They consist in the "rights" associated with the position, plus what may be called its accompaniments or perquisites. Often the rights, and sometimes the accompaniments, are functionally related to the duties of the position. (Rights as viewed by the incumbent are usually duties as viewed by other members of the community.) However, there may be a host of subsidiary rights and perquisites that are not essential to the function of the position and have only an indirect and symbolic connection with its duties, but which still may be of considerable importance in inducing people to seek the positions and fulfil the essential duties.

If the rights and perquisites of different positions in a society must be unequal, then the society must be stratified, because that is precisely what stratification means. Social inequality is thus an unconsciously evolved device by which societies insure that the most important positions are conscientiously filled by the most qualified persons. Hence every society, no matter how simple or complex, must differentiate persons in terms of both prestige and esteem, and must therefore possess a certain amount of institutionalized inequality.

It does not follow that the amount or type of inequality need be the same in all societies. This is largely a function of factors that will be discussed presently.

THE TWO DETERMINANTS OF POSITIONAL RANK

Granting the general function that inequality subserves, one can specify the two factors that determine the relative rank of different positions. In general those positions convey the best reward, and hence have the highest rank, which (a) have the greatest importance for the society and (b) require the greatest training or talent. The first factor concerns function and is a matter of relative significance; the second concerns means and is a matter of scarcity.

Differential functional importance. Actually a society does not need to reward positions in proportion to their functional importance. It merely needs to give sufficient reward to them to insure that they will be filled competently. In other words, it must see that less essential positions do not compete successfully with more essential ones. If a position is easily filled, it need not be heavily rewarded, even though important. On the other hand, if it is important but hard to fill, the reward must be high enough to get it filled anyway. Functional importance is therefore a necessary but not a sufficient cause of high rank being assigned to a position.

Differential scarcity of personnel. Practically all positions, no matter how acquired, require some form of skill or capacity for performance. This is implicit in the very notion of position, which implies that the incumbent must, by virtue of his incumbency, accomplish certain things.

There are, ultimately, only two ways in which a person's qualifications come about: through inherent capacity or through training. Obviously, in concrete activities both are always necessary, but from a practical standpoint the scarcity may lie primarily in one or the other, as well as in both. Some positions require innate talents of such high degree that the persons who fill them are bound to be rare. In many cases, however, talent is fairly abundant in the population but the training process is so long, costly, and elaborate that relatively few can qualify. Modern medicine, for example, is within the mental capacity of most individuals, but a medical education is so burdensome and expensive that virtually none would undertake it if the position of the M.D. did not carry a reward commensurate with the sacrifice.

If the talents required for a position are abundant and the training easy, the method of acquiring the position may have little to do with its duties. There may be, in fact, a virtually accidental relationship. But if the skills required are scarce by reason of the rarity of talent or the costliness of training, the position, if functionally important, must have an attractive power that will draw the necessary skills in competition with other positions. This means, in effect, that the position must be high in the social scale—must command great prestige, high salary, ample leisure, and the like.

How variations are to be understood. In so far as there is a difference between one system of stratification and another, it is attributable to whatever factors affect the two determinants of differential reward—namely, functional importance and scarcity of personnel. Positions important in one society may not be important in another, because the conditions faced by the societies, or their degree of internal development, may be different. The same conditions, in turn, may affect the question of scarcity; for in some societies the stage of development, or the external situation, may wholly obviate the necessity of certain kinds of skill or talent. Any particular system of stratification, then, can be understood as a product of the special conditions affecting the two aforementioned grounds of differential reward.

7.3 ROBERT MICHELS

The Iron Law of Oligarchy

Robert Michels (1876–1936), a German sociologist, Socialist, and economist, is best-known for his formulation of the "iron law of oligarchy," which argues that in all large organizations, oligarchy (the rule by a few) is inevitable. According to Michels, although they are initially committed to democracy, Socialist parties are no less oligarchic than conservative parties. In principle, the leaders are elected democratically, but once in power, they gain the knowledge and control of resources to remain in power. Michels argues that leaders, originally elected to serve the mass, eventually become "professional" leaders and attain an independence from the mass. The mass then lacks the necessary resources and skills to remove the leaders from power. Over time, the leaders in power promote officials of like thought and opinion, thus establishing a self-perpetuating leadership group or oligarchy.

Key Concept: the iron law of oligarchy

*T*he most formidable argument against the sovereignty of the masses is . . . derived from the mechanical and technical impossibility of its realization.

The sovereign masses are altogether incapable of undertaking the most necessary resolutions. The impotence of direct democracy, like the power of indirect democracy, is a direct outcome of the influence of number. In a polemic against Proudhon (1849), Louis Blanc asks whether it is possible for thirty-four millions of human beings (the population of France at that time) to carry on their affairs without accepting what the pettiest man of business finds necessary, the intermediation of representatives. He answers his own question by saying that one who declares direct action on this scale to be possible is a fool. . . .

There are, however, other reasons of a technical and administrative character which render impossible the direct self-government of large groups. If Peter wrongs Paul, it is out of the question that all the other citizens should hasten to the spot to undertake a personal examination of the matter in dispute,

143

and to take the part of Paul against Peter. By parity of reasoning, in the modern democratic party, it is impossible for the collectivity to undertake the direct settlement of all the controversies that may arise.

Hence the need for delegation, for the system in which delegates represent the mass and carry out its will. Even in groups sincerely animated with the democratic spirit, current business, the preparation and the carrying out of the most important actions, is necessarily left in the hands of individuals. It is well known that the impossibility for the people to exercise a legislative power directly in popular assemblies led the democratic idealists of Spain to demand, as the least of evils, a system of popular representation and a parliamentary state.

Originally the chief is merely the servant of the mass. The organization is based upon the absolute equality of all its members. Equality is here understood in its most general sense, as an equality of like men. In many countries, as in idealist Italy (and in certain regions in Germany where the socialist movement is still in its infancy), this equality is manifested, among other ways, by the mutual use of the familiar "thou," which is employed by the most poorly paid wage-labourer in addressing the most distinguished intellectual. This generic conception of equality is, however, gradually replaced by the idea of equality among comrades belonging to the same organization, all of whose members enjoy the same rights. The democratic principle aims at guaranteeing to all an equal influence and an equal participation in the regulation of the common interests. All are electors, and all are eligible for office. The fundamental postulate of the *Déclaration des Droits de l'Homme* [Declaration of the Rights of Man] finds here its theoretical application. All the offices are filled by election. The officials, executive organs of the general will, play a merely subordinate part, are always dependent upon the collectivity, and can be deprived of their office at any moment. The mass of the party is omnipotent. . . .

The technical specialization that inevitably results from all extensive organization renders necessary what is called expert leadership. Consequently the power of determination comes to be considered one of the specific attributes of leadership, and is gradually withdrawn from the masses to be concentrated in the hands of the leaders alone. Thus the leaders, who were at first no more than the executive organs of the collective will, soon emancipate themselves from the mass and become independent of its control.

Organization implies the tendency to oligarchy. In every organization, whether it be a political party, a professional union, or any other association of the kind, the aristocratic tendency manifests itself very clearly. The mechanism of the organization, while conferring a solidity of structure, induces serious changes in the organized mass, completely inverting the respective position of the leaders and the led. As a result of organization, every party or professional union becomes divided into a minority of directors and a majority of directed. . . .

As organization develops, not only do the tasks of the administration become more difficult and more complicated, but, further, its duties become enlarged and specialized to such a degree that it is no longer possible to take them all in at a single glance. In a rapidly progressive movement, it is not only the growth in the number of duties, but also the higher quality of these, which imposes a more extensive differentiation of function. Nominally, and according to the letter of the rules, all the acts of the leaders are subject to the ever vigilant criticism of the rank and file. In theory the leader is merely an employee bound by the instructions he receives. He has to carry out the orders of the mass, of which he is no more than the executive organ. But in actual fact, as the organization increases in size, this control becomes purely fictitious. The members have to give up the idea of themselves conducting or even supervising the whole administration, and are compelled to hand these tasks over to trustworthy persons specially nominated for the purpose, to salaried officials. The rank and file must content themselves with summary reports, and with the appointment of occasional special committees of inquiry. Yet this does not derive from any special change in the rules of the organization. It is by very necessity that a simple employee gradually becomes a "leader," acquiring a freedom of action which he ought not to possess. The chief then becomes accustomed to despatch important business on his own responsibility, and to decide various questions relating to the life of the party without any attempt to consult the rank and file. It is obvious that democratic control thus undergoes a progressive diminution, and is ultimately reduced to an infinitesimal minimum. In all the socialist parties there is a continual increase in the number of functions withdrawn from the electoral assemblies and transferred to the executive committees. In this way there is constructed a powerful and complicated edifice. The principle of division of labour coming more and more into operation, executive authority undergoes division and subdivision. There is thus constituted a rigorously defined and hierarchical bureaucracy. In the catechism of party duties, the strict observance of hierarchical rules becomes the first article. This hierarchy comes into existence as the outcome of technical conditions, and its constitution is an essential postulate of the regular functioning of the party machine.

It is indisputable that the oligarchical and bureaucratic tendency of party organization is a matter of technical and practical necessity. It is the inevitable product of the very principle of organization. Not even the most radical wing of the various socialist parties raises any objection to this retrogressive evolution, the contention being that democracy is only a form of organization and that where it ceases to be possible to harmonize democracy with organization, it is better to abandon the former than the latter. Organization, since it is the only means of attaining the ends of socialism, is considered to comprise within itself the revolutionary content of the party, and this essential content must never be sacrificed for the sake of form. . . .

The more solid the structure of an organization becomes in the course of the evolution of the modern political party, the more marked becomes the tendency to replace the emergency leader by the professional leader. Every party organization which has attained to a considerable degree of complication demands that there should be a certain number of persons who devote all their activities to the work of the party. The mass provides these by delegation, and the delegates, regularly appointed, become permanent representatives of the mass for the direction of its affairs. . . .

Leadership is a necessary phenomenon in every form of social life. Consequently it is not the task of science to inquire whether this phenomenon is good or evil, or predominantly one or the other. But there is great scientific value in the demonstration that every system of leadership is incompatible with the most essential postulates of democracy. We are now aware that the law of the historic necessity of oligarchy is primarily based upon a series of facts of experience. Like all other scientific laws, sociological laws are derived from empirical observation. In order, however, to deprive our axiom of its purely descriptive character, and to confer upon it that status of analytical explanation which can alone transform a formula into a law, it does not suffice to contemplate from a unitary outlook those phenomena which may be empirically established; we must also study the determining causes of these phenomena. Such has been our task.

Now, if we leave out of consideration the tendency of the leaders to organize themselves and to consolidate their interests, and if we leave also out of consideration the gratitude of the led towards the leaders, and the general immobility and passivity of the masses, we are led to conclude that the principal cause of oligarchy in the democratic parties is to be found in the technical indispensability of leadership.

The process which has begun in consequence of the differentiation of functions in the party is completed by a complex of qualities which the leaders acquire through their detachment from the mass. At the outset, leaders arise SPONTANEOUSLY; their functions are ACCESSORY and GRATUITOUS. Soon, however, they become PROFESSIONAL leaders, and in this second stage of development they are STABLE and IRREMOVABLE.

It follows that the explanation of the oligarchical phenomenon which thus results is partly PSYCHOLOGICAL; oligarchy derives, that is to say, from the psychical transformations which the leading personalities in the parties undergo in the course of their lives. But also, and still more, oligarchy depends upon what we may term the PSYCHOLOGY OF ORGANIZATION ITSELF, that is to say, upon the tactical and technical necessities which result from the consolidation of every disciplined political aggregate. Reduced to its most concise expression, the fundamental sociological law of political parties (the term "political" being here used in its most comprehensive significance) may be formulated in the following terms: "It is organization which gives birth to the dominion of the elected over the electors, of the mandataries over the mandators, of the delegates over the delegators. Who says organization, says oligarchy."

Every party organization represents an oligarchical power grounded upon a democratic basis. We find everywhere electors and elected. Also we find everywhere that the power of the elected leaders over the electing masses is almost unlimited. The oligarchical structure of the building suffocates the basic democratic principle. That which IS oppresses THAT WHICH OUGHT TO BE. For the masses, this essential difference between the reality and the ideal remains a mystery.

CHAPTER 8 Elites

8.1 C. WRIGHT MILLS

The Higher Circles

Radical sociologist C. Wright Mills (1916–1962) was a leader of mid-twentieth-century American sociological thought. He believed that social scientists should not be merely disinterested observers, a practice that Mills referred to as "abstracted empiricism," but that they should be activists asserting their social responsibility. In his book *The Power Elite* (Oxford University Press, 1956), Mills offers his view of the U.S. system of power. In the following excerpt from *The Power Elite,* he argues that there is a "power elite" in the United States that is composed of a small group of individuals who occupy powerful positions and exert a dominant influence on the country's decision-making process. Mills does not see this group as a deliberately organized conspiracy that is out to usurp power from democratically elected representatives. But by virtue of their positions at the upper levels of the military, the government, and various business organizations, they shape major policies and make the key decisions of the United States.

Mills notes that the American economy shifted from a system of small units to one that is dominated by 200 or so giant corporations that are interrelated politically and administratively. They are the key economic decisionmakers. Prior to World War II, the military had little or no influence, but since the 1950s, the military has exerted great influence and commanded major resources. Finally, the political leadership has become centralized and has taken on power that, in the past, was dispersed. According to Mills, the "power elite" interact socially and develop a common set of values and beliefs of what they believe is right and good for the United States.

Key Concept: the power elite

*T*he power elite is composed of men whose positions enable them to transcend the ordinary environments of ordinary men and women; they are in positions to make decisions having major consequences. Whether they do or do not make such decisions is less important than the fact that they do occupy such pivotal positions: their failure to act, their failure to make decisions, is itself an act that is often of greater consequence than the decisions they do make. For they are in command of the major hierarchies and organizations of modern society. They rule the big corporations. They run the machinery of the state and claim its prerogatives. They direct the military establishment. They occupy the strategic command posts of the social structure, in which are now centered the effective means of the power and the wealth and the celebrity which they enjoy.

The power elite are not solitary rulers. Advisers and consultants, spokesmen and opinion-makers are often the captains of their higher thought and decision. Immediately below the elite are the professional politicians of the middle levels of power, in the Congress and in the pressure groups, as well as among the new and old upper classes of town and city and region. Mingling with them, in curious ways which we shall explore, are those professional celebrities who live by being continually displayed but are never, so long as they remain celebrities, displayed enough. If such celebrities are not at the head of any dominating hierarchy, they do often have the power to distract the attention of the public or afford sensations to the masses, or, more directly, to gain the ear of those who do occupy positions of direct power. More or less unattached, as critics of morality and technicians of power, as spokesmen of God and creators of mass sensibility, such celebrities and consultants are part of the immediate scene in which the drama of the elite is enacted. But that drama itself is centered in the command posts of the major institutional hierarchies.

The truth about the nature and the power of the elite is not some secret which men of affairs know but will not tell. Such men hold quite various theories about their own roles in the sequence of event and decision. Often they are uncertain about their roles, and even more often they allow their fears and their hopes to affect their assessment of their own power. No matter how great their actual power, they tend to be less acutely aware of it than of the resistances of others to its use. Moreover, most American men of affairs have learned well the rhetoric of public relations, in some cases even to the point of using it when they are alone, and thus coming to believe it. The personal awareness of the actors is only one of the several sources one must examine in order to understand the higher circles. Yet many who believe that there is no elite, or at any rate none of any consequence, rest their argument upon what men of affairs believe about themselves, or at least assert in public.

There is, however, another view: those who feel, even if vaguely, that a compact and powerful elite of great importance does now prevail in America often base that feeling upon the historical trend of our time. They have felt, for example, the domination of the military event, and from this they infer that generals and admirals, as well as other men of decision influenced by them, must be enormously powerful. They hear that the Congress has again abdicated to a handful of men decisions clearly related to the issue of war or peace.

They know that the bomb was dropped over Japan in the name of the United States of America, although they were at no time consulted about the matter. They feel that they live in a time of big decisions; they know that they are not making any. Accordingly, as they consider the present as history, they infer that at its center, making decisions or failing to make them, there must be an elite of power.

On the other hand, those who share this feeling about big historical events assume that there is an elite and that its power is great. On the other hand, those who listen carefully to the reports of men apparently involved in the great decisions often do not believe that there is an elite whose powers are of decisive consequence.

Both views must be taken into account, but neither is adequate. The way to understand the power of the American elite lies neither solely in recognizing the historic scale of events nor in accepting the personal awareness reported by men of apparent decision. Behind such men and behind the events of history, linking the two, are the major institutions of modern society. These hierarchies of state and corporation and army constitute the means of power; as such they are now of a consequence not before equaled in human history—and at their summits, there are now those command posts of modern society which offer us the sociological key to an understanding of the role of the higher circles in America.

Within American society, major national power now resides in the economic, the political, and the military domains. Other institutions seem off to the side of modern history, and, on occasion, duly subordinated to these. No family is as directly powerful in national affairs as any major corporation; no church is as directly powerful in the external biographies of young men in America today as the military establishment; no college is as powerful in the shaping of momentous events as the National Security Council. Religious, educational, and family institutions are not autonomous centers of national power; on the contrary, these decentralized areas are increasingly shaped by the big three, in which developments of decisive and immediate consequence now occur.

Families and churches and schools adapt to modern life; governments and armies and corporations shape it; and, as they do so, they turn these lesser institutions into means for their ends. Religious institutions provide chaplains to the armed forces where they are used as a means of increasing the effectiveness of its morale to kill. Schools select and train men for their jobs in corporations and their specialized tasks in the armed forces. The extended family has, of course, long been broken up by the industrial revolution, and now the son and the father are removed from the family, by compulsion if need be, whenever the army of the state sends out the call. And the symbols of all these lesser institutions are used to legitimate the power and the decisions of the big three.

The life-fate of the modern individual depends not only upon the family into which he was born or which he enters by marriage, but increasingly upon the corporation in which he spends the most alert hours of his best years; not only upon the school where he is educated as a child and adolescent, but also upon the state which touches him throughout his life; not only upon the church in which on occasion he hears the word of God, but also upon the army in which he is disciplined.

If the centralized state could not rely upon the inculcation of nationalist loyalties in public and private schools, its leaders would promptly seek to modify the decentralized educational system. If the bankruptcy rate among the top five hundred corporations were as high as the general divorce rate among the thirty-seven million married couples, there would be economic catastrophe on an international scale. If members of armies gave to them no more of their lives than do believers to the churches to which they belong, there would be a military crisis.

Within each of the big three, the typical institutional unit has become enlarged, has become administrative, and, in the power of its decisions, has become centralized. Behind these developments there is a fabulous technology, for as institutions, they have incorporated this technology and guide it, even as it shapes and paces their developments.

The economy—once a great scatter of small productive units in autonomous balance—has become dominated by two or three hundred giant corporations, administratively and politically interrelated, which together hold the keys to economic decisions.

The political order, once a decentralized set of several dozen states with a weak spinal cord, has become a centralized, executive establishment which has taken up into itself many powers previously scattered, and now enters into each and every cranny of the social structure.

The military order, once a slim establishment in a context of distrust fed by state militia, has become the largest and most expensive feature of government, and, although well versed in smiling public relations, now has all the grim and clumsy efficiency of a sprawling bureaucratic domain.

In each of these institutional areas, the means of power at the disposal of decision makers have increased enormously; their central executive powers have been enhanced; within each of them modern administrative routines have been elaborated and tightened up.

As each of these domains becomes enlarged and centralized, the consequences of its activities become greater, and its traffic with the others increases. The decisions of a handful of corporations bear upon military and political as well as upon economic developments around the world. The decisions of the military establishment rest upon and grievously affect political life as well as the very level of economic activity. The decisions made within the political domain determine economic activities and military programs. There is no longer, on the one hand, an economy, and, on the other hand, a political order containing a military establishment unimportant to politics and to money-making. There is a political economy linked, in a thousand ways, with military institutions and decisions. On each side of the world-split running through central Europe and around the Asiatic rimlands, there is an ever-increasing interlocking of economic, military, and political structures. If there is government intervention in the corporate economy, so is there corporate intervention in the governmental process. In the structural sense, this triangle of power is the source of the interlocking directorate that is most important for the historical structure of the present.

The fact of the interlocking is clearly revealed at each of the points of crisis of modern capitalist society—slump, war, and boom. In each, men of decision are led to an awareness of the interdependence of the major institutional orders. In the nineteenth century, when the scale of all institutions was smaller, their liberal integration was achieved in the automatic economy, by an autonomous play of market forces, and in the automatic political domain, by the bargain and the vote. It was then assumed that out of the imbalance and friction that followed the limited decisions then possible a new equilibrium would in due course emerge. That can no longer be assumed, and it is not assumed by the men at the top of each of the three dominant hierarchies.

For given the scope of their consequences, decisions—and indecisions—in any one of these ramify into the others, and hence top decisions tend either to become co-ordinated or to lead to a commanding indecision. It has not always been like this. When numerous small entrepreneurs made up the economy, for example, many of them could fail and the consequences still remain local; political and military authorities did not intervene. But now, given political expectations and military commitments, can they afford to allow key units of the private corporate economy to break down in slump? Increasingly, they do intervene in economic affairs, and as they do so, the controlling decisions in each order are inspected by agents of the other two, and economic, military, and political structures are interlocked.

At the pinnacle of each of the three enlarged and centralized domains, there have arisen those higher circles which make up the economic, the political, and the military elites. At the top of the economy, among the corporate rich, there are the chief executives; at the top of the political order, the members of the political directorate; at the top of the military establishment, the elite of soldier-statesmen clustered in and around the Joint Chiefs of Staff and the upper echelon. As each of these domains has coincided with the others, as decisions tend to become total in their consequence, the leading men in each of the three domains of power—the warlords, the corporation chieftains, the political directorate—tend to come together, to form the power elite of America.

The higher circles in and around these command posts are often thought of in terms of what their members possess: they have a greater share than other people of the things and experiences that are most highly valued. From this point of view, the elite are simply those who have the most of what there is to have, which is generally held to include money, power, and prestige—as well as all the ways of life to which these lead. But the elite are not simply those who have the most, for they could not 'have the most' were it not for their positions in the great institutions. For such institutions are the necessary bases of power, of wealth, and of prestige, and at the same time, the chief means of exercising power, of acquiring and retaining wealth, and of cashing in the higher claims for prestige.

By the powerful we mean, of course, those who are able to realize their will, even if others resist it. No one, accordingly, can be truly powerful unless he has access to the command of major institutions, for it is over these institutional means of power that the truly powerful are, in the first instance, powerful.

Higher politicians and key officials of government command such institutional power; so do admirals and generals, and so do the major owners and executives of the larger corporations. Not all power, it is true, is anchored in and exercised by means of such institutions, but only within and through them can power be more or less continuous and important.

Wealth also is acquired and held in and through institutions. The pyramid of wealth cannot be understood merely in terms of the very rich; for the great inheriting families . . . are now supplemented by the corporate institutions of modern society: every one of the very rich families has been and is closely connected—always legally and frequently managerially as well—with one of the multi-million dollar corporations.

The modern corporation is the prime source of wealth, but, in latter-day capitalism, the political apparatus also opens and closes many avenues to wealth. The amount as well as the source of income, the power over consumers' goods as well as over productive capital, are determined by position within the political economy. If our interest in the very rich goes beyond their lavish or their miserly consumption, we must examine their relations to modern forms of corporate property as well as to the state; for such relations now determine the chances of men to secure big property and to receive high income.

Great prestige increasingly follows the major institutional units of the social structure. It is obvious that prestige depends, often quite decisively, upon access to the publicity machines that are now a central and normal feature of all the big institutions of modern America. Moreover, one feature of these hierarchies of corporation, state, and military establishment is that their top positions are increasingly interchangeable. One result of this is the accumulative nature of prestige. Claims for prestige, for example, may be initially based on military roles, then expressed in and augmented by an educational institution run by corporate executives, and cashed in, finally, in the political order, where, for General Eisenhower and those he represents, power and prestige finally meet at the very peak. Like wealth and power, prestige tends to be cumulative: the more of it you have, the more you can get. These values also tend to be translatable into one another: the wealthy find it easier than the poor to gain power; those with status find it easier than those without it to control opportunities for wealth.

If we took the one hundred most powerful men in America, the one hundred wealthiest, and the one hundred most celebrated away from the institutional positions they now occupy, away from their resources of men and women and money, away from the media of mass communication that are now focused upon them—then they would be powerless and poor and uncelebrated. For power is not of a man. Wealth does not center in the person of the wealthy. Celebrity is not inherent in any personality. To be celebrated, to be wealthy, to have power requires access to major institutions, for the institutional positions men occupy determine in large part their chances to have and to hold these valued experiences.

The people of the higher circles may also be conceived as members of a top social stratum, as a set of groups whose members know one another, see one another socially and at business, and so, in making decisions, take one another into account. The elite, according to this conception, feel themselves to be, and are felt by others to be, the inner circle of 'the upper social classes.' They form a more or less compact social and psychological entity; they have become self-conscious members of a social class. People are either accepted into this class or they are not, and there is a qualitative split, rather than merely a numerical scale, separating them from those who are not elite. They are more or less aware of themselves as a social class and they behave toward one another differently from the way they do toward members of other classes. They accept one another, understand one another, marry one another, tend to work and to think if not together at least alike.

C. Wright Mills

Systemic Power in Community Decision Making: A Restatement of Stratification Theory

In the following article, Clarence N. Stone discusses stratification theory with a focus on the relationship between community decision-making and what he calls "systemic power." He argues that high socioeconomic status groups dominate political decisions in complex ways. They influence decisionmakers directly through personal contact or through lobbyists, but they also have an indirect effect because decisionmakers are reinforced by the social and tangible benefits that come with favoring the powerful. Earlier analysts underestimated the influence of elite groups because they only took into account the results of the direct actions of groups. These analysts failed to note that elite groups have a contextual or situational influence on political life that predisposes decisionmakers to favor certain interests. Stone says that this systemic power is embedded in the social structure and is removed from open competition among groups and politics in the public view. Systemic power is the perennial bias of politicians and officials in favor of the interests of upper groups over lower groups.

Stone (b. 1935) is a political scientist who has intensively studied urban politics, especially in Atlanta, Georgia. He is also a professor of government, politics, and urban studies at the University of Maryland at College Park. He has performed painstaking research on how and why even reform administrations in cities favor business interests.

Key Concept: systemic power

In their continued considerations of political inequality, urban scholars are especially concerned with less visible influences surrounding community decision making, and have employed such concepts as potential power, nondecision making, and anticipated reactions. However, these concepts leave some patterns of influence unexplained. There is also a dimension of power in which durable features of the socioeconomic system confer advantages and disadvantages on groups in ways that predispose public officials to favor some interests at the expense of others. Public officials make their decisions in a context in which strategically important resources are hierarchically arranged. Because this system of stratification leaves public officials situationally dependent on upper-strata interests, it is a factor in all that they do. Consequently, system features lower the opportunity costs of exerting influence of some groups and raise them for others. Thus socioeconomic inequalities put various strata on different political footings.

Clarence N. Stone

Students of power have long probed beneath the surface fiction of political equality for the imbalances of influence that are invariably present in the governance of communities. But this search is complicated by the fact that power is often present without being visibly exercised. In trying to understand the less visible influences surrounding public decision making, scholars have variously developed such concepts as nondecisions, anticipated reactions, and indirect influence. Useful as they are, these concepts don't take us far enough. It seems that there is a dimension of power beyond what the accepted concepts suggest—a dimension best termed "systemic."

Consider these circumstances. Contrary to reasonable expectations, electoral strength, whether potential or manifest, appears to be an unreliable indicator of political power. Major business enterprises and other upper-strata interests seem to have an influence on local decisions not warranted by their numbers or their overt participation in political and governmental affairs. For example, while business influence in particular controversies is not very impressive (business interests are often divided or defeated), business influence seems to be important in a way not measured by victories and losses. Conversely, lower-strata groups seem to face fewer handicaps in politics than in other areas of community life (cf. Dahl, 1961, pp. 293–96), but they make little use of political activity to further their position and, when they do, they are often disappointed by the transitory nature of their influence.

Peter Bachrach and Morton Baratz (1970) confronted this problem of a less visible face of power, setting forth the notion of nondecision making. By this term, they meant the capacity of elite groups to restrict the scope of community decision making. G. William Domhoff (1978) has added the assertion that there is a national upper class based on corporate wealth which is able to control the agenda of public debate and maintain ideological dominance. However, nondecision making has proved difficult to research: critics charge that it is not possible to study non-events and that what in fact is studied is a special kind of decision making.

Whether the critics have fairly characterized nondecision making is debatable (see Crenson, 1971), but there does seem to be more to the "hidden face" of power than agenda control. Despite efforts to contain them, a variety of issues do surface; during the 1960s, for example, redistributive issues were prominent. The missing element in the community power puzzle seems to be in the predispositions of public officials. Why, when all of their actions are taken into account, do officials over the long haul seem to favor upper-strata interests, disfavor lower-strata interests, and sometimes act in apparent disregard of the contours of electoral power? Can this systemic pattern be treated in power terms?

In the discussion below, I will argue "yes" to this last question. The core of my argument is that we must take into account contextual forces—the facet of community decision making I label "systemic power." In brief, this argument runs as follows: public officials form their alliances, make their decisions and plan their futures in a context in which strategically important resources are hierarchically arranged—that is, officials operate in a stratified society. The system of stratification is a motivating factor in all that they do; it predisposes them to favor upper- over lower-strata interests. Systemic power therefore has to do with *the impact of the larger socioeconomic system on the predispositions of public officials.*

The class character of community decision making does not result from a conscious calculation. As Norton Long has argued, rationality is "a function of the parts rather than the whole" (1958, p. 251). What I shall elaborate below is the argument that because officials operate within a stratified system, they find themselves rewarded for cooperating with upper-strata interests and unrewarded or even penalized for cooperating with lower-strata interests. In selective ways described later, public officials experience strategic dependencies predisposing them to favor upper- over lower-strata interests. Thus some groups are in a position to receive official cooperation, while others encounter substantial resistance. Put another way, different strata operate from different footings and therefore face different opportunity costs (cf. Harsanyi, 1962). The particular interactions and relationships (the parts) yield an overall pattern of decision making that is unplanned and unforeseen. It does, however, bear a class imprint not predicted by pluralist theories of community power and it comes about in ways requiring no ruling elite.

The overall argument is developed in three steps: (1) a definition and explanation of the concept of systemic power, (2) a highlighting of systemic features underlying specified power imbalances, and (3) an examination of empirical findings bearing on the notion of systemic power used here.

SYSTEMIC POWER: TOWARD AN EXPLANATION AND DEFINITION

Everyone recognizes that system features in some way affect the distribution of power. But how does one relate those system features to the power relationships among determinate actors?

Power is most readily seen in overt and purposive activity among individuals. But students of politics (such as Anton, 1963) have long recognized that power relationships are more complex than what can be observed in that form:

1. Power is not only *interpersonal*; it is also *intergroup* (including relationships between classes and strata). Few would quarrel with this position.

2. Power is not only a matter of *intention*; it is also a matter of context, of the nature of or "logic" of the *situation*. Here there is a need for some clarification.

Most students of power agree that there is a phenomenon called "anticipated reactions." *A* may influence the behavior of *B* because *B* is fearful of the reactions of *A* to a given course of conduct; or *B* may be accommodating to *A* because *B* wants to stay in the good graces of *A* for future advantage. To illustrate, Robert Dahl observes that "elected leaders keep the real or imagined preferences of constituents constantly in mind in deciding what policies to adopt or reject" (1961, p. 164). In this latter instance especially, it is not necessary that the passive "actor" intend that its preferences be taken into account or even be conscious that a power relationship exists. Indeed, Dahl makes much of the indifference and unconcern of the electorate. All that is required for this to be a power relationship is that elected officials take into account preferences of the electorate because the electorate is in a position to give or withhold something of value—in this case, votes. Any actor may, just by possessing a politically useful resource, enjoy a power advantage.

Furthermore, it is not necessary that the superordinate member in a power relationship have gained that position by some intended activity. Inherited wealth is not politically valueless because it was inherited, nor is advantage gained through a fortuitous change in circumstances any less an advantage because the change was fortuitous. Power can therefore be situational in a twofold sense: (a) a participant need not make a conscious effort to get into a power position for that position to be power-relevant, and (b) the participant need not be aware of the particular consequences of the power position (cf. Oppenheim, 1978). This means therefore that, if the *situation* is such that *B* feels a need to be accommodating to *A*, then *A* had power over *B*, whether *A* sought that position or is even aware of it or not. Moreover, the strength of the relationship is not governed by motivation. In an anticipated reaction, the strength of the relationship is determined by the vulnerability of *B* to *A* (cf. Emerson, 1962). Vulnerability hinges on the *structure of the situation*, and that is separate from the motivation or effort that went into creating or even exploiting the situation. This is not to say that motivation, sharply defined intention, or conscious effort to gain an advantage are never important, only that they are not essential to a power relationship.

3. Power relationships are not only *direct*; they may also be *indirect*. Again, there is need for clarification, and there is also a need for keeping in mind the difference between the situational element of power and the indirect element of power.

Power is most often viewed as a conflict relationship. When there is direct conflict, the exercise of power is not in doubt. This is the standard "*A* gets *B* to do what *B* would not otherwise have done." This is a clear case of the "power over" relationship. But suppose there is no overt threat, not even an implicit threat to use sanctions. Rather, participants have an unequal opportunity to further their interests. *A* has a greater capacity to achieve goals than *C* has (excluding *B* from consideration for the time being). We say that *A* is more powerful than *C*—that, for example, Mayor Lee is more powerful than the corner grocer. But is this a power relationship since there is no *direct* conflict between *A* and *C*? This relationship has been treated as a "power to" rather than a "power over" relationship, and therefore not as a conflict relationship. However, the "power to" relationship is a conflict relationship if *A* and *C* are in *indirect* competition to achieve their goals. If *A*, by getting *B* to do *x* makes it unlikely that *C* can get *B* to do *y*, then there is a conflict relationship—but it is indirect because *A* and *C* are not competing directly with one another. This is implied in the nondecision-making argument. *A* excludes *C*'s items from the agenda of decision making, not only because *C*'s items may be threatening in some direct way, but *because the agenda is limited and there is competition for the space available*. An unequal capacity to achieve goals is therefore a conflict relationship to the extent that the actors are in competition for a limited opportunity to further their interests. If *A* uses superior resources to structure a pattern of agenda setting and *C* finds that s/he cannot change the agenda, *A* has exerted power over *C* even in the absence of direct conflict between *A* and *C*.

Defining Systemic Power.

For purposes of the present discussion, let us assume that we need be concerned only with durable, not transient, power conditions. Let us also assume that we are concerned only with intergroup power relationships. What we are looking for is a way to treat the durable features of the larger socioeconomic system as an element of the power relationships among groups.

TABLE 1

Types of Power Relationships

Elements in Relationship	Type of Relationship
Intergroup, intentional and direct	Decisional
Intergroup, situational and direct	Anticipated Reaction
Intergroup, intentional and indirect	Nondecision Making
Intergroup, situational and indirect	Systemic

By putting together the different elements of power in their various combinations (and concentrating on durable conditions), one may derive the following classification scheme. Systemic power appears as that type of power *furthest* removed from open competition (*direct* power relationships) and purposive activity (involving a conscious *intention*) among individuals (*interpersonal*). Yet it is made up of elements that are acknowledged to be aspects of power.

Systemic power can be defined as that dimension of power in which durable features of the socioeconomic system (the *situational* element) confer advantages and disadvantages on groups (the *intergroup* element) in ways predisposing public officials to favor some interests at the expense of others (the *indirect* element).

At the intergroup level, when situational and indirect elements of power are put together in the political context, the combination brings to light the situational dependency of official decision makers on one set of participants that prevents other participants from having an equal chance to further their interests through the political process. Beneficiaries of that situational dependency need not have made a conscious effort to create that dependency for political purposes. All that is necessary for that dependency relationship to qualify as part of a power relationship is that some visible gain be allocated to the beneficiary group and that the gain be, at least indirectly, at the expense of some competing group.

To be sure that the various dimensions of power are differentiated, let us trace the recession from direct and open conflict based on active intention. If a business organization contributes money and mounts a successful campaign to defeat a candidate, it is exercising decisional power. This represents an intentional use of resources under conditions of direct conflict to gain a specific objective.

Anticipated reactions differ from decisional power only in that while conflict is direct, it is not overt, but tacit. It arises from the structure of the situation rather than from an open and intentional mobilization of resources. Consider a hypothetical example. Because only the local chamber of commerce is capable of putting together an effective challenge, an incumbent administration interested in running for reelection courts the good favor of the chamber by being attentive to its interests. The mere presence of mobilizable resources produces results because the responding actor (the mayor) wants to avoid sanctions from the superordinate party (the chamber). Consequently, the chamber exercises power without any active effort.

In contrast to the above examples, nondecision making falls into the category of power relationships involving no direct conflict. The point made so forcefully by Peter Bachrach and Morton Baratz (1970) is that contending groups exercise power not only to influence the outcomes of specific issues but also to shape the context of decision making and thereby influence how, and even whether, an issue develops. It is important to remember that the superordinate party in nondecision making is not totally passive. We could, for example, observe a chamber of commerce promoting city manager government, or school administrators reinforcing the view that education is nonpolitical. Bear in mind, however, that what is being observed is not a superordinate party exercising power over a subordinate party (hence the power relationship is not one of direct conflict) but rather the superordinate party using resources to influence the context (institutions, procedures, and norms) of community decision making. Nondecision-making power differs from decisional power in that it is not a matter of winning particular decisional struggles but of determining how conflict will be shaped or opposition prevented (Frey, 1971). It is most telling when it so diffuses the conflict relationship that a direct and even tacit confrontation is avoided.

Systemic power differs from nondecision making on the important dimension of intention and situation. That is, like nondecision making, systemic power does not entail a relationship of direct conflict, but, unlike nondecision making, systemic power is *purely situational*. By this I mean both that members of the power relationship may be unaware of the particular consequences of their power position and that they need have made no active effort to build up or defend their power advantage. Systemic power, *as such*, involves no overt attempt to influence the context of decision making. It lies in the *imperatives of the situation* and requires no elite group engaged in changing or maintaining institutions, procedures, or norms. Because its operation is completely impersonal and deeply embedded in the social structure, this form of power can appropriately be termed "systemic."

How, then, can systemic power be studied? The answer is that its consequences can be observed. Like other elements of community power, systemic features impinge on the behavior of official decision makers, and that impingement can be translated into power terms by means of the concept "opportunity costs." As John Harsanyi (1962) has pointed out, if some actors encounter less resistance than others, they must expend fewer resources to achieve their goals—in short, their opportunity costs are lower. Hence their power position is stronger than the position of those actors who have higher opportunity costs. Now we can link that idea directly to systemic power. Because system features predispose officials to favor some interests and to oppose others, those system features lower the opportunity costs for some groups while raising them for others—thereby having an important impact on the community's overall set of power relationships.

The concept of opportunity costs makes it clear why influence is not proportional to the effort expended on political activities. If, for example, one candidate for public office has to make a great effort to be elected and another sails through with an easy campaign, we don't conclude that the first candidate was more powerful because s/he overcame more resistance. It is often the case that the weak must struggle while the strong have only to ask. And if those with few resources encounter official resistance, they may find that they quickly face political bankruptcy. Edward Banfield recounts how Mayor Richard Daley, on assuming office, wrote to three or four of Chicago's major business leaders, "asking them to list the things they thought most needed doing" (1961, p. 251). The poor of Woodlawn, by contrast, had to engage in protests, voter-registration drives, and other highly visible forms of political action to call attention to their concerns. The truly powerful are often able to achieve their aims with little effort whereas those who are less powerful must make a much greater effort to achieve the same results.

A method of analysis that looks only at conflict or even at amount of energy expended politically is therefore likely to concentrate mainly on the struggles of the less powerful to have some influence on decision makers. It would miss systemic power and overlook the advantages that some groups enjoy in the form of favorable predispositions of public officials. Hence we need a conception of power that encompasses more than direct conflict between two actors. Some power relationships are triadic, and that makes indirect conflict possible. The triad we are considering here has public officials at the focal point. Their tendency to cooperate with some interests and resist others is itself an aspect of community power through its effects on the opportunity costs involved in influencing decisions. Bear in mind that the *indirect* power relationship referred to is not between public officials and favored groups, but between favored and unfavored groups. Note also that if this indirect relationship leads to overt conflict, it is not the favored groups but rather public officials (the intervening presence in the triad) who are likely to be the target of discontent.

Community power relationships thus manifest themselves through the behavior of public officials. That is why recruitment patterns are so important. But systemic power refers to something more fundamental even than recruitment. It refers to the circumstance that officeholders (regardless of personal background, nature of electoral support, network of associations, etc.) are, by virtue of their position, more situationally dependent on some interests than others. Because this dependency is inherent in the situation, officials are inescapably predisposed to favor some interests over others.

The tendency for officials to favor some interests at the expense of others can be the result of many factors—overt pressure, anticipated reactions, or a nondecision process, for example. But the central point here is that one source of that tendency is a set of situational dependencies that grow out of the larger socioeconomic system. Because the impact of these dependencies is indirect and because they are not the product of overt and purposive political activity, they are often overlooked. However, systemic features do affect the power positions of competing groups with a stake in community decision making. By employing the notion of opportunity costs, we can see that systemic power does not mean that power is exercised by the system, but rather that *the system affects power relationships in ways that are situational and indirect.* . . .

CONCLUSION

The systemic power argument is at heart an argument about the behavior of public officials. They are the most active element in a triadic relationship in which high-strata interests enjoy a power advantage over lower-strata interests. As officials pursue their own interests, being especially mindful of the particular institutions and processes they are part of, they are guided by a set of strategic dependencies that grow out of a stratified socioeconomic system. This contextual force is what throws off the pluralist prediction that electoral competition and administrative fragmentation will yield shifting coalitions and unpatterned biases. The argument here suggests that, in governing, public officials are strongly drawn to the upper strata and their decisions reflect this attraction. Yet the systemic power argument differs from the ruling-class thesis. Systemic power is not a general form of upper-strata dominance through agenda control. Because the upper strata are strategically advantaged, their extraordinary influence is not so much exercised as it is selectively manifested in the predispositions and behavior of public officials. The argument here can be summarized briefly:

1. While public officials enjoy significant autonomy in decision making, their autonomy is constrained by the fact that they operate in the broad context of a highly stratified socioeconomic system.

2. This system predisposes officials to favor upper- over lower-strata interests.

3. *These predispositions grow out of public office holding itself;* public officeholders are motivated by a desire for career success. For the institutions they are affiliated with to flourish and for their individual careers to advance, officeholders pursue various policy objectives.

4. As officeholders pursue their objectives, the logic of their situation confers advantages on some groups, disadvantages on others. That is, officeholders are predisposed to accommodate some interests while resisting others. In this way, system features lower the opportunity costs for some groups and raise them for others—thereby having an impact on the overall distribution of power.

5. The system attributes that influence the predispositions of officeholders are of at least three kinds: economic, associational and social; and the impact of systemic power varies accordingly with the nature of the policy problem.

6. Systemic power is not absolutely controlling or always overriding; it is most evident in the least visible phases of policy making.

7. While systemic advantage is only a facet of the total community power picture, it has wide-ranging importance. It affects who has intimate access to decision making, which proposals are considered, and how they are promoted.

Public officeholders are predisposed to interact with and to favor those who can reciprocate benefits (cf. Blau, 1964). Thus they respond to dual pressures. Formal democracy conditions the highly visible actions and campaign strategies of public officials so that they are especially responsive to those of the numerous middle strata of society. Actual governing, however, heightens responsiveness to upper-strata interests, especially when policy activities are technically complex or so diffuse in time and place as to involve no single focused dramatic event—that is, where public oversight is least effective.

It should be acknowledged that there are important limitations of the systemic power argument. It is not intended to explain how the present system of stratification came into being. Rather, it focuses on the results of the system— how system features affect power relationships and the pattern of community decision making. The argument does help explain how the system of stratification is maintained. Advantage perpetuates itself. Public officeholders seldom find it feasible to challenge those who hold strategically important resources. As officeholders, their performance is tied closely to a need to cooperate with those who possess material, organizational, and cultural advantages. It is almost always easier to come to terms with the advantaged than to overthrow them. In their innermost selves, public officials may doubt that the system is just or even the best possible, but in their roles as public officials they nevertheless feel impelled to be "realistic" and accommodate to the existing distribution of strategically important resources.

The fragments of empirical evidence examined here suggest that socioeconomic inequalities do affect the behavior of public officials, and, in this way, leave a class imprint on policy decisions. The system of stratification thus seems to undercut the formal equalities of citizenship and put various groups on different political footings. In that way, socioeconomic inequalities become part of the total community power picture.

NOTE

This article is a revised version of a paper given at the 1979 annual meeting of the American Political Science Association in Washington, D.C. Numerous colleagues have provided helpful comments and words of encouragement. I am particularly indebted to Stephen Elkin for his comments and his willingness to read several drafts. Special thanks are also due Emma Jackson, Kathleen Kemp, Charles Levine, Louis Masotti, Richard Medley, Martin Shefter, Eric Uslaner, and Oran Young for their comments and suggestions. Finally, I wish to express my appreciation to the General Research Board of the University of Maryland for support.

REFERENCES

Anton, Thomas J. (1963). "Power, Pluralism, and Local Politics." *Administrative Science Quarterly* 7: 425–57.

Bachrach, Peter, and Morton S. Baratz (1970). *Power and Poverty*. New York: Oxford University Press.

Banfield, Edward C. (1961). *Political Influence*. New York: Free Press.

Blau, Peter (1964). *Exchange and Power in Social Life*. New York: John Wiley.

Crenson, Matthew A. (1971). *The Un-Politics of Air Pollution*. Baltimore: Johns Hopkins Press.

Dahl, Robert A. (1961). *Who Governs?* New Haven, Conn.: Yale University Press.

Domhoff, G. William (1978). *Who Really Rules? New Haven and Community Power Reexamined*. New Brunswick, N.J.: Transaction Books.

Emerson, Richard M. (1962). "Power-Dependence Relations." *American Sociological Review* 27: 31–40.

Frey, Frederick W. (1971). "Comment: On Issues and Non-Issues in the Study of Power." *American Political Science Review* 65: 1081–1101.

Harsanyi, John C. (1962). "The Measurement of Social Power, Opportunity Costs, and the Theory of Two Person Bargaining Games." *Behavioral Science* 7: 67–75.

Long, Norton (1958). "The Local Community as an Ecology of Games." *American Journal of Sociology* 64: 251–61.

Oppenheim, Felix E. (1978). " 'Power' Revisited." *Journal of Politics* 40: 598–608.

CHAPTER 9 The Poor

9.1 HERBERT J. GANS

The Uses of Poverty: The Poor Pay All

In chapter 7, selection 7.2, entitled "Some Principles of Stratification," Kingsley Davis and Wilbert E. Moore argue that social inequality is necessary and functional for society. In the following analysis, Herbert J. Gans reexamines the functional framework of social stratification and points out that the so-called positive functions are positive for affluent groups, but some of them are dysfunctional (negative) for the poor. Gans notes that it seems unimaginable to associate poverty with anything positive; nevertheless, poverty does provide various benefits for the affluent in society. For example, the poor ensure that the well-off do not have to perform the menial, underpaid, or dirty jobs. Further-more, by working for low wages the poor free the affluent for professional jobs and social activities. The poor also provide jobs for the middle class in social services, the law, and so on, and they provide a market for goods rejected by the affluent.

Gans (b. 1927) is the Robert S. Lynd Professor of Sociology at Columbia University and a former president of the American Sociological Association. He is a scholar and analyst of the class structure of the city, a city planner, and a student of ethnicity, as is evident in his long list of publications, spanning *The Urban Villagers* (Free Press, 1962) to *People, Plans and Policies* (Columbia University Press, 1991). His concept of *underclass* has been widely adopted. "The Uses of Poverty" addresses the much-debated issue of functionalism from a novel perspective.

Key Concept: the functions of poverty

*S*ome twenty years ago Robert K. Merton applied the notion of functional analysis to explain the continuing though maligned existence of the urban political machine: if it continued to exist, perhaps it fulfilled latent— unintended or unrecognized—positive functions. Clearly it did. Merton pointed out how the political machine provided central authority to get things done when a decentralized local government could not act, humanized the services of the impersonal bureaucracy for fearful citizens, offered concrete help (rather than abstract law or justice) to the poor, and otherwise performed services needed or demanded by many people but considered unconventional or even illegal by formal public agencies.

Today, poverty is more maligned than the political machine ever was; yet it, too, is a persistent social phenomenon. Consequently, there may be some merit in applying functional analysis to poverty, in asking whether it also has positive functions that explain its persistence.

Merton defined functions as "those observed consequences [of a phenomenon] which make for the adaptation or adjustment of a given [social] system." I shall use a slightly different definition; instead of identifying functions for an entire social system, I shall identify them for the interest groups, socioeconomic classes, and other population aggregates with shared values that "inhabit" a social system. I suspect that in a modern heterogeneous society, few phenomena are functional or dysfunctional for the society as a whole, and that most result in benefits to some groups and costs to others. Nor are any phenomena indispensable; in most instances, one can suggest what Merton calls "functional alternatives" or equivalents for them, i.e., other social patterns or policies that achieve the same positive functions but avoid the dysfunctions.

Associating poverty with positive functions seems at first glance to be unimaginable. Of course, the slumlord and the loan shark are commonly known to profit from the existence of poverty, but they are viewed as evil men, so their activities are classified among the dysfunctions of poverty. However, what is less often recognized, at least by the conventional wisdom, is that poverty also makes possible the existence or expansion of respectable professions and occupations, for example, penology, criminology, social work, and public health. More recently, the poor have provided jobs for professional and para-professional "poverty warriors," and for journalists and social scientists, this author included, who have supplied the information demanded by the revival of public interest in poverty.

Clearly, then, poverty and the poor may well satisfy a number of positive functions for many nonpoor groups in American society. I shall describe thirteen such functions—economic, social, and political—that seem to me most significant.

THE FUNCTIONS OF POVERTY

First, the existence of poverty ensures that society's "dirty work" will be done. Every society has such work: physically dirty or dangerous, temporary, dead-end and underpaid, undignified and menial jobs. Society can fill these jobs by paying higher wages than for "clean" work, or it can force people who have no other choice to do the dirty work—and at low wages. In America, poverty functions to provide a low-wage labor pool that is willing—or, rather, unable to be *unwilling*—to perform dirty work at low cost. Indeed, this function of the poor is so important that in some Southern states, welfare payments have been cut off during the summer months when the poor are needed to work in the fields. Moreover, much of the debate about the Negative Income Tax and the Family Assistance Plan has concerned their impact on the work incentive, by which is actually meant the incentive of the poor to do the needed dirty work if the wages therefrom are no larger than the income grant. Many economic activities that involve dirty work depend on the poor for their existence: restaurants, hospitals, parts of the garment industry, and "truck farming," among others, could not persist in their present form without the poor.

Second, because the poor are required to work at low wages, they subsidize a variety of economic activities that benefit the affluent. For example, domestics subsidize the upper middle and upper classes, making life easier for their employers and freeing affluent women for a variety of professional, cultural, civic, and partying activities. Similarly, because the poor pay a higher proportion of their income in property and sales taxes, among others, they subsidize many state and local governmental services that benefit more affluent groups. In addition, the poor support innovation in medical practice as patients in teaching and research hospitals and as guinea pigs in medical experiments.

Third, poverty creates jobs for a number of occupations and professions that serve or "service" the poor, or protect the rest of society from them. As already noted, penology would be minuscule without the poor, as would the police. Other activities and groups that flourish because of the existence of poverty are the numbers game, the sale of heroin and cheap wines and liquors, pentecostal ministers, faith healers, prostitutes, pawn shops, and the peacetime army, which recruits its enlisted men mainly from among the poor.

Fourth, the poor buy goods others do not want and thus prolong the economic usefulness of such goods—day-old bread, fruit and vegetables that would otherwise have to be thrown out, second-hand clothes, and deteriorating automobiles and buildings. They also provide incomes for doctors, lawyers, teachers, and others who are too old, poorly trained, or incompetent to attract more affluent clients.

In addition to economic functions, the poor perform a number of social functions.

Fifth, the poor can be identified and punished as alleged or real deviants in order to uphold the legitimacy of conventional norms. To justify the desirability of hard work, thrift, honesty, and monogamy, for example, the defenders of these norms must be able to find people who can be accused of being lazy, spendthrift, dishonest, and promiscuous. Although there is some evidence that the poor are about as moral and law-abiding as anyone else, they are more likely than middle-class transgressors to be caught and punished when they participate in deviant acts. Moreover, they lack the political and cultural power to correct the stereotypes that other people hold of them and thus continue to be thought of as lazy, spendthrift, etc., by those who need living proof that moral deviance does not pay.

Sixth, and conversely, the poor offer vicarious participation to the rest of the population in the uninhibited sexual, alcoholic, and narcotic behavior in which they are alleged to participate and which, being freed from the constraints of affluence, they are often thought to enjoy more than the middle classes. Thus many people, some social scientists included, believe that the poor not only are more given to uninhibited behavior (which may be true, although it is often motivated by despair more than by lack of inhibition) but derive more pleasure from it than affluent people (which research by Lee Rainwater, Walter Miller, and others shows to be patently untrue). However, whether the poor actually have more sex and enjoy it more is irrelevant; so long as middle-class people believe this to be true, they can participate in it vicariously when instances are reported in factual or fictional form.

Seventh, the poor also serve a direct cultural function when culture created by or for them is adopted by the more affluent. The rich often collect artifacts from extinct folk cultures of poor people; and almost all Americans listen to the blues, Negro spirituals, and country music, which originated among the Southern poor. Recently they have enjoyed the rock styles that were born, like the Beatles, in the slums; and in the last year, poetry written by ghetto children has become popular in literary circles. The poor also serve as culture heroes, particularly, of course, to the left; but the hobo, the cowboy, the hipster, and the mythical prostitute with a heart of gold have performed this function for a variety of groups.

Eighth, poverty helps to guarantee the status of those who are not poor. In every hierarchical society someone has to be at the bottom; but in American society, in which social mobility is an important goal for many and people need to know where they stand, the poor function as a reliable and relatively permanent measuring rod for status comparisons. This is particularly true for the working class, whose politics is influenced by the need to maintain status distinctions between themselves and the poor, much as the aristocracy must find ways of distinguishing itself from the *nouveaux riches.*

Ninth, the poor also aid the upward mobility of groups just above them in the class hierarchy. Thus a goodly number of Americans have entered the middle class through the profits earned from the provision of goods and services in the slums, including illegal or nonrespectable ones that upper-class and upper-middle-class businessmen shun because of their low prestige. As a result, members of almost every immigrant group have financed their upward mobility by providing slum housing, entertainment, gambling, narcotics, etc., to later arrivals—most recently to Blacks and Puerto Ricans.

Tenth, the poor help to keep the aristocracy busy, thus justifying its continued existence. "Society" uses the poor as clients of settlement houses and beneficiaries of charity affairs; indeed, the aristocracy must have the poor to demonstrate its superiority over other elites who devote themselves to earning money.

Eleventh, the poor, being powerless, can be made to absorb the costs of change and growth in American society. During the nineteenth century, they did the backbreaking work that built the cities; today, they are pushed out of their neighborhoods to make room for "progress." Urban renewal projects to hold middle-class taxpayers in the city and expressways to enable suburbanites to commute downtown have typically been located in poor neighborhoods, since no other group will allow itself to be displaced. For the same reason, universities, hospitals, and civic centers also expand into land occupied by the poor. The major costs of the industrialization of agriculture have been borne by the poor, who are pushed off the land without recompense; and they have paid a large share of the human cost of the growth of American power overseas, for they have provided many of the foot soldiers for Vietnam and other wars.

Twelfth, the poor facilitate and stabilize the American political process. Because they vote and participate in politics less than other groups, the political system is often free to ignore them. Moreover, since they can rarely support Republicans, they often provide the Democrats with a captive constituency that has no other place to go. As a result, the Democrats can count on their votes, and be more responsive to voters—for example, the white working class—who might otherwise switch to the Republicans.

Thirteen, the role of the poor in upholding conventional norms (see the *fifth* point, above) also has a significant political function. An economy based on the ideology of laissez faire requires a deprived population that is allegedly unwilling to work or that can be considered inferior because it must accept charity or welfare in order to survive. Not only does the alleged moral deviancy of the poor reduce the moral pressure on the present political economy to eliminate poverty but socialist alternatives can be made to look quite unattractive if those who will benefit most from them can be described as lazy, spendthrift, dishonest, and promiscuous.

Men and Jobs

Participant observation is a type of field study in which the researcher becomes a member of the group being studied. The results of this method can be at once simple and direct yet powerful and moving. Researcher Elliot Liebow's study of street corner men in a lower-class black neighborhood in Washington, D.C., conducted during the mid-1960s, is one such case. In the following selection from that study, which was published in 1967 and titled *Tally's Corner* (Little, Brown), Liebow explores the jobs available to this community and the street corner man's relationship to work. *Tally's Corner* became famous because of the detailed insights it provided on lower-class life.

Liebow (b. 1925) retired in 1984 as chief of the Center for Studies of Work and Mental Health at the National Institute of Mental Health and has since been active in social work. He is currently working on *Tell Them Who I Am: A Study of Homeless Women,* to be published by Free Press.

Key Concept: the man-job relationship is a tenuous one

A pickup truck drives slowly down the street. The truck stops as it comes abreast of a man sitting on a cast-iron porch, and the white driver calls out, asking if the man wants a day's work. The man shakes his head, and the truck moves on up the block, stopping again whenever idling men come within calling distance of the driver. At the Carry-out corner, five men debate the question briefly and shake their heads no to the truck. The truck turns the corner and repeats the same performance up the next street. In the distance, one can see one man, then another, climb into the back of the truck and sit down. In starts and stops, the truck finally disappears.

What is it we have witnessed here? A labor scavenger rebuffed by his would-be prey? Lazy, irresponsible men turning down an honest day's pay for an honest day's work? Or a more complex phenomenon, marking the intersection of economic forces, social values, and individual states of mind and body?

Let us look again at the driver of the truck. He has been able to recruit only two or three men from each 20 or 50 he contacts. To him, it is clear that the others simply do not choose to work. Singly or in groups, belly-empty or belly-full, sullen or gregarious, drunk or sober, they confirm what he has read, heard, and knows from his own experience: These men wouldn't take a job if it were handed to them on a platter.

Quite apart from the question of whether or not this is true of some of the men he sees on the street, it is clearly not true of all of them. If it were, he would not have come here in the first place; or, having come, he would have left with an empty truck. It is not even true of most of them, for most of the men he sees on the street this weekday morning do, in fact, have jobs. But since, at the moment, they are neither working nor sleeping, and since they hate the depressing room or apartment they live in, or because there is nothing to do there, or because they want to get away from their wives or anyone else living there, they are out on the street, indistinguishable from those who do not have jobs or do not want them. Some, like Boley, a member of a trash-collection crew in a suburban housing development, work Saturdays and are off on this weekday. Some, like Sweets, work nights cleaning up middle-class trash, dirt, dishes, and garbage, and mopping the floors of the office buildings, hotels, restaurants, toilets, and other public places dirtied during the day. Some men work for retail businesses, such as liquor stores, that do not begin the day until ten o'clock. Some laborers, like Tally, have already come back from the job, because the ground was too wet for pick and shovel, or because the weather was too cold for pouring concrete. Other employed men stayed off the job today for personal reasons: Clarence to go to a funeral at eleven this morning, and Sea Cat to answer a subpoena as a witness in a criminal proceeding.

Also on the street, unwitting contributors to the impression taken away by the truck driver, are the halt and the lame. The man on the cast-iron steps strokes one gnarled arthritic hand with the other and says he doesn't know whether or not he'll live long enough to be eligible for Social Security. He pauses, then adds matter-of-factly, "Most times, I don't care whether I do or don't." Stoopy's left leg was polio-withered in childhood. Raymond, who looks as if he could tear out a fire hydrant, coughs up blood if he bends or moves suddenly. The quiet man who hangs out in front of the Saratoga apartments has a steel hook strapped onto his left elbow. And, had the man in the truck been able to look into the wine-clouded eyes of the man in the green cap, he would have realized that the man did not even understand he was being offered a day's work.

Others, having had jobs and been laid off, are drawing unemployment compensation (up to $44 per week) and have nothing to gain by accepting work that pays little more than this and frequently less.

Still others, like Bumdoodle the numbers man, are working hard at illegal ways of making money—hustlers who are on the street to turn a dollar any way they can: buying and selling sex, liquor, narcotics, stolen goods, or anything else that turns up.

Only a handful remains unaccounted for. There is Tonk, who cannot bring himself to take a job away from the corner, because, according to the other men, he suspects his wife will be unfaithful if given the opportunity. There is Stanton, who has not reported to work for four days now, not since Bernice disappeared. He bought a brand-new knife against her return. She had done this twice before, he said, but not for so long and not without warning, and he had forgiven her. But this time, "I ain't got it in me to forgive her again." His rage and shame are there for all to see, as he paces the Carry-out and the corner, day and night, hoping to catch a glimpse of her.

And, finally, there are those like Arthur, able-bodied men who have no visible means of support, legal or illegal, who neither have jobs nor want them. The truck driver, among others, believes the Arthurs to be representative of all the men he sees idling on the street during his working hours. They are not, but they cannot be dismissed simply because they are a small minority. It is not enough to explain them away as being lazy or irresponsible, or both, because an able-bodied man with responsibilities who refuses work is, by the truck driver's definition, lazy and irresponsible. Such an answer begs the question. It is descriptive of the facts; it does not explain them.

Moreover, despite their small numbers, the don't-work-and-don't-want-to-work minority [are] especially significant, because they represent the strongest and clearest expression of those values and attitudes associated with making a living that, to varying degrees, are found throughout the street-corner world. These men differ from the others in degree rather than in kind, the principal difference being that they are carrying out the implications of their values and experiences to their logical, inevitable conclusions. In this sense, the others have yet to come to terms with themselves and the world they live in.

Putting aside, for the moment, what the men say and feel, and looking at what they actually do and the choices they make, getting a job, keeping a job, and doing well at it is clearly of low priority. Arthur will not take a job at all. Leroy is supposed to be on his job at 4:00 P.M.; but it is already 4:10, and he still cannot bring himself to leave the free games he has accumulated on the pinball machine in the Carry-out. Tonk started a construction job on Wednesday, worked Thursday and Friday, then didn't go back again. On the same kind of job, Sea Cat quit in the second week. Sweets had been working three months as a busboy in a restaurant, then quit without notice, not sure himself why he did so. A real-estate agent, saying he was more interested in getting the job done than in the cost, asked Richard to give him an estimate on repairing and painting the inside of a house, but Richard, after looking over the job, somehow never got around to submitting an estimate. During one period, Tonk would not leave the corner to take a job because his wife might prove unfaithful; Stanton would not take a job because his woman had been unfaithful.

Thus, the man–job relationship is a tenuous one. At any given moment, a job may occupy a relatively low position on the street-corner scale of real values. Getting a job may be subordinated to relations with women or to other nonjob considerations; the commitment to a job one already has is frequently shallow and tentative.

The reasons are many. Some are objective and reside principally in the job; some are subjective and reside principally in the man. The line between them, however, is not a clear one. Behind the man's refusal to take a job or his decision to quit one is not a simple impulse or value choice but a complex combination of assessments of objective reality, on the one hand, and values, attitudes, and beliefs drawn from different levels of his experience on the other.

Objective economic considerations are frequently a controlling factor in a man's refusal to take a job. How much the job pays is a crucial question but seldom asked. He knows how much it pays. Working as a stock clerk, a delivery boy, or even behind the counter of liquor stores, drug stores, and other retail businesses pays one dollar an hour. So, too, do most busboy, car-wash, janitorial, and other jobs available to him. Some jobs, such as dishwasher, may dip as low as 80 cents an hour, and others, such as elevator operator or work in a junk yard, may offer $1.15 or $1.25. Take-home pay for jobs such as these ranges from $35 to $50 a week, but a take-home pay of over $45 for a five-day week is the exception rather than the rule.

One of the principal advantages of these kinds of jobs is that they offer fairly regular work. Most of them involve essential services and are therefore somewhat less responsive to business conditions than are some higher-paying, less menial jobs. Most of them are also inside jobs not dependent on the weather, as are construction jobs and other higher-paying outside work.

Another seemingly important advantage of working in hotels, restaurants, office and apartment buildings, and retail establishments is that they frequently offer an opportunity for stealing on the job. But stealing can be a two-edged-sword. Apart from increasing the cost of the goods or services to the general public, a less obvious result is that the practice usually acts as a depressant on the employee's own wage level. Owners of small retail establishments and other employers frequently anticipate employee stealing and adjust the wage rate accordingly. Tonk's employer explained why he was paying Tonk $35 for a 55–60 hour workweek. These men will all steal, he said. Although he keeps close watch on Tonk, he estimates that Tonk steals from $35 to $40 a week. What he steals, when added to his regular earnings, brings his take-home pay to $70 or $75 per week. The employer said he did not mind this, because Tonk is worth that much to the business. But, if he were to pay Tonk outright the full value of his labor, Tonk would still be stealing $35–$40 per week, and this, he said, the business simply would not support.

This wage arrangement with stealing built-in, was satisfactory to both parties, with each one independently expressing his satisfaction. Such a wage–theft system, however, is not as balanced and equitable as it appears. Since the wage level rests on the premise that the employee will steal the unpaid value of his labor, the man who does not steal on the job is penalized. And, furthermore, even if he does not steal, no one would believe him; the employer and others believe he steals because the system presumes it.

Nor is the man who steals, as he is expected to, as well off as he believes himself to be. The employer may occasionally close his eyes to the worker's stealing but not often and not for long. He is, after all, a businessman and cannot always find it within himself to let a man steal from him, even if the man is stealing his own wages. Moreover, it is only by keeping close watch on the worker that the employer can control how much is stolen and thereby protect himself against the employee's stealing more than he is worth. From this viewpoint, then, the employer is not in wage–theft collusion with the employee. In the case of Tonk, for instance, the employer was not actively abetting the theft. His estimate of how much Tonk was stealing was based on what he thought Tonk was able to steal despite his own best efforts to prevent him from stealing anything at all. Were he to have caught Tonk in the act of stealing, he would, of course, have fired him from the job and perhaps called the police as well. Thus, in an actual, if not in a legal, sense, all the elements of entrapment are present. The employer knowingly provides the conditions that entice (force) the employee to steal the unpaid value of his labor, but, at the same time, he punishes him for theft if he catches him doing so.

Other consequences of the wage–theft system are even more damaging to the employee. Let us, for argument's sake, say that Tonk is in no danger of entrapment; that his employer is willing to wink at the stealing, and that Tonk, for his part, is perfectly willing to earn a little, steal a little. Let us say, too, that he is paid $35 a week and allowed to steal $35. His money income—as measured by the goods and services he can purchase with it—is, of course, $70. But not all of his income is available to him for all purposes. He cannot draw on what he steals to build his self-respect or to measure his self-worth. For this, he can draw only on his earnings—the amount given him publicly and voluntarily in exchange for his labor. His "respect" and "self-worth" income remains at $35— only half [of] that of the man who also receives $70 but all of it in the form of wages. His earnings publicly measure the worth of his labor to his employer, and they are important to others and to himself in taking the measure of his worth as a man.

With or without stealing, and quite apart from any interior processes going on in the man who refuses such a job or quits it casually and without apparent reason, the objective fact is that menial jobs in retailing or in the service trades simply do not pay enough to support a man and his family. This is not to say that the worker is underpaid; this may or may not be true. Whether he is or not, the plain fact is that, in such a job, he cannot make a living. Nor can he take much comfort in the fact that these jobs tend to offer more regular, steadier work. If he cannot live on the $45 or $50 he makes in one week, the longer he works, the longer he cannot live on what he makes.

Construction work, even for unskilled laborers, usually pays better, with the hourly rate ranging from $1.50 to $2.60 an hour. Importantly, too, good references, a good driving record, a tenth-grade (or any high school) education, previous experience, the ability to "bring police clearance with you" are not normally required of laborers as they frequently are for some of the jobs in retailing or in the service trades.

Construction work, however, has its own objective disadvantages. It is, first of all, seasonal work for the great bulk of the laborers, beginning early in the spring and tapering off as winter weather sets in. And, even during the season, the work is frequently irregular. Early or late in the season, snow or temperatures too low for concrete frequently sends the laborers back home, and, during late spring or summer, a heavy rain on Tuesday or Wednesday, leaving a lot of water and mud behind it, can mean a two- or three-day workweek for the pick-and-shovel men and other unskilled laborers.

The elements are not the only hazard. As the project moves from one construction stage to another, laborers—usually without warning—are laid off, sometimes permanently or sometimes for weeks at a time. The more fortunate or the better workers are told periodically to "take a walk for two, three days."

Both getting the construction job and getting to it are also relatively more difficult than is the case for the menial jobs in retailing and the service trades. Job competition is always fierce. In the city, the large construction projects are unionized. One has to have ready cash to get into the union to become eligible to work on these projects, and being eligible, one has to find an opening. Unless one "knows somebody"—say, a foreman or a laborer who knows the day before that they are going to take on new men in the morning—this can be a difficult and disheartening search.

Many of the nonunion jobs are in suburban Maryland or Virginia. The newspaper ads say "Report ready to work to the trailer at the intersection of Rte. 11 and Old Bridge Rd., Bunston, Virginia (or Maryland)," but this location may be 10, 15, or even 25 miles from the Carry-out. Public transportation would require two or more hours to get there, if it services the area at all. Without access to a car or to a car-pool arrangement, it is not worthwhile reading the ad. So the men do not. Jobs such as these are usually filled by word-of-mouth information, beginning with someone who knows someone or who is himself working there and looking for a paying rider. Furthermore, nonunion jobs in outlying areas tend to be smaller projects of relatively short duration and to pay somewhat less than scale.

Still another objective factor is the work itself. For some men, whether the job be digging, mixing mortar, pushing a wheelbarrow, unloading materials, carrying and placing steel rods for reinforcing concrete, or building or laying concrete forms, the work is simply too hard. Men such as Tally and Wee Tom can make such work look like child's play; some of the older work-hardened men, such as Budder and Stanton, can do it, too, though not without showing unmistakable signs of strain and weariness at the end of the workday. But those who lack the robustness of a Tally or the time-inured immunity of a Budder must either forego jobs such as these or pay a heavy toll to keep them. For Leroy, in his early twenties, almost six feet tall but weighing under 140 pounds, it would be as difficult to push a loaded wheelbarrow, or to unload and stack 96-pound bags of cement all day long, as it would be for Stoopy with his withered leg. . . .

Men who have been running an elevator, washing dishes, or "pulling trash" cannot easily move into laboring jobs. They lack the basic skills for "unskilled" construction labor, familiarity with tools and materials, and tricks of the trade without which hard jobs are made harder. Previously unused or untrained muscles rebel in pain against the new and insistent demands made upon them, seriously compromising the man's performance and testing his willingness to see the job through.

A healthy, sturdy, active man of good intelligence requires from two to four weeks to break in on a construction job. Even if he is willing somehow to bull his way through the first few weeks, it frequently happens that his foreman or the craftsman he services with materials and general assistance is not willing to wait that long for him to get into condition or to learn at a glance the difference in size between a rough 2" × 8" and a finished 2" × 10". The foreman and the craftsman are themselves "under the gun" and cannot "carry" the man when other men, who are already used to the work and who know the tools and materials, are lined up to take the job.

Sea Cat was "healthy, sturdy, active, and of good intelligence." When a judge gave him six weeks in which to pay his wife $200 in back child-support payments, he left his grocery-store job in order to take a higher-paying job as a laborer, arranged for him by a foreman friend. During the first week, the weather was bad, and he worked only Wednesday and Friday, cursing the elements all the while for cheating him out of the money he could have made. The second week, the weather was fair, but he quit at the end of the fourth day, saying frankly that the work was too hard for him. He went back to his job at the grocery store and took a second job working nights as a dishwasher in a restaurant, earning little, if any, more at the two jobs than he would have earned as a laborer and keeping at both of them until he had paid off his debts.

Tonk did not last as long as Sea Cat. No one made any predictions when he got a job in a parking lot; but, when the men on the corner learned he was to start on a road construction job, estimates of how long he would last ranged from one to three weeks. Wednesday was his first day. He spent that evening and night at home. He did the same on Thursday. He worked Friday and spent Friday evening and part of Saturday draped over the mailbox on the corner. Sunday afternoon, Tonk decided he was not going to report on the job the next morning. He explained that, after working three days, he knew enough about the job to know that it was too hard for him. He knew he wouldn't be able to keep up, and he'd just as soon quit now as get fired later.

Logan was a tall, 200-pound man in his late twenties. His back used to hurt him only on the job, he said, but now he can't straighten up for increasingly longer periods of time. He said he had traced this to the awkward walk he was forced to adopt by the loaded wheelbarrows, which pull him down into a half-stoop. He's going to quit, he said, as soon as he can find another job. If he can't find one real soon, he guesses he'll quit anyway. It's not worth it, having to walk bent over and leaning to one side. . . .

In summary of objective job considerations, then, the most important fact is that a man who is able and willing to work cannot earn enough money to support himself, his wife, and one or more children. A man's chances for working regularly are good only if he is willing to work for less than he can live on, and sometimes not even then. On some jobs, the wage rate is deceptively higher than on others; but the higher the wage rate, the more difficult it is to get the job, and the less the job security. Higher-paying construction work tends to be seasonal, and during the season, the amount of work available is highly sensitive to business and weather conditions and to the changing requirements of individual projects. Moreover, high-paying construction jobs are frequently beyond the physical capacity of some of the men, and some of the low-paying jobs are scaled down even lower in accordance with the self-fulfilling assumption that the man will steal part of his wages on the job.

CHAPTER 10 Racial and Sexual Inequality

10.1 WILLIAM JULIUS WILSON

The Black Community in the 1980s: Questions of Race, Class, and Public Policy

The position of African Americans in American society has changed significantly in some respects since the civil rights movement of the 1960s. African
Americans have more years of schooling, hold more political offices, are found
in a greater variety of jobs, and live in more varied neighborhoods as compared
to a quarter-century ago before the passage of the Civil Rights Act. That piece of
federal legislation outlawed discrimination in public accommodations or employment based on race, religion, national origin, or sex. But despite these
improvements, inequalities between blacks and whites persist. What currently
accounts for the disparities between blacks and whites? What exactly are the
problems facing the black community? Are the problems matters of race or
class? What is the future of race relations in the United States? Finally, how
should those who are committed to social reform proceed? Black sociologist
William Julius Wilson addresses these questions and more in the following
selection. Wilson (b. 1935) is the Lucy Flower Distinguished Service Professor of
Sociology and Public Policy and the director of the Center for the Study of
Urban Inequality at the University of Chicago. His work is known for being
challenging and provocative.

Key Concept: the underclass

Civil rights supporters are puzzled by recent developments in the black community. Despite the passage of antidiscrimination legislation and the creation of affirmative action programs, they sense that conditions are getting worse not better for the vast majority of black Americans. This perception emerges because of the constant flow of pessimistic reports concerning the sharp rise in black unemployment, the substantial decline of Blacks in the labor force, the steady drop in the black-white family income ratio, the consistent increase in the percentage of Blacks on the welfare roles, the remarkable growth of single-parent households, and the persistent problems of black crime and black victims of crime. The perception is reinforced by the almost uniform cry among black leaders that not only are conditions deteriorating, but white Americans have abandoned the cause of Blacks as well. In the face of these developments, there are noticeable signs that demoralization has set in among many Blacks who have come to believe that "nothing really works" and among many Whites who are otherwise committed to social reform.

However, a careful review of the issues makes it immediately clear that significant variations in the black experience tend not to be noted or appreciated and that the differing effect of policy programs on different segments of the black population are usually not specified. In this article, these issues are examined within the context of a broader framework of macroeconomic and political change. In the process I hope to focus on a series of mounting problems that are not receiving serious attention, but that have profound implications for the structure of the black community and for the future of race relations in America.

In the mid-1960s, a series of insightful articles were written by black and white intellectuals that raised questions about the direction and goals of the black protest movement. Basically, the authors of these articles made it clear that from 1955 to 1965, the chief objectives of the Civil Rights movement were to integrate public accommodations and to eliminate black disfranchisement. These were matters of constitutional rights and basic human dignity, matters that affected Blacks and other minorities exclusively and therefore could be defined and addressed simply as problems of civil rights. However, these authors noted that despite the spectacular victories in the area of civil rights, by the latter half of the 1960s a more complex and fundamental set of problems had yet to be attacked—problems of jobs, education, and housing that affected not only Blacks, but other minorities and Whites as well.

CHANGING DEFINITIONS OF THE PROBLEM

A consistent theme running throughout these articles is that in the period from 1955 to 1965, all Blacks, regardless of their station in life, were concerned about the banning of discrimination in public accommodations and in voting. As [civil rights leader] Bayard Rustin observed, "Ralph Bunch was as likely to be refused service in a restaurant or a hotel as any illiterate sharecropper. This common bond prevented the latent class differences and resentments from being openly expressed." However, it did not take long to realize that the group that had profited the most from the civil rights legislation up to 1965 were middle-class Blacks—Blacks who had competitive resources such as steady incomes, education, and special talents. As Kenneth Clark argued in 1967, "The masses of Negroes are now starkly aware of the fact that recent civil rights victories benefited a very small percentage of middle-class Negroes while their predicament remained the same or worsened."

What these observers were telling us in the mid-1960s is that a close examination of ghetto black discontent, most dramatically revealed in the riots of that period, revealed issues that transcended the creation and implementation of civil rights laws. "To the segregation by race," Bayard Rustin observed in 1967, "was now added segregation by class, and all the problems created by segregation and poverty—inadequate schooling, substandard and overcrowded housing, lack of access to jobs and job training, narcotics and crime—were greatly aggravated." In short, for ghetto Blacks the issue of human rights is far more important than the issue of civil rights. The late Martin Luther King, Jr., recognized this point in 1968 when shortly before his death he asked, "What good is it to be allowed to eat in a restaurant if you can't afford a hamburger?" It would not be unfair to suggest that he was probably influenced by the thoughts of Bayard Rustin who, four years earlier in his now classic article "From Protest to Politics," phrased the matter in much the same way: "What is the value of winning access to public accommodations for those who lack money to use them?"

Thus the removal of artificial racial barriers would not enable poor Blacks to compete equally with other groups in society for valued resources because of an accumulation of disadvantages flowing from previous periods of prejudice and discrimination, disadvantages that have been passed on from generation to generation. Basic structural changes in our modern industrial economy have compounded the problems of poor Blacks because education and training have become more important for entry into the more desirable and higher-paying jobs and because the increased reliance on labor-saving devices has contributed to a surplus of untrained black workers. In short, once the movement faced these more fundamental issues, argued Rustin in 1964, "it was compelled to expand its version beyond race relations to economic relations, including the role of education in society."

During the same period in which problems of structural inequality were being raised, scholars such as Kenneth Clark and Lee Rainwater were also raising important issues about the experiences of inequality. Both scholars sensitively examined the cumulative effects of chronic subordination and racial isolation on life and behavior in the urban ghettos. . . .

Indeed, what was both unique and important about Clark and Rainwater's studies was that their discussions of the experiences of inequality were inextricably tied to their discussions of the structure of inequality. Thus in reading their works one received a clear understanding of how the economic and social situations into which so many poor Blacks are born produce modes of adaptation and the creation of subcultural patterns that take the form of a "self perpetuating pathology." In other words, and in sharp contrast to approaches that simply "blame the victim" or which use a "culture of poverty" thesis to explain group disadvantages, the works of Clark and Rainwater not only presented a sensitive portrayal of the destructive features of ghetto life, they also provided a comprehensive analysis of the deleterious structural conditions that produce these features. . . .

BLACK COMMUNITY CHANGES SINCE 1960

Although the black population is often regarded as a monolithic socioeconomic group by social scientists and social commentators alike, since the end of World War II, and especially since 1960, Blacks have become increasingly differentiated along occupational lines. The proportion of employed black workers from 1960 to 1978 increased 10.7 percent and 9.6 percent in professional and technical positions and in clerical jobs, respectively, and decreased 13.4 percent and 5.0 percent in service workers and laborer jobs and in farm worker jobs, respectively.

However, these occupational changes only partly demonstrate the nature of internal change within the black population. The major problem is that occupational data on employed workers, which reveal substantial progress in the movement of black workers from lower-paying to higher-paying positions, fail to capture the relative decline in the economic position of poor Blacks during the last decade—a growing number of whom are either unemployed, underemployed, or outside the labor force altogether. Thus in order to more completely describe the range of experiences in the black community, I should like to conceptualize a black class structure that includes a middle class represented by white-collar workers and skilled blue-collar workers, a working class represented by semiskilled operatives, and a lower class represented by unskilled laborers and service workers. Within the lower class is an underclass population, a heterogeneous grouping at the very bottom of the economic class hierarchy. This underclass population includes those lower-class workers whose income falls below the poverty level, the long-term unemployed, discouraged workers who have dropped out of the labor market, and the more or less permanent welfare recipients.

Although the underclass constitutes the more impoverished segment of the lower class, I shall attempt to show that even full-time "lower-class" workers increasingly face structural barriers in advanced industrial society that trap them in menial, dead-end jobs. Nonetheless, the concept of "underclass" depicts a reality that is not fully captured in using the more general designation of "lower class." For example, unlike other families in the black community, the head of the household in underclass families is almost invariably a woman. The distinctive characteristics of the underclass are also reflected in the large number of unattached adult males who have no fixed address, who live mainly on the streets, and who roam from one place of shelter to another.

*William Julius
Wilson*

PROBLEMS OF EMPLOYMENT

The question of what happens to individuals who are trapped in depressed areas and are therefore denied access to the normal channels of economic opportunity and mobility takes on even greater meaning for the black poor today than in previous years. Poor black Americans, heavily concentrated in inner cities, have experienced a worsening of their economic position on the basis of nearly all the major labor-market indicators. The unemployment rates for both black men and black women from 1955 to 1978 have increased more rapidly at all age levels than those of comparable Whites, with black teenage unemployment showing the sharpest increase—from 13.4 percent in 1955 to 34.4 percent in 1978 for men, and from 19.2 percent in 1955 to 38.4 percent in 1978 for women. The unemployment rates of Blacks age 20 to 24 also reached very high proportions in 1978—20 percent for men and 21.3 percent for women—extending a trend of increasing joblessness that began in the mid-1960s. The significant rise in unemployment for younger Blacks stands in sharp contrast to the slight change in the rate of unemployment for Blacks 25 years old and over. Still, even the older Blacks had unemployment rates above those of their white counterparts. . . .

The high incidence of joblessness among Blacks as a group is partly related to the fact that they constitute a disproportionate percentage of workers employed in the lowest-paying jobs, such as service work and unskilled labor—jobs that have a high turnover and are susceptible to unemployment. Nonetheless, this fact alone cannot account for the rapid deterioration of the position of poor Blacks in the labor market; nor can their employment problems be adequately explained in terms of racial discrimination. These issues will be further clarified by considering the effect of basic shifts in the economy on the life chances of lower-class Blacks. But first let me pay special attention to changes that are occurring in poor black families, changes that have accompanied their worsening economic plight and that could have long-term effects on their future employment prospects.

POOR BLACK FAMILY

In 1969, black median family income was 61 percent that of Whites; by 1976 it had dropped to 59 percent; by 1977 to 57 percent; and by 1978, it had risen slightly to 59 percent, but was still below the ratio of 1969. However, it should be pointed out that the ratio of black to white median family income in male-headed homes was 72 percent in 1969, rose to 80 percent in 1976, declined to 75 percent in 1977, then climbed back up to 80 percent in 1978.

What should be underlined, therefore, is that the overall relative decline in black family income since 1969 has been accompanied by the sharp increase in female-headed homes during this period—from 28 percent in 1969, to 37 percent in 1976, to 39 percent in 1977, and finally to a staggering 40 percent in 1978. And when we take into account the fact that the median income of black male-headed families ($15,678) in 1978 was $9690 more than the median income of black female-headed families, it becomes clear why the recorded black-to-white family income ratio has declined in recent years. By 1978, the proportion of all poor black families headed by women had reached 74 percent.

The class-related features of black female-headed households cannot be overemphasized. I have already stated that what is distinctive about underclass black families is that the head of the household is almost invariably a woman. The powerful connection between class background and the structure of the black family is further revealed in these data. . . . Whereas 80.3 percent of all black families with incomes of less than $4000 and $6999 were headed by women in 1978, only 15.3 percent of those with incomes between $16,000 and $24,999 and 7.7 percent with incomes of $25,000 and more were headed by women. In metropolitan areas the differences in the proportion of black families with female heads was even greater, with extremes of 85.1 percent for those whose incomes were below $4000 and 7.6 percent for those whose incomes were $25,000 and more. Although . . . the factor of race is clearly associated with the difference in the makeup of black and white families, the relationship between type of family and level of income is much stronger among Blacks than among Whites.

Reflecting the rise in black female-headed families, the proportion of black children living with both parents has decreased sharply from 64 percent in 1970, to 56 percent in 1974, and finally, to 48.5 percent in 1978. An extremely high percentage of the black children who do not live with both parents are impoverished. . . .

The findings in this section and the ones presented in the previous sections have profound implications for both the future of race relations in this country and for the internal structure of the black community. They also raise serious questions about existing policy programs that have been designed to address matters of racial inequality.

In the next section, I should like to take a critical look at these programs and suggest why they have not sufficiently addressed the problems and experiences of underclass Blacks. In the process I hope to show that the problems of poor Blacks are closely related to changes in the modern American economy.

RACE, CLASS AND PUBLIC POLICY

Since World War II, political changes in the government and structural changes in the economy have both contributed to a gradual and continuous process of deracialization in the economic sector—in other words, a process in which racial distinctions gradually lose their importance in determining individual mobility in the United States. The expansion of the economy, on the one hand, facilitated the movement of Blacks from southern rural areas to the industrial centers of the nation and created job opportunities leading to greater occupational differentiation within the black community. On the other hand, the state, instead of reinforcing the racial barriers that were created during previous periods, has, in recent years, promoted racial equality. Partly in response to the pressure of increased black political resources—resources that were a result of the growing concentration of Blacks in large industrial cities—and partly in response to the pressures of black protest movements—pressures which in many ways were a manifestation of greater black political strength—the state has consistently intervened in behalf of Blacks with the enactment and enforcement of antidiscrimination legislation. In short, a combination of economic and political changes created greater economic mobility opportunities for a substantial segment of the black population.

The curious paradox, however, is that whereas economic growth since World War II enabled many Blacks to experience occupational mobility, recent structural shifts in the economy have diminished mobility opportunities for others. And whereas antidiscrimination legislation has removed many racial barriers, not all Blacks are in a position to benefit from them. Indeed the position of the black underclass has actually deteriorated during the very period in which the most sweeping antidiscrimination legislation and programs have been enacted and implemented. The net effect is a growing bifurcation between the "haves" and "have nots" in the black community.

Thus while poor Blacks are recording rising levels of unemployment, declining labor-force participation rates, sharp drops in employment—population ratios, and decreasing proportions with work experience, the number of Blacks in professional and managerial positions climbed to more than 1.8 million by the second quarter of 1980, over two and a half times the number in 1965 (728,000). Moreover, whereas prior to the late 1960s, the ratio of black income to white income actually decreased as educational attainment increased, today the reverse seems to be the case, especially for younger black males. In 1978, 25- to 29-year-old black males who graduated from high school earned on the average only 79 percent as much as their white counterparts—$9995 for Blacks and $12,678 for Whites—whereas those who graduated from college actually earned on the average more than comparable Whites—$15,217 for Blacks and $14,013 for Whites.

The failure to recognize these profound differences in the black experience, differences based on economic class position, often leads to policies that do not address the specific needs and concerns of those Blacks who are the most disadvantaged. For example, it has been argued in many quarters, and with rising insistence, that there should be a more vigorous enforcement of affirmative action programs to reverse the decline in the black-white family income ratio. However, as I have attempted to show, the recent relative decline in black family income is largely due to the growth of female-headed families, an overwhelming percentage of whom are impoverished. And, as I shall argue in more detail, affirmative action programs, which have helped to enhance the economic position of the more trained and educated Blacks, are not really designed to address the unique economic problem of poor Blacks. Indeed, even if all racial discrimination in labor-market practices were eliminated, unless there were a serious attempt to address the problems of structural barriers to decent jobs, the economic position of poor Blacks would not improve significantly. . . .

RACE, CLASS AND THE CITIES

The extent to which white-collar jobs are replacing blue-collar positions in central cities is illustrated in the data on the number of jobs in five selected occupational categories in 18 older northern cities. Whereas the professional, technical, and clerical employment increased by 291,055 positions from 1960 to 1970, blue-collar employment—craftsmen, operatives, and laborers—decreased by 749,774 positions. And the overwhelming majority of the jobs lost were the higher-paying blue-collar positions: craftsmen and operatives. There is also some indication that the blue-collar jobs decline in larger northern cities has accelerated. During the decade of the 1970s, Chicago lost more than 200,000 jobs, mostly in manufacturing, New York City lost 600,000 jobs during the 1970s despite the fact that the number of white-collar, professional, managerial and clerical jobs increased in Manhattan.

In considering these job shifts, it should be emphasized that roughly 60 percent of the unemployed Blacks in the United States reside in the central city, mostly within the cities' low-income areas. Conversely, there is much more dispersion among unemployed Whites, as approximately 40 percent live in suburban areas and an additional 30 percent reside in nonmetropolitan areas. Furthermore, the proportion of black men employed as laborers and service workers—occupational categories with a higher than average jobless ratio—is twice that of white workers employed in these jobs. In the final analysis, the lack of economic opportunity for lower-class Blacks means that they are forced to remain in economically depressed ghettos and their children are forced to attend inferior ghetto schools. This gives rise to a vicious circle as ghetto isolation and inferior opportunities in education reinforce their disadvantaged position in the labor market and contribute to the growing gap in the economic resources of the haves and have nots in the black community.

Given these basic economic realities, it is instructive to examine race-oriented policies and programs such as affirmative action. Of all the programs created to improve the economic position of Blacks, none has received as much attention as affirmative action. However, whereas affirmative action programs have contributed to the recent occupational mobility of trained and educated Blacks, they are not designed to break down color-blind barriers created by the shift from goods-producing to service-producing industries, the relocation of industries, the segmentation of the labor market, and the growth of technology and automation.

Furthermore, affirmative action programs are irrelevant to the problem of labor surplus in low-wage industries. Many of the dead-end and low-paying jobs in these industries do not generate racial competition between black and white workers because they are not in high demand and are now identified as "minority jobs." Because fewer black and white workers are willing to accept an economic arrangement that consigns them to dead-end, menial, and poorly paid jobs, low-wage service and manufacturing industries have increasingly used immigrant labor, including illegal aliens or undocumented workers from Mexico and other Latin American countries, to control labor problems and keep wages depressed.

If race-oriented policies are not designed to deal with the deteriorating economic condition of poor Blacks, then more attention has to focus on programs of economic reform. everything from growing unemployment to the growth of female-headed families can be traced to economic dislocation. As Lee Rainwater observed 14 years ago, unemployed men are more likely to abandon their families than are employed men. Indeed, the female-headed pattern in the ghetto symbolizes the poverty-stricken nature of the underclass. To repeat, the main problem is that the lower-class black family is in the throes of an economic depression and the rising percentage of female-headed families is one of the symptoms, not the cause, of that problem.

However, if a program of economic reform is to be meaningful, it has to be directed at improving the job prospects of both poor black men and poor black women. And considering the fact that most poor black families are now headed by women, it would even be advisable to include the creation of publicly financed daycare centers in this reform program so that women can avail themselves of job opportunities if and when they develop.

In suggesting the need for economic reform, I am fully aware that it will be more successful if it can generate conditions that guarantee sustained full employment. I am also aware of the difficulty entailed in trying to create such conditions. Unlike several other capitalist democracies, the United States does not have a system of central government planning to further economic growth, establish long-range industrial policy, and outline labor-market projections and to design land use, regional distribution of resources, and educational development. Accordingly, the government response to economic fluctuations is much more likely to be determined by short term political considerations, to reflect the interests of the more powerful and organized groups in society, and therefore to underrepresent the interests of the poor and the unemployed.

Moreover, even many of these committed to social reform have yet to recognize that current discrimination is not as central to the plight of the black poor as is the problem of economic dislocation. We only need to consider the fact that in the latter half of the 1970s, articulate black and white supporters of equal rights expressed far more concern and devoted far more attention to the *Bakke* case [in which a white applicant to a medical school charged that he was excluded in favor of a less qualified black student, in accordance with that school's affirmative action policy] than to the Humphrey Hawkins full-employment bill. If the nation is to avert serious domestic problems in the future, a shift in emphasis will soon have to occur. And a first step in that direction is to recognize what the problem is and where it is concentrated.

Socioeconomic Status in the Female World

Jessie Bernard (b. 1903) is a leading feminist sociologist, researcher, and writer. Her research interests lie in marriage, family, community, women, and sex, and her publications include *Women, Wives, Mothers* (Aldine de Gruyter, 1975) and *The Future of Marriage* (Yale University Press, 1982). In the following selection, she discusses what she calls "the female world" and how it compares and interacts with the male world. She explains that the three major dimensions for ranking people in American society and describing social inequalities—income, education, and occupational status—do not describe the female world very well, because many women have no income and only half have occupational titles. Only education is a dimension applicable to all women.

In addition to comparing the educational opportunities of men and women, Bernard contrasts the socioeconomic statuses and occupational distributions of women in the labor force with those of men. Her findings suggest that women, whether working in traditionally "female" jobs or working side by side with men, remain socially and psychologically separated from men. However, Bernard argues that greater understanding of the female world would positively affect women's status in the work force.

Key Concept: the female world

INTRODUCTION

Bernard Barber specifies several "dimensions of social stratification" such as education and knowledge, income or wealth, occupational prestige, religious and ritual purity, family and ethnicity, and power (1968, 292). The first three of these correspond to what Lipset calls the objective aspect of stratification (1968, 310) because they are amenable to measurement or scaling, and they are the ones usually used for operationalizing SES [socioeconomic status].

The unsuitability of SES as a variable for understanding the female world becomes evident when one considers that many women have no monetary income at all and that only about half of them have occupations that are recognized in the research literature. Most women, whatever other occupation they engage in, are housewives. Only the education dimension of SES includes all women.

187

Jessie Bernard

The use of SES as a research variable is practically standard, but a host of questions remain. Although the three "dimensions" are related to one another, they do not necessarily coincide, and a large apparatus of conceptual finagling is required to take care of the "status inconsistency" that results when a person is high on one dimension, low on another. High, for example, in education but low in income. Especially in the case of women, whose SES may be high as the wives of distinguished men but low on the basis of years of schooling. In this chapter we report on the distribution of these three standard variables or "dimensions" of SES in the female world, however defective they may be.

EDUCATION IN THE FEMALE WORLD

. . . Especially important for the female world has been the rise in the number of college-educated women, for exposure to college makes an enormous difference. It stimulates them to read and think and challenge. Women in the colleges early in the century were already leading the movement to reconceptualize the female world. They were fighting the first battles against the restraints of their Gemeinschaft, kin- and locale-oriented world, just beginning to challenge the "family claim" of the love-and/or-duty ethos. College-educated women have supplied an elite who have been pioneers shaping the course of the female world for over a century. They were the ones who first examined the changing conditions that made the ideology of the women's sphere an inadequate conceptualization. They were the first to see the necessity for expanding the love-and/or-duty ethos of the female world. They were the first to challenge the "selfishness" prescribed in that ethos. They were the first to wrestle with the marriage-versus-career issue. And in the 1970s and 1980s they have been the avant garde who have done the thinking, analyzing, and researching for the whole female world. . . .

Overall, the female population in the United States shows up well so far as the number of years of schooling is concerned (Table 1). In 1977, the median number of years of schooling was beyond high school graduation, 12.3. (For white women in 1976, it was 12.4 and for blacks just a year less, 11.4.) But for reasons just suggested, the most significant trend seems to be the increase in women exposed to college. From a small trickle—11,126 resident college students in 1869–1870—to almost a million and a half (1,467,000) in the fall of 1961. . . . At the turn of the century, about a third of the college population consisted of women. By 1968, about two-fifths (39 percent) of all college students aged fourteen to thirty-four were women; in 1978, about half were, many of them women returning to school after time out for children. Two-thirds of college students over thirty-four were women (Rich, 1979). . . . [A] kind of educational homogenization seems to be in process in the female world.

TABLE 1

Years of School Completed by Females, 1977

Years of Schooling	Percent of Females over Fourteen Years of Age
0	.7
1–4	2.0
5–8	16.0
9–12	57.9
13–16	20.2
17 or more	3.2

Source: Bureau of the Census, Educational Attainment in the United States: March 1977 and 1976. Series P-20, no. 314, issued Dec. 1977, Table 1, p. 7.

In the context of education as a dimension of socioeconomic status, the increase in the number of women in junior and community colleges—64.8 percent between 1960 and 1976—is of extraordinary significance. This figure reflects one of the most interesting trends reshaping the female world: the movement of women from even the lower socioeconomic levels into colleges. For a considerable part of the student body in these schools is contributed by women from just such socioeconomic levels. Continuing education programs in community colleges as well as in standard institutions make it possible for rapidly increasing numbers of women to be exposed to higher education. Wherever they can get in, whenever the hours are scheduled for their convenience and the tuition is tailored to their resources, they eagerly flock to the colleges. . . .

At the present time it would seem that the educational opportunities of the female population are similar if not identical to those of the male population. Actually, of course, the schools girls attend are not the same as the schools boys attend. . . . Education has different impacts, therefore, on women and men. Thus, for example, the income of a college-educated woman in 1976 was less than that of a male high-school dropout (Statistical Abstract, 1977, 452) while professionally or technically trained women received about the same income as male operatives (Table 2).

WEALTH AND INCOME IN THE FEMALE POPULATION

Ownership of the means of production has declined as a dimension of class since the time of Marx and especially since the control of the means of production has been separated from ownership. In any event, it has never been suitable for application to women. There is, to be sure, a myth that women own most of the wealth of the country in the form of stocks and bonds. It is not true.

TABLE 2

Median Annual Earnings by Sex and Occupation, 1976

Occupation	Females	Males
Professional, technical, kindred	11,072	16,939
Managers, Administrators, except farm	9,804	16,674
Sales	6,272	14,586
Clerical, kindred	8,128	12,843
Craft, kindred	7,765	13,638
Operatives	6,649	11,688
Laborers, except farm	7,613	10,104
Service workers, except household	5,840	10,036

Source: Statistical Abstract, 1977, 411.

TABLE 3

Income of Adult Females, 1976

Income	Percent
No income	26.7
Less than $2,000	22.1
$2,000–$3,999	17.3
$4,000–$6,999	15.3
$7,000–$9,000	9.5
$10,000–$14,999	6.6
$15,000+	2.5
	100.0

Source: Statistical Abstract of the United States, 1977, 451.

There is not much "power of the purse" in the female world. In 1970 women constituted only 30 percent of all shareholders and owned only 25 percent of all shares held by individuals and 16 percent of all shares (Women's Bureau, 1975, 179). And even the portion of the wealth registered in the name of women is often controlled by trustees, husbands, or other male guardians. The basis for the idea that women own most of the wealth of the country may inhere in the interesting fact that among the few female heads of families in the high-income brackets—$25,000 and over—women—probably the rich widows we hear so much about—receive almost twice as much income ($10,031) as male heads of husband-wife households ($5,123) on the average from dividends, pensions, and other regular payments (1970 Census, Sources and Structure of Family Income). It remains true, however, that within the female world, where wealth exists it is associated with social class, indirectly by means of influence, if not directly by way of power.

No more than wealth is income a wholly suitable dimension of social class in the female world. Not all women have incomes of their own (Table 3) and among those who have, most are in the lowest income brackets (Table 4). Clearly the husband's income must be taken into account. . . . [T]he assumption was made that the social status of a wife was that of her husband, which, in turn, was measured by his income. But being in a household with high social status as measured by income does not mean that the housewife herself has a high monetary income. Much of her "income" is in the form of maintenance or support. The monetary part may be in the form of allowances from her husband, determined by either bargaining or whim.

TABLE 4

Persons Fourteen Years of Age and over with Incomes

Income	Females	Males
Less than $2,000	30.1	12.3
$2,000–$3,999	23.6	11.3
$4,000–$6,999	20.8	15.2
$7,000–$9,999	13.0	13.7
$10,000–$14,999	9.0	20.6
$15,000 and over	3.4	27.0

Source: Statistical Abstract, 1977, 451.

A great many people work under conditions that they view as demeaning. But many nonemployed housewives at all income levels have felt especially degraded by the unilateral control of their monetary resources. There is a whole body of female lore dealing with the wheedling women must engage in to get money—when is the best time to ask for money; how to finagle bills and charge accounts to disguise expenditures; how to save secretly out of household allowances. Desire for escape from such humiliating conditions was found, in fact, to be a major motive or reward among blue-collar and service workers for entering the labor force. "I've never been good for asking my husband for anything. I don't want to have to ask anybody for anything. And I don't have to say 'Well, honey, can I have this or can I spend that?' [Working] gives me more money, even though what I'm making now isn't that much more. I feel a lot more independent" (Walshok, 1977, 16). And, "the first plus is having money of your own, which makes a hell of a difference." And, "I'm a very independent person. . . . It's my income you know, and I lose by dependence on other people." Understandably, with few exceptions, "none of the women indicated they would stop working even if they did not need the money. . . . The benefits of paid employment outweigh the benefits of homemaking." . . .

Whatever its source, size of income has widely ramifying implications. It influences life chances, determines access to prerogatives and amenities, to different kinds of life styles, and thus, indirectly, leads to differentiated social status. Although earned income in the female population is low, it is in a large number of cases enough to provide a woman with a modicum of economic independence if she wants it. And such potential economic independence makes a difference in both the female and the male world. We know, for example, that the marriage rate, age for age, is lower for women who are employed, for . . . jobs or careers constitute notable competition for marriage, especially if women find partners to live with and supply companionship and love. And if suitable job opportunities are available, divorce rates also rise (Moles and Levinger, 1979).

It is hard to emphasize too strongly how this income dimension of socioeconomic status impacts on women. The lack of money can influence the whole worldview of those suffering from it. There has to be pinching, scraping, saving. It is harder to be generous. Public services are often less graciously supplied, if they are forthcoming at all. A world in which so large a proportion does not have money of its own is bound to be different from one in which there are relatively few in this category. In any monetary exchange situation— characteristic of Gesellschaft—the odds are against the person with fewer monetary resources. The power of the purse is overwhelming. . . .

A SERIOUSLY FLAWED CONCEPTUALIZATION

The inappropriateness of current models of socioeconomic status becomes clear when we apply the occupational dimension of socioeconomic status to the female world. Housewife, the most important occupation in the female world— in terms of the number engaged in it as well as of sociological importance—is not even included. Most women, whether or not they are in the labor force, are housewives at least part-time and about half of all adult women—those not in the labor force—are full-time housewives. There is, to be sure, an enormous corpus of research dealing with the household, especially by home economists, and a long history dealing with the cult of domesticity in the nineteenth century. . . . But what is relevant here is that as an occupation, housewifery does not appear in any of the research on occupation as a dimension of socioeconomic status; it is not even viewed as within the economy because it is not operated on a cash-nexus basis. "It would serve no purpose . . . to include housewives in a count of a country's working force," we are told, because including them "would have no relevance for the significant economic problems of our times" (Jaffe and Stewart, 1951, 14, 18). This occupation is outside the Gesellschaft and therefore outside the male world's concern. . . .

Because "occupation housewife" is not included in the standard research on occupations, when we speak of the occupational dimension of the female world we are speaking only of that half of adult women—51.1 percent—who have jobs in the labor force. In Table 5, a column in which all the percentages are halved has been added to portray the fact that housewives are omitted, and another occupational category, "housewife," has been added containing the (roughly) half of adult women who are probably full-time housewives. . . .

TABLE 5

Women by Major Occupation, 1977

Major Occupation	Proportion of Employed Women	Proportion of All Women*
Professional and Technical	16.1	8
Managers and Administrators	5.7	3
Sales Workers	6.7	3
Clerical Workers	35.1	18
Craft and Kindred Workers	1.6	.8
Operatives	11.7	6
Nonfarm Laborers	.1	.05
Service Workers	20.8	11
Farm Workers	.1	.05
Housewives		50
	100.0	

Source: Bureau of the Census, Statistical Abstract of the United States, 1977, p. 406.

*In 1977, when this table was prepared, fewer than half of all women (47.4 percent) were in the labor force, but the relative numbers in various occupations are roughly approximate. The proportion of women in the labor force was 51.1 percent in June 1979 (Bureau of Labor Statistics, 1979, Table 3A) and was projected to reach 54.8 percent in 1990 (Smith, ed., 1979, 14).

THE OCCUPATIONAL DISTRIBUTION OF WOMEN IN THE LABOR FORCE

The increasing participation of women in the labor force is one of the best documented and most salient trends in the female world as well as in the male world. It reverses the old ideological tenet with respect to women's sphere. In the nineteenth century female labor-force participation was hailed by avant-garde women as a counter to the restrictive and deteriorating women's sphere ideology; in the twentieth, as an ethical obligation (Myrdal and Klein, 1956). Actually women, then as now, have entered the labor force because they were needed there: the economy could not have developed as it did without them. . . .

The occupational distribution of the half of all adult women in the labor force is quite different from that of men. A far larger proportion are in service and so-called helping kinds of work, reflecting the traditional love-and/or-duty ethos of female culture. "As the focus for female aspirations the three 'k's' of an earlier generation—Kinder, Küche, Kirche [children, kitchen and church]—have been replaced by the three 'h's'—healing, helping, and home management. The professions now open to women are in the main in the service sector, calling for 'warm hearts' and 'beautiful bodies' " (Schork, 1978, p. 33).

There are important concomitants to the occupational distribution of women quite apart from the income aspect, for work itself has ramifying influences on personality. Almost fifty years ago, sociologist Pitirim Sorokin reminded us how our work influenced all aspects of our personality, from the physical to the ideological. "Occupation," he said, "marks a whole organism and shapes it, making it conform to its nature. . . . [Occupation] stigmatizes the movement and habitual posture of the body. . . . Still greater is the occupational influence on the processes and on the character of one's evaluations, beliefs, and practical judgments, opinions, ethics, and whole ideology" (1927, 320–321). . . . Although women are said to have little aspiration for upward occupational mobility, in connection with the influence of work on behavior, it is interesting to note that men and women in the same work situation seem to respond in similar ways. That the kind of work engaged in has similar impact on psychological functioning for women and for men was shown in a study by Joanne Miller and her associates (1978, draft). And another study, this time of managers, found male and female managers psychologically very much alike. It reported no difference in "critical thinking, temperament, values, intelligence, verbal abilities or leadership style" (Quinn, 1978).

The joker is, however, that men and women are rarely in the same position. The *ceteris paribus* [other things being equal] fallacy is involved. Thus Miller and her associates are careful to note that "women's job conditions differ from men's. Our data indicate that, compared to men, women are significantly more closely supervised and significantly less likely to be owners, to occupy a high position in a supervisory hierarchy, to do complex work with data, things, or people, to work under time pressure, to work long hours, to do heavy work, to be held responsible for things outside their control, and to expect dramatic changes in their job circumstances" (draft, 1978). . . .

THE SCENARIO ACCORDING TO THE "IMMIGRANT" ANALOGY

James March, an economist, has noted that women enter the male world as, in effect, "immigrants." This is a vivid figure of speech with interesting implications. A classic study of European immigrants to the United States more than half a century ago, for example, described the many ways immigrants, most of them peasants with rural—Gemeinschaft—backgrounds, had had to change in order to cope with their new—usually urban, Gesellschaft—world (Park and Miller, 1921). The analogy may not be close, but in some ways it is suggestive. Like European immigrants to the United States, women bring with them "old country" ways from the female world when they "immigrate" to the male world. As the Lowell girls did. Or as the secretary does when she functions as a "wife." In fact, for many women, labor-force participation constitutes simply a change of site for performing their traditional function of serving their families. To pay for home improvements, for example, or for the children's college education. Such employment does not lead to independence from authority of the husband or demands of the children (Cowan, 1974, 250). Nor departure from the female world. Their work is just a part of their service to the family. And since the kind of work they do is so often in jobs that are subservient, even passive, they do not violate the prescribed role patterns of the female world. They carry their female world with them into the labor force. The male world remains the same. . . .

But even when women have not been segregated into enclaves on the work scene, they have nevertheless lived in a different work world from that of men. Working with men in the same shop or on the same assembly line or in the same office does not mean living in the same world. Even when they are not spatially separated from the male work world, women are socially and psychologically separated. Rosabeth Moss Kanter has shown, for example, that in one of the corporations she observed women were given less encouragement from their superiors to improve and less encouragement to advance; the company was less aware of their contributions (1977, 125). They were not as likely as men to be seen as material for promotion. Thus, a sample of management men predicted no promotion for about a fifth of the women, contrasted with only 6 percent of the men (143). It was a self-fulfilling prophecy. Fewer opportunities for advancement were offered; less advancement was achieved.

There are different hazards in the work site for women. Sexual harassment, for example, is rare in the male work world; it is a common, everyday hazard in the female (Farley, 1978). The work site does not homogenize the female and the male worlds, nor does it "Americanize" or "masculinize" the female world.

Women are increasingly knocking at the doors of traditionally all-male kinds of skilled blue-collar jobs because they pay better. But even the women who succeed do not thereby enter the male world. In fact, Mary Wolshak has found that their lives are very much like those of other women in even the most segregated female jobs. True, "many describe their husbands as ambivalent or nonsupportive and some of their male coworkers are downright hostile to their new careers"; still, "most report that they carry the full burden of household tasks in addition to their physical labors on the job" (in Fisher, 1978, 33). The norms of the female world still control their behavior, whether at the work site or at home.

Because the economic rewards are so much greater in the male world than in the female world, some women in the labor force reject the female world; they see it as an encumbrance to their own success in the male world; they want none of it. They want to discard their "old country" ways, as successful immigrants did, and take on those of the "new country." They want to be "assimilated." Thus a considerable spate of books began to appear in the 1970s to teach women the rules of the game as played in the male world so that they would know how it operated and learn how to deal with it. . . .

A small, but indeterminate, number of women may, indeed, succeed in "cracking" the male world, in truly becoming "one of the boys." They may indeed have a male identity, feel like men, enjoy the male style of sociality. . . .

A somewhat larger number of women may think they live in the male world until something happens that shows how wide the chasm really is. One such woman, for example, could pub-crawl with men, romp with them, even attend burlesque shows with them. But when one evening ended in a visit to a brothel? Women may become "role-wise." They may, in fact, think like men, act like men, live by the rules of the male world. They may reject identification with other women and certainly with the female world. For all intents and purposes they are "men." But they are almost never truly "in." Almost never completely accepted. Nor does their presence change the nature, structure, or functioning of the male world. Though they are in the male world in the sense that they participate in it, they are not truly "of" it. And that is the bottom line.

In terms of practical procedures, women will no doubt continue to be in though not of the male world. But the growth in recognition and understanding of the female world by both women and men will have its impact on both sexes in the work force. With the support that comes from knowledge and understanding of the female world, women will feel stronger, less defensive, supported by the legitimacy of their perspective. The overwhelming male consensus will begin to show cracks.

REFERENCES

Barber, Bernard. "Social Stratification: Introduction." *International Encyclopedia of the Social Sciences*, vol. 15. New York: Macmillan, 1968, 228–295.

Cowan, Ruth Schartz. "A Case Study of Technological and Social Change: The Washing Machine and the Working Wife." In Mary Hartman and Lois W. Banner, eds., *Clio's Consciousness Raised*. New York: Harper Torchbooks, 1974, 245–253.

Farley, Lin. *Sexual Shakedown: Sexual Harassment of Women on the Job*. New York: McGraw-Hill, 1978.

Fisher, Anne E. *Women's Worlds, NIMH—Supported Research on Women*. Orockville, Maryland: National Institute of Mental Health, 1978.

Jaffe, Abram L., and Charles D. Stewart. *Manpower Resources and Utilization, Principles of Labor Force Analysis*. New York: Wiley, 1951.

Kanter, Rosabeth Moss. *Women and Men of the Corporation*. New York: Basic Books, 1977.

Lipset, Martin Seymour. "Social Class." *International Encyclopedia of the Social Sciences*, vol. 15. New York: Macmillan, 1968, 296–316.

Miller, Joanne, Carol Schooler, Melvin L. Kohn, and Karen A. Miller. "Women and Work: The Psychological Effects of Occupational Conditions." 1978. Draft.

Moles, Oliver. "Marital Dissolution and Public Assistance Payments." In George Levinger and Oliver Moles, eds., *Divorce and Separation*. New York: Basic Books, 1979.

Myrdal, Alva, and Viola Klein. *Women's Two Roles*. London: Routledge and Kegan Paul, 1956.

Park, Robert E., and Herbert A. Miller. *Old World Traits Transplanted*. New York: Harper, 1921.

Quinn, Jane Bryant. "Managerial Men and Women Are Found Remarkably Alike." *The Washington Post*, July 17, 1978.

Rich, Spencer. "Enrollment Hits New Low for the 70s." *The Washington Post*, May 13, 1979.

Smith, Ralph E., ed., *The Subtle Revolution*. Washington, D.C.: The Urban Institute, 1979.

Sorokin, Pitrim. *Social and Cultural Dynamics.* Englewood Cliffs, N.J.: Bedminster Press, 1962.

Statistical Abstract of the United States 1977. Washington, D.C.: Government Printing Office, 1977.

Walshok, Mary Lindenstein. "Occupational Values and Family Roles: A Descriptive Study of Women Working in Blue-Collar and Service Occupations." Paper presented at a seminar at the National Institute of Mental Health. February 1977.

Women's Bureau. *Handbook of Women Workers.* Washington, D.C.: Government Printing Office, 1975.

PART FOUR

Social Institutions

CHAPTER 11 The Polity

11.1 CHARLES PETERS

From Ouagadougou to Cape Canaveral: Why the Bad News Doesn't Travel Up

Why is it that the top executive of an organization is often the last to know about problems that significantly interfere with the organization's success and at times are highly perilous to human life? Why is the leadership often protected from bad news?

In the following selection, investigative journalist Charles Peters discusses some of the problems associated with getting bad news to the top by examining specific cases, including the fatal *Challenger* flight in 1986. One of the major difficulties, according to Peters, is the fear of subordinates that such information ("the bad news") will have a deleterious effect on their positions and prospects in the company. He notes, for example, that people who do not have high stakes in their positions, such as temporary employees, are more honest and open about problems than are careerists. Another reason is that middle-level employees often feel that it is their responsibility to solve problems rather than to communicate them to higher-ups.

To prevent this problem, Peters suggests that an independent evaluator should be established to inspect and evaluate projects. A sociologist would note, however, that solving this problem through external evaluators implies that organizations cannot or will not solve this problem themselves. This raises the question of "how rational are organizations after all?"

Peters (b. 1926) is the founder and editor in chief of *The Washington Monthly*. He is a leading advocate of neoliberalism, and his "A Neoliberal's Manifesto," *The Washington Monthly* (May 1983), describes a political program that is designed to promote individual initiative, overcome bureaucratic practices, and foster a new sense of national unity.

Key Concept: system of information cutoffs

*E*veryone is asking why the top NASA officials who decided to launch the fatal Challenger flight had not been told of the concerns of people down below, like Allan McDonald and the other worried engineers at Morton Thiokol.

In the first issue of *The Washington Monthly,* Russell Baker and I wrote, "In any reasonably large government organization, there exists an elaborate system of information cutoffs, comparable to that by which city water systems shut off large water-main breaks, closing down, first small feeder pipes, then larger and larger valves. The object is to prevent information, particularly of an unpleasant character, from rising to the top of the agency, where it may produce results unpleasant to the lower ranks.

"Thus, the executive at or near the top lives in constant danger of not knowing, until he reads it on Page One some morning, that his department is hip-deep in disaster."

This seemed to us to be a serious problem for government, no only because the people at the top didn't know but because the same system of cut-offs operated to keep Congress, the press, and the public in the dark. (Often it also would operate to keep in the dark people within the organization but outside the immediate chain of command—this happened with the astronauts, who were not told about the concern with the O-rings.)

I first became aware of this during the sixties, when I worked at the Peace Corps. Repeatedly I would find that a problem that was well-known by people at lower and middle levels of the organization, whose responsibility it was, would be unknown at the top of the chain of command or by anyone outside.

The most serious problems of the Peace Corps had their origins in Sargent Shriver's desire to get the organization moving. He did not want it to become mired in feasibility studies, he wanted to get volunteers overseas and into action fast. To fulfill his wishes, corners were cut. Training was usually inadequate in language, culture, and technical skills. Volunteers were selected who were not suited to their assignments. For example, the country then known as Tanganyika asked for surveyors, and we sent them people whose only connection with surveying had been holding the rod and chain while the surveyor sighted through his gizmo. Worse, volunteers were sent to places where no job at all awaited them. These fictitious assignments were motivated sometimes by the host official's desire to please the brother-in-law of the president of the United States and sometimes by the official's ignorance of what was going on at the lower levels of his own bureaucracy.

But subordinates would not tell Shriver about the problems. There were two reasons for this. One was fear. They knew that he wanted action, not excuses, and they suspected that their careers would suffer if he heard too many of the latter. The other reason was that they felt it was their job to solve problems, not burden the boss with them. They and Shriver shared the view expressed by Deke Slayton, the former astronaut, when he was asked about the failure of middle-level managers to tell top NASA officials about the problems they were encountering:

"You depend on managers to make a decision based on the information they have. If they had to transmit all the fine detail to the top people, it wouldn't get launched but once every ten years."

The point is not without merit. It is easy for large organizations to fall into "once every ten years" habits. Leaders who want to avoid that danger learn to set goals and communicate a sense of urgency about meeting them. But what many of them never learn is that once you set those goals you have to guard against the tendency of those down below to spare you not only "all the fine detail" but essential facts about significant problems.

For instance, when Jimmy Carter gave the Pentagon the goal of rescuing the Iranian hostages, he relied on the chain of command to tell him if there were any problems. So he did not find out until after the disaster at Desert One that the Delta Commandos thought the Marine pilots assigned to fly the helicopters were incompetent.

In NASA's case chances have been taken with the shuttle from the beginning—the insulating thermal tiles had not gone through a reentry test before the first shuttle crew risked their lives to try them out—but in recent years the pressure to cut corners has increased markedly. Competition with the European Ariane rocket and the Reagan administration's desire to see agencies like NASA run as if they were private businesses have led to a speedup in the launch schedule, with a goal of 14 this year and 24 by 1988.

"The game NASA is playing is the maximum tonnage per year at the minimum costs possible," says Paul Cloutier, a professor of space physics. "Some high officials don't want to hear about problems," reports *Newsweek*, "especially if fixing them will cost money."

Under pressures like these, the NASA launch team watched Columbia, after seven delays, fall about a month behind schedule and then saw Challenger delayed, first by bad weather, then by damaged door handles, and then by bad weather again. Little wonder that Lawrence Mulloy, when he heard the warnings from the Thiokol engineers, burst out: "My God, Thiokol, when do you want me to launch? Next April?"

Mulloy may be one of the villains of this story, but it is important to realize that you need Lawrence Mulloys to get things done. It is also important to realize that, if you have a Lawrence Mulloy, you must protect yourself against what he might fail to do or what he might do wrong in his enthusiastic rush to get the job done.

And you can't just ask him if he has any doubts. If he's a gung-ho type, he's going to suppress the negatives. When Jimmy Carter asked General David Jones to check out the Iran rescue plan, Jones said to Colonel Beckwith: "Charlie, tell me what you really think about the mission. Be straight with me."

"Sir, we're going to do it!" Beckwith replied. "We want to do it, and we're ready."

John Kennedy received similar confident reports from the chain of command about the readiness of the CIA's Cuban Brigade to charge ashore at the Bay of Pigs and overthrow Fidel Castro. And Sargent Shriver had every reason to believe that the Peace Corps was getting off to a fabulous start, based on what his chain of command was telling him.

With Shriver, as with NASA's senior officials, the conviction that everything was A-OK was fortified by skillful public relations. Bill Moyers was only one of the geniuses involved in this side of the Peace Corps. At NASA, Julian Scheer began a tradition of inspired PR that endured until Challenger. These were men who could sell air conditioning in Murmansk. The trouble is they also sold their bosses the same air conditioning. Every organization has a tendency to believe its own PR—NASA's walls are lined with glamorizing posters and photographs of the shuttle and other space machines—and usually the top man is the most thoroughly seduced because, after all, it reflects the most glory on him.

Favorable publicity and how to get it is therefore the dominant subject of Washington staff meetings. The minutes of the Nuclear Regulatory Commission show that when the reactor was about to melt down at Three Mile Island, the commissioners were worried less about what to do to fix the reactor than they were about what they were going to say to the press.

One of the hottest rumors around Washington is that the White House had put pressure on NASA to launch so that the president could point with pride to the teacher in space during his State of the Union speech. The White House denies this story, and my sources tell me the denial is true. But NASA had—and this is fact, not rumor—put pressure on *itself* by asking the president to mention Christa McAuliffe. In a memorandum dated January 8, NASA proposed that the president say:

"Tonight while I am speaking to you, a young elementary school teacher from Concord, New Hampshire, is taking us all on the ultimate field trip as she orbits the earth as the fist citizen passenger on the space shuttle. Christa McAuliffe's journey is a prelude to the journeys of other Americans living and working together in a permanently manned space station in the mid-1990s. Mrs. McAuliffe's week in space is just one of the achievements in space we have planned for the coming year."

The flight was scheduled for January 23. It was postponed and postponed again. Now it was January 28, the morning of the day the speech was to be delivered, the last chance for the launch to take place in time to have it mentioned by the president. NASA officials must have feared they were about to lose a PR opportunity of stunning magnitude, an opportunity to impress not only the media and the public but the agency's two most important constituencies, the White House and the Congress. Wouldn't you feel pressure to get that launch off this morning so that the president could talk about it tonight? . . .

Sargent Shriver liked good press as much as, if not more than, the next man. But he also had an instinct that the ultimate bad press would come if the world found out about your disaster before you had a chance to do something to prevent it. He and an assistant named William Haddad decided to make sure that Shriver got the bad news first. Who was going to find it out for them? Me.

It was July 1961. They decided to call me an evaluator and send me out to our domestic training programs and later overseas to find out what was really going on. My first stop was the University of California at Berkeley where our Ghana project was being trained. Fortunately, except for grossly inadequate language instruction, this program was excellent. But soon I began finding serious deficiencies in other training programs and in our projects abroad.

Shriver was not always delighted by these reports. Indeed, at one point I heard I was going to be fired. I liked my job, and I knew that the reports that I and the other evaluators who had joined me were writing were true. I didn't want to be fired. What could I do?

I knew he was planning to visit our projects in Africa. So I prepared a memorandum that contrasted what the chain of command was saying with what I and my associates were reporting. Shriver left for Africa. I heard nothing for several weeks. Then came a cable from Somalia: "Tell Peters his reports are right." I knew then that, however much Shriver wanted to hear the good news and get good publicity, he could take the bad news. The fact that he could take the bad news meant that the Peace Corps began to face its problems an do something about them before they became a scandal.

NASA did the opposite. A 1983 reorganization shifted the responsibility for monitoring flight safety from the chief engineer in Washington to the field. This may sound good. "We're not going to micromanage," said James M. Beggs, then the NASA administrator. But the catch is that if you decentralize, you must maintain the flow of information from the field to the top so that the organization's leader will know what those decentralized managers are doing. What NASA's reorganization did, according to safety engineers who talked to Mark Tapscott of *The Washington Times*, was to close off "an independent channel with authority to make things happen at the top."

I suspect what happened is that the top NASA administrators, who were pushing employees down below to dramatically increase the number of launches, either consciously or unconsciously did not want to be confronted with the dangers they were thereby risking.

This is what distinguishes the bad leaders from the good. The good leader, realizing that there is a natural human tendency to avoid bad news, traps himself into having to face it. He encourages whistleblowers instead of firing them. He visits the field himself and talks to the privates and lieutenants as well as the generals to find out the real problems. He can use others to do this for him, as Shriver used me, or as Franklin Roosevelt used his wife Eleanor and Harry Hopkins, and as they in turn used Lorena Hickock[1] to find out what the New Deal was really accomplishing. But he must have some independent knowledge of what's going on down below in order to have a feel for whether the chain of command is giving him the straight dope.

What most often happens, of course, is that the boss, if he goes to the field at all, talks only to the colonels and generals. Sometimes he doesn't want to know what the privates know. He may be hoping that the lid can be kept on whatever problems are developing, at least until his watch is over, so that he won't be blamed when they finally surface. Or he may have a very good idea that bad things are being done and simply wants to retain "deniability," meaning that the deed cannot be traced to him. The story of Watergate is filled with "Don't tell me" and "I don't want to know."

When NASA's George Hardy told Thiokol engineers that he was appalled by their verbal recommendation that the launch be postponed and asked Thiokol to reconsider and make another recommendation, Thiokol, which

Hardy well knew was worried about losing its shuttle contract, was in effect being told, "Don't tell me" or "Don't tell me officially so I won't have to pass bad news along and my bosses will have deniability."

In addition to the leader himself, others must be concerned with making him face the bad news. This includes subordinates. Their having the courage to speak out about what is wrong is crucial, and people like Bruce Cook of NASA and Allan McDonald of Thiokol deserve great credit for having done so. But it is a fact that none of the subordinates who knew the danger to the shuttle took the next step and resigned in protest so that the public could find out what was going on in time to prevent disaster. The almost universal tendency to place one's own career above one's moral responsibility to take a stand on matters like these has to be one of the most depressing facts about bureaucratic culture today. . . .

Certainly the process of getting bad news from the bottom to the top can be helped by institutionalizing it, as it was in the case of the Peace Corps Evaluation Division, and by hiring to perform it employees who have demonstrated courage and independence as well as the ability to elicit the truth and report it clearly.

Two other institutions that can help this process are the Congress and the White House. But the staff they have to perform this function is tiny. The White House depends on the OMB [Office of Management and Budget] to tell it what the executive branch is doing. Before the Challenger exploded, the OMB had four examiners to cover science and space. The Senate subcommittee on Space, Science and Technology had a staff of three. Needless to say, they had not heard about the O-rings.

Another problem is lack of experience. Too few congressmen and too few of their staff have enough experience serving in the executive branch to have a sense of the right question to ask. OMB examiners usually come aboard straight from graduate school, totally innocent of practical experience in government.

The press shares this innocence. Only a handful of journalists have worked in the bureaucracy. Like the members of Congress, they treat policy formulation as the ultimate reality: Congress passed this bill today; the president signed that bill. That's what the TV reporters on the Capitol steps and the White House lawn tell us about. But suppose the legislation in question concerns coal mine safety. Nobody is going to know what it all adds up to until some members of Congress and some members of the press go down into the coal mine to find out if conditions actually are safer or if only more crazy regulations have been added.

Unfortunately, neither the congressmen nor the press display much enthusiasm for visits to the mines. Yet this is what I found to be the key to getting the real story about the Peace Corps. I had to go to Ouagadougou and talk to the volunteers at their sites before I could really know what the Peace Corps was doing and what its problems were. I wasn't going to find out by asking the public affairs office.

But that's where most reports go and sit all day—outside Larry Speakes's office or its equivalent throughout the government.

Because the reporters don't know any better, they don't press the Congress to do any better. What journalists could do is make the public aware of how little attention Congress devotes to what is called "oversight," i.e., finding out what the programs it has authorized are actually doing. If the press would publicize the nonperformance of this function, it is at least possible that the public would begin to reward the congressmen who perform it consistently and punish those who ignore it by not reelecting them.

But the press will never do this until it gets itself out of Larry Speakes's office. Woodward and Bernstein didn't get the Watergate story by talking to Ron Ziegler, or, for that matter, by using other reportorial techniques favored by the media elite, like questioning Richard Nixon at a press conference or interviewing other administration luminaries at fancy restaurants. They had to find lower-level sources like Hugh Sloan, just as the reporters who finally got the NASA story had to find the Richard Cooks and Allan McDonalds. . . .

There are a couple of reasons, however, to hope that the performance of the press will improve. The coverage of business news has become increasingly sophisticated about the way institutional pressures affect executive and corporate behavior, mainly because the comparison of our economy with Japan's made the importance of cultural factors so obvious. And on defense issues, visits to the field are increasingly common as reporters attempt to find out whether this or that weapon works.

But these are mere beachheads. They need to be radically expanded to include the coverage of all the institutions that affect our lives, especially government. This may seem unlikely, but if the press studies the Challenger case, I do not see how it can avoid perceiving the critical role bureaucratic pressure played in bringing about the disaster. What the press must then realize is that similar pressures vitally influence almost everything this government does, and that we will never understand why government fails until we understand those pressures and how human beings in public office react to them.

NOTE

1. See Political Booknotes, May 1981, page 58. Other articles concerned with the issues raised here: "The Shriver Prescription: How Government Can Find Out What It's Doing," November 1972; "How Carter Can Find Out What the Government Is Doing," January 1977; "Blind Ambition in the White House," March 1977; "The Prince and His Courtiers," March 1971; "Why the White House Press Didn't Get the Watergate Story," July/August 1973. The latter two are included in the fourth edition of *Inside the System* (Holt Rinehart), the foreword of which, by Richard Rovere, describes evaluation in the Peace Corps. More about Peace Corps evaluation can be found in *A Moment in History*, by Brent Ashabranner (Doubleday) and *The Bold Experiment*, by Gerard Rice (Notre Dame). *Blowing the Whistle* (Praeger) is a collection of *Washington Monthly* articles dealing with employees who speak up. Also see *The Culture of Bureaucracy*, (Holt Rinehart) and *How Washington Really Works* (Addison-Wesley).

The Science of "Muddling Through"

The heart and soul of politics is decision-making, and a major focus of political sociology is on how decisions are made. Some of the impressive techniques for making decisions convey the impression that policy decision-making is a highly refined art that can result in rational decisions, assuming that administrators are not perverted by special interests. In the following selection, Charles E. Lindblom shows that policy decision-making is really a process of "muddling through" by making relatively low-risk small changes to policies that were followed in the past. Then, surprisingly, he goes on to argue that muddling through is the best way to make decisions.

In his analysis, Lindblom compares two models of decision-making. The first model, the "rational comprehensive" method, is nearly impossible to utilize in formulating real policies. However, it was much promoted in the social science literature of the late 1950s. The most widely utilized model by administrators is "the successive limited comparison" method. Within the context of the American political system of incremental change, it is far more workable and effective, according to Lindblom.

Lindblom (b. 1917) is the Sterling Professor of Economics and Political Science at Yale University, where he has been teaching since 1946. A leading political scientist and economist, his research interests lie in planning and political development, and his many publications include *Politics and Markets: The World's Political-Economic Systems* (Basic Books, 1977).

Key Concept: successive limited comparisons

*S*uppose an administrator is given responsibility for formulating policy with respect to inflation. He might start by trying to list all related values in order of importance, e.g., full employment, reasonable business profit, protection of small savings, prevention of a stock market crash. Then all possible policy outcomes could be rated as more or less efficient in attaining a maximum of these values. This would of course require a prodigious inquiry into values held by members of society and an equally prodigious set of calculations on how much of each value is equal to how much of each other value. He could then proceed to outline all possible policy alternatives. In a third step, he would undertake systematic comparison of his multitude of alternatives to determine which attains the greatest amount of values.

Charles E. Lindblom

In comparing policies, he would take advantage of any theory available that generalized about classes of policies. In considering inflation, for example, he would compare all policies in the light of the theory of prices. Since no alternatives are beyond his investigation, he would consider strict central control and the abolition of all prices and markets on the one hand and elimination of all public controls with reliance completely on the free market on the other, both in the light of whatever theoretical generalizations he could find on such hypothetical economies.

Finally, he would try to make the choice that would in fact maximize his values.

An alternative line of attack would be to set as his principal objective, either explicitly or without conscious thought, the relatively simple goal of keeping prices level. This objective might be compromised or complicated by only a few other goals, such as full employment. He would in fact disregard most other social values as beyond his present interest, and he would for the moment not even attempt to rank the few values that he regarded as immediately relevant. Were he pressed, he would quickly admit that he was ignoring many related values and many possible important consequences of his policies.

As a second step, he would outline those relatively few policy alternatives that occurred to him. He would then compare them. In comparing his limited number of alternatives, most of them familiar from past controversies, he would not ordinarily find a body of theory precise enough to carry him through a comparison of their respective consequences. Instead he would rely heavily on the record of past experience with small policy steps to predict the consequences of similar steps extended into the future.

Moreover, he would find that the policy alternatives combined objectives or values in different ways. For example, one policy might offer price level stability at the cost of some risk of unemployment; another might offer less price stability but also less risk of unemployment. Hence, the next step in his approach—the final selection—would combine into one the choice among values and the choice among instruments for reaching values. It would not, as in the first method of policy-making, approximate a more mechanical process of choosing the means that best satisfied goals that were previously clarified and ranked. Because practitioners of the second approach expect to achieve their goals only partially, they would expect to repeat endlessly the sequence just described, as conditions and aspirations changed and as accuracy of prediction improved.

BY ROOT OR BY BRANCH

For complex problems, the first of these two approaches is of course impossible. Although such an approach can be described, it cannot be practiced except for relatively simple problems and even then only in a somewhat modified form. It assumes intellectual capacities and sources of information that men simply do not possess, and it is even more absurd as an approach to policy when the time and money that can be allocated to a policy problem is limited, as is always the case. Of particular importance to public administrators is the fact that public agencies are in effect usually instructed not to practice the first method. That is to say, their prescribed functions and constraints—the politically or legally possible—restrict their attention to relatively few values and relatively few alternative policies among the countless alternatives that might be imagined. It is the second method that is practiced.

Curiously, however, the literatures of decision-making, policy formulation, planning, and public administration formalize the first approach rather than the second, leaving public administrators who handle complex decisions in the position of practicing what few preach. For emphasis I run some risk of overstatement. True enough, the literature is well aware of limits on man's capacities and of the inevitability that policies will be approached in some such style as the second. But attempts to formalize rational policy formulation—to lay out explicitly the necessary steps in the process—usually describe the first approach and not the second.

The common tendency to describe policy formulation even for complex problems as though it followed the first approach has been strengthened by the attention given to, and success enjoyed by, operations research, statistical decision theory, and systems analysis. The hallmarks of these procedures, typical of the first approach, are clarity of objective, explicitness of evaluation, a high degree of comprehensiveness of overview, and, wherever possible, quantification of values for mathematical analysis. But these advanced procedures remain largely the appropriate techniques of relatively small-scale problem-solving where the total number of variables to be considered is small and value problems restricted. Charles Hitch, head of the Economics Division of RAND Corporation, one of the leading centers for application of these techniques, has written:

> I would make the empirical generalization from my experience at RAND and elsewhere that operations research is the art of sub-optimizing, i.e., of solving some lower-level problems, and that difficulties increase and our special competence diminishes by an order of magnitude with every level of decision making we attempt to ascend. The sort of simple explicit model which operations researchers are so proficient in using can certainly reflect most of the significant factors influencing traffic control on the George Washington Bridge, but the proportion of the relevant reality which we can represent by any such model or models in studying, say, a major foreign-policy decision, appears to be almost trivial. [1]

Accordingly, I propose in this paper to clarify and formalize the second method, much neglected in the literature. This might be described as the method of *successive limited comparisons*. I will contrast it with the first approach, which might be called the rational-comprehensive method. More impressionistically and briefly—and therefore generally used in this article—they could be characterized as the branch method and root method, the former continually building out from the current situation, step-by-step and by small degrees; the latter starting from fundamentals anew each time, building on the past only as experience is embodied in a theory, and always prepared to start completely from the ground up.

Let us put the characteristics of the two methods side by side in simplest terms.

Rational-Comprehensive (Root)

1a. Clarification of values or objectives distinct from and usually prerequisite to empirical analysis of alternative policies.
2a. Policy-formulation is therefore approached through means-end analysis: First the ends are isolated, then the means to achieve them are sought.
3a. The test of a "good" policy is that it can be shown to be the most appropriate means to desired ends.
4a. Analysis is comprehensive; every important relevant factor is taken into account.
5a. Theory is often heavily relied upon.

Assuming that the root method is familiar and understandable, we proceed directly to clarification of its alternative by contrast. In explaining the second, we shall be describing how most administrators do in fact approach complex questions, for the root method, the "best" way as a blueprint or model, is in fact not workable for complex policy questions, and administrators are forced to use the method of successive limited comparisons.

INTERTWINING EVALUATION AND EMPIRICAL ANALYSIS (1B)

The quickest way to understand how values are handled in the method of successive limited comparisons is to see how the root method often breaks down in *its* handling of values or objectives. The idea that values should be clarified, and in advance of the examination of alternative policies, is appealing. But what happens when we attempt it for complex social problems? The first difficulty is that on many critical values or objectives, citizens disagree, congressmen disagree, and public administrators disagree. Even where a fairly specific objective is prescribed for the administrator, there remains considerable room for disagreement on sub-objectives. Consider, for example, the conflict with respect to locating public housing, described in [Martin] Meyerson and [Edward C.] Banfield's study of the Chicago Housing Authority—disagreement which occurred despite the clear objective of providing a certain number of public housing units in the city. Similarly conflicting are objectives in highway location, traffic control, minimum wage administration, development of tourist facilities in national parks, or insect control.

1b. Selection of value goals and empirical analysis of the needed action are not distinct from one another but are closely intertwined.
2b. Since means and ends are not distinct, means-end analysis is often inappropriate or limited.
3b. The test of a "good" policy is typically that various analysts find themselves directly agreeing on a policy (without their agreeing that it is the most appropriate means to an agreed objective).
4b. Analysis is drastically limited:
   i) Important possible outcomes are neglected.
   ii) Important alternative potential policies are neglected.
   iii) Important affected values are neglected.
5b. A succession of comparisons greatly reduces or eliminates reliance on theory.

Administrators cannot escape these conflicts by ascertaining the majority's preference, for preferences have not been registered on most issues; indeed, there often *are* no preferences in the absence of public discussion sufficient to bring an issue to the attention of the electorate. Furthermore, there is a question of whether intensity of feeling should be considered as well as the number of persons preferring each alternative. By the impossibility of doing otherwise, administrators often are reduced to deciding policy without clarifying objectives first.

Even when an administrator resolves to follow his own values as a criterion for decisions, he often will not know how to rank them when they conflict with one another, as they usually do. Suppose, for example, that an administrator must relocate tenants living in tenements scheduled for destruction. One objective is to empty the buildings fairly promptly, another is to find suitable accommodation for persons displaced, another is to avoid friction with residents in other areas in which a large influx would be unwelcome, another is to deal with all concerned through persuasion if possible, and so on.

How does one state even to himself the relative importance of these partially conflicting values? A simple ranking of them is not enough; one needs ideally to know how much of one value is worth sacrificing for some of another value. The answer is that typically the administrator chooses—and must choose—directly among policies in which these values are combined in different ways. He cannot first clarify his values and then choose among policies.

A more subtle third point underlies both the first two. Social objectives do not always have the same relative values. One objective may be highly prized in one circumstance, another in another circumstance. If, for example, an administrator values highly both the dispatch with which his agency can carry through its projects *and* good public relations, it matters little which of the two possibly conflicting values he favors in some abstract or general sense. Policy questions arise in forms which put to administrators such a question as: Given the degree to which we are or are not already achieving the values of dispatch and the values of good public relations, is it worth sacrificing a little speed for a happier clientele, or is it better to risk offending the clientele so that we can get on with our work? The answer to such a question varies with circumstances.

The value problem is, as the example shows, always a problem of adjustments at a margin. But there is no practicable way to state marginal objectives or values except in terms of particular policies. That one value is preferred to another in one decision situation does not mean that it will be preferred in another decision situation in which it can be had only at great sacrifice of another value. Attempts to rank or order values in general and abstract terms so that they do not shift from decision to decision end up by ignoring the relevant marginal preferences. The significance of this third point thus goes very far. Even if all administrators had at hand an agreed set of values, objectives, and constraints, and an agreed ranking of these values, objectives, and constraints, their marginal values in actual choice situations would be impossible to formulate.

Unable consequently to formulate the relevant values first and then choose among policies to achieve them, administrators must choose directly among alternative policies that offer different marginal combinations of values. Somewhat paradoxically, the only practicable way to disclose one's relevant marginal values even to oneself is to describe the policy one chooses to achieve them. Except roughly and vaguely, I know of no way to describe—or even to understand—what my relative evaluations are for, say, freedom and security, speed and accuracy in governmental decisions, or low taxes and better schools than to describe my preferences among specific policy choices that might be made between the alternatives in each of the pairs. . . .

NON-COMPREHENSIVE ANALYSIS (4B)

Ideally, rational-comprehensive analysis leaves out nothing important. But it is impossible to take everything important into consideration unless "important" is so narrowly defined that analysis is in fact quite limited. Limits on human intellectual capacities and on available information set definite limits to man's capacity to be comprehensive. In actual fact, therefore, no one can practice the rational-comprehensive method for really complex problems, and every administrator faced with a sufficiently complex problem must find ways drastically to simplify.

An administrator assisting in the formulation of agricultural economic policy cannot in the first place be competent on all possible policies. He cannot even comprehend one policy entirely. In planning a soil bank program, he cannot successfully anticipate the impact of higher or lower farm income on, say, urbanization—the possible consequent loosening of family ties, possible consequent eventual need for revisions in social security and further implications for tax problems arising out of new federal responsibilities for social security and municipal responsibilities for urban services. Nor, to follow another line of repercussions, can he work through the soil bank program's effects on prices for agricultural products in foreign markets and consequent implications for foreign relations, including those arising out of economic rivalry between the United States and the U.S.S.R.

In the method of successive limited comparisons, simplification is systematically achieved in two principal ways. First, it is achieved through limitation of policy comparisons to those policies that differ in relatively small degree from policies presently in effect. Such a limitation immediately reduces the number of alternatives to be investigated and also drastically simplifies the character of the investigation of each. For it is not necessary to undertake fundamental inquiry into an alternative and its consequences; it is necessary only to study those respects in which the proposed alternative and its consequences differ from the status quo. The empirical comparison of marginal differences among alternative policies that differ only marginally is, of course, a counterpart to the incremental or marginal comparison of values discussed above.

Relevance as Well as Realism

It is a matter of common observation that in Western democracies public administrators and policy analysts in general do largely limit their analyses to incremental or marginal differences in policies that are chosen to differ only incrementally. They do not do so, however, solely because they desperately need some way to simplify their problems; they also do so in order to be relevant. Democracies change their policies almost entirely through incremental adjustments. Policy does not move in leaps and bounds.

The incremental character of political change in the United States has often been remarked. The two major political parties agree on fundamentals; they offer alternative policies to the voters only on relatively small points of difference. Both parties favor full employment, but they define it somewhat differently; both favor the development of water power resources, but in slightly different ways; and both favor unemployment compensation, but not the same level of benefits. Similarly, shifts of policy within a party take place largely through a series of relatively small changes, as can be seen in their only gradual acceptance of the idea of governmental responsibility for support of the unemployed, a change in party positions beginning in the early 30's and culminating in a sense in the Employment Act of 1946.

Party behavior is in turn rooted in public attitudes, and political theorists cannot conceive of democracy's surviving in the United States in the absence of fundamental agreement on potentially disruptive issues, with consequent limitation of policy debates to relatively small differences in policy.

Since the policies ignored by the administrator are politically impossible and so irrelevant, the simplification of analysis achieved by concentrating on policies that differ only incrementally is not a capricious kind of simplification. In addition, it can be argued that, given the limits on knowledge within which policy-makers are confined, simplifying by limiting the focus to small variations from present policy makes the most of available knowledge. Because policies being considered are like present and past policies, the administrator can obtain information and claim some insight. Non-incremental policy proposals are therefore typically not only politically irrelevant but also unpredictable in their consequences. . . .

*Charles E.
Lindblom*

SUCCESSIVE COMPARISON AS A SYSTEM

Successive limited comparisons is, then, indeed a method or system; it is not a failure of method for which administrators ought to apologize. None the less, its imperfections, which have not been explored in this paper, are many. For example, the method is without a built-in safeguard for all relevant values, and it also may lead the decision-maker to overlook excellent policies for no other reason than that they are not suggested by the chain of successive policy steps leading up to the present. Hence, it ought to be said that under this method, as well as under some of the most sophisticated variants of the root method—operations research, for example—policies will continue to be as foolish as they are wise.

Why then bother to describe the method in all the above detail? Because it is in fact a common method of policy formulation, and is, for complex problems, the principal reliance of administrators as well as of other policy analysts. And because it will be superior to any other decision-making method available for complex problems in many circumstances, certainly superior to a futile attempt at superhuman comprehensiveness.

NOTE

1. "Operations Research and National Planning—A Dissent," 5 *Operations Research* 718 (October, 1957).

CHAPTER 12 The Corporate World

12.1 MARK DOWIE

Pinto Madness

It may be difficult to imagine that some of the leaders of American industries—persons who contribute to and perform good deeds for the community—would contemplate taking actions that would result in the deaths of innocent men, women, and children. Nevertheless, in the following excerpt, Mark Dowie describes how the leaders of the Ford Motor Company deliberately produced a new car that they knew was potentially lethal. In their judgment, the $11 per car required to install a safety device that would make it safer was too costly.

In the early 1970s, Ford put the Pinto on the market to compete with foreign companies for the compact car market. When struck from the rear at relatively low speed, however, the car consistently exploded into a ball of fire. Minor changes would have corrected the flaw and saved lives, but it took nearly seven years of litigation to institute the safety standard that would force Ford to install a device that would prevent this type of accident. Finally, in 1978, all Pintos produced between 1971 and 1976 were recalled.

In "Pinto Madness," for which he won the National Magazine Award from Columbia University School of Journalism, Dowie describes with some incredulity the lengths to which Ford went to protect its investment. His forte as an investigative journalist lies in exposing business and government practices that are legal "but nonetheless reprehensible." Dowie (b. 1939) has also won numerous other journalism awards for his investigative reporting. The story of the Ford Pinto is a good sociological case study on corporate decision-making.

Key Concept: cost-benefit analysis

*O*ne evening in the mid-1960s, Arjay Miller was driving home from his office in Dearborn, Michigan, in the four-door Lincoln Continental that went with his job as president of the Ford Motor Company. On a crowded highway, another car struck his from the rear. The Continental spun around and burst into flames. Because he was wearing a shoulder-strap seat belt, Miller was unharmed by the crash, and because his doors didn't jam he escaped the flaming wreck. But the accident made a vivid impression on him. Several months later, on July 15, 1965, he recounted it to a U.S. Senate subcommittee that was hearing testimony on auto safety legislation. "I still have burning in my mind the image of that gas tank on fire," Miller said. He went on to express an almost passionate interest in controlling fuel-fed fires in cars that crash or roll over. He spoke with excitement about the fabric gas tank Ford was testing at that very moment. "If it proves out," he promised the senators, "it will be a feature you will see in our standard cars."

Almost seven years after Miller's testimony, a woman, whom for legal reasons we will call Sandra Gillespie, pulled onto a Minneapolis highway in her new Ford Pinto. Riding with her was a young boy, whom we'll call Robbie Carlton. As she entered a merge lane, Sandra Gillespie's car stalled. Another car rear-ended hers at an impact speed of 28 miles per hour. The Pinto's gas tank ruptured. Vapors from it mixed quickly with the air in the passenger compartment. A spark ignited the mixture and the car exploded in a ball of fire. Sandra died in agony a few hours later in an emergency hospital. Her passenger, 13-year-old Robbie Carlton, is still alive; he has just come home from another futile operation aimed at grafting a new ear and nose from skin on the few unscarred portions of his badly burned body. (This accident is real; the details are from police reports.)

Why did Sandra Gillespie's Ford Pinto catch fire so easily, seven years after Ford's Arjay Miller made his apparently sincere pronouncements—the same seven years that brought more safety improvements to cars than any other period in automotive history? An extensive investigation by *Mother Jones* over the past six months has found these answers:

Fighting strong competition from Volkswagen for the lucrative small-car market, the Ford Motor Company rushed the Pinto into production in much less than the usual time.

Ford engineers discovered in pre-production crash tests that rear-end collisions would rupture the Pinto's fuel system extremely easily.

Because assembly-line machinery was already tooled when engineers found this defect, top Ford officials decided to manufacture the car anyway—exploding gas tank and all—*even though Ford owned the patent on a much safer gas tank.*

For more than eight years afterwards, Ford successfully lobbied, with extraordinary vigor and some blatant lies, against a key government safety standard that would have forced the company to change the Pinto's fire-prone gas tank.

By conservative estimates Pinto crashes have caused 500 burn deaths to people who would not have been seriously injured if the car had not burst into flames. . . .

Ford knows the Pinto is a firetrap, yet it has paid out millions to settle damage suits out of court, and it is prepared to spend millions more lobbying against safety standards. With a half million cars rolling off the assembly lines each year, Pinto is the biggest-selling subcompact in America, and the company's operating profit on the car is fantastic. Finally, in 1977, new Pinto models have incorporated a few minor alterations necessary to meet that federal standard Ford managed to hold off for eight years. Why did the company delay so long in making these minimal inexpensive improvements?

Ford waited eight years because its internal "cost-benefit analysis," *which places a dollar value on human life,* said it wasn't profitable to make the changes sooner.

Before we get to the question of how much Ford thinks your life is worth, let's trace the history of the death trap itself. Although this particular story is about the Pinto, the way in which Ford made its decision is typical of the U.S. auto industry generally. There are plenty of similar stories about other cars made by other companies. But this case is the worst of them all. . . .

Mother Jones has studied hundreds of reports and documents on rear-end collisions involving Pintos. These reports conclusively reveal that if you ran into that Pinto you were following at over 30 miles per hour, the rear end of the car would buckle like an accordion, right up to the back seat. The tube leading to the gas-tank cap would be ripped away from the tank itself, and gas would immediately begin sloshing onto the road around the car. The buckled gas tank would be jammed up against the differential housing which contains four sharp protruding bolts likely to gash holes in the tank and spill still more gas. The welded seam between the main body frame and the wheel well would split, allowing gas to enter the interior of the car.

Now all you need is a spark from a cigarette, ignition, or scraping metal, and both cars would be engulfed in flames. If you gave the Pinto a really good whack—say, at 40 mph—chances are excellent that its doors would jam and you would have to stand by and watch its trapped passengers burn to death.

This scenario is no news to Ford. Internal company documents in our possession show that Ford has crash-tested the Pinto at a top-secret site more than 40 times and that *every* test made at over 25 mph without special structural alteration of the car has resulted in a ruptured fuel tank. Despite this, Ford officials denied having crash-tested the Pinto.

Eleven of these tests, averaging a 31-mph impact speed, came before Pintos started rolling out of the factories. Only three cars passed the test with unbroken fuel tanks. In one of them an inexpensive light-weight metal baffle was placed so those bolts would not perforate the tank. (Don't forget about that baffle which costs about a dollar and weighs about a pound. It plays an important role in our story later on.) In another successful test, a piece of steel was placed between the tank and the bumper. In the third test car the gas tank was lined with a rubber bladder. But none of these protective alterations was used in the mass-produced Pinto.

In preproduction planning, engineers seriously considered using in the Pinto the same kind of gas tank Ford uses in the Capri. The Capri tank rides over the rear axle and differential housing. It has been so successful in over 50 crash tests that Ford used it in its Experimental Safety Vehicle, which withstood rear-end impacts of 60 mph. So why wasn't the Capri tank used in the Pinto? Or, why wasn't that baffle placed between the tank and the axle—something that would have saved the life of Sandra Gillespie and hundreds like her. Why was a car known to be a serious fire hazard deliberately released to production in August of 1970?

Whether Ford should manufacture subcompacts at all was the subject of a bitter two-year debate at the company's Dearborn headquarters. The principals in the corporate struggle were the then-president Semon "Bunky" Knudsen, whom Henry Ford II had hired away from General Motors, and Lee Iacocca, a spunky young turk who had risen fast within the company on the enormous success of the Mustang. Iacocca argued forcefully that Volkswagen and the Japanese were going to capture the entire American subcompact market unless Ford put out its own alternative to the VW Beetle. Bunky Knudsen said, in effect: let them have the small-car market; Ford makes good money on medium and large models. But he lost the battle and later resigned. Iacocca became president and almost immediately began a rush program to produce the Pinto.

Like the Mustang, the Pinto became known in the company as "Lee's car." Lee Iacocca wanted that little car in the showrooms of America with the 1971 models. So he ordered his engineering vice president, Bob Alexander, to oversee what was probably the shortest production planning period in modern automotive history. The normal time span from conception to production of a new car model is about 43 months. The Pinto schedule was set at just under 25.

Design, styling, product planning, advance engineering and quality assurance all have flexible time frames, and engineers can pretty much carry these on simultaneously. Tooling, on the other hand, has a fixed time frame of about 18 months. Normally, an auto company doesn't begin tooling until the other processes are almost over. *But Iacocca's speed-up meant Pinto tooling went on at the same time as product development.* So when crash tests revealed a serious defect in the gas tank, it was too late. The tooling was well under way.

When it was discovered the gas tank was unsafe, did anyone go to Iacocca and tell him? "Hell no," replied an engineer who worked on the Pinto, a high company official for many years, who, unlike several others at Ford, maintains a necessarily clandestine concern for safety. "That person would have been fired. Safety wasn't a popular subject around Ford in those days. With Lee it was taboo. . . .

As Lee Iacocca was fond of saying, "Safety doesn't sell."

Heightening the anti-safety pressure on Pinto engineers was an important goal set by Iacocca known as "the limits of 2,000." The Pinto was not to weigh an ounce over 2,000 pounds and not to cost a cent over $2,000. "Iacocca enforced these limits with an iron hand," recalls the engineer quoted earlier. So, even when a crash test showed that that one-pound, one-dollar piece of metal stopped the puncture of the gas tank, it was thrown out as an extra cost and extra weight.

People shopping for subcompacts are watching every dollar. "You have to keep in mind," the engineer explained, "that the price elasticity on these subcompacts is extremely tight. You can price yourself right out of the market by adding $25 to the production cost of the model. And nobody understands that better than Iacocca."

Blame for Sandra Gillespie's death, Robbie Carlton's unrecognizable face and all the other injuries and deaths in Pintos since 1970 does not rest on the shoulders of Lee Iacocca alone. For, while he and his associates fought their battle against a safer Pinto in Dearborn, a larger war against safer cars raged in Washington. One skirmish in that war involved Ford's successful eight-year lobbying effort against Federal Motor Vehicle Safety Standard 301, the rear-end provisions of which would have forced Ford to redesign the Pinto.

But first some background:

During the early '60s, auto safety legislation became the *bête-noire* of American big business. The auto industry was the last great unregulated business, and if *it* couldn't reverse the tide of government regulation, the reasoning went, no one could. . . .

[But] by 1965, most pundits and lobbyists saw the handwriting on the wall and prepared to accept government "meddling" in the last bastion of free enterprise. Not Henry [Ford II]. With bulldog tenacity, he held out for defeat of the legislation to the very end, loyal to his grandfather's invention and to the company that makes it. But the Safety Act passed the House and Senate unanimously, and was signed into law by Lyndon Johnson in 1966.

While lobbying for and against legislation is pretty much a process of high-level back-slapping, press-conferencing and speech-making, fighting a regulatory agency is a much subtler matter. Henry headed home to lick his wounds in Grosse Pointe, Michigan, and a planeload of the Ford Motor Company's best brains flew to Washington to start the "education" of the new federal auto safety bureaucrats.

Their job was to implant the official industry ideology in the minds of the new officials regulating auto safety. Briefly summarized, that ideology states that auto accidents are caused not by *cars*, but by people and highway conditions. . . .

In light of an annual death rate approaching 50,000, they are forced to admit that driving is hazardous. But the car is, in the words of Arjay Miller, "the safest link in the safety chain."

Before the Ford experts left Washington to return to drafting tables in Dearborn they did one other thing. They managed to informally reach an agreement with the major public servants who would be making auto safety decisions. This agreement was that "cost-benefit" would be an acceptable mode of analysis by Detroit and its new regulators. . . .

Cost-benefit analysis was used only occasionally in government until President Kennedy appointed Ford Motor Company President Robert Mc-Namara to be Secretary of Defense. McNamara, originally an accountant, preached cost benefit with all the force of a Biblical zealot. Stated in its simplest terms, cost-benefit analysis says that if the cost is greater than the benefit, the project is not worth it—no matter what the benefit. Examine the cost of every action, decision, contract, part, or change, the doctrine says, then carefully evaluate the benefits (in dollars) to be certain that they exceed the cost before you begin a program or pass a regulation.

As a management tool in a business in which profits count over all else, cost-benefit analysis makes a certain amount of sense. Serious problems arise, however, when public officials who ought to have more than corporate profits

TABLE 1

219

What's Your Life Worth? Societal Cost Components for Fatalities, 1972 NHTSA Study

Mark Dowie

Component	1971 Costs
Future productivity losses	
Direct	$132,000
Indirect	41,300
Medical costs	
Hospital	700
Other	425
Property damage	1,500
Insurance administration	4,700
Legal and court	3,000
Employer losses	1,000
Victim's pain and suffering	10,000
Funeral	900
Assets (lost consumption)	5,000
Miscellaneous accident cost	200
Total per fatality: $200,725	

Here is a chart from a federal study showing how the National Highway Traffic Safety Administration has calculated the value of a human life. The estimate was arrived at under pressure from the auto industry. The Ford Motor Company has used it in cost-benefit analyses arguing why certain safety measures are not "worth" the savings in human lives. The calculation above is a breakdown of the estimated cost to society every time someone is killed in a car accident. We were not able to find anyone, either in the government or at Ford, who could explain how the $10,000 figure for "pain and suffering" had been arrived at.

at heart apply cost-benefit analysis to every conceivable decision. The inevitable result is that they must place a dollar value on human life.

Ever wonder what your life is worth in dollars? Perhaps $10 million? Ford has a better idea: $200,000.

Remember, Ford had gotten the federal regulators to agree to talk auto safety in terms of cost-benefit. But in order to be able to argue that various safety costs were greater than their benefits, Ford needed to have a dollar value figure for the "benefit." Rather than coming up with a price tag itself, the auto industry pressured the National Highway Traffic Safety Administration to do so. And in a 1972 report the agency determined that a human life lost on the highway was worth $200,725 [Table 1]. Inflationary forces have recently pushed the figure up to $278,000.

Furnished with this useful tool, Ford immediately went to work using it to prove why various safety improvements were too expensive to make.

Nowhere did the company argue harder that it should make no changes than in the area of rupture-prone fuel tanks. Not long after the government arrived at the $200,725-per-life figure, it surfaced, rounded off to a cleaner $200,000, in an internal Ford memorandum. This cost-benefit analysis argued that Ford should not make an $11-per-car improvement that would prevent 180 fiery deaths a year.

TABLE 2

*Benefits and Costs Relating to Fuel Leakage Associated with the Static
Rollover Test Portion of FMVSS 208*

Benefits

Savings: 80 burn deaths, 180 serious burn injuries, 2,100 burned
  vehicles.
Unit cost: $200,000 per death, $67,000 per injury, $700 per vehicle.
Total benefit: 180 × ($200,000) + 180 × ($67,000) + 2,100 × ($700) =
  $49.5 million.

Costs

Sales: 11 million cars, 1.5 million light trucks.
Unit cost: $11 per car, $11 per truck.
Total cost: 11,000,000 × ($11) + 1,500,000 × ($11) = $137 million.

This cold calculus [Table 2] is buried in a seven-page company memorandum entitled "Fatalities Associated with Crash-Induced Fuel Leakage and Fires."

The memo goes on to argue that there is no financial benefit in complying with proposed safety standards that would admittedly result in fewer auto fires, fewer burn deaths and fewer burn injuries. Naturally, memoranda that speak so casually of "burn deaths" and "burn injuries" are not released to the public. They are very effective, however, with Department of Transportation officials indoctrinated in McNamarian cost-benefit analysis.

All Ford had to do was convince men like John Volpe, Claude Brinegar and William Coleman (successive Secretaries of Transportation during the Nixon-Ford years) that certain safety standards would add so much to the price of cars that fewer people would buy them. This could damage the auto industry, which was still believed to be the bulwark of the American economy. "Compliance to these standards," Henry Ford II prophesied at more than one press conference, "will shut down the industry."

The Nixon Transportation Secretaries were the kind of regulatory officials big business dreams of. They understood and loved capitalism and thought like businessmen. Yet, best of all, they came into office uninformed on technical automotive matters. And you could talk "burn injuries" and "burn deaths" with these guys, and they didn't seem to envision children crying at funerals and people hiding in their homes with melted faces. Their minds appeared to have leapt right to the bottom line—more safety meant higher prices, higher prices meant lower sales and lower sales meant lower profits.

So when J. C. Echold, Director of Automotive Safety (chief anti-safety lobbyist) for Ford wrote to the Department of Transportation—which he still does frequently, at great length—he felt secure attaching a memorandum that in effect says it is acceptable to kill 180 people and burn another 180 every year, *even though we have the technology that could save their lives for $11 a car.*

Furthermore, Echold attached this memo, confident, evidently, that the Secretary would question neither his low death/injury statistics nor his high cost estimates. But it turns out, on closer examination, that both these findings were misleading.

First, note that Ford's table shows an equal number of burn deaths and burn injuries. This is false. All independent experts estimate that for each person who dies by an auto fire, many more are left with charred hands, faces and limbs. Andrew McGuire of the Northern California Burn Center estimates the ratio of burn injuries to deaths at ten to one instead of the one to one Ford shows here. Even though Ford values a burn at only a piddling $67,000 instead of the $200,000 price of life, the true ratio obviously throws the company's calculations way off.

The other side of the equation, the alleged $11 cost of a fire-prevention device, is also a misleading estimation. One document that was *not* sent to Washington by Ford was a "Confidential" cost analysis *Mother Jones* has managed to obtain, showing that crash fires could be largely prevented for considerably *less* than $11 a car. The cheapest method involves placing a heavy rubber bladder inside the gas tank to keep the fuel from spilling if the tank ruptures. Goodyear had developed the bladder and had demonstrated it to the automotive industry. We have in our possession crash-test reports showing that the Goodyear bladder worked well. On December 2, 1970 (*two years before* Echold sent his cost-benefit memo to Washington), Ford Motor Company ran a rear-end crash test on a car with the rubber bladder in the gas tank. The tank ruptured, but no fuel leaked. On January 15, 1971, Ford again tested the bladder and again it worked. The total purchase and installation cost of the bladder would have been $5.08 per car. That $5.08 could have saved the lives of Sandra Gillespie and several hundred others.

When a federal regulatory agency like the National Highway Traffic Safety Administration (NHTSA) decides to issue a new standard, the law usually requires it to invite all interested parties to respond before the standard is enforced—a reasonable enough custom on the surface. However, the auto industry has taken advantage of this process and has used it to delay lifesaving emission and safety standards for years. In the case of the standard that would have corrected that fragile Pinto fuel tank, the delay was for an incredible eight years.

The particular regulation involved here was Federal Motor Vehicle Safety Standard 301. Ford picked portions of Standard 301 for strong opposition back in 1968 when the Pinto was still in the blueprint stage. The intent of 301, and the 300 series that followed it, was to protect drivers and passengers *after* a crash occurs. Without question the worst postcrash hazard is fire. So Standard 301 originally proposed that all cars should be able to withstand a fixed barrier impact of 20 mph (that is, running into a wall at that speed) without losing fuel.

When the standard was proposed, Ford engineers pulled their crash-test results out of their files. The front ends of most cars were no problem—with minor alterations they could stand the impact without losing fuel. "We were already working on the front end," Ford engineer Dick Kimble admitted. "We knew we could meet the test on the front end." But with the Pinto particularly, a 20-mph rear-end standard meant redesigning the entire rear end of the car.

With the Pinto scheduled for production in August of 1970, and with $200 million worth of tools in place, adoption of this standard would have created a minor financial disaster. So Standard 301 was targeted for delay, and, with some assistance from its industry associates, Ford succeeded beyond its wildest expectations: the standard was not adopted until the 1977 model year. Here is how it happened:

There are several main techniques in the art of combating a government safety standard: a) make your arguments in succession, so the feds can be working on disproving only one at a time; b) claim that the real problem is not X but Y (we already saw one instance of this in "the problem is not cars but people"); c) no matter how ridiculous each argument is, accompany it with thousands of pages of highly technical assertions it will take the government months or, preferably, years to test. Ford's large and active Washington office brought these techniques to new heights and became the envy of the lobbyists' trade.

The Ford people started arguing against Standard 301 way back in 1968 with a strong attack of technique b). Fire, they said, was not the real problem. Sure, cars catch fire and people burn occasionally. But statistically auto fires are such a minor problem that NHTSA should really concern itself with other matters.

Strange as it may seem, the Department of Transportation (NHTSA's parent agency) didn't know whether or not this was true. So it contracted with several independent research groups to study auto fires. The studies took months, often years, which was just what Ford wanted. The completed studies, however, showed auto fires to be more of a problem that Transportation officials ever dreamed of. A Washington research firm found that 400,000 cars were burning up every year, burning more than 3,000 people to death. Furthermore, auto fires were increasing five times as fast as building fires. Another study showed that 35 per cent of all fire deaths in the U.S. occurred in automobiles. Forty per cent of all fire department calls in the 1960s were to vehicle fires—a public cost of $350 million a year, a figure that, incidentally, never shows up in cost-benefit analyses.

Another study was done by the Highway Traffic Research Institute in Ann Arbor, Michigan, a safety think-tank funded primarily by the auto industry (the giveaway there is the words "highway traffic" rather than "automobile" in the group's name). It concluded that 40 per cent of the lives lost in fuel-fed fires could be saved if the manufacturers complied with proposed Standard 301. Finally, a third report was prepared for NHTSA. This report indicated that the Ford Motor Company makes 24 per cent of the cars on the American road, yet these cars account for 42 per cent of the collision-ruptured fuel tanks.

Ford lobbyists then used technique a)—bringing up a new argument. Their line then became: yes, perhaps burn accidents do happen, but rear-end collisions are relatively rare (note the echo of technique b) here as well). Thus Standard 301 was not needed. This set the NHTSA off on a new round of analyzing accident reports. The government's findings finally were that rear-end collisions were seven and a half times more likely to result in fuel spills than were front-end collisions. So much for that argument.

By now it was 1972; NHTSA had been researching and analyzing for four years to answer Ford's objections. During that time, nearly 9,000 people burned to death in flaming wrecks. Tens of thousands more were badly burned and scarred for life. And the four-year delay meant that well over 10 million new unsafe vehicles went on the road, vehicles that will be crashing, leaking fuel and incinerating people well into the 1980s.

Ford now had to enter its third round of battling the new regulations. On the "the problem is not X but Y" principle, the company had to look around for something new to get itself off the hook. One might have thought that, faced with all the latest statistics on the horrifying number of deaths in flaming accidents, Ford would find the task difficult. But the company's rhetoric was brilliant. The problem was not burns, but . . . impact! Most of the people killed in these fiery accidents, claimed Ford, would have died whether the car burned or not. They were killed by the kinetic force of the impact, not the fire.

And so once again, the ball bounced into the government's court and the absurdly pro-industry NHTSA began another slow-motion response. Once again it began a time-consuming round of test crashes and embarked on a study of accidents. The latter, however, revealed that a large and growing number of corpses taken from burned cars involved in rear-end crashes contained no cuts, bruises or broken bones. They clearly would have survived the accident unharmed if the cars had not caught fire. This pattern was confirmed in careful rear-end crash tests performed by the Insurance Institute for Highway Safety. A University of Miami study found an inordinate number of Pintos burning on rear-end impact and concluded that this demonstrated "a clear and present hazard to all Pinto owners."

Pressure on NHTSA from Ralph Nader and consumer groups began mounting. The industry-agency collusion was so obvious that Senator Joseph Montoya (D-N.M.) introduced legislation about Standard 301. NHTSA waffled some more and again announced its intentions to promulgate a rear-end collision standard.

Waiting, as it normally does, until the last day allowed for response, Ford filed with NHTSA a gargantuan batch of letters, studies and charts now arguing that the federal testing criteria were unfair. Ford also argued that design changes required to meet the standard would take 43 months, which seemed like a rather long time in light of the fact that the entire Pinto was designed in about two years. Specifically new complaints about the standard involved the weight of the test vehicle, whether or not the brakes should be engaged at the moment of impact and the claim that the standard should only apply to cars, not trucks or buses. Perhaps the most amusing argument was that the engine should not be idling during crash tests, the rationale being that an idling engine meant that the gas tank had to contain gasoline and that the hot lights needed to film the crash might ignite the gasoline and cause a fire.

Some of these complaints were accepted, others rejected. But they all required examination and testing by a weak kneed NHTSA, meaning more of those 18-month studies the industry loves so much. So the complaints served their real purpose—delay; all told, an eight-year delay, while Ford manufactured more than three million profitable, dangerously incendiary Pintos. . . .

In 1977, however, an incredibly sluggish government has at last instituted Standard 301. Now Pintos will have to have rupture-proof gas tanks. Or will they?

To everyone's surprise, the 1977 Pinto recently passed a rear-end crash test in Phoenix, Arizona, for NHTSA. The agency was so convinced the Pinto would fail that it was the first car tested. Amazingly, it did not burst into flame.

"We have had so many Ford failures in the past," explained agency engineer Tom Grubbs, "I felt sure the Pinto would fail."

How did it pass?

Remember that one-dollar, one-pound metal baffle that was on one of the three modified Pintos that passed the pre-production crash tests nearly ten years ago? Well, it is a standard feature on the 1977 Pinto. In the Phoenix test it protected the gas tank from being perforated by those four bolts on the differential housing.

We asked Grubbs if he noticed any other substantial alterations in the rear-end structure of the car. "No," he replied, "the [baffle] seems to be the only noticeable change over the 1976 model."

But was it? What Tom Grubbs and the Department of Transportation didn't know when they tested the car was that it was manufactured in St. Thomas, Ontario. Ontario? The significance of that becomes clear when you learn that Canada has for years had extremely strict rear-end collision standards.

Tom Irwin is the business manager of Charlie Rossi Ford, the Scottsdale, Arizona, dealership that sold the Pinto to Tom Grubbs. He refused to explain why he was selling Fords made in Canada when there is a huge assembly plant much closer by in California. "I know why you're asking that question, and I'm not going to answer it," he blurted out. "You'll have to ask the company." . . .

The Department of Transportation is considering buying an American Pinto and running the test again. For now, it will only say that the situation is under investigation.

Whether the new American Pinto fails or passes the test, Standard 301 will never force the company to test or recall the more than two million pre-1977 Pintos still on the highway. Seventy or more people will burn to death in those cars every year for many years to come. If the past is any indication, Ford will continue to accept the deaths. . . .

The original draft of the Motor Vehicle Safety Act provided for criminal sanction against a manufacturer who willfully placed an unsafe car on the market. Early in the proceedings the auto industry lobbied the provision out of the bill. Since then, there have been those damage settlements, of course, but the only government punishment meted out to auto companies for non-compliance to standards has been a minuscule fine, usually $5,000 to $10,000. One wonders how long the Ford Motor Company would continue to market lethal cars were Henry Ford II and Lee Iacocca serving 20-year terms in Leavenworth for consumer homicide.

This article was published in September of 1977, and in February 1978 a jury awarded a sixteen-year-old boy, badly burned in a rear-end Pinto accident, $128 million in damages (the accident occurred in 1973 in Santa Ana, Calif.). That was the largest single personal injury judgment in history.

On May 8, 1978, the Department of Transportation announced that tests conducted in response to this article showed conclusively that the Pinto was defective in all respects described in the article and called for a recall of all 1971 to 1976 Pintos—the most expensive recall in automotive history.

Mark Dowie

Managers

Rosabeth Moss Kanter (b. 1943), sociologist, consultant, and one of the preeminent scholars of organizations, is a professor of management at Harvard University Business School and the first woman editor of the Harvard Business Review. She is a prolific writer and has done pioneering work on communes and organizations, which is exemplified in her work *Men and Women of the Corporation* (Basic Books, 1977), an analysis of (among other things) the problems of the token woman in the organization. In her recent works, *The Change Masters: Innovation for Productivity in the American Corporation* (Simon & Schuster, 1983) and *Teaching Elephants to Dance: The Post-Entrepreneurial Revolution in Strategy, Management, and Careers* (Simon & Schuster, 1989), she continues to offer new insights on the process of change, power, and empowerment.

The selection that follows examines the impact of uncertainty on the process of management. Kanter says that most bureaucratic principles are necessarily modified when they are applied to large corporations. For example, in the upper levels of the corporate hierarchy, the separation of the individual and his or her position is not clear-cut. Kanter argues that, contrary to the bureaucratic function of ensuring operational efficiency, neither the institutionalization of bureaucracy nor the routinization of the work in bureaucratic organizations has eliminated uncertainty. She shows how this leads to a quest for homogeneity within the managerial circle, which facilitates trust among like individuals but diminishes the role of merit and blurs official and personal roles.

Key Concept: similarity of outlook

> The corporation seems to seek an arrangement which is surely an anomaly in human society, that of homosexual reproduction.
>
> —Wilbert Moore, *The Conduct of the Corporation*

Managers at Indsco [not the real name of the company] had to look the part. They were not exactly cut out of the same mold like paper dolls, but the similarities in appearance were striking. Even this relatively trivial matter revealed the extent of conformity pressures on managers. Not that there were formal dress rules in this enlightened company, like the legendary IBM uniforms, but there was an informal understanding all the same. The norms were unmistakable, after a visitor saw enough managers, invariably white and male, with a certain shiny, clean-cut look. The only beards, even after beards became merely daring rather than radical, were the results of vacation-time experiments on camping trips, except (it was said), for a few in R & D—"but we know that scientists do strange things," a sales manager commented. An inappropriate appearance could be grounds for complaint to higher management. A new field supervisor was visited by his boss for a "chat about setting a good example for the guys" after his longish hair, curling the slightest way down the nape of his neck, caused comment. "Appearance makes a big difference in the response you get around this company," the boss insisted. Another executive was upset because a staff expert he frequently called upon for help seemed to change his appearance or hairstyle with each fashion wind. "What are you trying to do now?" he once asked the staffer exasperatedly. "We get used to you one way, then you have to change. Why must you always be changing?"

If differences in appearance were not easily tolerated in the ranks of those called managers, neither were a wide range of other sorts of differences. It is not news that social conformity is important in managerial careers. There is ample evidence from organizational studies that leaders in a variety of situations are likely to show preference for socially similar subordinates and help them get ahead. As Clark Kerr and his colleagues wrote, "Incumbents in the managerial hierarchy seek as new recruits those they can rely upon and trust. They demand that the newcomers be loyal, that they accept authority, and that they conform to a prescribed pattern of behavior."

Unlike a more communal environment, where eccentrics can be lovingly tolerated because trust is based on mutual commitments and deep personal knowledge, those who run the bureaucratic corporation often rely on outward manifestations to determine who is the "right sort of person." Managers tend to carefully guard power and privilege for those who fit in, for those they see as "their kind." Wilbert Moore was commenting on this phenomenon when he used the metaphor of a "bureaucratic kinship system" to describe the corporation—but a kinship system based on "homosexual reproduction," in which men reproduce themselves in their own image. The metaphor is apt. Because of the *situation* in which managers function, because of the position of managers in the corporate structure, social similarity tends to become extremely important to them. The structure sets in motion forces leading to the replication of managers as the same kind of social individuals. And the men who manage reproduce themselves in kind.

Conformity pressures and the development of exclusive management circles closed to "outsiders" stem from the degree of uncertainty surrounding managerial positions. Bureaucracies are social inventions that supposedly reduce the uncertain to the predictable and routine. Yet much uncertainty remains—many situations in which individual people rather than impersonal procedures must be trusted. "Uncertainty," James Thompson wrote in a recent major statement on organizations, "appears as the fundamental problem for complex organizations, and coping with uncertainty as the essence of the administrative process." Thompson identified three sources of uncertainty in even the most perfect of machine-like bureaucracies: a lack of cause-effect understanding in the culture at large (limiting the possibility for advance planning); contingencies caused by the fact that the bureaucracy is not alone, so that outcomes of organizational action are in part determined by action of other elements in the environment; and the interdependence of parts, the human interconnections inside the organization itself, which can never fully be reduced to predictable action. The requirements for a perfectly technically "rational" bureaucracy that never has to rely on the personal discretion of a single individual can never be met: complete knowledge of all cause-effect relationships plus control over all of the relevant variables. Thus, sources of uncertainty that are inherent in human institutions mean that some degree of reliance on individual persons must always be present.

It is ironic that in those most impersonal of institutions the essential communal problem of trust remains. For wherever there is uncertainty, *someone* (or some group) must decide, and thus, there must be personal discretion. And discretion raises not technical but human, social, and even communal questions: trust, and its origins in loyalty, commitment, and mutual understanding based on the sharing of values. It is the uncertainty quotient in managerial work, as it has come to be defined in the large modern corporation, that causes management to become so socially restricting: to develop tight inner circles excluding social strangers; to keep control in the hands of socially homogeneous peers; to stress conformity and insist upon a diffuse, unbounded loyalty; and to prefer ease of communication and thus social certainty over the strains of dealing with people who are "different."

If conditions of uncertainty mean that people have to be relied on, then people fall back on social bases for trust. The greater the uncertainty, the greater the pressures for those who have to trust each other to form a homogeneous group. At different times in an organization's history, and at different places in its structure, a higher degree of uncertainty brings with it more drive for social similarity. If this issue can be understood theoretically and in its historical manifestations, then the present-day behavior of Indsco's managers makes more sense.

UNCERTAINTY, DISCRETION, AND THE NEED FOR TRUST

Uncertainty is a feature of the early stages of organizations. The beginnings of all organizations, even those for which there are preexisting models, involve a set of choices requiring discretion on the part of decision-makers, so new organizations almost invariably begin by choosing a homogeneous rather than a diversified group to make initial decisions. Similarity of outlook guarantees at least some basis for trust and mutual understanding. If beginnings always tend to create pressures for similarity among those who begin, then the organizations that start without maps, guides, or the accumulated experience of those who have been there before—the organizations that must invent the models— are even more likely to face the trust issue.

The first large corporations had the uncertainty of how to proceed to organize, as well as the uncertainty of any beginning. How to organize was a task equaling, if not surpassing, in importance the task of coordinating whatever was organized. The early corporations also had to bring under control the potential for violations of trust inherent in instances of manager disloyalty or misbehavior—the possibility that the first managers would become so caught up in their own power they would forget their larger purposes.

Closed inner circles in which trust is assumed can be achieved by two kinds of homogeneity: similarity of social background and characteristics, or similarity of organizational experience. The latter is possible, of course, only when the organization or its models are no longer new—when organizational routines have been established and people have remained in their positions long enough to make shared socialization and shared experience a meaningful basis for trust. However, when organizations are new or changing rapidly, elites have to fall back on social homogeneity—on being part of the same social circle. In the military, for example, Oscar Grusky found that slower turnover of managerial personnel, when there was time for shared understanding to develop, was associated with homogeneity of organizational experience; but rapid turnover, signifying rapid change, was associated with greater homogeneity of their social characteristics. For the first corporations, then, we would expect social similarity to be a factor in the selection of trusted managers, and management to evolve as a socially closed circle. . . .

Discretion and Hierarchy Today

There is still a great deal of personal discretion required in positions with a high uncertainty quotient. Uncertainty can stem from either the time-span of decisions and the amount of information that must be collected, or from the frequency with which non-routine events occur and must be handled. The impossibility of specifying contingencies in advance, operating procedures for all possible events, leaves an organization to rely on personal discretion. (It is also this pressure that partly accounts for the desire to centralize responsibility in a few people who can be held accountable for discretionary decisions.) Commented a sales manager at Indsco, "The need for flexibility is primary in my job. The situation changes from minute to minute. One minute it's a tank truck that collapsed. Another it's a guy whose wife just had a hysterectomy and is going to die. . . . I'm dealing with such different problems all the time."

The importance of discretion increases with closeness to the top of a hierarchical organization. Despite the institutionalization and routinization of much of the work of large organizations and despite the proliferation of management experts, uncertainty remains a generic condition, increasing with rank. Jobs are relatively unstructured, tasks are non-routine, and decisions must be made about a variety of unknown elements. Issues such as "direction" and "purpose" cannot be reduced to rational formulae. Organizational improvement, or even maintenance, is not a simple matter that can be summarized in statements about "the ten functions of managers" or techniques of operation. If the "big picture" can be viewed from the top, it also looks bigger and fuzzier. Computers have not necessarily reduced the uncertainty of decisions at the top; in some cases, they have merely increased the amount of information that decision-makers must take into account. A major executive of Indsco confessed in a meeting that "we don't know how to manage these giant structures; and I suspect no one does. They are like dinosaurs, lumbering on of their own accord, even if they are no longer functional."

Criteria for "good decisions" or good management performance also get less certain closer to the top. The connection between an upper management decision and a factor such as production efficiency several layers below or gross sales is indirect, if it is even apparent. (An Indsco division president said, "In the 1960s we thought we were really terrific. We patted ourselves on the back a lot because every decision was so successful. Business kept on expanding. Then came the recession, and we couldn't do anything to stop it. We had been lucky before. Everything turned to gold in the 1960s. But it became clear that we don't know the first thing about how to make this enterprise work.")

Financial measures of performance are sometimes even artifactual because of the juggling of figures; for example, when and how a loss is recorded. There are also a variety of dilemmas in trying to evaluate the success of managers: qualitative versus quantitative measures, short-run versus long-run outcomes. Decisions that look good in the short term might be long-term disasters, but by that time the failure can be blamed on other factors, and those responsible for the decisions might be so entrenched in power that they now call the shots anyway. A former public relations manager at DuPont formulated what he called the Law of Inverse Certainty: "The more important the management decision, the less precise the tools to deal with it . . . and the longer it will take before anyone knows it was right." One example was a rigid cost cutter who helped increase profits by eliminating certain functions; by the time the company began to feel the loss of those functions, he had been promoted and was part of the inner power group. Someone else picked up the pieces.

The uncertainty up the ranks, like the uncertainty of beginnings, also puts trust and homogeneity at a premium. The personal loyalty normally demanded of subordinates by officials is most intense at the highest levels of organizations, as others have also noted. The lack of structure in top jobs makes it very important for decision-makers to work together closely in at least the harmony of shared understanding and a degree of mutual trust. Since for an organization to function at all requires that, to some extent, people will pull together around decisions, the solidarity that can be mustered through common membership in social networks, and the social control this provides, is a helpful supplement for decision-makers. Indeed, homogeneity of class and ethnic background and prior social experiences is one important "commitment mechanism" found to build a feeling of communion among members of viable utopian communities. Situational pressures, then, place a great emphasis on personal relations and social homogeneity as functional elements in the carrying out of managerial tasks. And privilege is also kept within a small circle. . . .

COMMUNICATION AND THE PREFERENCE FOR SOCIAL CERTAINTY

The tasks of managers constitute a "social event," as William Henry put it, "not an individual event." One psychologist explained it this way: "The individual manager does not have a clearly bounded job with neatly defined authorities and responsibilities. Rather, he is placed in the middle of a system of relationships, out of which he must fashion an organization which will accomplish his objectives." Research on executive time use support these propositions. In one study, four executives in England were found to spend 80 percent of their time talking. A Harvard Business School study estimated that 50 to 60 percent of a department head's time was spent talking to men other than his immediate subordinates. Robert Dubin found that in several samples as little as 28 percent down to 6.3 percent of an executive's time was actually spent making decisions as opposed to other kinds of more social activities. . . .

[In a small study of Indsco managers] there were several striking features of the communication dominating managerial tasks, because of the sheer size, complexity, and geographic spread of the organization: Communication had to be rapid, since each episode was squeezed in among many more. It had to be accurate, since it was part of a network of interdependencies and contingencies. And it had to travel long distances, sometimes by impersonal means and through channels where people were not directly known to one another. Common language and common understanding were thus very important. People had neither the time nor the backlog of joint experience to make appropriate calibrations for differences in meaning systems or messages that seemed incomprehensible.

The structure of communication involved in managerial jobs generated a desire for smooth social relationships and a preference for selection of those people with whom communication would be easiest. Indsco managers identified social and interpersonal skills as important characteristics of the "effective manager." After a group generated their list of twenty-four such attributes in a meeting, someone pointed out that missing from the list was "knowing the business you're in." But then another manager replied that he knew of many effective executives who knew nothing about their product or field. "Winning acceptance" and being able to communicate seemed much more important. And the group agreed that no one without peer acceptance could get ahead.

One way to ensure acceptance and ease of communication was to limit managerial jobs to those who were socially homogeneous. Social certainty, at least, could compensate for some of the other sources of uncertainty in the tasks of management. It was easier to talk to those of one's kind who had shared experiences—more certain, more accurate, more predictable. Less time could be spent concentrating on subtle meanings, and more time (such an overloaded resource for managers) on the task. . . .

There was a decided wish to avoid those people with whom communication was felt to be uncomfortable, those who took time to figure out or seemed unpredictable in their conduct. Deviants and nonconformists were certainly suspect for this reason. Even people who looked different raised questions, because the difference in appearance might signify a different realm and range of meanings in communication. . . .

Women were decidedly placed in the category of the incomprehensible and unpredictable. There were many reports that managers felt uncomfortable having to communicate with women. "It took more time," they said. "You never knew where you stood." "They changed their minds all the time; I never knew what they'd do from one minute to the next." "With women's lib around, I never know what to call them, how to treat them." "They're hard to understand." "It takes a lot of toe testing to be able to communicate." "I'm always making assumptions that turn out to be wrong." Some managers were willing to admit that this was "90 percent my problem, mostly in my head." But this was another example of the preference for dealing with people who were similar. The structure of the managerial role made it more comfortable to try to exclude those people seen as "different." A homogeneous network reinforced the inability of its members to incorporate heterogeneous elements. . . .

THE DEMAND FOR LOYALTY: MANAGEMENT AS TOTAL DEVOTION

There has traditionally been no such thing as a part-time manager. Women's advocacy agencies trying to find more part-time opportunities for women have discovered the concept very difficult to sell for managerial jobs. In addition, full time for a manager is not confined to normal working hours; in some cases, it literally means every waking hour. Managers have a great deal of discretion over how they use their time and when they leave their desk and sometimes even where they work; but the organizational situation surrounding business management has made it among the most absorptive and time-consuming careers. In the midst of organizations supposedly designed around the specific and limited contractual relationships of a bureaucracy, managers may face, instead, the demand for personal attachment and a generalized, diffuse, unlimited commitment.

The importance of loyalty in corporate careers was made clear in several different places on my sales force survey. Nearly half of those responding (42 percent) indicated that they had considered leaving Indsco within the last six months; only 5 percent said that they had never considered leaving. But in response to an open-ended question about why they had stayed, 17 percent of the potential leavers wrote that they had stayed out of *loyalty* to the company, even in the absence of concrete rewards such as a better job at Indsco. Another set of items asked people to rate themselves in terms of their strength on twenty-seven personal characteristics, on a five-point scale, running from "very strong" to "weak, need improvement." "Loyal" netted the highest mean rating (1.9), beating out "ambitious" (in second place with a mean rating of 2.1), and only closely followed by "helpful" and "friendly" (tied at 2.2). ("Knows business trends" received the lowest mean rating, at 3.1). Loyalty was thus an important part of the self-perception of Indsco's upper-level workers, and it showed in their acceptance of demands for unbounded commitment. . . .

Managers routinely felt that too many people were making too many demands on their time: "There's *no way* this is a forty-hour week." "When I walk through the office five people will say, 'Slow down.' " "It's a juggling act. There are twenty balls up in the air at any one time." "There's no such thing as relaxing or thinking time." "Part of *my* time I have to spend placating my wife for all the rest of the time I'm not spending with her." "Going up the line, it doesn't get better." Sixty-hour work weeks were typical. Sales managers agreed that even though some functions do not spend as much time traveling as do people in sales, they spend more time in team meetings. Furthermore, the tendency of Indsco to do more and more work through committees and task forces puts an additional pressure on managers. They were on committees to work on transportation, packaging, training, corporate relocation, minority relations, or to solve particular organizational problems. The immediate response to any problem in the corporation was to form a committee, and managers were likely to get an announcement in the mail that they were appointed to one. In the sales force survey, 83 percent of 205 respondents reported that they now did what they considered "extra work," beyond the bounds of a reasonable working day.

Some managers and professionals work so hard because the organization piles on tasks; others do it to get ahead; still others because they love the work. When asked why they did extra work, the sales force respondents indicated it was because of the work load (46 percent), commitment to the company (24 percent), or interest in the work itself (21 percent). (It is striking that interest in job content was mentioned with least frequency.) In any case, many companies resemble Indsco in actively encouraging work-absorption. A first-line manager told this story, which sent sympathetic chords through a group at Indsco to whom I showed it: "I used to work for another firm, and they really pushed for production, which was okay with me. I can work as hard as the next guy. My line produced as much as any of the others and more than most. You won't believe this, but upper management expected you to come in on Sundays too—not to work, but just to be seen on the premises—supposed to show how much you loved the damn place. . . . Well, I have a family. What are you supposed to do, live at the plant? Lots of the foremen came down to the lounge on Sunday and drank coffee for a couple of hours. I did a few times, and then said to hell with it—it's not worth it. . . . I started to get passed over on promotions, and I finally asked why. My boss said they weren't sure about my attitude and for me to think about it. Attitude! How does that grab you? So I quit and came here."

The organization's demands for a diffuse commitment from managers is another way to find concrete measures of trust, loyalty, and performance in the face of uncertainties. It is the answer to a series of questions about control over the performance of people given responsibility for the organization's fate. *Question:* How do managers show they are trustworthy? *Answer:* By showing they care about the company more than anything else. *Question:* How does the organization know managers are doing their jobs and that they are making the best possible decisions? *Answer:* Because they are spending every moment at it and thus working to the limits of human possibility. *Question:* When has a manager finished the job? *Answer:* Never. Or at least, hardly ever. There is always something more that could be done. . . .

IMPLICATIONS

Management becomes a closed circle in the absence of better, less exclusionary responses to uncertainty and communication pressures. Forces stemming from organizational situations help foster social homogeneity as a selection criterion for managers and promote social conformity as a standard for conduct. Concerned about giving up control and broadening discretion in the organization, managers choose others that can be "trusted." And thus they reproduce themselves in kind. Women are occasionally included in the inner circle when they are part of an organization's ruling family, but more usually this system leaves women out, along with a range of other people with discrepant social characteristics. Forces insisting that trust means total dedication and non-diffuse loyalty also serve to exclude those, like women, who are seen as incapable of such a single-minded attachment.

There is a self-fulfilling prophecy buried in all of this. The more closed the circle, the more difficult it is for "outsiders" to break in. Their very difficulty in entering may be taken as a sign of incompetence, a sign that the insiders were right to close their ranks. The more closed the circle, the more difficult it is to share power when the time comes, as it inevitably must, that others challenge the control by just one kind. And the greater the tendency for a group of people to try to reproduce themselves, the more constraining becomes the emphasis on conformity. It would seem a shame, indeed, if the only way out of such binds lay in increasing bureaucratization—that is, in a growth in routinization and rationalization of areas of uncertainty and a concomitant decline in personal discretion. But somehow corporations must grapple with the problem of how to reduce pressures for social conformity in their top jobs.

CHAPTER 13 The Family

13.1 ARLENE S. SKOLNICK AND JEROME H. SKOLNICK

Family in Transition

Why are American families having so many problems? Why is divorce so prevalent? Why are so many families classified by analysts as dysfunctional? In the following selection, family sociologists Arlene S. Skolnick and Jerome H. Skolnick use a historical approach to understand the modern American family and to provide answers to these questions.

According to the Skolnicks, in the process of becoming modern, the American family has lost many of its functions: Economic production has moved out of the home to the office or factory; education has been largely taken over by educational institutions; and the family has lost much of its control over the socialization process, which is increasingly shared with schools and peer groups. In addition to the loss of these family functions, new technologies and profound social-psychological changes have taken place, which affect all aspects of contemporary family life. The Skolnicks discuss, for example, how the reduction of infant mortality and improved contraception techniques have had a major impact on parent-child relations and on women's occupations. They argue that because of these and other such trends, marriages have become more intimate but also more troubled.

Arlene H. Skolnick (b. 1933) is a research psychologist for the Institute of Human Development at the University of California, Berkeley. Jerome H. Skolnick (b. 1931) is the Claire Clements Dean's Professor of Law, Jurisprudence, and Social Policy Program at the University of California, Berkeley, where he has been teaching since 1970.

Key Concept: functions of the family

[With regard to some of the commonly held assumptions about the nuclear family, one] half-myth concerns the image of the family as happy and harmonious. This myth sees the family as the focus of everything good and warm in human relationships, a center of love, solidarity, harmony, where each person fulfills personal needs while contributing to the well-being of other family members. The anthropologist Ray Birdwhistell calls this the "sentimental model" of the family (1966). The myth recognizes unhappy and unloving families, but assumes these are exceptions to the usual. Family problems are accordingly attributed to the personal shortcomings of the individual family members.

Now, to say the idea of the happy family is a myth—or half myth—is not to say that love and joy do not exist in family life, or that many people do not find their deepest satisfactions in their families. Rather, the myth omits important, if unpleasant, aspects of family life. Yet Western society has not always assumed the sentimental model of the family. From the Bible to the fairy tale, from Greek tragedy through Shakespeare to Eugene O'Neill to the soap opera, there is a tragic tradition portraying the family as a high-voltage, emotional setting, charged with love and hate, tenderness and spite. There is also a low comedy tradition. George Orwell once pointed out that the world of henpecked husbands and tyrannical mothers-in-law is as much a part of the Western cultural heritage as Greek drama. Although the comic tradition tends to portray men's discontents rather than women's, it scarcely views the family as a setting for ideal happiness.

Social theorists have not always portrayed the family as harmoniously fulfilling the needs of its members and society. Around the turn of the century, the founders of sociology took it for granted that conflict was a basic part of social life; individuals, classes, and social institutions would struggle to promote their own interests and values. Freud and Simmel offered conflict theories of the family. They argued that intimate relations inevitably involve antagonism as well as love, and it is this mixture of strong positive and negative feelings that sets close relationships apart from less intimate ones.

In recent years, family scholars in a number of areas have been reviving these older ideas about the family. Some scholars have even been studying such family violence as child abuse and wife beating to understand better the realistic strains of family life. Long-known facts about family violence have not until recently been incorporated into a general analysis of the family. For example, more policemen are killed and injured dealing with family fights than any other kind of situation; of all the relationships between murderers and their victims the family relationship is most common (Steinmetz and Straus 1974). Recent studies of family violence reveal that it is much more widespread than had been assumed, cannot easily be attributed to mental illness and is not confined to the lower classes. Family violence seems to be a product of psychological tensions and external stresses affecting all families at all social levels.

The study of family interaction has also undermined the traditional image of the happy, harmonious family. About two decades ago, researchers and therapists began to bring mental patients and their families together to watch how they behaved with one another. Was there something about family interaction that could explain the behavior of disturbed offspring? Strange as it may seem, whole family groups had not been systematically studied before.

At first, it did appear that there were many "pathogenic" features in such families, for example: a parent expressing affection in words, but nonverbal hostility; alliances between different family members; family secrets; one family member singled out as a scapegoat to blame for the family's troubles; parents caring for children only as reflections of themselves; parents making belittling and sarcastic statements to children. As more and more families began to be studied, such patterns were found common to many if not all families, not just those with a schizophrenic child. As comparisons were made, it became harder to perceive between "normal" families and those with mentally ill offspring. Although family processes discovered by this line of research may not, in themselves, teach us much about the causes of mental illness, they represent an important discovery about the nature of family life: so-called "normal" families can often be, in the words of one study, "difficult environments for interaction."

New historical studies of family life also cast doubt on the myth of family tranquility. Historians have found great variability in family values and behavior. Issues such as premarital sexuality, illegitimacy, infanticide, and generational conflict emerge as part of family life itself rather than as a separate category of deviance. . . .

David Hunt's (1970) study of child-rearing practices in early modern France found what would be considered by today's standards widespread mistreatment of children, or as he puts it a "breakdown in parental care," although his study was limited to upper class families. Rather than being an instinctive trait, tender feelings toward infants—the sense that a baby is a precious individual—seem to emerge only when infants have a decent chance of surviving, and adults experience life conditions offering enough security to avoid the feeling that children are competing with them in a struggle for survival. Throughout many centuries of European history, both these conditions were lacking. In the allocation of scarce resources, European society, as one historian put it, preferred adults to children (Trexler 1973, p. 110).

Thus, perhaps the most shocking finding of the new historical studies is the prevalence of infanticide throughout European history. Infanticide has long been attributed to primitive or Asian peoples, or assumed to be the desperate act of an unwed mother. It now appears that infanticide provided a major means of birth control in all societies lacking reliable contraception, Europe included, and that it was practiced by families on legitimate children. Historians now believe that rises and falls in fertility may actually reflect variations in infanticide rates (Shorter 1973).

PREDICAMENTS OF THE MODERN FAMILY

In sum, the new studies of the family reveal that previous thinking about the family had been too one-sided in emphasizing family harmony and adjustment, and the mutual benefits flowing between family and society. The study of family interaction shows that intimacy provides not only love and care, but often tension and conflict as well; and that these are inseparable parts of intimate relationships. The historical studies highlight the family's vulnerabilities to particular social, cultural, and economic contexts.

With these perspectives in mind, let us turn again to the question of the family in contemporary America. It seems to us that most laymen and social scientists who try to explain the current state of the family—some would call a crisis—fail to go far enough into history. They trace present events to the upheavals of the 1960s, such as the sexual revolution and women's liberation. By implication, the family patterns of the 1950s with their seeming stability and tranquility are taken as the normal state of the family. Current trends are treated as exceptions calling for special explanation. We hold a contrary view. It seems to us that the so-called radical ideas of the late twentieth century recapitulate an earlier ferment surrounding women's rights, male and female sex roles, sexuality, and the relations between the individual, the family, and the society. This ferment began in the last half of the nineteenth century and continued through the 1920s. The worldwide upheavals of the depression, followed by World War II, interrupted these trends. The family togetherness era of the 1950s, with the baby boom, and the increased domesticity of women, also appears to have been the product of a special set of economic, demographic, and historical circumstances (Ryder 1974).

Since the turn of the century family scholars have been debating the impact of modernization on the family. An earlier generation of scholars saw the family being undermined by its loss of economic functions in urban-industrial societies. Developments such as the movement of population from country to city, the shift of manufacturing from home to factory, and the emergence of public schools and day nurseries convinced scholars and laymen that the family had outlived its usefulness. For the first time in history, men and women could find work and satisfy basic needs without family ties of blood or marriage. On the whole, scholars lamented the passing of the family, while some feminists applauded it.

Succeeding generations of family scholars scoffed at the predictions of family disintegration. Although acknowledging that the family no longer served as workplace, school, or hospital, they judged its remaining functions to be more important than ever. The family nurtured and raised children, and provided refuge for adults from the impersonality and competition of public and industrial life.

Ties to the family one grew up in (the family of origin) may have "weakened" from what they were in the past, but the conjugal family—the family of one's spouse and children—was more emotionally close than ever. As one recent statement of this view put it, "the individual in a developed society has a greater need for emotional support and . . . the conjugal family is more exclusively the source of that support" (Ryder 1974, p. 123).

It now appears that both views were both right and wrong. Those who thought that the possibility of living as an autonomous individual in a mass society would undermine family life were correct. But they were wrong about how attractive life as an atomistic individual would prove for large numbers of people. Most reject it. Those who argued that the conditions of urban-industrial society create exceptional needs for nurturant, intimate, and enduring relationships were also correct. But they never understood that those same social conditions would make it difficult for the family to fulfill such needs. Thus, family ties have become more intense than they were in the past, and yet, at the same time, they have become more fragile.

To understand the dilemma, it is necessary to take a deeper look at how the social, cultural, and economic changes involved in modernization have affected the psychological qualities of individuals, families, and the community. Although the changes and dilemmas to be discussed below exist to some extent in all societies with advanced technologies and a high degree of urbanization (that is, in the Soviet Union and Eastern Europe as well as the United States), they may be found in their purest and most acute form under advanced capitalism, particularly in America.

THE RISE OF THE MODERN FAMILY

Modern family life in America and Europe contrasts sharply with family life in past eras in those societies, and also with the family systems of "traditional" or premodern societies. Although Europeans have never had the large, organized kin groups found in non-Western societies, kinship ties exerted much stronger constraints over the individual before the modern era. In preindustrial societies, work and marriage were not matters of individual choice. A person's economic and marital destiny was determined by hereditary status, tradition, and economic necessity. Continuity of marriages and conformity to prescribed behavior, within the family and outside, were enforced by severe economic, familial, and community sanctions.

Another extremely important aspect of family life in past times was its embeddedness in the community. The home was not set off as a private place, a refuge for the members of the immediate family to restore themselves from the work struggles in the outside world. There was no world of work outside the home—family members were fellow workers. Nor did the world outside one's front door consist of strangers or half-strangers, such as neighbors often are today. Rather, people lived in a community of people known since childhood and with whom one would expect to have dealings for the rest of one's life. These outsiders could enter the household freely, and were entitled, and even obligated, to intervene if relations between parents and children and husbands and wives were not as they should be.

Modernization liberates the individual from the restrictions of family, kin, and communities. W. J. Goode (1963) writes that whenever the modern pattern of work and family replaces the traditional one, it is accompanied by an ideology of liberation. Modernization promises freedom of opportunity to find work that suits one's talents, freedom to marry for love and dissolve the marriage if it fails to provide happiness, and greater equality in the family between husband and wife, and between parents and children.

The freedom of modern family life is bought at the price of fragility and instability in family ties. The removal of kin as a source of economic and social control means that the whole structure of family life comes to rest on a very fragile basis: the mutual feelings of two individuals. As Georg Simmel (1950, pp. 118-144) has shown, the couple or dyad is not only the most intimate of social relationships, it is also the most unstable. In traditional systems, the inevitable tensions of marriage are "contained" by kin and community pressures, by low expectations concerning the romance or happiness to be found in marriage (See Goode 1966, p. 493). Further, when families were also working units, the family members—children as well as the husband and wife—were held together by their dependence on each other's labors.

In short, modernization implies not merely economic or technological change, but also profound social and psychological change. It affects all aspects of life: physical environment, the types of communities people live in, the way they view the world, the way they organize their daily lives, the emotional quality of family relationships, down to the most private aspects of individual psychological experience.

In addition to promoting the ideology of individualism, modern technological societies change the inner experience of the self. The modernized individual possesses a heightened awareness of his or her own individuality. By contrast, the person living in an unchanging, traditional social world, where there are no alternatives to the influence of family and community, can take that world for granted and live with a minimum of self-awareness. Moreover, much of daily life in modern society is spent in narrow roles such as student, worker, customer, client. The individual begins to experience himself or herself as a replaceable role player (Berger, Berger, and Kellner, 1973; Davis 1973). As we become aware of a discrepancy between the role we are playing and our "real" and whole selves, we come to have a need for a private world, a set of social relations where we can express those aspects of ourselves that must be repressed in role demands of work and public behavior. Although the need for intimacy increases, the structural conditions creating that need make it more difficult to satisfy. At the same time, other conditions associated with modern life place additional strains on family relations.

EMOTIONAL TENSIONS IN THE MODERN FAMILY

Even those family scholars who stress the vital functions played by the family in modern societies acknowledge that societies also create strains on families. T. Parsons, for example, noted that when the family and the home no longer functioned as an economic unit, women, children, and old people were placed in an ambiguous position outside the occupational world. For children, the shift to industrial work, and the removal of the father from the home, also meant that the mother became a more central figure. Little boys could no longer observe and participate in their father's work.

Long before the days of women's liberation, social scientists were pointing to incongruities in women's family roles. In many ways, modernization has increased the work load of the housewife. Although she no longer has to make the family's clothing, bread, soap, and other necessities, child care has become more directly centered on the mother alone than it was when the home was a workplace and kin or community members were close at hand. Numerous studies have shown that housewives work extremely long hours, and that labor-saving devices have not really lightened the labor of the housewife: As W. J. Goode (1963) points out, most of these inventions have only raised the standards for cleanliness. For example, the washing machine brought back into the home a job that at one time was sent out to laundries; furthermore, people now have more clothing than they did in the past and expect it to be cleaned more often. (The personal bath was once a weekly ritual also.)

Despite the heavy burdens and the vital importance of housework, it isn't considered real work in a society equating work with paycheck. That the wife and the children are dependents of the husband creates the potential for strain in family relationships. Money is traditionally one of the leading topics for family arguments. The exchange of the husband's money for the wife's services makes it possible for each to feel exploited by the other. Thus, there are the traditional male worries that the wife is squandering his hard-earned money, that she is enjoying a free and easy life while he is chained to the office or factory. On the other hand, there is the pattern of "secondary poverty"—where the husband makes an adequate income, but the wife and children live at a poorer level because he doesn't provide them with enough to live on (Young 1952).

Some writers have argued that privacy is the key to understanding the plight of the modern family. Anthropologists note that only among Eskimos is there a comparable degree of isolation in nuclear families as they go about their daily round (Stephens 1963), and that isolation breeds tension and emotional instability, particularly in mothers (Minturn and Lambert et al. 1964). R. S. Weiss (1973) found that even people with close family relationships could feel lonely if they did not also have social networks of friends, co-workers, neighbors, and so on.

Looking at the American family in historical perspective, Barbara Laslett (1973) argues that family privacy is a relatively recent phenomenon. In the past, when families were larger, servants, boarders, and lodgers were common. Households were more open to the community, and the family possessed a more public character. Observation by outsiders implied more social control over family behavior, and also more social support. Thus, a husband and wife might be constrained from arguing with each other in front of outsiders; similarly the need to argue might arise less often than it does now, since a husband and wife are more apt to behave circumspectly in the presence of others. Like King Midas's touch, family privacy is a dream of affluence that turns out to unexpected costs when fulfilled. The single nuclear family's

> . . . major burden is its rootlessness, its aloneness with its tasks. Parents are somewhere else; the business you can't trust; the neighbors you never see; and friends are a help, when you see them, but never enough. Sometimes, late at night, the parent wakes up and on a sea of silence hears the ship creak, feels it drift, fragile and solitary, with its cargo of lives. (Napier 1972, p. 540)

CONTRADICTORY DEMANDS AND VALUES

. . . The new morality of fun and games often reunites the family in activities that everyone can enjoy, but also pulls family members apart in its emphasis on individual pursuit of enjoyment. Also, to the extent that fun morality teaches us that family life should be fun, it imposes a paradoxical demand: we are obligated to have a good time (see Wolfstein 1954). In the past, one could live up to demands of marriage and parenthood by doing one's duty. Now, duty is not enough. We are under obligation to enjoy all aspects of family life. As a result, pleasurable activities, even sex itself, become permeated by the work ethic: Am I a competent sexual performer? Is my spouse? Do I enjoy my children as much as I am supposed to?

DEMOGRAPHIC CHANGE

. . . The reduction of infant and child mortality released women from the demands of constant child bearing, and the development of contraceptives made it possible for them to control their fertility. Thus, women today are living longer, having fewer children, and having them earlier than in previous generations. The result of these changes is the increase in the number of married women at work. In the past, with later marriage and more children, the time the last child left home would be close to the end of the average mother's life expectancy. Today the average woman can look forward to three or four decades without maternal responsibilities. Since the prevailing assumptions about women are based on the notion that they are constantly involved with pregnancy, child rearing, and related domestic concerns, the current ferment about women's roles may be seen as a way of bringing cultural attitudes in line with existing social realities.

The changes noted above also have profound implications for marriage. With earlier marriage and longer life spans, the duration of marriage has nearly doubled, from about 25 or 27 years, to about 50. With the decline in the number of children, marriage becomes more of a personal relationship between husband and wife, and less of a union of a mother and father preoccupied with the needs of their offspring. The prospect of 50 years with the same person increases tensions in marriage and makes it more likely that dissatisfaction will lead to divorce. Furthermore, in a rapidly changing society, the couple who seemed to be well-suited to each other in their early twenties may find themselves growing in different ways and at different rates later on. . . .

DOMESTIC RELATIONS AND SOCIAL CHANGE

There is little reason to expect that these trends affecting family life will be soon reversed. It is not likely, for example, that divorce will again be regarded as an offense against public decency, that virginity will be considered the normal condition of unmarried women, that population pressures will reverse themselves and demand that women devote most of their lives to child bearing.

REFERENCES

Berger, P.; Berger, Brigitte; and Kellner, H. 1973. *The Homeless Mind: Modernization and Consciousness.* New York: Random House.

Birdwhistell, R. L. 1966. "The American Family: Some Perspectives." *Psychiatry,* 29, pp. 203–212.

Davis, M. S. 1973. *Intimate Relations.* New York: The Free Press.

Goode, W. J. 1963. *World Revolution and Family Patterns.* New York: The Free Press.

_____. 1966. "Family Disorganization." In *Contemporary Social Problems,* 2nd ed., edited by R. K. Merton and R. A. Nisbet, pp. 493–522. New York: Harcourt, Brace, and World.

Hunt, D. 1970. *Parents and Children in History: The Psychology of Family Life in Early Modern France.* New York: Basic Books.

Laslett, B. 1973. "The Family as a Public and Private Institution." *Journal of Marriage and the Family,* 35, pp. 480–494.

Minturn, L., Lambert, W. E. et al. 1964. *Mothers of Six Cultures.* New York: John Wiley.

Napier, A. 1972. Introduction to section four in *The Book of Family Therapy,* edited by A. Farber, M. Mendelsohn, and A. Napier. New York: Science House.

Ryder, N. B. 1974. "The Family in Developed Countries." *Scientific American,* September, pp. 123–132.

Shorter, E. 1973. "Infanticide in the Past." *History of Childhood Quarterly,* Summer, pp. 178–180.

Simmel, G. 1950. *The Sociology of Georg Simmel,* edited by K. Wolf. New York, The Free Press, 1950.

Steinmetz, K., and Straus, M. A. (eds.). 1974. *Violence in the Family.* New York: Dodd, Mead and Co.

Stephens, W. N. 1963. *The Family in Cross-Cultural Perspective.* New York: World.

Trexler, R. C. 1973. "Infanticide in Florence: New Sources and First Results." *History of Childhood Quarterly,* Summer, pp. 98–116.

Weiss, R. S. 1973. *Loneliness: The Experience of Emotional and Social Isolation.* Cambridge, Mass.: M.I.T. Press.

Wolfenstein, M. 1954. "Fun Morality: An Analysis of Recent American Child-Training Literature." In *Childhood in Contemporary Cultures,* edited by M. Mead and M. Wolfenstein. Chicago: University of Chicago Press, pp. 168–178.

Young, M. 1952. "Distribution of Income Within the Family." *British Journal of Sociology,* III, pp. 305–321.

13.2 PETER L. BERGER AND HANSFRIED KELLNER

Marriage and the Construction of Reality

In the past, when marriage and the family were embedded in the community, neighbors, friends, and relatives supported and assisted the family. Community norms guarded against divorce, affairs, and other threats to the family. As a result, the stability of marriages and families appeared less problematic than it does today.

In contemporary society, the strain on most marriages is great, and the marital relationship is fragile. Consequently the establishment of an identity as a couple is very important. In the following excerpt, Peter L. Berger and Hansfried Kellner discuss the process through which two individuals modify, redefine, and transform their pasts and construct a new mutual reality for themselves. This reality is different from each individual's perception of the past or future. According to the authors, spouses create a new identity for themselves as a couple and validate each other's constructions of reality.

Berger (b. 1929), a sociologist with wide-ranging interests, supports what he calls "methodological atheism," which argues that explanations of society and social life should be based on scientific study. He is the director of the Institute for the Study of Economic Culture at Boston University and the author of *The Heretical Imperative: Contemporary Possibilities of Religious Affirmation* (Doubleday, 1979), which was nominated for the 1980 American Book Award. Kellner (b. 1937?) is a professor of sociology at the University of Darmstadt in West Germany.

Key Concept: constructing a mutual reality in marriage

*E*ver since Durkheim it has been a commonplace of family sociology that marriage serves as a protection against anomie [normlessness] for the individual. Interesting and pragmatically useful though this insight is, it is but the negative side of a phenomenon of much broader significance. If one speaks of *anomic* states, then one ought properly to investigate also the *nomic* processes that, by their absence, lead to the aforementioned states. If, consequently, one

245

finds a negative correlation between marriage and anomie, then one should be led to inquire into the character of marriage as a *nomos*-building instrumentality, that is, of marriage as a social arrangement that creates for the individual the sort of order in which he can experience his life as making sense. It is our intention here to discuss marriage in these terms. While this could be done in a macrosociological perspective, dealing with marriage as a major social institution related to other broad structures of society, our focus will be microsociological, dealing primarily with the social processes affecting the individuals in any specific marriage, although, of course, the larger framework of these processes will have to be understood. In what sense this discussion can be described as microsociology of knowledge will hopefully become clearer in the course of it.[1]

Marriage is obviously only *one* social relationship in which this process of *nomos*-building takes place. It is, therefore, necessary to first look in more general terms at the character of this process. In doing so, we are influenced by three theoretical perspectives—the Weberian perspective on society as a network of meanings, the Meadian perspective on identity as a social phenomenon, and the phenomenological analysis of the social structuring of reality especially as given in the work of Schutz and Merleau-Ponty.[2] Not being convinced, however, that theoretical lucidity is necessarily enhanced by terminological ponderosity, we shall avoid as much as possible the use of the sort of jargon for which both sociologists and phenomenologists have acquired dubious notoriety.

The process that interests us here is the one that constructs, maintains and modifies a consistent reality that can be meaningfully experienced by individuals. In its essential forms this process is determined by the society in which it occurs. Every society has its specific way of defining and perceiving reality—its world, its universe, its overarching organization of symbols. This is already given in the language that forms the symbolic base of the society. Erected over this base, and by means of it, is a system of ready-made *typifications* [stereotypical explanations of events in the world], through which the innumerable experiences of reality come to be ordered.[3] These typifications and their order are held in common by the members of society, thus acquiring not only the character of objectivity, but being taken for granted as *the* world *tout court*, the only world that normal men can conceive of.[4] The seemingly objective and taken-for-granted character of the social definitions of reality can be seen most clearly in the case of language itself, but it is important to keep in mind that the latter forms the base and instrumentality of a much larger world-erecting process.

The socially constructed world must be continually mediated to and actualized by the individual, so that it can become and remain indeed *his* world as well. The individual is given by his society certain decisive cornerstones for his everyday experience and conduct. Most importantly, the individual is supplied with specific sets of typifications and criteria of relevance, predefined for him by the society and made available to him for the order of his everyday life. This order or (in line with our opening considerations) nomic apparatus is biographically cumulative. It begins to be formed in the individual from the

*Peter L. Berger
and Hansfried
Kellner*

earliest stages of socialization on, then keeps on being enlarged and modified by himself throughout his biography.[5] While there are individual biographical differences making for differences in the constitution of this apparatus in specific individuals, there exists in the society an overall consensus on the range of differences deemed to be tolerable. Without such consensus, indeed, society would be impossible as a going concern, since it would then lack the ordering principles by which alone experience can be shared and conduct can be mutually intelligible. This order, by which the individual comes to perceive and define his world, is thus not chosen by him, except perhaps for very small modifications. Rather, it is discovered by him as an external datum, a ready-made world that simply is *there* for him to go ahead and live in, though he modifies it continually in the process of living in it. Nevertheless, this world is in need of *validation*, perhaps precisely because of an ever-present glimmer of suspicion as to its social manufacture and relativity. This validation, while it must be undertaken by the individual himself, requires ongoing interaction with others who co-inhabit this same socially constructed world. In a broad sense, *all* the other co-inhabitants of this world serve a validating function. Every morning the newspaper boy validates the widest coordinates of my world and the mailman bears tangible validation of my own location within these coordinates. However, some validations are more significant than others. Every individual requires the ongoing validation of his world, including crucially the validation of his identity and place in this world, by those few who are his truly significant others.[6] Just as the individual's deprivation of relationship with his significant others will plunge him into anomie, so their continued presence will sustain for him that *nomos* by which he can feel at home in the world at least most of the time. Again in a broad sense, all the actions of the significant others and even their simple presence serve this sustaining function. In everyday life, however, the principal method employed is speech. In this sense, it is proper to view the individual's relationship with his significant others as an ongoing conversation. As the latter occurs, it validates over and over again the fundamental definitions of reality once entered into, not, of course, so much by explicit articulation, but precisely by taking the definitions silently for granted and conversing about all conceivable matters on this taken-for-granted basis. Through the same conversation the individual is also made capable of adjusting to changing and new social contexts in his biography. In a very fundamental sense it can be said that one converses one's way through life.

If one concedes these points, one can now state a general sociological proposition: the plausibility and stability of the world, as socially defined, is dependent upon the strength and continuity of significant relationships in which conversation about this world can be continually carried on. Or, to put it a little differently: *the reality of the world is sustained through conversation with significant others*. This reality-bestowing force of social relationships depends on the degree of their nearness,[7] that is, on the degree to which social relationships occur in face-to-face situations and to which they are credited with primary significance by the individual. In any empirical situation, there now emerge obvious sociological questions out of these considerations, namely, questions about the patterns of the world-building relationships, the social forms taken by the conversation with significant others. Sociologically, one must ask how these relationships are *objectively* structured and distributed, and one will also want to understand how they are *subjectively* perceived and experienced.

With these preliminary assumptions stated we can now arrive at our main thesis here. Namely, we would contend that marriage occupies a privileged status among the significant validating relationships for adults in our society. Put slightly differently: marriage is a crucial nomic instrumentality in our society. We would further argue that the essential social functionality of this institution cannot be fully understood if this fact is not perceived.

We can now proceed with an ideal-typical analysis of marriage, that is, seek to abstract the essential features involved. Marriage in our society is a *dramatic* act in which two strangers come together and redefine themselves. The drama of the act is internally anticipated and socially legitimated long before it takes place in the individual's biography, and amplified by means of a pervasive ideology, the dominant themes of which (romantic love, sexual fulfillment, self-discovery and self-realization through love and sexuality, the nuclear family as the social site for these processes) can be found distributed through all strata of the society. The actualization of these ideologically predefined expectations in the life of the individual occurs to the accompaniment of one of the few traditional rites of passage that are still meaningful to almost all members of the society. It should be added that, in using the term "strangers," we do not mean, of course, that the candidates for the marriage come from widely discrepant social backgrounds—indeed, the data indicate that the contrary is the case. The strangeness rather lies in the fact that, unlike marriage candidates in many previous societies, those in ours typically come from different face-to-face contexts—in the terms used above, they come from different areas of conversation. They do not have a shared past, although their pasts have a similar structure. In other words, quite apart from prevailing patterns of ethnic, religious and class endogamy [or marriage within the same group], our society is typically exogamous [involving marriage between those who differ] in terms of nomic relationships. Put concretely, in our mobile society the significant conversation of the two partners previous to the marriage took place in social circles that did not overlap. With the dramatic redefinition of the situation brought about by the marriage, however, all significant conversation for the two new partners is now centered in their relationship with each other—and, in fact, it was precisely with this intention that they entered upon their relationship.

It goes without saying that this character of marriage has its root in much broader structural configurations of our society. The most important of these, for our purposes, is the crystalization of a so-called private sphere of existence, more and more segregated from the immediate controls of the public institutions (especially the economic and political ones), and yet defined and utilized as the main social area for the individual's self-realization.[8] It cannot be our purpose here to inquire into the historical forces that brought forth this phenomenon, beyond making the observation that these are closely connected with the industrial revolution and its institutional consequences. The public institutions now confront the individual as an immensely powerful and alien world, incomprehensible in its inner workings, anonymous in its human character. If only through his work in some nook of the economic machinery, the individual must find a way of living in this alien world, come to terms with

*Peter L. Berger
and Hansfried
Kellner*

its power over him, be satisfied with a few conceptual rules of thumb to guide him through a vast reality that otherwise remains opaque to his understanding, and modify its anonymity by whatever *human relations* he can work out in his involvement with it. It ought to be emphasized, against some critics of "mass society," that this does not inevitably leave the individual with a sense of profound unhappiness and lostness. It would rather seem that large numbers of people in our society are quite content with a situation in which their public involvements have little subjective importance, regarding work as a not too bad necessity and politics as at best a spectator sport. It is usually only intellectuals with ethical and political commitments who assume that such people must be terribly desperate. The point, however, is that the individual in this situation, no matter whether he is happy or not, will turn elsewhere for the experiences of self-realization that do have importance for him. The private sphere, this interstitial area created (we would think) more or less haphazardly as a by-product of the social metamorphosis [or unfolding] of industrialism, is mainly where he will turn. It is here that the individual will seek power, intelligibility and, quite literally, a name—the apparent power to fashion a world, however Lilliputian, that will reflect his own being: a world that, seemingly having been shaped by himself and thus unlike those other worlds that insist on shaping him, is translucently intelligible to him (or so he thinks); a world in which, consequently, he is *somebody*—perhaps even, within its charmed circle, a lord and master. What is more, to a considerable extent these expectations are not unrealistic. The public institutions have no need to control the individual's adventures in the private sphere, as long as they really stay within the latter's circumscribed limits. The private sphere is perceived, not without justification, as an area of individual choice and even autonomy. This fact has important consequences for the shaping of identity in modern society that cannot be pursued here. All that ought to be clear here is the peculiar location of the private sphere within and between the other social structures. In sum, it is above all and, as a rule, only in the private sphere that the individual can take a slice of reality and fashion it into his world. If one is aware of the decisive significance of this capacity and even necessity of men to externalize themselves in reality and to produce for themselves a world in which they can feel at home, then one will hardly be surprised at the great importance which the private sphere has come to have in modern society.[9]

The private sphere includes a variety of social relationships. Among these, however, the relationships of the family occupy a central position and, in fact, serve as a focus for most of the other relationships (such as those with friends, neighbors, fellow-members of religious and other voluntary associations). . . . [T]he central relationship in this whole area is the marital one. It is on the basis of marriage that, for most adults in our society, existence in the private sphere is built up. It will be clear that this is not at all a universal or even a cross culturally wide function of marriage. Rather . . . marriage in our society [has] taken on a very peculiar character and functionality. It has been pointed out that marriage in contemporary society has lost some of its older functions and taken on new ones instead.[10] This is certainly correct, but we would prefer to state the matter a little differently. Marriage and family used to be firmly embedded in a matrix of wider community relationships, serving as extensions and particularizations of the latter's social controls. There were few separating barriers between the world of the individual family and the wider community, a fact even to be seen in the physical conditions under which the family lived before the industrial revolution.[11] The same social life pulsated through the house, the street and the community. In our terms, the family and within it the marital relationship were part and parcel of a considerably larger area of conversation. In our contemporary society, by contrast, each family constitutes its own segregated subworld, with its own controls and its own closed conversation.

This fact requires a much greater effort on the part of the marriage partners. Unlike an earlier situation in which the establishment of the new marriage simply added to the differentiation and complexity of an already existing social world, the marriage partners now are embarked on the often difficult task of constructing for themselves the little world in which they will live. To be sure, the larger society provides them with certain standard instructions as to how they should go about this task, but this does not change the fact that considerable effort of their own is required for its realization. The monogamous character of marriage enforces both the dramatic and the precarious nature of this undertaking. Success or failure hinges on the present idiosyncrasies and the fairly unpredictable future development of these idiosyncrasies of *only two individuals* (who, moreover, do not have a shared past)—as Simmel has shown, the most unstable of all possible social relationships.[12] Not surprisingly, the decision to embark on this undertaking has a critical, even cataclysmic connotation in the popular imagination, which is underlined as well as psychologically assuaged by the ceremonialism that surrounds the event.

Every social relationship requires *objectivation*, that is, requires *a process by which subjectively experienced meanings become objective to the individual and*, in interaction with others, *become common property* and thereby massively objective.[13] The degree of objectivation will depend on the number and the intensity of the social relationships that are its carriers. A relationship that consists of only two individuals called upon to sustain, by their own efforts, an ongoing social world will have to make up in intensity for the numerical poverty of the arrangement. This, in turn, accentuates the drama and the precariousness. The later addition of children will add to the, as it were, density of objectivation taking place within the nuclear family, thus rendering the latter a good deal less precarious. It remains true that the establishment and maintenance of such a social world make extremely high demands on the principal participants.

The attempt can now be made to outline the ideal-typical process that takes place as marriage functions as an instrumentality for the social construction of reality. The chief protagonists of the drama are two individuals, each with a biographically accumulated and available stock of experience.[14] As members of a highly mobile society, these individuals have already internalized a degree of readiness to redefine themselves and to modify their stock of experience, thus bringing with them considerable psychological capacity for entering new relationships with others.[15] Also, coming from broadly similar sectors of the larger society (in terms of region, class, ethnic and religious affiliations), the two individuals will have organized their stock of experience in similar fashion. In other words, *the two individuals have internalized the same overall world, including the general definitions and expectations of the marriage relationship itself.* Their society has provided them with a taken-for-granted image of marriage and has socialized them into an anticipation of stepping into the taken-for-granted roles of marriage. All the same, *these relatively empty projections now have to be actualized, lived through and filled with experiential content* by the protagonists. This will require a dramatic change in their definitions of reality and of themselves.

Peter L. Berger and Hansfried Kellner

As of the marriage, most of each partner's actions must now be projected in conjunction with those of the other. Each partner's definitions of reality must be continually correlated with the definitions of the other. The other is present in nearly all horizons of everyday conduct. Furthermore, the identity of each now takes on a new character, having to be constantly matched with that of the other, indeed being typically perceived by the people at large as being symbiotically conjoined with the identity of the other. In each partner's psychological economy of significant others, the marriage partner becomes the other *par excellence*, the nearest and most decisive co-inhabitant of the world. Indeed, all other significant relationships have to be almost automatically reperceived and regrouped in accordance with this drastic shift.

In other words, from the beginning of the marriage each partner has new modes in his meaningful experience of the world in general, of other people and of himself. By definition, then, marriage constitutes a nomic rupture. In terms of each partner's biography, the event of marriage initiates a new nomic process. Now, the full implications of this fact are rarely apprehended by the protagonists with any degree of clarity. There rather is to be found the notion that one's world, one's other-relationships and, above all, oneself have remained what they were before—only, of course, that world, others and self will now be shared with the marriage partner. It should be clear by now that this notion is a grave misapprehension. Just because of this fact, marriage now propels the individual into an unintended and unarticulated development, in the course of which the nomic transformation takes place. What typically *is* apprehended are certain objective and concrete problems arising out of the marriage—such as tensions with in-laws, or with former friends, or religious differences between the partners, as well as immediate tensions between them. These are apprehended as external, situational and practical difficulties. What is *not* apprehended is the subjective side of these difficulties, namely, the transformation of *nomos* and identity that has occurred and that continues to go on, so that all problems and relationships are experienced in a quite new way, that is, experienced within a new and ever-changing reality.

Take a simple and frequent illustration—the male partner's relationships with male friends before and after the marriage. It is a common observation that such relationships, especially if the extramarital partners are single, rarely survive the marriage, or, if they do, are drastically redefined after it. This is typically the result of neither a deliberate decision by the husband nor deliberate sabotage by the wife. What rather happens, very simply, is a slow process in which the husband's image of his friend is transformed as he keeps talking about this friend with his wife. Even if no actual talking goes on, the mere presence of the wife forces him to see his friend differently. This need not mean that he adopts a negative image held by the wife. Regardless of what image she holds or is believed by him to hold, it will be different from that held by the husband. This difference will enter into the joint image that now must needs be fabricated in the course of the ongoing conversation between the marriage partners—and, in due course, must act powerfully on the image previously held by the husband. Again, typically, this process is rarely apprehended with any degree of lucidity. The old friend is more likely to fade out of the picture by slow degrees, as new kinds of friends take his place. The process, if commented upon at all within the marital conversation, can always be explained by socially available formulas about "people changing," "friends disappearing" or oneself "having become more mature." This process of conversational liquidation is especially powerful because it is one-sided—the husband typically talks with his wife about his friend, but *not* with his friend about his wife. Thus the friend is deprived of the defense of, as it were, counterdefining the relationship. *This dominance of the marital conversation over all others is one of its most important characteristics.* It may be mitigated by a certain amount of protective segregation of some non-marital relationships (say "Tuesday night out with the boys," or "Saturday lunch with mother"), but even then there are powerful emotional barriers against the sort of conversation (conversation *about* the marital relationship, that is) that would serve by way of counterdefinition.

Marriage thus posits a new reality. The individual's relationship with this new reality, however, is a dialectical one—he acts upon it, in collusion with the marriage partner, and it acts back upon both him and the partner, welding together their reality. Since, as we have argued before, the objectivation that constitutes this reality is precarious, the groups with which the couple associates are called upon to assist in co-defining the new reality. The couple is pushed towards groups that strengthen their new definition of themselves and the world, avoids those that weaken this definition. This in turn releases the commonly known pressures of group association, again acting upon the marriage partners to change their definitions of the world and of themselves. Thus the new reality is not posited once and for all, but goes on being redefined not only in the marital interaction itself but also in the various maritally based group relationships into which the couple enters.

In the individual's biography marriage, then, brings about a decisive phase of socialization that can be compared with the phases of childhood and adolescence. This phase has a rather different structure from the earlier ones. There the individual was in the main socialized into already existing patterns. Here he actively collaborates rather than passively accommodates himself. Also, in the previous phases of socialization, there was an apprehension of entering into a new world and being changed in the course of this. In marriage there is little apprehension of such a process, but rather the notion that the world has remained the same, with only its emotional and pragmatic connotations having changed. This notion, as we have tried to show, is illusionary.

The reconstruction of the world in marriage occurs principally in the course of conversation, as we have suggested. *The implicit problem of this conversation is how to match two individual definitions of reality.* By the very logic of the relationship, a common overall definition must be arrived at—otherwise the conversation will become impossible and, *ipso facto*, the relationship will be endangered. Now, this conversation may be understood as the working away of an ordering and typifying apparatus—if one prefers, an objectivating apparatus. Each partner ongoingly contributes his conceptions of reality, which are then "talked through," usually not once but many times, and in the process become objectivated by the conversational apparatus. The longer this conversation goes on, the more massively real do the objectivations become to the partners. In the marital conversation a world is not only built, but it is also kept in a state of repair and ongoingly refurnished. The subjective reality of this world for the two partners is sustained by the same conversation. The nomic instrumentality of marriage is concretized over and over again, from bed to breakfast table, as the partners carry on the endless conversation that feeds on nearly all they individually or jointly experience. Indeed, it may happen eventually that no experience is fully real unless and until it has been thus "talked through."

This process has a very important result—namely, *a hardening or stabilization of the common objectivated reality.* It should be easy to see now how this comes about. The objectivations ongoingly performed and internalized by the marriage partners become ever more massively real, as they are confirmed and reconfirmed in the marital conversation. The world that is made up of these objectivations at the same time gains in stability. For example, the images of other people, which before or in the earlier stages of the marital conversation may have been rather ambiguous and shifting in the minds of the two partners, now become hardened into definite and stable characterizations. A casual acquaintance, say, may sometimes have appeared as lots of fun and sometimes as quite a bore to the wife before her marriage. Under the influence of the marital conversation, in which this other person is frequently "discussed," she will now come down more firmly on one or the other of the two characterizations, or on a reasonable compromise between the two. In any of these three options, though, she will have concocted with her husband a much more stable image of the person in question than she is likely to have had before her marriage, when there may have been no conversational pressure to make a definite option at all. The same process of stabilization may be observed with regard to self-definitions as well. In this way, the wife in our example will not only be pressured to assign stable characterizations to others but also to herself. Previously uninterested politically, she now identifies herself as liberal. Previously alternating between dimly articulated religious positions, she now declares herself an agnostic. Previously confused and uncertain about her sexual emotions, she now understands herself as an unabashed hedonist in this area. And so on and so forth, with the same reality—and identity—stabilizing process at work on the husband. Both world and self thus take on a firmer, more reliable character for both partners.

Furthermore, it is not only the ongoing experience of the two partners that is constantly shared and passed through the conversational apparatus. The same *sharing extends into the past.* The two distinct biographies, as subjectively apprehended by two individuals who have lived through them, are overruled and reinterpreted in the course of their conversations. Sooner or later, they will "tell all"—or, more correctly, they will tell it in such a way that it fits into the self-definitions objectivated in the marital relationship. The couple thus construct not only present reality but reconstruct past reality as well, fabricating a common memory that integrates the recollections of the two individual pasts.[16] The comic fulfillment of this process may be seen in those cases when one partner "remembers" more clearly what happened in the other's past than the other does—and corrects him accordingly. Similarly, there occurs a *sharing of future horizons*, which leads not only to stabilization, but inevitably to a narrowing of the future projections of each partner. Before marriage the individual typically plays with quite discrepant daydreams in which his future self is projected.[17] Having now considerably stabilized his self-image, the married individual will have to project the future in accordance with this maritally defined identity. This narrowing of future horizons begins with the obvious external limitation that marriage entails, as, for example, with regard to vocational and career plans. However, it extends also to the more general possibilities of the individual's biography. To return to a previous illustration, the wife, having "found herself" as a liberal, an agnostic and a "sexually healthy" person, *ipso facto* liquidates the possibilities of becoming an anarchist, a Catholic or a Lesbian. At least until further notice she has decided upon who she is—and, by the same token, upon who she will be. The stabilization brought about by marriage thus affects that total reality in which the partners exist. In the most far-reaching sense of the word, the married individual "settles down"—and *must* do so, if the marriage is to be viable, in accordance with its contemporary institutional definition.

It cannot be sufficiently strongly emphasized that this process is typically unapprehended, almost automatic in character. The protagonists of the marriage drama do *not* set out deliberately to create their world. Each continues to live in a world that is taken for granted—and keeps its taken-for-granted character even as it is metamorphosed. The new world that the married partners, Prometheuslike, have called into being is perceived by them as the normal world in which they have lived before. Reconstructed present and reinterpreted past are perceived as a continuum, extending forward into a commonly projected future. *The dramatic change that has occurred remains in bulk, unapprehended and unarticulated.* And where it forces itself upon the individuals' attention, it is retrojected into the past, explained as having always been there, though perhaps in a hidden way. Typically, the reality that has been "invented" within the marital conversation is subjectively perceived as a "discovery." Thus the partners "discover" themselves and the world, "who they really are," "what they really believe," "how they really feel, and always have felt, about so-and-so." This retrojection of the world being produced all the time by themselves serves to enhance the stability of this world and at the same time to assuage the "existential anxiety" that, probably inevitably, accompanies the perception that nothing but one's own narrow shoulders supports the universe in which one has chosen to live. . . .

The use of the term "stabilization" should not detract from the insight into the difficulty and precariousness of this world-building enterprise. Often enough, the new universe collapses *in statu nascendi*. Many more times it continues over a period, swaying perilously back and forth as the two partners try to hold it up, finally to be abandoned as an impossible undertaking. If one conceives of the marital conversation as the principal drama and the two partners as the principal protagonists of the drama, then one can look upon the other individuals involved as the supporting chorus for the central dramatic action. Children, friends, relatives and casual acquaintances all have their part in reinforcing the tenuous structure of the new reality. It goes without saying that the *children form the most important part of this supporting chorus.* Their very existence is predicated on the maritally established world. The marital partners themselves are in charge of their socialization *into* this world, which to them has a pre-existent and self-evident character. They are taught from the beginning to speak precisely those lines that lend themselves to a supporting chorus, from their first invocations of "Daddy" and "Mummy" on to their adoption of the parents' ordering and typifying apparatus that now defines *their* world as well. The marital conversation is now in the process of becoming a family symposium, with the necessary consequence that its objectivations rapidly gain in density, plausibility and durability.

In sum: the process that we have been inquiring into is, ideal-typically, one in which reality is crystallized, narrowed and stabilized. Ambivalences are converted into certainties. Typifications of self and of others become settled. Most generally, possibilities become facticities. What is more, this process of transformation remains, most of the time, unapprehended by those who are both its authors and its objects.[18]

NOTES

1. The present article has come out of a larger project on which the authors have been engaged in collaboration with three colleagues in sociology and philosophy. The project is to produce a systematic treatise that will integrate a number of now separate theoretical strands in the sociology of knowledge.
2. Cf. especially Max Weber, *Wirtschaft und Gesellschaft* (Tuebingen: Mohr 1956), and *Gesammelte Aufsaetze zur Wissenschaftslehre* (Tuebingen: Mohr 1951); George H. Mead, *Mind, Self and Society* (University of Chicago Press 1934); Alfred Schutz, *Der sinnhafte Aufbau der sozialen Welt* (Vienna: Springer, 2nd ed. 1960) and *Collected Papers*, 1 (The Hague: Nijhoff 1962); Maurice Merleau-Ponty, *Phénoménolgie de la perception* (Paris: Gallimard 1945) and *La structure du comportement* (Paris: Presses universitaires de France 1953).
3. Cf. Schutz, *Aufbau*, 202–20 and *Collected Papers*, I, 3–27, 283–6.
4. Cf. Schutz, *Collected Paper*, I, 207–28.
5. Cf. especially Jean Piaget, *The Child's Construction of Reality* (Routledge & Kegan Paul 1955).
6. Cf. Mead, *op. cit.*, 135–226.
7. Cf. Schutz, *Aufbau*, 181–95.
8. Cf. Arnold Gehlen, *Die Seele im technischen Zeitalter* (Hamburg: Rowohlt 1957), 57–69 and *Anthropologische Forschung* (Hanburg: Rowohlt 1961), 69–77, 127–40; Helmut Schelsky, *Soziologie der Sexualitaet* (Hamburg: Rowohlt 1955), 102–33. Also cf. Thomas Luckmann, "On religion in modern society," *Journal for the Scientific Study of Religion* (Spring 1963), 147–62.
9. In these considerations we have been influenced by certain presuppositions of Marxian anthropology, as well as by the anthropological work of Max Scheler,

Helmuth Plessner and Arnold Gehlen. We are indebted to Thomas Luckmann for the clarification of the social-psychological significance of the private sphere.

10. Cf. Talcott Parsons and Robert Bales, *Family: Socialization and Interaction Process* (London: Routledge & Kegan Paul 1956), 3–34, 353–96.

11. Cf. Philippe Aries, *Centuries of Childhood* (New York: Knopf 1962), 339–410.

12. Cf. Georg Simmel (Kurt Wolff ed.), *The Sociology of Georg Simmel* (New York: Collier-Macmillan 1950), 118–44.

13. Cf. Schutz, *Aufbau*, 29–36, 149–53.

14. Cf. Schutz, *Aufbau*, 186–92, 202–10.

15. David Riesman's well-known concept of "other-direction" would also be applicable here.

16. Cf. Maurice Halbwachs, *Les Cadres sociaux de la memoire* (Paris: Presses universitaires de France 1952), especially 146–77; also cf. Peter Berger, *Invitation to Sociology—A Humanistic Perspective* (Garden City, N.Y.: Doubleday-Anchor 1963), 54–65 (available in Penguin).

17. Cf. Schultz, *Collected Papers*, I, 72–3, 79–82.

18. The phenomena here discussed could also be formulated effectively in terms of the Marxian categories of reification and false consciousness. Jean-Paul Sartre's recent work, especially *Critique de la raison dialectique*, seeks to integrate these categories within a phenomenological analysis of human conduct. Also cf. Henri Lefebvre, *Critique de la vie quotidienne* (Paris: l'Arche 1958–61).

CHAPTER 14 Other Institutions: Religion, Education, and Health Care

14.1 ROSE LAUB COSER AND LEWIS COSER

Jonestown as a Perverse Utopia

Religious organizations take many forms, including those of sects and cults. According to the relevant literature, sects are small groups that (usually) withdraw from and reject the secular culture. Members form a separatist religious group and sometimes set up a utopian community. They emphasize fundamentalist teachings and see themselves as the only group who has access to the "truth." Membership in a sect requires a so-called conversion experience, abandoning the past, and an emotional commitment to the leader or prophet (a charismatic figure) who alone determines all the proper behavior and social relations of the followers.

Rose Laub Coser (b. 1916), sociologist, taught at the State University of New York at Stony Brook for 20 years. She is the author of *Life in the Ward* (Michigan State University Press, 1962), and her research interests include bureaucratic organization, socialization, and social structure. Lewis Coser (b. 1913), sociologist, also taught at the State University of New York at Stony Brook for 20 years.

258

*Chapter 14
Other
Institutions:
Religion,
Education, and
Health Care*

He is noted for his theory on social structure equilibrium, which states that conflict is the locus of social dynamics and change, but it also maintains a balance of powers (equilibrium). His research interests include political sociology, sociological theory, and organizations concerned with exacting total loyalties from their members, such as the commune known as Jonestown.

In the following excerpt, Coser and Coser discuss the People's Temple that was established by Jim Jones in San Francisco and eventually transferred to Guyana, presumably so its followers could lead a better, purer life of devotion to God and equality. But in November 1979 this utopian community of 911 men, women, and children ended tragically in mass suicide or murder. The Cosers argue that the commune was never a pure cult or sect but was structured much like a concentration camp. It instilled dependency and infantilism in its members.

The Cosers' analysis suggests that when people are cut off from the emotional bonds with their fellow human beings, isolated from others, and unable to test reality, their psychic energies cease to function. Unable to relate to others, each individual becomes "an atom unto itself."

Key Concept: utopian commune

*F*or 20 days, until December 8 [1978], the Jonestown horror story made first-page news in the *New York Times*. In the course of five hours, 911 adults and children were killed or killed themselves. There had been no threat on their lives from the outside, nor was there any strong transcendental cause that leader or followers meant to serve. The leader had claimed he wanted "socialism" and "Marxism," and had mixed his missionary zeal with religion because he allegedly believed the followers "needed it." So for years he gave them "opium for the people," and in the end cyanide.

The questions that are usually being asked are: What kind of people were those commune members? Were they without roots? Were they the rejects of society—the drug addicts, the convicts, the prostitutes, those not embedded in the social fabric of their society? And who was the leader? What manner of man commanded such obedience? How did he grow up in the small town where he was born? Had he given signs of such wickedness earlier in his life?

It turned out that the followers were of all kinds. There were the poor, the rich, and those of the middle. There were convicts and there were lawyers; there were the elderly and young prostitutes; there were physicians and nurses, blacks and whites. There were those with weak moral beliefs, and those with a strong social conscience. The answers about the characteristics of the members are not satisfactory. At best they tell us who was attracted to Jim Jones, but they cannot tell us why they obeyed him unto death.

Nor do the characteristics of the leader tell us much. It is interesting to hear that as a child he killed animals, and said mass after their death; and that his mother had predicted her son would be a messiah. But surely, the Jekyll-Hyde personality is a frequent figure, and many people have fantasies of omnipotence. Some even become murderers, and occasionally there is one who manages to kill as many as a dozen people. But they do not kill, or are not capable of killing, almost a thousand people in one sweep. This is hard work. While psychological predispositions in the leader and his followers explain some of their mutual attraction, they cannot fully explain this horrible success story.

Let us turn from personal to structural characteristics. Perverse as it was, Jonestown was a species of the genus, *utopian commune.* Ever since the industrial revolution and earlier—already in antiquity—usually at times of widespread discontent with the quality of life, blueprints for a more satisfying social organization were drawn up, from *The Republic to Utopia* (which coined the generic name) to *Looking Backward.* These utopias transcended the here-and-now, served as guidelines for social criticism and as foci for human strivings. Yet, as Lewis Coser and Henry Jacoby wrote years ago, "We are appalled to discover that many of the rationalistic fantasies of the world improvers contain a large admixture of what we now recognize as totalitarianism" (*Common Cause,* February 1951).

Not only blueprints but actual experiments in utopian living attracted over the years the socially committed and the morally courageous, the physically and psychologically deprived, and those yearning for a new morality. Yet, in most communes morals and social relations tended to become regulated from above; personal and public allegiances were monopolized by a central authority; and what had started out as an experiment in liberation usually ended in an experiment in the total absorption of personality. Communes have an innate tendency to become, as one of the authors wrote, *greedy institutions.*

Communes did not usually end in the destruction of their members, and some of those inspired by vigorous religious beliefs even managed to survive for several generations. But most ended in splits, fights between factions, acrid disputes, mutual recriminations, and sordid intrigues between rival leaders. Their isolation from other social institutions, their inward orientation, the absorption of the members' total personality often led to a disintegration of the commune, even as it deprived members of the ability to sustain personal relations both within and without.

Jonestown was a community isolated by design. In a sense, if not literally, it was an incestuous community. To survive for even the short period it did, it operated in secrecy, erected strong barriers around itself. Rank-and-file members had to break all ties with the outside. This prevented interference from nonbelievers, but mainly it prevented reality testing. Any personal or social values members brought with them from their previous lives were destroyed. Finally, any personal relations, whether sexual or otherwise affective, were broken up. This assured the absence of interpersonal allegiances. It also assured complete dependency, similar to the dependency of a newborn child, on one person, and one person only.

THE ISOLATED SOCIETY: "WE HAD NOWHERE TO GO."

Anthropologists and sociologists are generally agreed on the proposition that society is possible because libidinal energies and affective orientations, within

260

*Chapter 14
Other
Institutions:
Religion,
Education, and
Health Care*

or between generations, are directed outward, so that self-sufficiency is prevented. This is the basis for the incest taboo. A certain amount of what Philip Slater has called "libidinal diffusion" (*American Sociological Review,* 1963) is necessary for social survival, since it facilitates exchange among various units of a society. Groups that monopolize affective energies within themselves tend to be subject to inner decay and to have low survival value. Jonestown is a case in point. Isolated from any but the minimum contact with the outside world, Jonestown's members had no place to go: no place to go to test reality, no place to go with libidinal cathexis except to one man, no place to go to obtain or receive support except from him.

Jonestown seems to have been incestuous in more than the figurative sense. The leader, who was called "Dad," had sexual relations with the commune's members, that is, his "children," men or women, sometimes as many as 16 a day, as he bragged to Charles Gary. He explained that he did this "to assure their loyalty to him." By working to monopolize the affect of the community's members, and making them withdraw their libidinal energy not only from outside relationships but inside as well, Jones completed his efforts at reducing his followers to a narcissistic stage of infantile dependency that Bruno Bettelheim had shown to develop among inmates of concentration camps.

There was hardly any contact with the outside on the part of rank-and-file members. Nobody could leave the premises except some trusted aides who could go as far as the Georgetown headquarters, where control of movement was as tight as it could possibly be. Ron Javers describes the physical isolation from the plane that took him to Port Kaituma—a six-mile jeep ride from Jonestown:

> At some points the trees were so thick we couldn't see the ground. . . . Elsewhere there were large stretches of flat, deep, red mud. There were no roads. It was startling to realize how isolated people could be only 150 miles from the capital. There was no way to get to Jonestown except by air or by a long boat trip along the Atlantic coast and up the Kaituma River.*

The isolation of the site was a criterion for selection when Jones first conceived of the settlement. From its early days, the People's Temple tried to erect boundaries or break relations with the rest of society (even as Jones tried to influence, cajole, or threaten politicians and the press). Several times he had picked up and moved when outside intrusions became threatening. Around 1965 in Redwood City, it became known that there were guards around the Temple church and dogs along the fences.

There was isolation from the media as well. Jones controlled the news and the members' access to it. When *New West* magazine was to appear with disclosures about the doings at the Temple, and he departed for Guayana, he instructed his aides to buy out the magazine from newsstands in Oakland, San Francisco, and Los Angeles, where a copy might fall into the hands of Temple members or their relatives. He also instructed his aides to forbid followers to

---

*Marshall Kilduff and Ron Javers, *Suicide Cult* (New York: Bantam Books, 1978). All subsequent quotes and factual material not otherwise identified are from this book.

read newspapers or watch television. Later, in Jonestown, members were asked to listen to news broadcasts selectively, and had to write out their reactions and send them to "Dad."

Without newspapers and with only occasional news that had to be "understood" in a prescribed manner, surrounded by the jungle—how would it ever be possible for any rank-and-file member to test reality? How could anyone have looked for evidence of the alleged fact that mercenaries were waiting in the woods to invade the settlement and torture its members? There was no place to go with one's cognitive assessments if not into the jungle—even if, as is doubtful, the need for such assessment were perceived by the members who anyhow "knew" that they must depend on "Dad."

Isolation could not be maintained without secrecy. In the mid-'60s in Redwood Valley, the Temple members' children were said to lie, and to be evasive at school about what they did at the Temple. Isolation and secrecy, if they are to be organizational requirements, must be enjoined upon and upheld by all individual members. Temple members often had to forgo bidding their relatives good-bye when they left for Guayana. Often departing members were called in the morning and told they would leave for Guayana the same night. People would call their children to tell them they would be leaving on a trip immediately, and refuse to say where they were going or how long they would be gone. Relatives of those who had gone to Jonestown without leaving word were met with silence when they made inquiries at the San Francisco Temple.

While isolation and secrecy were organizational requirements for Jones's designs, they served social and psychological purposes as well. Group members who break up all relationships on the outside will be dependent on staying with that group. Not only will it be difficult for them to return home if they so desire, but their whole cognitive and affective orientation will be inward-directed so that the outside world fades from view—much as in cases of confinement to concentration camps, long-term imprisonment or hospitalization, even though in these cases the inmates do not join voluntarily.

Temple members who made the trip signed away to the church, as many before them had done, their cars, homes, and other possessions. When they arrived at Jonestown, whatever money they had left was confiscated together with their passports. Already in San Francisco church members had been talked into cashing their life-insurance policies and turning the money over to the Temple, or into signing over power-of-attorney. Way back in Indiana couples had been persuaded to sell their houses and turn the money over to the church. The well-to-do had to give up their means of survival on the outside. The poor had to contribute an ever larger percentage of meager earnings.

All this money made the People's Temple a viable operation. But it served other purposes as well: it deprived members of all means of independence. Jones wanted the money not only for selfish or organizational purposes: it became a problem merely to dispose of the wealth that piled up. "Jim was giving the stuff away just to get rid of it," one former member said. People who were deprived of their money would have no options but to stay with the Temple. "The Temple ended up with everything I had," said Jeannie Mills. "That's what made it so hard to leave. *We had nowhere to go* and nothing to fall back on."

262

*Chapter 14
Other
Institutions:
Religion,
Education, and
Health Care*

Having no place to go, and having invested all their emotional life in the Temple, the stage was set for binding people to the Total Institution that was to be Jonestown. To assure its survival, however, two more things had to be accomplished: the remaking of personal values, and the prevention of solidarity within the settlement. These, paradoxically, led to its destruction.

THE INVERTEBRATE: "I KNOW I'M LIKE A BANANA."

Having no place to go was not enough. Not *wanting* to go would be better. And so we read in one of those required letters of confession: "I'm an elitist and anarchist. . . . I've come a little way. . . . Here I don't have any intention of becoming a traitor or going back to the United States" (Avis G., quoted in the *New York Times*, November 29).

People's behavior as well as their personal attitudes and moral values had to come under the scrutiny of all. Individuals had to submit to physical and mental humiliations and more: they had to humiliate themselves. Former Temple members report that men and women would be forced to strip off their clothes at the public meetings and say they were homosexuals or lesbians.

Already in San Francisco Jones spent much of his time presiding over such "catharsis" sessions, which were grueling, drawn-out spells of emotional dissection by the followers:

> Why did she wear such new clothes when there were millions of people starving? Wasn't it true that he wanted to make love to another man's wife? Admit it! How could anyone complain about working until dawn after getting off work when Father is in such pain for us all.

Beatings, torture, mutual accusations and confessions—techniques that had started way back in San Francisco—remind us of the social-psychological processes in the concentration camps as described by Bruno Bettelheim. At Jonestown, those who, like Bettelheim's camp inmates,

> did not develop a childlike dependency were accused of threatening the security of the group. . . . The regression into childlike behavior was inescapable. . . . [They] lived, like children, only in the immediate present; they lost their feeling for the sequence of time; they became unable to plan for the future. . . . They were unable to establish durable object relations. Friendships developed as quickly as they broke off. [*Journal of Abnormal and Social Psychology*, 1943.]

For the acceptance of the new life, everything that had to do with the personal life of the past or of the present—relatives, friends, social, personal, and intimate values—had to be defiled. "When your name was called, people would scream, 'Get down there,' and swear. It was hostile," said a former member. "Everyone related to you was required to run up and accuse you." Any loyalties, any solidarity, any relatedness between the members of the

Temple had to be broken up, and mutual accusations, hostilities, and mandatory denunciations were used to bring this about. Nobody could trust anybody. Not being permitted to establish relationships with one another, they soon became incapable of doing so, like Don F., who wrote in one of his mandatory letters of confession: "Now I know I'm like a banana, just one of the bunch. I have come a long way" (*New York Times*, November 29).

"SEX WAS ONE OF JIM'S SPECIALTIES FOR PULLING PEOPLE APART."

Children were removed from their parents, spouses separated, matches made and broken up. Family ties within the church were always kept under Jones's direct control. Jones knew that the most effective way to control personal relationships is to control libidinal attractions. When he bragged to his lawyer, Charles Gary, about having sex with 14 women and 2 men in that one day, he explained that this was to assure their loyalty to him.

Jones ordered marriages ended and rearranged. Many of his marathon six-hour sermons dwelled on sex, including directions to members to swear off relations. Already in the church he had established a kind of spy group that regulated everything including hand holding, forced divorces and shotgun marriages. A high school boy seen talking to a girl who did not belong to the Temple would be called before the assembly to talk at length about his sex life.

"Sex was one of Jim's specialties for pulling people apart," said a former member. For married couples, Jones would often have another form of advice: abstention. Couples were forced apart and told not to engage in sexual intercourse because it was evil.

Lewis Coser has argued elsewhere that such manifestly opposite sexual patterns as abstinence and sexual promiscuity serve the same purposes (*Greedy Institutions*, Free Press, 1974). Both promiscuity and celibacy help prevent stable dyadic bonds, for such bonds detract from emotional attachment to the community and its leaders. Whether members refrain from all sexual relations, as did the Shakers, or whether there is a controlled form of promiscuity, as in Oneida [which was a utopian community established in 1840 in which the adult members all considered themselves married to one another], is sociologically unimportant. What these communities share is a deliberate attempt to prevent dyadic personal relationships so that emotional energies will be purposely channeled. A similar pattern prevails in other totalistic communes today, for example, at Synanon. A recent *New York Times* report (December 10, 1978) describes the policies introduced by its leader, Mr. Dederich. They include forced vasectomies for male members, mandatory abortions for women, and orders from Mr. Dederich for more than 230 married couples to divorce and switch to other partners within the group.

"I'M DEAD INSIDE"

Chapter 14
Other
Institutions:
Religion,
Education, and
Health Care

The problem, it seems to us, is that emotional energies cannot simply be "channeled" for the common or not so common good. Arbitrary and unpredictable interference with them leads to their being damaged at best and destroyed at worst. The latter happened in Jonestown. When people are cut off from emotional bonds with their fellows they have no psychic energies left that can be mobilized even in situations of extreme peril. How many were there among the hundreds of adults in line for cyanide who asked themselves like Odell Rhodes, "How can I get out of here?" as he later reported? Could he not at least have made eye contact with someone who had similar feelings? It seems that at the high point of the ceremony of self-immolation everyone was but an atom unto itself, unable to relate even in imagination to others who might share some doubts. They must all have felt, as Odell Rhodes later stated about himself, "dead inside" (*New York Times*, November 29).

Jonestown was more "greedy" an institution than has probably ever existed. It successfully "devoured" its members by making total claims on them and by encompassing their whole personality. By claiming, and receiving, undivided loyalty, and by reducing the claims of competing roles and allegiances, it succeeded not merely in totally absorbing members within its boundaries but in reducing them to human pulp as well. Not only did it erect insurmountable boundaries between the inside and the outside, between the "reborn" collective present of the members and their "disreputable" private past; it also succeeded in maiming them by breaking up any mutual attachments, sexual or otherwise. The stable relationship, *voila l'ennemi*.

Even as we recoil in horror at the unfolding of the Jonestown story it behooves us not to look at it in isolation. It did, after all, unfold at this time and in this place. While it would be fatuous to blame what happened on "American society," we must keep in mind that the damned and the lost and the hopeful who flocked to Jones and the People's Temple did so because the society in which they lived had failed to provide satisfactory bonds, meaningful community, and fraternal solidarities. To Jones's followers, the society felt like a desert devoid of love; so they turned to the People's Temple, which they saw as an oasis. Although their quest turned out to be a delusion, we cannot deny that their need was acute.

14.2 CHRISTOPHER J. HURN

Theories of Schooling and Society: The Functional and Radical Paradigms

What function does education have in society? In the following selection, Christopher J. Hurn explores this essential sociological question by reviewing two theories of schooling. He calls them the functional and the radical paradigms of schooling. Until the late 1960s, the functional paradigm was widely accepted. According to this theory, schools provide an effective means for "sorting and selecting talented people so that the most able and motivated attain the highest status positions." Schools teach the knowledge, skills, and norms that enable students to become useful workers and citizens. It is the key to the equal opportunity society and the ladder of success. Most sociologists, however, have come to regard this functionalist view as more ideal than real. And that's where the radical paradigm comes in. This paradigm views schools in an entirely different light. In this theory, schooling is not as benign as the functionalists describe it. Schools in a capitalist society are repressive and perpetuate inequality. To illustrate the radical paradigm, Hurn discusses the theories of Ivan Illich and neo-Marxists Samuel Bowles and Herbert Gintis. This selection provides a comprehensive look at contemporary sociological theories of schooling. Hurn (b. 1938), noted for his work on society and education, is an associate professor in the Department of Sociology at the University of Massachusetts—Amherst.

Key Concept: the role of schooling in society

*S*ociological theories of schooling, indeed, are closely related to implicit common sense ideas about education and its function in modern society—a group of more or less coherent ideas, rather than a set of tightly knit theoretical propositions.

265

266

*Chapter 14
Other
Institutions:
Religion,
Education, and
Health Care*

Until ten years ago discussion of theories of schooling in modern society would have made little sense. The contest between groups of competing ideas, each claiming to offer an explanation of what schools do and why they do it, is fairly recent. Until a decade or so ago one major interpretation of the role of schooling in modern society prevailed almost unchallenged. This theory, which I shall call the *functional paradigm*, offers both an explanation and a justification for the role of educational institutions. In simplest terms, the functional paradigm argues that schools are essential institutions in modern society because they perform two crucial functions: first, schools represent a rational way of sorting and selecting talented people so that the most able and motivated attain the highest status positions; second, schools teach the kind of cognitive skills and norms essential for the performance of most roles in a society increasingly dependent upon knowledge and expertise. The functional paradigm is largely an elaboration of these two apparently straightforward propositions.

Although these beliefs are still very widely held, still constituting the core of what might be called the liberal orthodoxy in educational thought, they have lost some of the taken-for-granted character that they possessed a decade or so ago. Most obviously, the image of constantly expanding schooling meeting the needs of an increasingly complex and knowledge-dependent society (an image implicit in some of the cruder formulations of the functional paradigm) has been questioned in recent years. . . . The many successful efforts at educational reform in the last fifteen years—attempts to create schools that unleash the natural intelligence or creativity of students and attempts to reduce class and race differences in educational performance—have led more and more educators and social scientists to question the optimistic assumptions about the direction of educational change that lie at the heart of the functional paradigm.

Most fundamentally, however, this dominant theory of schooling and society has recently been challenged by a new, much less sanguine account. This theory, which I shall call the *radical paradigm*, portrays schools not as more or less rational instruments for sorting and selecting talented people, but as institutions that perpetuate inequality and convince lower class groups of their inferiority. In the radical paradigm what is important about schooling is not the cognitive and intellectual skills schools teach, but the class-related values and attitudes that they reinforce. In this view, schools are instruments of elite domination, agencies that foster compliance and docility rather than independent thought and humane values.[1]

THE FUNCTIONAL PARADIGM OF SCHOOLING

The functional paradigm of schooling is not the work of any one individual theorist, nor does it consist exclusively of the ideas of sociologists. In its most general form the functional paradigm has long been part of the conventional wisdom of liberal intellectuals in Western society and, to a large extent, part of the working assumptions of the great majority of all who have thought and written about schooling in Western societies until quite recently. . . .

267

Christopher J.
Hurn

Modern Society—The Functional View

At the heart of the functional paradigm is an analysis of what adherents to the model see as the unique character of the modern Western world and the crucial role that schooling plays in that world. The paradigm sees modern Western societies differing from most previous societies in at least three crucial respects.

The Meritocratic Society. First, in modern societies occupational roles are (and should be) achieved rather than ascribed. Contemporary intellectuals have long regarded the inheritance of occupational roles, and more broadly the inheritance of social status, as anathema. People believe high status positions should be achieved on the basis of merit rather than passed on from parent to child. The children of the poor should have equal opportunity to achieve high status with more privileged children. And in all Western societies, particularly since World War II, governments have responded to this belief by trying to increase equality of opportunity: by expanding higher education, introducing universalistic rules for employment intended to discourage nepotism, and legislating elimination of discrimination on the basis of religion, race, and sex. The functional paradigm, therefore, sees modern society as *meritocratic:* a society where ability and effort count for more than privilege and inherited status. . . .

The Expert Society. . . . The functional paradigm sees modern society as an "expert" society: one that depends preeminently on rational knowledge for economic growth, requiring more and more highly trained individuals to fill the majority of occupational positions. Schools perform two crucial functions in this view of society. The research activities of universities and colleges produce the new knowledge that underpins economic growth and social progress. And extensive schooling both equips individuals with specialized skills and provides a general foundation of cognitive knowledge and intellectual sophistication to permit the acquisition of more specialized knowledge.

The Democratic Society. Finally, the functional paradigm portrays contemporary society as a democratic society moving gradually toward the achievement of humane goals: toward social justice, a more fulfilling life for all citizens, and the acceptance of diversity. Implicit in the functional paradigm, therefore, is a particular kind of political liberalism; a view that does not deny the evils and inequities of the present society, but does believe that progress has been made and will continue to be made. Increasing levels of education are at the core of this conception of progress. An educated citizenry is an informed citizenry, less likely to be manipulated by demagogues, more likely to make responsible and informed political decisions and to be actively involved in the political process. Education reduces intolerance and prejudice, and increases support for civil liberties; it is, in other words, an essential bulwark of a democratic society

268

*Chapter 14
Other
Institutions:
Religion,
Education, and
Health Care*

dedicated to freedom and justice. And a more educated society, finally, will be a better society in another sense; a society dedicated not only to economic growth and material wealth, but also to the pursuit of social justice. The educated society is concerned with the quality of life and the conditions that make individual fulfillment possible.

Schooling and Society

In this general form, then, the functional paradigm is an account of what are the most distinctive and important features of modern society and a set of assertions about the role schooling plays in sustaining and supporting these features. At the same time it is the theory of what schools do, how schools are changing and will change in the future, and a justification for high levels of society commitment to schooling.[2] This model views the close relationship between schooling and future status in contemporary society as an essentially rational process of adaptation: a process where the needs of the increasingly complex society for talented and expert personnel are met by outputs from the educational system in the form of cognitive skills and the selection of talented individuals.[3] And if only the most uncritical supporters of the paradigm would assert that such a process of social selection in schools is perfectly meritocratic or that disadvantaged groups have identical opportunities to those afforded to more privileged students, there is some general confidence that the direction of educational change has been in a meritocratic direction. From this perspective the net effect of the expansion of schooling has been to increase the percentage of poor but talented students who reach high status positions, with the assumption that further expansion of schooling will move us closer toward a society of equal opportunity. What schools teach is also, although imperfectly, a functional adaptation to the needs of the social order. As the nature of the modern economy increasingly demands (even in middle or lower status occupations) more sophisticated cognitive skills and flexibility and adaptability in the work force, so pedagogical techniques and curricula shift away from rote memorization and moral indoctrination to concern with cognitive development and intellectual flexibility. In this respect the functional paradigm is not necessarily traditional and politically conservative, as critics sometimes allege. . . . People often use functional paradigm arguments to attack traditional schools and to call for a new more rational school system to better meet the needs of the contemporary world.

But if the functional paradigm is not necessarily politically conservative, it certainly does portray the major features of contemporary society in fundamentally benign terms.[4] Inequality, for example, is often seen as a necessary device for motivating talented individuals to achieve high status positions. And while it is recognized by most observers that the correlation between ability and high status is far from perfect, they see the problem of inequality in contemporary society as one of raising barriers to the mobility of talent rather than as a problem of redistributing wealth from high status positions to low status positions.[5] That talent in turn tends to be conceived as one dimensional, underlying both success in school and success in life. And if many liberals within this tradition argue that there are "vast reserves of untapped talent" among disadvantaged groups, others more pessimistically conclude that such talent is inherently scarce.

DIFFICULTIES IN THE FUNCTIONAL PARADIGM

The set of assumptions I have described are still influential among social scientists, policy makers, and educators, but they have lost some of the taken-for-granted character of a decade or more ago. The rate of educational expansion has declined; past projections of the need for college graduates have been confounded by a surplus of unemployed or underemployed degree holders. In the face of these developments it becomes more difficult to argue that industrial societies require ever-increasing percentages of highly educated individuals. But the difficulties of the functional paradigm are more fundamental than those posed by the current (and possibly temporary) imbalance between educational outputs and the supply of high status jobs. In the past decade a substantial body of research has developed that poses a challenge to almost all the main assertions of the paradigm—to the link between schooling and jobs, the assumption of an increasing meritocratic society, and arguments about increasing opportunities for the mobility of talented, but underprivileged youth.

THE RADICAL PARADIGM

I have shown that the model of schooling and society that dominated much thought about education until quite recently is beset with serious difficulties. Schools do undoubtedly teach cognitive skills and increase the intellectual sophistication of their students, but it is not clear that it is these skills that explain the relationship between schooling, occupational status, and earnings. The available evidence does not suggest that United States society is substantially more meritocratic than in the past. Nor is there much evidence to indicate that increased resources devoted to schooling have resulted in more favorable opportunities for the talented children of disadvantaged parents to obtain high status positions. Simply put, the expansion of schooling does not seem to have worked in the way the functional paradigm suggests that it should work.

The radical paradigm offers a very different interpretation of schooling in its relationship to society. Like the functional paradigm the radical paradigm sees schools and society as closely linked . . . but it stresses the links between schools and the demands of elites rather than the needs of the whole society. It

270

*Chapter 14
Other
Institutions:
Religion,
Education, and
Health Care*

also stresses the connection between schooling and the learning of docility and compliance rather than the acquisition of cognitive skills. If the functional paradigm sees schools as more or less efficient mechanisms for sorting and selecting talented people and for producing cognitive skills, the radical paradigm sees schools as serving the interests of elites, as reinforcing existing inequalities, and as producing attitudes that foster acceptance of this status quo.

The Intellectual Background

The functional paradigm took shape at a time when the climate of intellectual opinion was predominantly optimistic about the main features of contemporary society and its likely future evolution. Modern society was viewed as increasingly rational and meritocratic, a society where prejudice, racism, intolerance, and the ignorance that fostered these evils would gradually disappear. Schools taught, sustained, and nurtured essentially modern cosmopolitan values and attitudes. Schools, at least the best schools, worked to emancipate children from parochialism, from an unreflecting respect for the traditions of the past, and from ignorance and prejudice. The new mathematics of the late 1960s, with its stress on understanding the principles of logic rather than the mere acquisition of immediately useful skills, and the new English curriculum, with its use of modern novels that invited frank discussion of contemporary moral issues, both symbolized a commitment to modern, liberal, and cosmopolitan ideals. The best schools, at least, taught rationality; they developed the ability to handle moral complexity and to tolerate ambiguity. If the prisons of ignorance, prejudice, and unthinking respect for the past prevented many parents from entering this new world, schools were agencies of emancipation for the next generation. In the modern world, schools do not merely reproduce the values, attitudes, and skills of the past, they are "active agents" in creating a more liberal, a more rational, and a more humane society.

. . . The liberal model of modern society—a world admittedly full of serious imperfection, but nevertheless moving in a fundamentally progressive direction—was replaced, for more and more intellectuals, by a model of society requiring urgent and wholesale surgery to avoid disaster. The new, more skeptical vision saw greedy business corporations intent on destroying the environment, cynical and corrupt politicians concerned with their own power and privilege, and entrenched racism and sexism in virtually every social institution. Instead of a model of society where authority was based on expertise and competence, this radical vision defined a society where powerful elites manipulate public opinion to preserve their own entrenched position. . . .

The rejection of the liberal model of society implied a more skeptical interpretation of what schools teach and the role that schooling plays in modern society. Instead of teaching the values and attitudes essential to the functioning of a modern, liberal, democratic policy, schools were seen as institutions that teach middle class morality—unthinking patriotism, good work habits, good manners. Rather than teaching students to think for themselves, schools teach conformity to business values. Instead of teaching the cognitive skills needed by the complex nature of modern occupations, schools teach a narrow technocratic vision of the world. Successful students are not more creative or more intelligent than others; they are successful because they have learned to play by the official rules of the game. They have learned to work the system to their own advantage, to conform to the officially established definitions of knowledge and truth.

None of these ideas, perhaps, is distinctively radical. The observation that institutions subvert the aims that they profess is not necessarily radical nor even particularly novel. Nor can all those who complain that schools teach passivity and compliance be regarded as radical theorists. The boundaries between the functional and the radical paradigm, therefore, are not always clear-cut. Perhaps most distinctive, however, is the radical paradigm's attribution of the source of schools' failings. The radical paradigm assumes that the failure of schools is inevitable because of the organization of contemporary capitalist society. Schools are not imperfect institutions in the process of gradual transformation toward new and more humane ends. The defects of schooling, rather, are a reflection of a social order demanding repression and requiring the perpetuation of inequality. . . .

Within these general guiding assumptions are important disagreements among radical theorists. On the one hand some writers (many of the popular school critics fall into this category) imply that a fundamental of schooling reconstruction is conceivable within existing capitalist society. School reform can, in this view, serve as a catalyst of broader social change because a reconstructed school system will produce individuals intolerant of exploitation, repression, and racism.[6] Many of the progressives in the early decades of this country made such an argument, though in less strident form.

A second, and often specifically Marxist argument, asserts that revolutionary social change must precede the reconstruction of educational institutions.[7] From this perspective any attempt to create a more "humane" and liberated school will inevitably be extinguished or emasculated by the vested interests that elites have in preventing such outcomes. These elites may tolerate or even encourage such innovations as new or more "rational" curricula, open classrooms, or nondirective teaching styles, but more fundamental changes in the social organization of schools that affect the whole population rather than only a privileged minority are not possible in contemporary capitalist society. The theories of Ivan Illich and the theories of Samuel Bowles and Herbert Gintis are perhaps the two most important exemplars of the radical paradigm. They illustrate different approaches toward the problem of repressive schooling in a repressive society.

Ivan Illich's Theory of Schooling

The publication of Ivan Illich's *Deschooling Society* in the *New York Review of Books* in 1969 was a watershed in thought about schooling in Western society.[8]

272

*Chapter 14
Other
Institutions:
Religion,
Education, and
Health Care*

Before Illich, of course, radical criticism of schools had become fashionable among many intellectuals. . . . Illich's work, however, is distinctive in calling for the abolition of schooling rather than reform. Illich argues that societies should not require compulsory schooling in any form and maintains that legislation should forbid employers from hiring individuals on the basis of the amount of their schooling.

Illich calls for an abandonment of this faith in universal schooling on several grounds. He argues that there is no conceivable way that poor countries can close the schooling gap between themselves and rich countries. To place faith in schooling is, for a poor country, to be condemned to perpetual inferiority. Most poor countries in Asia, Africa, and Latin America simply do not have the resources to provide five years of elementary schooling for all students, let alone universal secondary schooling. And if the idealistic goal of universal schooling is chimerical, the pursuit of that goal actually heightens inequalities and increases the sense of inferiority that many people in poor countries experience. The effect of educational expansion in poor countries is to close opportunities to those who have little or no schooling. The most important knowledge that children who attend school in Brazil for two years will learn, Illich suggests, is a sense of their own inadequacy and inferiority. The child will learn that mobility, success, and self-worth require more schooling than most children can achieve. Rather than seeing compulsory schooling as indispensable for the creation of literacy in the population, Illich sees schooling as a status symbol of modernization that will condemn much of the world's population to a sense of their own lack of self-worth.[9]

The solution for rich and poor countries alike is to abolish compulsory schooling and to set up alternative "convivial" institutions to foster true educational goals. The state must cease to require that children go to school, and equally important, employers must be forbidden inquiry into a person's scholastic experience—grades, examination results, degrees, and so on. Instead employers must hire people on the basis of competence for a particular job. To replace schools, a network of alternative institutions must be established and individuals given vouchers permitting them to purchase units of instruction at whatever centers they choose to attend. They can attend skill centers teaching literacy, computational skills, or specific vocational skills. The resources of computer technology can be used to assemble groups of people with similar interests who wish to exchange ideas and information. Individuals who wish to discuss a particular play of Shakespeare, for example, will be put in touch with other individuals with the same interests. Those who wish to acquire the most recent knowledge in agricultural technology can be matched with those who wish to teach.[10] Illich believes that attendance at these convivial institutions must not be made a condition for future employment or future status. The link between educational credentials and occupational status must be broken.

Illich's work stands the liberal conventional wisdom about the effects of schooling on its head. The expansion of schooling in the modern world heightens inequalities between nations and between individuals within society. The close connection between educational attainment and occupational status characteristic of the modern world is not a sign that our society has become more rational and more competence based. Rather, the connection reflects a misplaced conviction that schooling is synonymous with education and that scholastic credentials indeed certify competence. Finally, the belief that the expansion of schooling underlies any just, humane, and democratic order is altogether incorrect. Western societies, despite their professed principles, are fundamentally undemocratic and inhumane. They are dedicated to the pursuit of material affluence, where decisions are increasingly made by individuals with technical knowledge rather than by elected officials, and individual lives are increasingly governed by large bureaucracies over which people have no control. Schools teach the inevitability of this present social order; they are essential props of the bureaucratic and technological world view of Western society. They may encourage questioning and dissent within that world view— questions about means and methods rather than ends—but they have the effect of discouraging alternative and more democratic visions of society.[11]

THE NEO-MARXIST THEORIES OF BOWLES AND GINTIS

The work of Bowles and Gintis, while making many of the same substantive assertions about the effects of schooling, differs profoundly in methods and procedures from Illich's analysis. Illich is not a social scientist. He cites virtually no empirical evidence for the sweeping conclusions that he draws. He gives no footnotes, making it virtually impossible to know the basis for many of his generalizations. He exaggerates deliberately, perhaps in an effort to provoke the reader to question the conventional wisdom. Bowles and Gintis, by contrast, are highly competent social scientists. Their book *Schooling in Capitalist America* is packed with charts and tables and careful reasoning on the basis of empirical evidence.

Reinforcing Inequality

Bowles and Gintis' major argument . . . is that the educational system reinforces class inequalities in contemporary society. Different social classes in America tend to attend different neighborhood schools. Both the value preferences of parents and the different financial resources available to different communities mean that schools catering to working class students will teach different values and different personal qualities than schools serving higher status populations. These latter schools are not "better" or "freer" in any absolute sense, but high status schools communicate to their students the distinctive values and attitudes required by high status occupations in modern capitalist societies. The great majority of occupations in contemporary society, Bowles and Gintis believe, require a loyal and compliant work force to perform tasks with little responsibility and discretion. Most schools, therefore, teach

274

*Chapter 14
Other
Institutions:
Religion,
Education, and
Health Care*

their students to follow orders reliably, to take explicit directions, to be punctual, and to respect the authority of the teacher and of the school. Such schools, which satisfy the preference of most parents for discipline and good manners in their children, channel students to manual and lower level white-collar occupations. But schools serving more elite groups are only superficially less repressive. Such schools encourage students to work at their own pace without continuous supervision, to work for the sake of long-term future rewards, and to internalize rules of behavior rather than depend on specific and frequent instructions. These qualities are essential to effective performance in middle or high status positions in large organizations. But work in such organizations permits only limited freedom and autonomy. Workers may question specific procedures, but not the purpose of the organization; employees may be flexible and innovative, but they must be loyal. The capitalist society requires that all schools teach the values of individual achievement, material consumption, and the inevitability of the present social order. Free schools are therefore impossible in a repressive society.[12]

Bowles and Gintis decisively reject the meritocratic hypothesis, with its assumption that schools are efficient ways of selecting talented people. Instead schools work to *convince* people that selection is meritocratic. It is essential for the legitimacy of the capitalist order that the population be convinced that people in high status positions do deserve these positions, that they are more talented and harder workers than others. Schools are an essential prop of this legitimacy. Selection for particular tracks within a school must appear to be made on the basis of ability and intelligence, and such purportedly objective criteria as IQ and grades serve this function. But these criteria mask the fact that success in schooling, and of course success in later life, is strongly related to social class and shows no indication of becoming less closely related over time. The correlation between college graduation and social class in the last twenty years, they report, has remained unchanged despite the rapid expansion of higher education. Schools remain institutions that reproduce and legitimate existing inequalities between social classes. This state of affairs will continue indefinitely in capitalist societies unless capitalism itself is abolished. Reforms in the educational system alone cannot reduce inequalities in the life chances of different social classes. The premise of liberal educational reform—that educational expansion and improved schooling can create equality of opportunity—is false. Schools that liberate, diminishing rather than reinforcing the handicaps of inequality, can only be achieved after a revolution in the distribution of power and the ownership of the means of production in contemporary capitalist society.

NOTES

1. The clearest statements of this argument are in Samuel Bowles and Herbert Gintis, *Schooling in capitalist America* (New York: Basic Books, 1976); Martin Carnoy (Ed.), *Schooling in a corporate society* (New York: McKay, 1975), pp. 1–37; Maurice Levitas,

Marxist perspective in the sociology of education (London: Routledge & Kegan Paul, 1974).

2. See the justifications for educational expansion given in Clark Kerr et al., *Industrialism and industrial man* (New York: Oxford, 1964).
3. The "schooling is rational as well as moral" argument is best represented in the reports of the Carnegie Commission on Higher Education, Clark Kerr (Ed.), *A digest of reports of the Carnegie Commission on Higher Education* (New York: McGraw-Hill, 1974).
4. Much of what I have called the *functional paradigm* is described as the *progress paradigm* by Phillip Wexler in *The sociology of education: Beyond equality* (Indianapolis: Bobbs Merrill, 1976).
5. See Wexler, *Sociology of education,* for an excellent discussion of how the central problem of early research in the sociology of education was conceived as one of erasing barriers to the mobility of talent.
6. See, for example, Neil Postman and Charles Weingartner, *Teaching as a subversive activity* (New York: Dell, 1969), chap 1.
7. This is essentially Bowles and Gintis's argument.
8. Later published by Harper & Row in 1971.
9. These arguments are stated somewhat less polemically by Everett Reimer in *School is dead* (New York: Doubleday, 1971).
10. It is not clear how Illich, who is opposed to any kind of "institutionalized values," proposes to prevent these alternative "convivial" institutions from developing the "dry rot" that afflicts existing institutions.
11. As he writes, "School is the advertising agency which makes you believe you need the society as it is." Ivan Illich, *Deschooling society.* New York: Harper & Row, 1971, p. 163.
12. See their comments on the free school movement, Bowles and Gintis, *Schooling,* p. 254.

Christopher J. Hurn

On Being Sane in Insane Places

In the labeling theory of deviance, the designation of a person as a deviant by officials has extensive consequences, including changes in the behavior of others toward that person. The result may well be to make that person become what he or she has been labeled. This theory has been applied to mental illness: It posits that when people are labeled as mentally ill they will be treated as such. Subsequently, they will see themselves as mentally ill, thus confirming the label. In the following paper, D. L. Rosenhan tests another aspect of the labeling theory and raises an important issue: How does one tell the difference between a mentally healthy person and a mentally ill person?

In Rosenhan's experiment, healthy people presented themselves to 12 mental hospitals claiming they had symptoms that are associated with schizophrenia. Upon admission to the hospitals, they ceased to show these symptoms and behaved as they normally would. Nevertheless, Rosenhan found that throughout their stays, they were treated as mentally ill, in accordance with the initial diagnosis of schizophrenia. They were all eventually discharged with the label of "schizophrenia in remission." Thus, a long period without schizophrenia symptoms did not earn them the label of "sane."

Rosenhan expands on the details of this study and suggests that the label "mentally ill," once placed upon a person, will remain with that person regardless of his or her behavior, because the label influences the way other people interpret his or her sane behavior. Rosenhan's study also calls attention to the fact that the diagnosis of mental illness is difficult when there are no clear manifestations of psychosis and that such diagnoses have unacceptably large margins of error.

Rosenhan (b. 1929) is a professor of law and psychology at Stanford University. He is a social psychologist whose work is concerned with clinical and personality matters.

Key Concept: labeling theory

*I*f sanity and insanity exist, how shall we know them?

The question is neither capricious nor itself insane. However much we may be personally convinced that we can tell the normal from the abnormal, the evidence is simply not compelling. It is commonplace, for example, to read about murder trials wherein eminent psychiatrists for the defense are contradicted by equally eminent psychiatrists for the prosecution on the matter of the defendant's sanity. More generally, there are a great deal of conflicting data on the reliability, utility, and meaning of such terms as "sanity," "insanity," "mental illness," and "schizophrenia." Finally, as early as 1934, [Ruth] Benedict suggested that normality and abnormality are not universal. What is viewed as normal in one culture may be seen as quite aberrant in another. Thus, notions of normality and abnormality may not be quite as accurate as people believe they are. . . .

At its heart, the question of whether the sane can be distinguished from the insane (and whether degrees of insanity can be distinguished from each other) is a simple matter: do the salient characteristics that lead to diagnoses reside in the patients themselves or in the environments and contexts in which observers find them? From Bleuler, through Kretchmer, through the formulators of the recently revised *Diagnostic and Statistical Manual* of the American Psychiatric Association, the belief has been strong that patients present symptoms, that those symptoms can be categorized, and, implicitly, that the sane are distinguishable from the insane. More recently, however, this belief has been questioned. Based in part on theoretical and anthropological considerations, but also on philosophical, legal and therapeutic ones, the view has grown that psychological categorization of mental illness is useless at best and downright harmful, misleading, and pejorative at worst. Psychiatric diagnoses, in this view, are in the minds of the observers and are not valid summaries of characteristics displayed by the observed.

Gains can be made in deciding which of these is more nearly accurate by getting normal people (that is, people who do not have, and have never suffered, symptoms or serious psychiatric disorders) admitted to psychiatric hospitals and then determining whether they were discovered to be sane and, if so, how. . . .

This article describes such an experiment. Eight sane people gained secret admission to 12 different hospitals. Their diagnostic experiences constitute the data of the first part of this article; the remainder is devoted to a description of their experiences in psychiatric institutions. . . .

PSEUDOPATIENTS AND THEIR SETTINGS

The eight pseudopatients were a varied group. One was a psychology graduate student in his 20's. The remaining seven were older and "established." Among them were three psychologists, a pediatrician, a psychiatrist, a painter, and a housewife. Three pseudopatients were women, five were men. All of them employed pseudonyms, lest their alleged diagnoses embarrass them later. Those who were in mental health professions alleged another occupation in

278

*Chapter 14
Other
Institutions:
Religion,
Education, and
Health Care*

order to avoid the special attentions that might be accorded by staff, as a matter of courtesy or caution, to ailing colleagues. With the exception of myself (I was the first pseudopatient and my presence was known to the hospital administrator and chief psychologist and, so far as I can tell, to them alone), the presence of pseudopatients and the nature of the research program was not known to the hospital staff. . . .

After calling the hospital for an appointment, the pseudopatient arrived at the admissions office complaining that he had been hearing voices. Asked what the voices said, he replied that they were often unclear, but as far as he could tell they said "empty," "hollow," and "thud." The voices were unfamiliar and were of the same sex as the pseudopatient. The choice of these symptoms was occasioned by their apparent similarity to existential symptoms. Such symptoms are alleged to arise from painful concerns about the perceived meaninglessness of one's life. It is as if the hallucinating person were saying, "My life is empty and hollow." The choice of these symptoms was also determined by the *absence* of a single report of existential psychoses in the literature.

Beyond alleging the symptoms and falsifying name, vocation, and employment, no further alterations of person, history, or circumstances were made. The significant events of the pseudopatient's life history were presented as they had actually occurred. Relationships with parents and siblings, with spouse and children, with people at work and in school, consistent with the aforementioned exceptions, were described as they were or had been. Frustrations and upsets were described along with joys and satisfactions. These facts are important to remember. If anything, they strongly biased the subsequent results in favor of detecting sanity, since none of their histories or current behaviors were seriously pathological in any way.

Immediately upon admission to the psychiatric ward, the pseudopatient ceased simulating *any* symptoms of abnormality. In some cases, there was a brief period of mild nervousness and anxiety, since none of the pseudopatients really believed that they would be admitted so easily. Indeed, their shared fear was that they would be immediately exposed as frauds and greatly embarrassed. Moreover, many of them had never visited a psychiatric ward; even those who had nevertheless had some genuine fears about what might happen to them. Their nervousness, then, was quite appropriate to the novelty of the hospital setting, and it abated rapidly.

Apart from that short-lived nervousness, the pseudopatient behaved on the ward as he "normally" behaved. The pseudopatient spoke to patients and staff as he might ordinarily. Because there is uncommonly little to do on a psychiatric ward, he attempted to engage others in conversation. When asked by staff how he was feeling, he indicated that he was fine, that he no longer experienced symptoms. He responded to instructions from attendants to calls for medication (which was not swallowed), and to dining-hall instructions. Beyond such activities as were available to him on the admissions ward, he spent his time writing down his observations about the ward, its patients, and the staff. Initially these notes were written "secretly," but as it soon became clear that no one much cared, they were subsequently written on standard tablets of paper in such public places as the dayroom. No secret was made of these activities. . . .

279

*D. L.
Rosenhan*

THE NORMAL ARE NOT DETECTABLY SANE

Despite their public "show" of sanity, the pseudopatients were never detected. Admitted, except in one case, with a diagnosis of schizophrenia, each was discharged with a diagnosis of schizophrenia "in remission." The label "in remission" should in no way be dismissed as a formality, for at no time during any hospitalization had any question been raised about any pseudopatient's simulation. Nor are there any indications in the hospital records that the pseudopatient's status was suspect. Rather, the evidence is strong that, once labeled schizophrenic, the pseudopatient was stuck with that label. If the pseudopatient was to be discharged, he must naturally be "in remission"; but he was not sane, nor, in the institution's view, had he ever been sane. . . .

Finally, it cannot be said that the failure to recognize the pseudopatients' sanity was due to the fact that they were not behaving sanely. While there was clearly some tension present in all of them, their daily visitors could detect no serious behavioral consequences—nor, indeed, could other patients. It was quite common for the patients to "detect" the pseudopatients' sanity. During the first three hospitalizations, when accurate counts were kept, 35 of a total of 118 patients on the admissions ward voiced their suspicions, some vigorously. "You're not crazy. You're a journalist, or a professor [referring to the continual note-taking]. You're checking up on the hospital." While most of the patients were reassured by the pseudopatient's insistence that he had been sick before he came in but was fine now, some continued to believe that the pseudopatient was sane throughout his hospitalization. The fact that the patients often recognized normality when staff did not raises important questions.

Failure to detect sanity during the course of hospitalization may be due to the fact that physicians operate with a strong bias toward what statisticians call the type 2 error. This is to say that physicians are more inclined to call a healthy person sick (a false positive, type 2) than a sick person healthy (a false negative, type 1). The reasons for this are not hard to find: it is clearly more dangerous to misdiagnose illness than health. Better to err on the side of caution, to suspect illness even among the healthy.

But what holds for medicine does not hold equally well for psychiatry. Medical illnesses, while unfortunate, are not commonly pejorative. Psychiatric diagnoses, on the contrary, carry with them personal, legal, and social stigmas. It was therefore important to see whether the tendency toward diagnosing the sane insane could be reversed. The following experiment was arranged at a research and teaching hospital whose staff had heard these findings but doubted that such an error could occur in their hospital. The staff was informed

280

Chapter 14
Other
Institutions:
Religion,
Education, and
Health Care

that at some time during the following 3 months, one or more pseudopatients would attempt to be admitted into the psychiatric hospital. Each staff member was asked to rate each patient who presented himself at admission or on the ward according to the likelihood that the patient was a pseudopatient. A 10-point scaled was used, with a 1 and 2 reflecting high confidence that the patient was a pseudopatient.

Judgments were obtained on 193 patients who were admitted for psychiatric treatment. All staff who had had sustained contact with or primary responsibility for the patient—attendants, nurses, psychiatrists, physicians, and psychologists—were asked to make judgments. Forty-one patients were alleged, with high confidence, to be pseudopatients by at least one member of the staff. Twenty-three were considered suspect by at least one psychiatrist. Nineteen were suspected by one psychiatrist *and* one other staff member. Actually, no genuine pseudopatient (at least from my group) presented himself during this period. . . .

THE STICKINESS OF PSYCHODIAGNOSTIC LABELS

Beyond the tendency to call the healthy sick—a tendency that accounts better for diagnostic behavior or admission than it does for such behavior after a lengthy period of exposure—the data speak to the massive role of labeling in psychiatric assessment. Having once been labeled schizophrenic, there is nothing the pseudopatient can do to overcome the tag. The tag profoundly colors others' perceptions of him and his behavior.

From one viewpoint, these data are hardly surprising, for it has long been known that elements are given meaning by the context in which they occur. Gestalt psychology made this point vigorously, and Asch demonstrated that there are "central" personality traits (such as "warm" versus "cold") which are so powerful that they markedly color the meaning of other information in forming an impression of a given personality. "Insane," "schizophrenic," "manic-depressive," and "crazy" are probably among the most powerful of such central traits. Once a person is designated abnormal, all of his other behaviors and characteristics are colored by that label. Indeed, that label is so powerful that many of the pseudopatients' normal behaviors were overlooked entirely or profoundly misinterpreted. Some examples may clarify this issue.

Earlier I indicated that there were no changes in the pseudopatient's personal history and current status beyond those of name, employment, and, where necessary, vocation. Otherwise, a veridical description of personal history and circumstances was offered. Those circumstances were not psychotic. How were they made consonant with the diagnosis of psychosis? Or were those diagnoses modified in such a way as to bring them into accord with the circumstances of the pseudopatient's life, as described by him?

As far as I can determine, diagnoses were in no way affected by the relative health of the circumstances of a pseudopatient's life. Rather, the reverse occurred: the perception of his circumstances was shaped entirely by the diagnosis. A clear example of such translation is found in the case of a pseudopatient who had had a close relationship with his mother but was rather remote from his father during his early childhood. During adolescence and beyond, however, his father became a close friend, while his relationship with his mother cooled. His present relationship with his wife was characteristically close and warm. Apart from occasional angry exchanges, friction was minimal. The children had rarely been spanked. Surely there is nothing especially pathological about such a history. Indeed, many readers may see a similar pattern in their own experiences, with no markedly deleterious consequences. Observe, however, how such a history was translated in the psychopathological context, this from the case summary prepared after the patient was discharged.

> This white 39-year-old male . . . manifests a long history of considerable ambivalence in close relationships, which begins in early childhood. A warm relationship with his mother cools during his adolescence. A distant relationship to his father is described as becoming very intense. Affective stability is absent. His attempts to control emotionality with his wife and children are punctuated by angry outbursts and, in the case of the children, spankings. And while he says that he has several good friends, one senses considerable ambivalence embedded in those relationships also. . . .

The facts of the case were unintentionally distorted by the staff to achieve consistency with a popular theory of the dynamics of a schizophrenic reaction. Nothing of an ambivalent nature had been described in relations with parents, spouse, or friends. To the extent that ambivalence could be inferred, it was probably not greater than is found in all human relationships. It is true the pseudopatient's relationships with his parents changed over time, but in the ordinary context that would hardly be remarkable—indeed, it might very well be expected. Clearly, the meaning ascribed to his verbalizations (that is, ambivalence, affective instability) was determined by the diagnosis: schizophrenia. An entirely different meaning would have been ascribed if it were known that the man was "normal." . . .

One tacit characteristic of psychiatric diagnosis is that it locates the sources of aberration within the individual and only rarely within the complex of stimuli that surrounds him. Consequently, behaviors that are stimulated by the environment are commonly misattributed to the patient's disorder. For example, one kindly nurse found a pseudopatient pacing the long hospital corridors. "Nervous, Mr. X?" she asked. "No, bored," he said.

The notes kept by pseudopatients are full of patient behaviors that were misinterpreted by well-intentioned staff. Often enough, a patient would go "berserk" because he had, wittingly or unwittingly, been mistreated by, say, an attendant. A nurse coming upon the scene would rarely inquire even cursorily into the environmental stimuli of the patient's behavior. Rather, she assumed that his upset derived from his pathology, not from his present interactions with other staff members. Occasionally, the staff might assume that the patient's family (especially when they had recently visited) or other patients had stimulated the outburst. But never were the staff found to assume that one of themselves or the structure of the hospital had anything to do with a patient's

282

*Chapter 14
Other
Institutions:
Religion,
Education, and
Health Care*

behavior. One psychiatrist pointed to a group of patients who were sitting outside the cafeteria entrance half an hour before lunchtime. To a group of young residents he indicated that such behavior was characteristic of the oral-acquisitive nature of the syndrome. It seemed not to occur to him that there were very few things to anticipate in a psychiatric hospital besides eating.

A psychiatric label has a life and an influence of its own. Once the impression has been formed that the patient is schizophrenic, the expectation is that he will continue to be schizophrenic. When a sufficient amount of time has passed, during which the patient has done nothing bizarre, he is considered to be in remission and available for discharge. But the label endures beyond discharge, with the unconfirmed expectation that he will behave as a schizophrenic again. Such labels, conferred by mental health professionals, are as influential on the patient as they are on his relatives and friends, and it should not surprise anyone that the diagnosis acts on all of them as a self-fulfilling prophecy. Eventually, the patient himself accepts the diagnosis, with all of its surplus meanings and expectations, and behaves accordingly.

The inferences to be made from these matters are quite simple. Much as Zigler and Phillips have demonstrated that there is enormous overlap in the symptoms presented by patients who have been variously diagnosed,[1] so there is enormous overlap in the behaviors of the sane and the insane. The sane are not "sane" all of the time. We lose our tempers "for no good reason." We are occasionally depressed or anxious, again for no good reason. And we find it difficult to get along with one or another person—again for no reason that we can specify. Similarly, the insane are not always insane. Indeed, it was the impression of the pseudopatients while living with them that they were sane for long periods of time—that the bizarre behaviors upon which their diagnoses were allegedly predicated constituted only a small fraction of their total behavior. If is makes no sense to label ourselves permanently depressed on the basis of an occasional depression, then it takes better evidence than is presently available to label all patients insane or schizophrenic on the basis of bizarre behaviors or cognitions.

NOTE

1. E. Zigler and L. Phillips, *J. Abnorm. Soc. Psychol.* **63,** 69 (1961).

PART FIVE

Society and Social Change

CHAPTER 15 Population and Environment

15.1 PAUL R. EHRLICH AND ANNE H. EHRLICH

World Population Crisis

Paul R. Ehrlich (b. 1932) is a population biologist, a writer, and the Bing Professor of Population Studies at Stanford University, where he has taught since 1976. He is a member of the National Academy of Sciences and a fellow of the American Academy of Arts and Sciences. Anne H. Ehrlich (b. 1933) is a biological research associate, a writer, and a senior research associate in biological sciences at Stanford University. Together, the Ehrlichs have written a number of books, including *The Population Explosion* (Simon & Schuster, 1990) and *Population, Resources, Environment: Issues in Human Ecology* (W. H. Freeman, 1970).

   The problems of overpopulation, hunger, and starvation in developing countries receive major, though sporadic, attention in the mass media. But the media say little about how the highly industrialized countries contribute to the problem. To be sure, the rate of population growth is lower in these countries, but the resources consumed are significantly higher. In the following selection, the Ehrlichs expand on this point and examine the possible consequences of allowing population growth to continue unchecked, particularly in the developed countries. They point out, for example, that the average person in the United States consumes the equivalent of 10,000 kg of coal per year compared to the average of 600 kg of coal for people in Asia and 425 kg of coal in Africa. The authors warn that economic growth is not limitless and that unless societies become aware of the full environmental effects of current economic practices and take rather radical actions, the premature death of billions of people may follow.

Key Concept: overpopulation

Most people realize that unless something is done soon about the nuclear arms race, civilization may well be destroyed. Understandably, then, a prime focus of attention is on issues that seem immediately related to the possible triggering of a large-scale thermonuclear exchange, such as the deployment of weapons, the adequacy of command and control systems, arms control negotiations in Geneva, and so on.

But those who are concerned with the human predicament should not lose sight of more basic problems that influence nation-states. While we struggle to prevent the nuclear arms race from ending the world with a bang, more subtle global trends may lead to the same end within a century or so, but with a whimper. Moreover, these trends aggravate the conditions that breed conflict, thus increasing the chances that nuclear weapons will be used. They include:

- destruction and dispersion of the one-time bonanza of "capital" (fossil fuels, rich soils, other species, and so forth) that humanity inherited;
- environmental deterioration, including the decay of the systems that provide civilization with the "income" resources that are the only alternative to consuming our capital stock;
- the widening gap between rich and poor nations and related patterns of migration;
- the persistence of economic inequality within nations;
- the rise of ethnic and religious separatism;
- persisting high levels of hunger and unemployment; and
- the relatively slow and geographically spotty progress in ending racism, sexism, and religious prejudice.

All those negative trends are interrelated, and interwoven with them is one of the most basic causes of the human predicament—unprecedented continued growth in human numbers in an already overpopulated world. When the two of us were born in the early 1930s, only two billion people existed; by 1987, five billion will.

This year the population will grow by more than 84 million people—a record number—and each year in the immediate future will see a new record increment. A great deal of attention has been paid to a small decrease in the global growth rate since the early 1960s, a drop from about 2.2 percent annual natural increase to around 1.7 percent. But with that growth rate applied to an ever-larger population base, the absolute annual increase continues to escalate. The ecological systems that support humanity respond primarily to absolute numbers, not rates; those numbers will be a major determinant of how long civilization can be sustained.

Earth is overpopulated today by a very simple standard: humanity is able to support itself—often none too well, at that—only by consuming its capital. This consumption involves much more than the widely publicized depletion of stocks of fossil fuels and dispersion of other high-grade mineral resources. Much more critical are the erosion of deep, rich agricultural soils, the diminution of our fresh water supply by pollution and mismanagement of groundwater, and the loss of much of the diversity of other life-forms that share the earth with us. All these are intimately involved in providing humans with nourishment from the only significant source of income, the radiant energy of the sun, which, converted by photosynthetic plants into the energy of chemical bonds, supports essentially all life on the planet.

Two crucial points must be remembered. The first is that with today's technology, humanity could not support anything like its current numbers without continually using its nonrenewable resource subsidy. The second is that while exploiting that capital subsidy, civilization is continually degrading the systems that supply its income. Consider only the accelerating extermination of other organisms, which is intimately connected with brute increase in the human population and its exploitation of the planet.

Those organisms are working parts of the ecosystems that provide society with a wide variety of indispensable services, including regulation of the composition of the atmosphere, amelioration of weather, the generation and preservation of soils, the cycling of nutrients essential to agriculture and forestry, disposal of wastes, control of the vast majority of potential crop pests and carriers of human diseases, provision of food from the sea, and maintenance of a vast genetic library, from which humans have already drawn the very basis of civilization, and whose potential has barely been tapped.

All of these services are directly or indirectly involved in providing necessities to humanity derived from our solar income. Ecologists standardly measure that income in terms of net primary productivity. Net primary productivity is the total amount of the energy bound each year by plants in the process of photosynthesis, minus the portion of that chemical energy that the plants themselves must use to run their own life processes. The global net primary productivity can be viewed as the basic food supply for the entire animal world, including *Homo sapiens*, as well as a major source of structural materials, fibers, medicines, and other things of importance to humanity.

The relationship between current human population size and this basic income source is revealed by the answer to a simple question: How much of global net primary productivity is now being coopted by *Homo sapiens*, just one of five to 30 million animal species that completely depend upon it? Humanity not only directly consumes a disproportionate share, but it also reduces production by replacing natural ecosystems with generally less productive, human-managed or disrupted ones. Humanity coopts about 40 percent of terrestrial net primary productivity today, and an additional few percent in aquatic systems.

For technical reasons, it will prove very difficult to increase human exploitation of the oceans significantly, as the decline of per capita yields of food from the sea since 1970 indicates. It is on land that civilization must seek the income to support ever-growing numbers of people. The population is now growing at a rate that, if continued, would double it in about 42 years. Even if *Homo sapiens* could persist after wiping out most of the other animals, population growth clearly would soon carry it past the limits of Earth's short-term human carrying capacity, and a population crash would ensue.

Economic and social systems also respond to absolute numbers as well as to rates of growth. There is every reason to believe that most aspects of these systems have long since passed the point where economies of scale become diseconomies of scale. Twenty years ago, C. P. Snow, commenting on the declining quality of English telephone services, generated what we might call Snow's Law: "The difficulties of a service increase roughly by the square of the number of people using it."

That growing numbers of people are deleterious can be seen in the increased costs of supplying them with goods. If today's population were of constant size, it still would have to run continually, like the Red Queen, to stay in place. Technology would have to be constantly improved to compensate for depleted supplies of fuels, declining quality of ores, and deterioration of soils, and to protect people from the environmental consequences of using both old and new technologies. But today's population is growing. Each additional person, on average, must be cared for by using lower-quality resources that must be transported further, and by food grown on more marginal land. Supplying the additional energy needed for these tasks creates both economic and environmental problems.

Although population growth rates are highest in poor countries, overpopulation and continuing population growth in rich countries are the prime threat to global resources and environmental systems, simply because the average individual in rich nations has a large impact on resources and environment. One of the best available measures of that impact is a nation's per capita use of commercially produced energy. In the United States, the average person uses the commercial energy equivalent of about 10,000 kilograms of coal annually. In contrast, an average South American uses about 1,000 kilograms, an Asian about 600, and an African about 425. By this measure, the birth of an average baby in the United States will be about 200 times as disastrous for the world as the birth of an average Bangladeshi, who will consume the commercial equivalent of some 45 kilograms of coal annually.

This does not mean that population growth in poor nations is harmless. But, as a great oversimplification, one can say that population growth in less developed countries primarily harms those countries, while that in industrialized nations harms the world as a whole. Consider what it means for poor countries such as Bangladesh or Kenya to double their populations in 25 and 17 years, respectively, as they are currently doing. If those nations are to maintain their present standards of living, low as they are, they will have to duplicate every amenity for the support of human beings in that time period. Among other things, that means doubling their food production, their supply of teachers, doctors, engineers, and scientists, and the capacity of housing, hospitals, road and rail systems, and manufacturing plants. It would be a daunting task for a rich nation such as the United States, with abundant capital, incredibly rich soils, good supplies of most other resources, fine transport and communications systems, vast industrial capacity, and a largely educated and literate population. Most poor nations have none of these things.

Indeed, even without further growth, most less developed countries face massive problems in the near future just because of their age structures. In Mexico, for instance, about half of the labor force is unemployed or underemployed. That is bad enough, but in the next 15 years Mexico will have to find jobs for perhaps 10 million people if the unemployment rate is not to increase, and 20 million people if the number of unemployed is not to rise. Those numbers are not based on future population growth, but on people already born. Today there are over 30 million Mexicans under the age of 15.

In the face of all these factors, why is the population component so often ignored in discussions of the human predicament? One possible reason is evolutionary. Evolutionary success has meant, and means today, outbreeding your friends and neighbors.

Animal populations have often increased in size to the point where they exceeded the carrying capacity of their environments, which, in turn, led to catastrophic population declines or extinctions. *Homo sapiens* is the first of billions of species that has developed the ability both to detect the relation of its population size to carrying capacity and, through birth control, to adjust its numbers to fit within that capacity.

Yet, problems of overpopulation were rarely present or perceived over most of the millions of years that human beings were evolving into the most successful of the great apes. Throughout our evolutionary history, the emphasis has been on successful reproduction. People therefore have great difficulty facing the fact that either humanity must consciously halt population growth and then gradually reduce its numbers, or nature will end the explosion of human numbers with a catastrophic population crash. Decreasing the death rate goes with the evolutionary grain, and in the past century our species has been extraordinarily successful at it. Avoiding disaster by humanely causing a compensating decline in the birth rate, unfortunately for humanity, goes against long-evolved prejudices.

A second evolutionary reason is that the human nervous system developed little capacity to detect gradual trends in the environment—trends that only created significant changes after decades or centuries. Over most of our history, our ancestors did not need to respond adaptively to such changes, but to sudden or rapid alterations in their environments. So our nervous systems evolved a high capacity to detect the sudden appearance of tigers and the crack of falling trees and a low capacity to respond to growth in human numbers, nuclear arms, or environmental damage from acid rains.

The inability of people to register change over long periods often leads them to ignore history, to believe that the world has not and will not change. It allows economists to think that there have always been and always will be high rates of economic growth. Even those who admit that there must be ultimate limits to growth struggle to keep their world constant by assuming, against all the evidence, that those limits are so far in the future that they can be safely ignored.

There is no longer any substitute for analysis; the world can no longer afford to believe such myths as that economic growth can be infinite, contraception is immoral, and more nuclear weapons will prevent nuclear war. All the educational mechanisms that society can deploy must be focused on teaching people to understand the physical and biological constraints on human activities, to recognize and deal with long-term trends, and to perceive the connections between various aspects of the human predicament. Then everyone will recognize that problems as seemingly disconnected as Star Wars [strategic defense strategy first proposed by Ronald Reagan] and the population bomb are simply different aspects of a general problem of social organization.

15.2 LESTER R. BROWN, CHRISTOPHER FLAVIN, AND EDWARD C. WOLF

Earth's Vital Signs

Lester R. Brown (b. 1934), an agricultural economist and writer, is the founder, president, and senior researcher at the Worldwatch Institute in Washington, D.C., a private, nonprofit research organization devoted to the analysis of global environmental issues. His annual *State of the World* reports remain his most highly regarded and popular works.

Christopher Flavin (b. 1955) is the vice president for research at the Worldwatch Institute. He also serves on the advisory committee of the Energy Conservation Coalition and is a member of the International Solar Energy Society and the Society for International Development. His research focuses on solutions to global environmental problems, particularly on sustainable development and on slowing climate change, and he has written extensively on new energy technologies and policies.

Edward C. Wolf (b. 1959) is a former senior researcher at the Worldwatch Institute and a former writer and editor with Conservation International in Washington, D.C. He is currently a graduate student in forest ecology at the University of Washington, Seattle.

In the following paper, Brown, Flavin, and Wolf argue that shrinking forests, expanding deserts, and topsoil erosion bodes ill for mankind. The physical condition of the Earth is affected by numerous and varied human activities, but the most significant today are energy use and population growth. The authors feel that these require immediate international attention.

Brown, Flavin, and Wolf discuss the harmful effects of several current world problems, such as the rapid increase of population growth in Third World countries and certain monetary interests that have led to environmental exploitation and the rapid transformation of habitats such as the Amazon. They then argue that to prevent some of these consequences, it is imperative that these issues be addressed immediately, and they offer some radical solutions.

Key Concept: sustainability

*I*n giving the earth a physical examination, checking its vital signs, we find that the readings are not reassuring: The planet's forests are shrinking, its deserts expanding, and its soils eroding—all at record rates.

TABLE 1

Vital Signs

Lester R.
Brown et al.

Forest Cover	Tropical forests shrinking by 11 million hectares per year; 31 million hectares in industrial countries damaged, apparently by air pollution or acid rain.
Topsoil on Cropland	An estimated 26 billion tons lost annually in excess of new soil formation.
Desert Area	Some 6 million hectares of new desert formed annually by land mismanagement.
Lakes	Thousands of lakes in the industrial north now biologically dead; thousands more dying.
Fresh Water	Underground water tables falling in parts of Africa, China, India, and North America as demand for water rises above aquifer recharge rates.
Species Diversity	Extinctions of plant and animal species together now estimated at several thousand per year; one-fifth of all species may disappear over next 20 years.
Ground-water Quality	Some 50 pesticides contaminate groundwater in 32 American states; some 2,500 U.S. toxic waste sites need cleanup; extent of toxic contamination unknown.
Climate	Mean temperature projected to rise between 1.5° and 4.5° C between now and 2050.
Sea Level	Projected to rise between 1.4 meters (4.7 feet) and 2.2 meters (7.1 feet) by 2100.
Ozone Layer in Upper Atmosphere	Growing "hole" in the earth's ozone layer over Antarctica each spring suggests gradual global depletion could be starting.

Source: Compiled by Worldwatch Institute from various sources.

Each year, thousands of plant and animal species disappear, many before they are named or cataloged. The ozone layer in the upper atmosphere that protects us from ultraviolet radiation is thinning. The temperature of the earth appears to be rising, posing a threat of unknown dimensions to virtually all the life-support systems on which humanity depends.

All human activities affect the earth's physical condition, but two are disproportionately important: energy use and population growth. Heavy dependence on fossil fuels has caused a buildup of carbon dioxide in the atmosphere that threatens to warm the earth. Pollutants from fossil-fuel burning have also led to acidification and the death of lakes and forests. Advances in human health have led to unprecedented reproductive success and a growth of population that in many countries is overwhelming local life-support systems.

Many of the world's problems, including ozone depletion and climate protection, cannot be solved without international action. In these areas, any one country's efforts to change would be overwhelmed without global cooperation. This sense of international responsibility marked the September 1987 signing in Montreal of international accords to limit the production of chloro-fluorocarbons to protect the earth's ozone layer. These accords, although modest in scope, were a signal achievement and could become a model for future agreements.

The world has come a long way from the mid-1970s, when environmental concerns were considered something that only the rich could afford to worry about. Today, they are concerns no one can afford to ignore.

THE EARTH'S ANNUAL PHYSICAL

Table 1 depicts the earth's vital signs—the current state of the world's physical health.

Tree cover is one of the most visible indicators of the earth's health and, because trees are an integral part of basic life-support systems, one of the most vital. The loss of trees on sloping land can accelerate rainfall runoff and increase soil erosion, diminishing land productivity and aggravating local flooding. Where tree cutting exceeds regrowth, deforestation releases carbon that contributes to the buildup of atmospheric CO_2 and a warming of the earth.

One consequence of declining tree cover and expanding agriculture is accelerated soil erosion. Despite topsoil's essential economic role, only a few countries regularly monitor these losses. As erosion continues, land gradually loses its inherent productivity, threatening the livelihood of those who depend on it.

The health of the earth's inhabitants cannot be separated from that of the planet itself. Contaminations by industrial chemicals in communities such as Love Canal in the United States and Seveso in Italy have led to permanent evacuations. In Brazil, where concentrations of industrial wastes along the southern coast have reached life-threatening levels, the industrial city of Cubatão is locally referred to as the "Valley of Death."

Another of the earth's vital indicators, the amount of carbon dioxide and other greenhouse gases in the atmosphere, can be measured rather precisely. Since 1958, careful recordings have shown that the atmospheric CO_2 concentration is rising each year. This increase, combined with that of trace gases, may be warming the earth more rapidly than had been anticipated.

As forests disappear, as soils erode, and as lakes and soil acidify and become polluted, the number of plant and animal species diminishes. This reduction in the diversity of life on earth may well have unforeseen long-term consequences.

POPULATION GROWTH AND LAND DEGRADATION

The annual increment of births over deaths has climbed from 74 million in 1970 to 83 million in 1987. During the 1990s, it is projected to surpass 90 million before moderating as the next century begins. Most of the annual increment has been concentrated in the Third World, where human demands often overtax local life-support systems already.

When annual population additions are coupled with heightened stress on local life-support systems, shortages of food, fodder, and fuel can emerge almost overnight. Development economists typically focus on changes in the rate of population growth, but a more vital sign is the relationship between population size and the sustainable yield of local forests, grasslands, and croplands. If the demands of a local population surpass these sustainable yields, the systems will continue to deteriorate even if population growth stops.

In the Third World, continuous population growth and skewed land distribution drive land-hungry farmers onto marginal land that is highly erodible and incapable of sustaining cultivation over the long term.

A DESTRUCTIVE ENERGY PATH

Energy trends are an important indicator of the world's economic and ecological health. The trends since early 1986 point to a partial resurgence of growth in world oil consumption and continued growth in coal use. Although oil ministers and coal operators are undoubtedly cheered by this turn of events, it is in fact an ominous one. Any additional energy growth will add to the dangerous chemistry experiment we are conducting on the earth's atmosphere. Lakes, estuaries, forests, human health, and the climate itself are now at risk.

By the early 1980s, activities such as generating electricity, driving automobiles, and producing steel were releasing into the atmosphere over 5 billion tons of carbon, close to 10 million tons of sulfur, and lesser quantities of nitrogen oxides each year. Carbon emissions closely track world energy trends, but because coal releases more carbon than does either oil or natural gas, the shift to coal accelerates the rise in carbon emissions. At a time when climatological evidence points to a need to reduce carbon emissions, they are actually rising.

Developing countries are also among the victims of environmental damage from the use of fossil fuels. China, for instance, is suffering from its massive use of coal. Since China generally lacks both tall smokestacks and pollution-control equipment, cities and surrounding farmland will likely suffer severe damage from coal-fired air pollution. The Third World as a whole will have to exert enormous effort in order to avoid the apparent environmental fate of Eastern Europe.

In developing energy strategies, policy makers should consider the benefits of reducing acidification and CO_2 emission together. The combined societal cost of acidification and climate warming of the sort projected may justify a

more fundamental redirection of the world's energy systems than any seriously
considered to date.

THE CLIMATIC CONSEQUENCES

As indicated in Table 1, the earth's mean temperature will rise over the next
decades. Two of the most serious effects of the projected warming would be the
impact on agriculture and sea level. Meteorological models, though they remain
sketchy, suggest that two of the world's major food-producing regions—the
North American heartland and the grain-growing regions of the Soviet Union—
are likely to experience a decline in soil moisture during the summer growing
season as a result of increased evaporation.

A somewhat more predictable result of a hotter earth is a rise in sea level.
This would hurt most in Asia, where rice is produced on low-lying river deltas
and floodplains. Without heavy investments in dikes and seawalls to protect the
rice fields from saltwater intrusion, even a relatively modest one-meter rise
would markedly reduce harvests.

The detailed effects of climate change cannot be predicted with great
accuracy. We do know, however, that human civilization has evolved within a
narrow range of climate conditions. Any major departure from those conditions
will cause enormous hardship and require incalculable investments during the
adjustment. Because some of the most important changes could occur abruptly,
with little warning, most of the costs would simply have to be borne by an
unwitting society. Ways to avoid massive climate change now deserve serious
consideration.

RECLAIMING THE FUTURE

Assessing the threats to the future of the planet's life-support systems can
easily lead to apathy or despair, particularly in view of policy makers' preoccupation with the East-West political conflict and global economic issues. Yet,
we can do something about the planet's deteriorating physical condition. Some
of the steps needed to restore its health, including investment in energy
efficiency, reforestation, and population stabilization, can be sketched out.

A sustainable future requires that a series of interlocking issues be dealt
with simultaneously. For instance, it may be impossible to avoid a mass
extinction of species as long as the Third World is burdened with debt. And the
resources needed to arrest the physical deterioration of the planet may not be
available unless the international arms race can be reversed.

The immediate effects of population growth and land degradation are
largely local, but the climate alteration linked to fossil-fuel combustion is

incontestably global. Just as land degradation can threaten local efforts to raise living standards, so, too, climate alteration can overwhelm progress at the global level. Efforts to adjust the global economy to a much warmer earth—with the accompanying changes in rainfall patterns, evaporation rates, and sea level—eventually could absorb all available investment capital.

CONSERVING SOIL

Restoring two of the earth's life-support systems—its soil and trees—will require heavy capital investments and strong commitments by political leaders. The expenditures sketched here are rough estimates at best intended only to convey the magnitude of the effort needed.

As of the early 1980s, American farmers and the U.S. Department of Agriculture together were spending just over $1 billion per year to control erosion on cropland. Despite this effort, a detailed soil survey conducted in 1982 showed farmers were losing 3.1 billion tons of topsoil annually from water and wind erosion, some 2 billion tons in excess of tolerable levels of soil loss. For every ton of grain they produced, American farmers were losing six tons of their topsoil.

Congress responded to this clearly documented threat and the runaway costs of farm price-support programs with the landmark Conservation Reserve program. For the first time, policy was designed to control excessive production *and* to cut soil losses by idling land. The USDA agreed to pay farmers an average of $48 per acre each year for land enrolled in the reserve to compensate them for net income from the crops the land would otherwise have produced.

Reaching a goal of converting 40 million acres of highly erodible cropland to grassland or woodland by 1990 will cost the U.S. Treasury $2 billion per year once the full area is retired.

Erosion on the land planted to grass or trees during the first year of the cropland conversion program was estimated to decline from an average of 29 tons per acre to two tons. If this rate prevailed on all the land to be enrolled in the reserve, excessive erosion would be reduced by over 1 billion tons. This would leave just under 1 billion tons to be eliminated on the remaining 30% of the cropland still eroding excessively.

In summary, annual expenditures of roughly $3 billion would be required for the United States to stabilize the soils on its cropland once the program is fully in place by 1990.

Extrapolating these data, we estimate that global expenditures to protect the cropland base would total some $24 billion per year. Although this is obviously a large sum, it is less than the U.S. government paid farmers to support crop prices in 1986. As an investment in future food supplies for a world expecting 3–5 billion more people, $24 billion is one that humanity can ill afford not to make.

PLANTING TREES

Adding trees to the global forest stock is a valuable investment in our economic future, whether to satisfy growing firewood needs in the Third World or to stabilize soil and water regimes in watersheds where land degradation and disruptions of the hydrological cycle are undermining local economies.

Considering that some trees would serve both ecological and fuelwood objectives, a total of 120 million hectares might need to be planted. An additional 30 million hectares will be needed to satisfy demand for lumber, paper, and other forest products. If this tree-planting goal is to be achieved by the end of the century, the effort would need to reach total plantings of 17 million hectares, at a cost of $6.8 billion, per year.

It should be noted that tree planting which restores watersheds, thereby conserving soil and water, complements the expenditures on soil erosion by farmers on their cropland.

SLOWING POPULATION GROWTH

The success of efforts to save topsoil and restore tree cover both depend heavily on slowing population growth. Indeed, countries with populations expanding at 2%–4% per year may find it almost impossible to restore tree cover, protect their soils, and take other steps toward a sustainable development path.

Providing family-planning services in response to unsatisfied demand is often the quickest and most cost-effective step countries can take to secure life-support systems. World Bank surveys show that 50%–90% of the Third World women interviewed want either to stop childbearing altogether or to delay the birth of another child. This suggests an enormous unsatisfied demand for contraceptive services. The Bank estimates that providing family-planning services to all those in need would entail expenditures of roughly $8 billion per year by the end of the century.

Fertility declines most rapidly when family-planning services are introduced into a society already enjoying broad-based economic and social gains. The social indicator that correlates most closely with fertility decline is the education of women. Providing elementary education for the estimated 120 million school-age children not now in school would cost roughly $50 each or $6 billion per year. Providing literacy training for those women who are illiterate and beyond school age would require an additional estimated $2 billion per year.

A second social indicator that closely correlates with declines in birth rates is infant mortality. It is rare for birth rates to drop sharply if infant survival remains low. Substantial gains in reducing infant mortality can be achieved with relatively modest investments. Immunizing the 55% of the world's children not now protected from diphtheria, measles, polio, and tuberculosis would cost roughly $2 billion per year. Training mothers in oral rehydration therapy (used to treat infants with diarrhea), in basic hygiene, and in the health advantages of breastfeeding would cost another $1 billion per year. These efforts would markedly lower infant death and in the process stimulate interest in reducing family size.

STABILIZING THE EARTH'S CLIMATE

The central issue for policy makers is whether to follow a business-as-usual energy policy and risk having to adapt the global economy to the changed climate, or to take steps to slow the warming. Unfortunately, the costs of adapting to the global warming could one day siphon off so much investment capital that economic progress would come to a halt and living standards would begin to decline.

The most costly adjustments now anticipated would be those needed to protect coastal areas from the rising sea. Some sense of the magnitude of these expenses is offered by Bangladesh.

Unlike the Netherlands, which spends 6% of its gross national product to maintain a complex set of dikes, seawalls, and other structures to protect the nation from the sea, Bangladesh cannot afford this approach. Consequently, it has paid a heavy toll in human lives. In 1970, some 300,000 people were killed in a single cyclone; 10,000 people were killed and 1.3 million affected by a storm surge in 1985. The willingness of Bangladeshis to resettle in such high-risk areas reflects a keen land hunger—one that will intensify if the population increases, as projected, from 106 million in 1988 to 305 million late in the next century.

One thing is clear: If the projected warming is to be minimized, the buildup of CO_2 and the trace gases that contribute to the greenhouse effect must be slowed, and quickly, by raising the efficiency of energy use, shifting from fossil fuels to renewable energy sources and reversing deforestation.

The United States uses twice as much energy to produce a dollar's worth of goods and services as Japan does. If the United States were to double fuel-efficiency standards for vehicles to over 50 miles per gallon by the end of the century—a level that can be achieved with cars now on the market—global carbon emissions would drop measurably.

Replacing existing technologies with more efficient ones is merely the first step. Beyond this, economic systems can be redesigned so that some sectors can be sustained with relatively little energy. For example, although fuel-inefficient cars can be replaced with more-efficient ones, the large gains in transport efficiency will come from designing communities where residents do not depend on automobiles.

Countries that rely heavily on renewable energy typically use several different sources. Among the largest is Brazil, a country that relies heavily on hydropower for electricity, alcohol fuels for transport, and charcoal for steel smelting. Altogether renewable energy sources account for some 60% of Brazil's total energy use, making it the first large industrializing economy to rely primarily on renewables.

But Brazil ranks fourth in CO_2 emissions. The reason is not because it is a heavy user of fossil fuels, but because it is burning its rain forest to make way for cattle ranching and crop production. The vast Amazon rain forest helps shape continental climate patterns; unrestrained forest clearing would therefore adversely affect rainfall and temperatures in the important agricultural regions to the south.

Expenditures in energy efficiency and renewable energy sufficient to head off the global warming cannot easily be estimated, in contrast to those on soil conservation and population stabilization. Having only a sense that the costs of climate change are enormous, we recommend a tripling in the annual investment in energy efficiency during the 1990s and a doubling in investment in developing renewable energy resources.

These investment levels, which offer immediate environmental and economic gains, should be viewed as minimal. If the economic disruption associated with the global warming passes the threshold of political acceptability, then investments far greater than those outlined here will be made to reduce fossil-fuel use.

INVESTING IN ENVIRONMENTAL SECURITY

To continue with a more or less business-as-usual attitude—to accept the loss of tree cover, the erosion of soil, the expansion of deserts, the loss of plant and animal species, the depletion of the ozone layer, and the buildup of greenhouse gases—implies acceptance of economic decline and social disintegration. In a world where progress depends on a complex set of national and international economic ties, such disintegration would bring human suffering on a scale that has no precedent. The threat posed by continuing environmental deterioration is no longer a hypothetical one. Dozens of countries will have lower living standards at the end of the 1980s than at the beginning.

The momentum inherent in population growth, the forces of land degradation, and the changing chemistry of the atmosphere make it difficult to get the world on a sustainable development path. The scale of these challenges and the urgency with which they must be addressed require that they be moved to the center of governmental agendas.

Through decisions about existing and prospective technologies, humanity has far more control over the rate of global warming than is commonly recognized. In addition to direct influence over the activities that produce CO_2

TABLE 2

Investments Needed for Sustainability (Figures in billions of dollars)

Lester R. Brown et al.

Year	Protecting Topsoil on Cropland	Reforest-ing the Earth	Slowing Population Growth	Raising Energy Efficiency	Developing Renewable Energy	Retiring Third World Debt	Total
1990	4	2	13	5	2	20	46
1991	9	3	18	10	5	30	75
1992	14	4	22	15	8	40	103
1993	18	5	26	20	10	50	129
1994	24	6	28	25	12	50	145
1995	24	6	30	30	15	40	145
1996	24	6	31	35	18	30	144
1997	24	6	32	40	21	20	143
1998	24	7	32	45	24	10	142
1999	24	7	32	50	27	10	150
2000	24	7	33	55	30	0	149

Source: Worldwatch Institute.

and the land uses that sequester carbon from the atmosphere, accelerating progress toward population stabilization can reduce the numbers dependent on activities that put climate stability at risk. The many factors that will shape future energy demand and the pattern of human activities in generations to come cannot be forecast with any certainty, but investing some $150 billion per year in areas that broaden human options in the face of enormous uncertainty would be a reasonable down payment on environmentally sustainable global economy. (See Table 2.)

Two barriers now stand in the way of ensuring that capital and political will are available on the scale needed. One is the profound misallocation of capital implicit in global military expenditures of $900 billion each year. (See Table 3.) The other is the unmanageable Third World debt that burdens the world economy. Unless these obstacles are overcome, funds on the scale needed to ensure sustainable development will not be available.

ENTERING A NEW ERA

In some important respects, the world situation today resembles that during the mid-1940s. The scale of human suffering as a result of the Great Depression and World War II gave the international community the resolve to address the weaknesses inherent in the global system.

TABLE 3

Alternative Global-Security Budgets (Figures in billions of dollars)

Year	Global Security Defined in Military Terms — Current Military Expenditures Continued	Global Security Defined in Sustainable Development Terms		
		Military Expenditures	Expenditures to Achieve Sustainable Development	Total Security Expenditures
1990	900	854	46	900
1991	900	825	75	900
1992	900	797	103	900
1993	900	771	129	900
1994	900	755	145	900
1995	900	755	145	900
1996	900	756	144	900
1997	900	757	143	900
1998	900	758	142	900
1999	900	750	150	900
2000	900	751	149	900

Source: Worldwatch Institute.

This period of crisis produced some visionaries—leaders who were able to engineer an effective response to the new threats to progress. One was General George Marshall, U.S. Secretary of State from 1947 to 1949. When he proposed in 1947 that the United States launch a massive international assistance plan to rebuild Europe, including Germany, the conventional image of postwar relationships was turned upside down. Instead of plundering the defeated enemy, the United States held out a helping hand, launching a massive reconstruction of victors and vanquished alike, an effort that led to a generation of European prosperity.

Initiatives of comparable boldness are needed in the late 1980s. The world may not have the financial resources both to sustain the arms race and to make the investments needed to return the world to a sustainable development path. The deterioration of the earth's life-support systems is threatening, but the psychological toll of failing to reverse it could also be high. Such a failure would lead to a loss of confidence in political institutions and would risk widespread demoralization—a sense that our ability to control our destiny is slipping away.

If, on the other hand, the world can mobilize along the lines discussed here, the trends that threaten to undermine the human future can be reversed. If widespread concern motivates political action, and if the needed changes in national priorities, national policies, and individual lifestyles take root, then—and only then—can we expect sustained improvements in the human condition.

CHAPTER 16 Community

16.1 ROBERT REDFIELD

Antecedents of Urban Life: The Folk Society

Perhaps the most important distinction made in sociology is between close, face-to-face, informal, primary relationships and more distant, formal, secondary relationships. This distinction has a rich intellectual heritage in sociology. Over a century ago, the German sociologist Ferdinand Toennies distinguished between preindustrial society, which he characterized as *Gemeinschaft,* or "community," and industrial society, which he characterized as *Gesellschaft,* a more impersonal and limited association. About a half century later, Robert Redfield similarly differentiated between the preindustrial folk society and life in an industrial society, based on his work in a preindustrial community in Mexico.

Redfield (1897–1958), a cultural anthropologist and ethnologist, was a pioneer in the study of cultural and social change between folk and urban societies. He was the Robert Maynard Hutchins Distinguished Service Professor at the University of Chicago and a recognized authority on Middle American folk culture.

In the following excerpt, Redfield discusses the folk society, which he characterizes as small, geographically isolated, homogenous, cooperative, and having a high level of solidarity. Interpersonal relations are face-to-face, emotional, familial, and include the whole person. Personal interaction in Redfield's folk society contrasts markedly with the way most people interact when they encounter each other in modern cities.

Key Concept: folk society

*T*he conception of a 'primitive society' which we ought to form," wrote Sumner, "is that of small groups scattered over a territory."[1] The folk society is a small society. There are no more people in it than can come to know each other well, and they remain in long association with each other. . . .

The folk society is an isolated society. Probably there is no real society whose members are in complete ignorance of the existence of people other than themselves; the Andamanese, although their islands were avoided by navigators for centuries, knew of outsiders and occasionally came in contact with Malay or Chinese visitors. Nevertheless, the folk societies we know are made up of people who have little communication with outsiders, and we may conceive of the ideal folk society as composed of persons having communication with no outsider.

This isolation is one half of a whole of which the other half is intimate communication among the members of the society. . . .

The people who make up a folk society are much alike. Having lived in long intimacy with one another and with no others, they have come to form a single biological type. The somatic homogeneity of local, inbred populations has been noted and studied. Since the people communicate with one another and with no others, one man's learned ways of doing and thinking are the same as another's. Another way of putting this is to say that, in the ideal folk society, what one man knows and believes is the same as what all men know and believe. Habits are the same as customs. In real fact, of course, the differences among individuals in a primitive group and the different chances of experience prevent this ideal state of things from coming about. Nevertheless, it is near enough to the truth for the student of a real folk society to report it fairly well by learning what goes on in the minds of a few of its members, and a primitive group has been presented, although sketchily, as learned about from a single member. The similarity among the members is found also as one generation is compared with its successor. Old people find young people doing, as they grow up, what the old people did at the same age, and what they have come to think right and proper. This is another way of saying that, in such a society, there is little change.

The members of the folk society have a strong sense of belonging together. The group that an outsider might recognize as composed of similar persons different from members of other groups is also the group of people who see their own resemblances and feel correspondingly united. Communicating intimately with each other, each has a strong claim on the sympathies of the others. Moreover, against such knowledge as they have of societies other than their own, they emphasize their own mutual likeness and value themselves as compared with others. They say of themselves "we" as against all others, who are "they."

Thus, we may characterize the folk society as small, isolated, nonliterate, and homogeneous, with a strong sense of group solidarity. . . .

There is not much division of labor in the folk society: What one person does is what another does. In the ideal folk society, all the tools and ways of production are shared by everybody. The "everybody" must mean "every adult man" or "every adult woman," for the obvious exception to the homogeneity of the folk society lies in the differences between what men do and know and what women do and know. These differences are clear and unexceptional (as compared with our modern urban society, where they are less so). "Within the local group there is no such thing as a division of labor save as between the sexes," writes Radcliffe-Brown about the Andaman Islanders. " . . . Every man is expected to be able to hunt pig, to harpoon turtle and to catch fish, and also to cut a canoe, to make bows and arrows and all the other objects that are made by men."[2] So, all men share the same interests and have, in general, the same experience of life.

We may conceive, also, of the ideal folk society as a group economically independent of all others: The people produce what they consume and consume what they produce. Few, if any, real societies are completely in this situation; some Eskimo groups, perhaps, most closely approach it. Although each little Andamanese band could get along without getting anything from any other, exchange of goods occurred between bands by a sort of periodic gift-giving.

The foregoing characterizations amount, roughly, to saying that the folk society is a little world off by itself, a world in which the recurrent problems of life are met by all its members in much the same way. This statement, while correct enough, fails to emphasize an important, perhaps the important, aspect of the folk society. The ways in which the members of the society meet the recurrent problems of life are conventionalized ways; they are the results of long intercommunication within the group in the face of these problems; and these conventionalized ways have become interrelated within one another so that they constitute a coherent and self-consistent system. Such a system is what we mean in saying that the folk society is characterized by a "culture." A culture is an organization or integration of conventional understandings. It is, as well, the acts and the objects, insofar as they represent the type of characteristic of that society, that express and maintain these understandings. In the folk society, this integrated whole, this system, provides for all the recurrent needs of the individual from birth to death and of the society through the seasons and the years. The society is to be described, and distinguished from others, largely by presenting this system. . . .

What is done in the ideal folk society is done not because somebody or some people decided, at once, that it should be done but because it seems "necessarily" to flow from the very nature of things. There is, moreover, no disposition to reflect upon traditional acts and consider them objectively and critically. In short, behavior in the folk society is traditional, spontaneous, and uncritical. In any real folk society, of course, many things are done as a result of decision as to that particular action, but as to that class of actions tradition is the sufficient authority. The Indians decide now to go on a hunt; but it is not a matter of debate whether or not one should, from time to time, hunt.

The folkways are the ways that grow up out of long and intimate association of men with each other; in the society of our conception, all the ways are folkways. Men act with reference to each other by understandings that are tacit and traditional. There are no formal contracts or other agreements. The rights and obligations of the individual do not come about by special arrangement; they are, chiefly, aspects of the position of the individual as a person of one sex or the other, one age group or another, one occupational group or another, and as one occupying just that position in a system of relationships that are traditional in the society. The individual's status is thus, in large part, fixed at birth; it changes as he lives, but it changes in ways that were "foreordained" by the nature of his particular society. The institutions of the folk society are of the sort that has been called "crescive"; they are not of the sort that is created deliberately for special purposes, as was the juvenile court. So, too, law is made up of the traditional conceptions of rights and obligations and the customary procedures whereby these rights and obligations are assured; legislation has no part in it. . . .

Behavior in the folk society is highly conventional, custom fixes the rights and duties of individuals, and knowledge is not critically examined or objectively and systematically formulated; but it must not be supposed that primitive man is a sort of automaton in which custom is the mainspring. It would be as mistaken to think of primitive man as strongly aware that he is constrained by custom. Within the limits set by custom, there is invitation to excel in performance. There is lively competition, a sense of opportunity, and a feeling that what the culture moves one to do is well worth doing. "There is no drabness in such a life. It has about it all the allurements of personal experience, very much one's own, of competitive skill, of things well done."[3] The interrelations and high degree of consistency among the elements of custom that are presented to the individual declare to him the importance of making his endeavors in the directions indicated by tradition. The culture sets goals that stimulate action by giving great meaning to it.

It has been said that the folk society is small, and that its members have lived in long and intimate association with one another. It has also been said that, in such societies, there is little critical or abstract thinking. These characteristics are related to yet another characteristic of the folk society: Behavior is personal, not impersonal. A "person" may be defined as that social object which I feel to respond to situations as I do, with all the sentiments and interests that I feel to be my own; a person is myself in another form, his qualities and values are inherent within him, and his significance for me is not merely one of utility. A "thing," on the other hand, is a social object that has no claim upon my sympathies, that responds to me, as I conceive it, mechanically; its value for me exists insofar as it serves my end. In the folk society, all human beings admitted to the society as treated as persons; one does not deal impersonally ("thing-fashion") with any other participant in the little world of that society. Moreover, in the folk society much besides human beings is treated personally. The pattern of behavior that is first suggested by the inner experience of the individual—his wishes, fears, sensitiveness, and interests of all sorts—is projected into all objects with which he comes into contact. Thus, nature, too, is treated personally: The elements, the features of the landscape, the animals, and especially anything in the environment that, by its appearance or behavior, suggests that it has the attributes of mankind—to all these are attributed qualities of the human person.

In short, the personal and intimate life of the child in the family is extended, in the folk society, into the social world of the adult and even into inanimate objects. It is not merely that relations in such a society are personal; it is also that they are familial. The first contact made as the infant becomes a person are with other persons; moreover, each of these first persons, he comes to learn, has a particular kind of relation to him that is associated with that one's genealogical position. The individual finds himself fixed within a constellation of familial relationships. The kinship connections provide a pattern in terms of which, in the ideal folk society, all personal relations are conventionalized and categorized. All relations are personal. But relations are not, in content of specific behavior, the same for everyone. As a mother is different from a father, and a grandson from a nephew, so are these classes of personal relationship, originating in genealogical connection, extended outward into all relationships whatever. In this sense, the folk society is a familial society. . . .

The real primitive and peasant societies differ very greatly as to the forms assumed by kinship. Nevertheless, it is possible to recognize two main types. In one of these, the connection between husband and wife is emphasized, while neither one of the lineages, matrilineal or patrilineal, is singled out as contrasted with the other. In such a folk society, the individual parental family is the social unit, and connections with relatives outside this family are of secondary importance. Such family organization is common where the population is small, the means of livelihood are by precarious collection of wild food, and larger units cannot permanently remain together because the natural resources will not allow it. But, where a somewhat larger population remains together, either in a village or in a migratory band, there often, although by no means always, is found an emphasis upon one line of consanguine connection rather than the other with subordination of the conjugal connection. There results a segmentation of the society into equivalent kinship units. These may take the form of extended domestic groups or joint families (as in China) or may include many households of persons related in part through recognized genealogical connection and in part through the sharing of the same name or other symbolic designation (in the latter case, we speak of the groups as clans). Even in societies where the individual parental family is an independent economic unit, as in the case of the eastern Eskimo, husband and wife never become a new social and economic unit with the completeness that is characteristic of our own society. When a marriage in primitive society comes to an end, the kinsmen of the dead spouse assert upon his property a claim they have never given up. On the whole, we may think of the family among folk peoples as made up of persons consanguinely connected. Marriage is, in comparison with what we in our society directly experience, an incident in the life of the individual who is born, brought up, and dies with his blood kinsmen. In such a society, romantic love can hardly be elevated to a major principle.

Insofar as the consanguine lines are well defined (and, in some cases, both lines may be of importance to the individual), the folk society may be thought of as composed of families rather than of individuals. It is the familial groups that act and are acted upon. There is strong solidarity within the kinship group, and the individual is responsible to all his kin as they are responsible to him. "The clan is a natural mutual aid society. . . . A member belongs to the clan, he is not his own; if he is wrong, they will right him; if he does wrong, the responsibility is shared by them."[4] Thus, in folk societies wherein the tendency to maintain consanguine connection has resulted in joint families or clans, it is usual to find that injuries done by an individual are regarded as injuries against his kinship group, and the group takes the steps to right the wrong. The step may be revenge regulated by custom or a property settlement. A considerable part of primitive law exists in the regulation of claims by one body of kin against another. The fact that the folk society is an organization of families rather than an aggregation of individuals is further expressed in many of those forms of marriage in which a certain kind of relative is the approved spouse. The customs by which, in many primitive societies, a man is expected to marry his deceased brother's widow or a woman to marry her deceased sister's husband express the view of marriage as an undertaking between kinship groups. One of the spouses having failed by death, the undertaking is to be carried on by some other representative of the family group. Indeed, in the arrangements for marriage—the selection of spouses by the relatives, in bride-price, dowry, and in many forms of familial negotiations leading to a marriage—the nature of marriage as a connubial form of social relations between kindreds finds expression.

It has been said in foregoing paragraphs that behavior in the folk society is traditional, spontaneous, and uncritical, that what one man does is much the same as what another man does, and that the patterns of conduct are clear and remain constant throughout the generations. It has also been suggested that the congruence of all parts of conventional behavior and social institutions with each other contributes to the sense of rightness that the member of the folk society feels to inhere in his traditional ways of action. In the well-known language of Sumner, the ways of life are folkways; furthermore, the folkways tend to be also mores—ways of doing or thinking to which attach notions of moral worth. The value of every traditional act or object or institution is, thus, something that the members of the society are not disposed to call into question; and, should the value be called into question, the doing so is resented. This characteristic of the folk society may be briefly referred to by saying that it is a sacred society. In the folk society, one may not, without calling into effect negative social sanctions, challenge as valueless what has come to be traditional in that society.

Presumably, the sacredness of social objects had its source, in part at least, in the mere fact of habituation; probably the individual organism becomes early adjusted to certain habits, motor and mental, and to certain associations between one activity and another or between certain sense experiences and certain activities, and it is almost physiologically uncomfortable to change or even to entertain the idea of change. There arises "a feeling of impropriety of certain forms, of a particular social or religious value, or a superstitious fear of change."[5] Probably the sacredness of social objects in the folk society is related also to the fact that, in such well-organized cultures, acts and objects suggest the traditions, beliefs, and conceptions that all share. There is reason to suppose that, when what is traditionally done becomes less meaningful because people no longer know what the acts stand for, life becomes more secular. In the repetitious character of conventional action (aside from technical action), we have ritual; in its expressive character, we have ceremony; in the folk society, ritual tends also to be ceremonious, and ritual-ceremony tends to be sacred, not secular.

NOTES

1. W. G. Sumner, *Folkways* (Boston: Ginn & Co., 1907), p. 12.
2. A. R. Radcliffe-Brown, *The Andaman Islanders* (Cambridge: At the University Press, 1933), p. 43.
3. A. A. Goldenweiser, "Individual, Pattern and Involution," *Essays in Honor of A. L. Kroeber* (Berkeley: University of California Press, 1936), p. 102.
4. Edwin W. Smith and Andrew Murray Dale, *The Ila-Speaking Peoples of Northern Rhodesia* (London: Macmillan, 1920), I, p. 296.
5. Franz Boas, *Primitive Art* (Oslo, 1927), p. 150.

Urbanism as a Way of Life

Louis Wirth (1897–1952), a 1930s University of Chicago sociologist, was a theorist and a founder of the International Sociological Society. Wirth contributed heavily to the study of social organization, mass society, minorities, the sociology of knowledge, and urbanism as a way of life. He was also among the first to introduce the concept of social planning. He was well aware of the dangers of political engineering through public opinion and stressed democracy as a process of intercommunication, discussion, debate, negotiation, compromise, and toleration.

In the following selection, Wirth discusses his view of urbanism as it emerged in Chicago during the 1920s and 1930s. Wirth defines the city as a densely populated area of socially heterogeneous individuals. In a far-ranging discussion, he provides an understanding, directly and indirectly, of why social relations in the city are anonymous and thus limited to specific activities. His theory explains how and why urbanism is conducive to social mobility, leveling, and a breakdown of caste lines and why it creates heterogeneity and the demise of the homogeneous community.

Key Concept: heterogeneity

For sociological purposes a city may be defined as a relatively *large, dense,* and permanent settlement of socially *heterogeneous* individuals. On the basis of the postulates which this minimal definition suggests, a theory of urbanism may be formulated in the light of existing knowledge concerning social groups.

A THEORY OF URBANISM

In the pages that follow we shall seek to set forth a limited number of identifying characteristics of the city. Given these characteristics we shall then indicate what consequences or further characteristics follow from them in the light of general sociological theory and empirical research. We hope in this manner to arrive at the essential propositions comprising a theory of urbanism. Some of these propositions can be supported by a considerable body of already available research materials; others may be accepted as hypotheses for which a certain amount of presumptive evidence exists, but for which more ample and exact verification would be required. At least such a procedure will, it is hoped, show what in the way of systematic knowledge of the city we now have and what are the crucial and fruitful hypotheses for future research. . . .

Size of the Population Aggregate

Ever since Aristotle's *Politics*, it has been recognized that increasing the number of inhabitants in a settlement beyond a certain limit will affect the relationships between them and the character of the city. Large numbers involve, as has been pointed out, a greater range of individual variation. Furthermore, the greater the number of individuals participating in a process of interaction, the greater is the *potential* differentiation between them. The personal traits, the occupations, the cultural life, and the ideas of the members of an urban community may, therefore, be expected to range between more widely separated poles than those of rural inhabitants.

That such variations should give rise to the spatial segregation of individuals according to color, ethnic heritage, economic and social status, tastes and preferences, may readily be inferred. The bonds of kinship, of neighborliness, and the sentiments arising out of living together for generations under a common folk tradition are likely to be absent or, at best, relatively weak in an aggregate the members of which have such diverse origins and backgrounds. Under such circumstances competition and formal control mechanisms furnish the substitutes for the bonds of solidarity that are relied upon to hold a folk society together.

Increase in the number of inhabitants of a community beyond a few hundred is bound to limit the possibility of each member of the community knowing all the others personally. Max Weber, in recognizing the social significance of this fact, pointed out that from a sociological point of view large numbers of inhabitants and density of settlement mean that the personal mutual acquaintanceship between the inhabitants which ordinarily inheres in a neighborhood is lacking. The increase in numbers thus involves a changed character of the social relationships. As [Georg] Simmel points out:

> [If] the unceasing external contact of numbers of persons in the city should be met by the same number of inner reactions as in the small town, in which one knows almost every person he meets and to each of whom he has a positive relationship, one would be completely atomized internally and would fall into an unthinkable mental condition.

The multiplication of persons in a state of interaction under conditions which make their contact as full personalities impossible produces that segmentalization of human relationships which has sometimes been seized upon by students of the mental life of the cities as an explanation for the "schizoid" character of urban personality. This is not to say that the urban inhabitants have fewer acquaintances than rural inhabitants, for the reverse may actually be true; it means rather that in relation to the number of people whom they see and with whom they rub elbows in the course of daily life, they know a smaller proportion, and of these they have less intensive knowledge.

Characteristically, urbanites meet one another in highly segmental roles. They are, to be sure, dependent upon more people for the satisfactions of their life-needs than are rural people and thus are associated with a greater number of organized groups, but they are less dependent upon particular persons, and their dependence upon others is confined to a highly fractionalized aspect of the other's round of activity. This is essentially what is meant by saying that the city is characterized by secondary rather than primary contacts. The contacts of the city may indeed be face to face, but they are nevertheless impersonal, superficial, transitory, and segmental. The reserve, the indifference, and the blasé outlook which urbanites manifest in their relationships may thus be regarded as devices for immunizing themselves against the personal claims and expectations of others.

The superficiality, the anonymity, and the transitory character of urban-social relations make intelligible, also, the sophistication and the rationality generally ascribed to city-dwellers. Our acquaintances tend to stand in a relationship of utility to us in the sense that the role which each one plays in our life is overwhelmingly regarded as a means for the achievement of our own ends. Whereas, therefore, the individual gains, on the one hand, a certain degree of emancipation or freedom from the personal and emotional controls of intimate groups, he loses, on the other hand, the spontaneous self-expression, the morale, and the sense of participation that comes with living in an integrated society. This constitutes essentially the state of *anomie* or the social void to which [Emile] Durkheim alludes in attempting to account for the various forms of social disorganization in technological society. . . .

In a community composed of a larger number of individuals than can know one another intimately and can be assembled in one spot, it becomes necessary to communicate through indirect mediums and to articulate individual interests by a process of delegation. Typically in the city, interests are made effective through representation. The individual counts for little, but the voice of the representative is heard with a deference roughly proportional to the numbers for whom he speaks. . . .

Density

As in the case of numbers, so in the case of concentration in limited space, certain consequences of relevance in sociological analysis of the city emerge. Of these only a few can be indicated.

As Darwin pointed out for flora and fauna and as Durkheim noted in the case of human societies, an increase in numbers when area is held constant (i.e., an increase in density) tends to produce differentiation and specialization, since only in this way can the area support increased numbers. Density thus reinforces the effect of numbers in diversifying men and their activities and in increasing the complexity of the social structure.

On the subjective side, as Simmel has suggested, the close physical contact of numerous individuals necessarily produces a shift in the mediums through which we orient ourselves to the urban milieu, especially to our fellow-men. Typically, our physical contacts are close but our social contacts are distant. The urban world puts a premium on visual recognition. We see the uniform which denotes the role of the functionaries and are oblivious to the personal eccentricities that are hidden behind the uniform. We tend to acquire and develop a sensitivity to a world of artefacts and become progressively farther removed from the world of nature.

We are exposed to glaring contrasts between splendor and squalor, between riches and poverty, intelligence and ignorance, order and chaos. The competition for space is great, so that each area generally tends to be put to the use which yields the greatest economic return. Place of work tends to become dissociated from place of residence, for the proximity of industrial and commercial establishments makes an area both economically and socially undesirable for residential purposes.

Density, land values, rentals, accessibility, healthfulness, prestige, aesthetic consideration, absence of nuisances such as noise, smoke, and dirt determine the desirability of various areas of the city as places of settlement for different sections of the population. Place and nature of work, income, racial and ethnic characteristics, social status, custom, habit, taste, preference, and prejudice are among the significant factors in accordance with which the urban population is selected and distributed into more or less distinct settlements. Diverse population elements inhabiting a compact settlement thus tend to become segregated from one another in the degree in which their requirements and modes of life are incompatible with one another and in the measure in which they are antagonistic to one another. Similarly, persons of homogeneous status and needs unwittingly drift into, consciously select, or are forced by circumstances into, the same area. The different parts of the city thus acquire specialized functions. The city consequently tends to resemble a mosaic of social worlds in which the transition from one to the other is abrupt. The juxtaposition of divergent personalities and modes of life tends to produce a relativistic perspective and a sense of toleration of differences which may be regarded as prerequisites for rationality and which lead toward the secularization of life.

The close living together and working together of individuals who have no sentimental and emotional ties foster a spirit of competition, aggrandizement, and mutual exploitation. To counteract irresponsibility and potential disorder, formal controls tend to be resorted to. Without rigid adherence to predictable routines a large compact society would scarcely be able to maintain itself. The clock and the traffic signal are symbolic of the basis of our social order in the urban world. Frequent close physical contact, coupled with great social distance, accentuates the reserve of unattached individuals toward one another and, unless compensated for by other opportunities for response, gives rise to loneliness. The necessary frequent movement of great numbers of individuals to a congested habitat gives occasion to friction and irritation. Nervous tensions which derive from such personal frustrations are accentuated by the rapid tempo and the complicated technology under which life in dense areas must be lived.

Heterogeneity

The social interaction among such a variety of personality types in the urban milieu tends to break down the rigidity of caste lines and to complicate the class structure, and thus induces a more ramified and differentiated framework of social stratification than is found in more integrated societies. The heightened mobility of the individual, which brings him within the range of stimulation by a great number of diverse individuals and subjects him to fluctuating status in the differentiated social groups that compose the social structure of the city, tends toward the acceptance of instability and insecurity in the world at large as a norm. This fact helps to account, too, for the sophistication and cosmopolitanism of the urbanite. No single group has the undivided allegiance of the individual. The groups with which he is affiliated do not lend themselves readily to a simple hierarchical arrangement. By virtue of his different interests arising out of different aspects of social life, the individual acquires membership in widely divergent groups, each of which functions only with reference to a single segment of his personality. Nor do these groups easily permit of a concentric arrangement so that the narrower ones fall within the circumference of the more inclusive ones, as is more likely to be the case in the rural community or in primitive societies. Rather the groups with which the person typically is affiliated are tangential to each other or intersect in highly variable fashion.

CHAPTER 17 Social Movements and Collective Behavior

17.1 MANCUR OLSON, JR.

The Logic of Collective Action

Mancur Olson, Jr. (b. 1932), economist, is a professor of economics at the University of Maryland and a consultant to the RAND Corporation in Santa Monica, California, and to the Institute of Defense Analysis in Washington, D.C. His publications include *Changing Unemployment Rates in Europe and the United States: Institutional Structure and Regional Variation* (University of Maryland, 1989) and *The Logic of Collective Action: Public Goods and the Theory of Groups* (Harvard University Press, 1971), which is excerpted here.

It is often assumed that members of a group with a common interest would naturally act collectively to pursue that interest. In the selection that follows, however, Olson shows that this assumption is false. It is very difficult for most people to act collectively in their own behalf. The reason is that it is usually rational for individuals not to contribute any effort or money to the pursuit of their collective goal but to let others carry the load, since the noncontributors and contributors share equally in the gains. There are conditions, however, under which collective action is much more likely, and Olson spells them out. Unfortunately for democratic ideals, these conditions make it easier for small elite groups to organize for their interests than it is for large disadvantaged groups.

Key Concept: rational self-interest

314

*Chapter 17
Social
Movements and
Collective
Behavior*

*I*t is often taken for granted, at least where economic objectives are involved, that groups of individuals with common interests usually attempt to further those common interests. Groups of individuals with common interests are expected to act on behalf of their common interests much as single individuals are often expected to act on behalf of their personal interests. This opinion about group behavior is frequently found not only in popular discussions but also in scholarly writings. Many economists of diverse methodological and ideological traditions have implicitly or explicitly accepted it. This view has, for example, been important in many theories of labor unions, in Marxian theories of class action, in concepts of "countervailing power," and in various discussions of economic institutions. It has, in addition, occupied a prominent place in political science, at least in the United States, where the study of pressure groups has been dominated by a celebrated "group theory" based on the idea that groups will act when necessary to further their common or group goals. Finally, it has played a significant role in many well-known sociological studies. . . .

But it is *not* in fact true that the idea that groups will act in their self-interest follows logically from the premise of rational and self-interested behavior. . . . Indeed, unless the number of individuals in a group is quite small, or unless there is coercion or some other special device to make individuals act in their common interest, *rational, self-interested individuals will not act to achieve their common or group interests.* In other words, even if all of the individuals in a large group are rational and self-interested, and would gain if, as a group, they acted to achieve their common interest or objective, they will still not voluntarily act to achieve that common or group interest. The notion that groups of individuals will act to achieve their common or group interests, far from being a logical implication of the assumption that the individuals in a group will rationally further their individual interests, is in fact inconsistent with that assumption. . . .

If the members of a large group rationally seek to maximize their personal welfare, they will *not* act to advance their common or group objectives unless there is coercion to force them to do so, or unless some separate incentive, distinct from the achievement of the common or group interest, is offered to the members of the group individually on the condition that they help bear the costs or burdens involved in the achievement of the group objectives. Nor will such large groups form organizations to further their common goals in the absence of the coercion or the separate incentives just mentioned. These points hold true even when there is unanimous agreement in a group about the common good and the methods of achieving it. . . .

None of the statements made above fully applies to small groups, for the situation in small groups is much more complicated. In small groups there may very well be some voluntary action in support of the common purposes of the individuals in the group, but in most cases this action will cease before it reaches the optimal level for the members of the group as a whole. In the sharing of the costs of efforts to achieve a common goal in small groups, there is however a surprising tendency for the "exploitation" of the *great* by the *small*. . . .

315

Mancur Olson, Jr.

THE PURPOSE OF ORGANIZATION

. . . The kinds of organizations that are the focus of this study are *expected* to further the interests of their members. Labor unions are expected to strive for higher wages and better working conditions for their members; farm organizations are expected to strive for favorable legislation for their members; cartels are expected to strive for higher prices for participating firms; the corporation is expected to further the interests of its stockholders; and the state is expected to further the common interests of its citizens (though in this nationalistic age the state often has interests and ambitions apart from those of its citizens). . . .

Just as those who belong to an organization or a group can be presumed to have a common interest, so they obviously also have purely individual interests, different from those of the others in the organization or group. All of the members of a labor union, for example, have a common interest in higher wages, but at the same time each worker has a unique interest in his personal income, which depends not only on the rate of wages but also on the length of time that he works.

PUBLIC GOODS AND LARGE GROUPS

The combination of individual interests and common interests in an organization suggests an analogy with a competitive market. The firms in a perfectly competitive industry, for example, have a common interest in a higher price for the industry's product. Since a uniform price must prevail in such a market, a firm cannot expect a higher price for itself unless all of the other firms in the industry also have this higher price. But a firm in a competitive market also has an interest in selling as much as it can, until the cost of producing another unit exceeds the price of that unit. In this there is no common interest; each firm's interest is directly opposed to that of every other firm, for the more other firms sell, the lower the price and income for any given firm. In short, while all firms have a common interest in a higher price, they have antagonistic interests where output is concerned. This can be illustrated with a simple supply-and-demand model. For the sake of a simple argument, assume that a perfectly competitive industry is momentarily in a disequilibrium position, with price exceeding marginal cost for all firms at their present output. Suppose, too, that all of the adjustments will be made by the firms already in the industry rather

316

*Chapter 17
Social
Movements and
Collective
Behavior*

than by new entrants, and that the industry is on an inelastic portion of its demand curve. Since price exceeds marginal cost for all firms, output will increase. But as all firms increase production, the price falls; indeed, since the industry demand curve is by assumption inelastic, the total revenue of the industry will decline. Apparently each firm finds that with price exceeding marginal cost, it pays to increase its output, but the result is that each firm gets a smaller profit. Some economists in an earlier day may have questioned this result, but the fact that profit-maximizing firms in a perfectly competitive industry can act contrary to their interests as a group is now widely understood and accepted. A group of profit-maximizing firms can act to reduce their aggregate profits because in perfect competition each firm is, by definition, so small that it can ignore the effect of its output on price. Each firm finds it to its advantage to increase output to the point where marginal cost equals price and to ignore the effects of its extra output on the position of the industry. It is true that the net result is that all firms are worse off, but this does not mean that every firm has not maximized its profits. If a firm, foreseeing the fall in price resulting from the increase in industry output, were to restrict its own output, it would lose more than ever, for its price would fall quite as much in any case and it would have a smaller output as well. A firm in a perfectly competitive market gets only a small part of the benefit (or a small share of the industry's extra revenue) resulting from a reduction in that firm's output.

For these reasons it is now generally understood that if the firms in an industry are maximizing profits, the profits for the industry as a whole will be less than they might otherwise be. And almost everyone would agree that this theoretical conclusion fits the facts for markets characterized by pure competition. The important point is that this is true because, though all the firms have a common interest in a higher price for the industry's product, it is in the interest of each firm that the other firms pay the cost—in terms of the necessary reduction in output—needed to obtain a higher price.

About the only thing that keeps prices from falling in accordance with the process just described in perfectly competitive markets is outside intervention. Government price supports, tariffs, cartel agreements, and the like may keep the firms in a competitive market from acting contrary to their interests. Such aid or intervention is quite common. It is then important to ask how it comes about. How does a competitive industry obtain government assistance in maintaining the price of its product?

Consider a hypothetical, competitive industry, and suppose that most of the producers in that industry desire a tariff, a price-support program, or some other government intervention to increase the price for their product. To obtain any such assistance from the government, the producers in this industry will presumably have to organize a lobbying organization; they will have to become an active pressure group. This lobbying organization may have to conduct a considerable campaign. If significant resistance is encountered, a great amount of money will be required. Public relations experts will be needed to influence the newspapers, and some advertising may be necessary. Professional organizers will probably be needed to organize "spontaneous grass roots" meetings among the distressed producers in the industry, and to get those in the industry to write letters to their congressmen. The campaign for the government assistance will take the time of some of the producers in the industry, as well as their money.

There is a striking parallel between the problem the perfectly competitive industry faces as it strives to obtain government assistance, and the problem it faces in the marketplace when the firms increase output and bring about a fall in price. *Just as it was not rational for a particular producer to restrict his output in order that there might be a higher price for the product of his industry, so it would not be rational for him to sacrifice his time and money to support a lobbying organization to obtain government assistance for the industry. In neither case would it be in the interest of the individual producer to assume any of the costs himself. A lobbying organization, or indeed a labor union or any other organization, working in the interest of a large group of firms or workers in some industry, would get no assistance from the rational, self-interested individuals in that industry.* This would be true even if everyone in the industry were absolutely convinced that the proposed program was in their interest (though in fact some might think otherwise and make the organization's task yet more difficult).

Although the lobbying organization is only one example of the logical analogy between the organization and the market, it is of some practical importance. There are many powerful and well-financed lobbies with mass support in existence now, but these lobbying organizations do not get that support because of their legislative achievements. The most powerful lobbying organizations now obtain their funds and their following for other reasons, as later parts of this study will show. . . .

Almost any government is economically beneficial to its citizens, in that the law and order it provides is a prerequisite of all civilized economic activity. But despite the force of patriotism, the appeal of the national ideology, the bond of a common culture, and the indispensability of the system of law and order, no major state in modern history has been able to support itself through voluntary dues or contributions. Philanthropic contributions are not even a significant source of revenue for most countries. Taxes, *compulsory* payments by definition, are needed. Indeed, as the old saying indicates, their necessity is as certain as death itself.

If the state, with all of the emotional resources at its command, cannot finance its most basic and vital activities without resort to compulsion, it would seem that large private organizations might also have difficulty in getting the individuals in the groups whose interests they attempt to advance to make the necessary contributions voluntarily.

The reason the state cannot survive on voluntary dues or payments, but must rely on taxation, is that the most fundamental services a nation-state provides are, in one important respect, like the higher price in a competitive market: they must be available to everyone if they are available to anyone. The basic and most elementary goods or services provided by government, like defense and police protection, and the system of law and order generally, are such that they go to everyone or practically everyone in the nation. It would obviously not be feasible, if indeed it were possible, to deny the protection provided by the military services, the police, and the courts to those who did not voluntarily pay their share of the costs of government, and taxation is accordingly necessary. The common or collective benefits provided by govern-

318

*Chapter 17
Social
Movements and
Collective
Behavior*

ments are usually called "public goods" by economists, and the concept of public goods is one of the oldest and most important ideas in the study of public finance. A common, collective, or public good is here defined as any good such that, if any person X_4 in a group, $X_1, \ldots, X_4, \ldots, X_{98}$ consumes it, it cannot feasibly be withheld from the others in that group. In other words, those who do not purchase or pay for any of the public or collective good cannot be excluded or kept from sharing in the consumption of the good, as they can where noncollective goods are concerned.

Students of public finance have, however, neglected the fact that *the achievement of any common goal or the satisfaction of any common interest means that a public or collective good has been provided for that group.* The very fact that a goal or purpose is *common* to a group means that no one in the group is excluded from the benefit or satisfaction brought about by its achievement. . . . It is of the essence of an organization that it provides an inseparable, generalized benefit. It follows that the provision of public or collective goods is the fundamental function of organizations generally. A state is first of all an organization that provides public goods for its members, the citizens; and other types of organizations similarly provide collective goods for their members.

And just as a state cannot support itself by voluntary contributions, or by selling its basic services on the market, neither can other large organizations support themselves without providing some sanction, or some attraction distinct from the public good itself, that will lead individuals to help bear the burdens of maintaining the organization. The individual member of the typical large organization is in a position analogous to that of the firm in a perfectly competitive market, or the taxpayer in the state: his own efforts will not have a noticeable effect on the situation of his organization, and he can enjoy any improvements brought about by others whether or not he has worked in support of his organization.

There is no suggestion here that states or other organizations provide *only* public or collective goods. Governments often provide noncollective goods like electric power, for example, and they usually sell such goods on the market much as private firms would do. Moreover, as later parts of this study will argue, large organizations that are not able to make membership compulsory *must also* provide some noncollective goods in order to give potential members an incentive to join. Still, collective goods are the characteristic organization goods, for ordinary noncollective goods can always be provided by individual action, and only where common purposes or collective goods are concerned is organization or group action ever indispensable. . . .

[C]ertain small groups can provide themselves with collective goods without relying on coercion or any positive inducements apart from the collective good itself. This is because in some small groups each of the members, or at least one of them, will find that his personal gain from having the collective good exceeds the total cost of providing some amount of that collective good; there are members who would be better off if the collective good were provided, even if they had to pay the entire cost of providing it themselves, than they would be if it were not provided. In such situations there is a presumption that the collective good will be provided. Such a situation will exist only when the benefit to the group from having the collective good exceeds the total cost by more than it exceeds the gain to one or more individuals in the group. Thus, in a very small group, where each member gets a substantial proportion of the total gain simply because there are few others in the group, a collective good can often be provided by the voluntary, self-interested action of the members of the group. In smaller groups marked by considerable degrees of inequality—that is, in groups of members of unequal "size" or extent of interest in the collective good—there is the greatest likelihood that a collective good will be provided; for the greater the interest in the collective good of any single member, the greater the likelihood that that member will get such a significant proportion of the total benefit from the collective good that he will gain from seeing that the good is provided, even if he has to pay all of the cost himself.

Even in the smallest groups, however, the collective good will not ordinarily be provided on an optimal scale. That is to say, the members of the group will not provide as much of the good as it would be in their common interest to provide. Only certain special institutional arrangements will give the individual members an incentive to purchase the amounts of the collective good that would add up to the amount that would be in the best interest of the group as a whole. This tendency toward suboptimality is due to the fact that a collective good is, by definition, such that other individuals in the group cannot be kept from consuming it once any individual in the group has provided it for himself. Since an individual member thus gets only part of the benefit of any expenditure he makes to obtain more of the collective good, he will discontinue his purchase of the collective good before the optimal amount for the group as a whole has been obtained. In addition, the amounts of the collective good that a member of the group receives free from other members will further reduce his incentive to provide more of that good at his own expense. Accordingly, *the larger the group, the farther it will fall short of providing an optimal amount of a collective good.*

This suboptimality or inefficiency will be somewhat less serious in groups composed of members of greatly different size or interest in the collective good. In such unequal groups, on the other hand, there is a tendency toward an arbitrary sharing of the burden of providing the collective good. The largest member, the member who would on his own provide the largest amount of the collective good, bears a disproportionate share of the burden of providing the collective good. The smaller member by definition gets a smaller fraction of the benefit of any amount of the collective good he provides than a larger member, and therefore has less incentive to provide additional amounts of the collective good. Once a smaller member has the amount of the collective good he gets free from the largest member, he has more than he would have purchased for himself, and has no incentive to obtain any of the collective good at his own expense. In small groups with common interests there is accordingly *a surprising tendency for the "exploitations" of the great by the small.* . . .

The most important single point about small groups in the present context, however, is that they may very well be able to provide themselves with a collective good simply because of the attraction of the collective good to the individual members. In this, small groups differ from larger ones. The larger a group is, the farther it will fall short of obtaining an optimal supply of any collective good, and

320

*Chapter 17
Social
Movements and
Collective
Behavior*

the less likely that it will act to obtain even a minimal amount of such a good. In short, the larger the group, the less it will further its common interests. . . .

The analog to atomistic competition in the nonmarket situation is the very large group, which will here be called the "latent" group. It is distinguished by the fact that, if one member does or does not help provide the collective good, no other one member will be significantly affected and therefore none has any reason to react. Thus an individual in a "latent" group, by definition, cannot make a noticeable contribution to any group effort, and since no one in the group will react if he makes no contribution, he has no incentive to contribute. Accordingly, large or "latent" groups have no incentive to act to obtain a collective good because, however valuable the collective good might be to the group as a whole, it does not offer the individual any incentive to pay dues to any organization working in the latent group's interest, or to bear in any other way any of the costs of the necessary collective action.

Only a *separate and "selective" incentive* will stimulate a rational individual in a latent group to act in a group-oriented way. In such circumstances group action can be obtained only through an incentive that operates, not indiscriminately, like the collective good, upon the group as a whole, but rather *selectively* toward the individuals in the group. The incentive must be "selective" so that those who do not join the organization working for the group's interest, or in other ways contribute to the attainment of the group's interest, can be treated differently from those who do. These "selective incentives" can be either negative or positive, in that they can either coerce by punishing those who fail to bear an allocated share of the costs of the group action, or they can be positive inducements offered to those who act in the group interest. A latent group that has been led to act in its group interest, either because of coercion of the individuals in the group or because of positive rewards to those individuals, will here be called a "mobilized" latent group. Large groups are thus called "latent" groups because they have a latent power or capacity for action, but that potential power can be realized or "mobilized" only with the aid of "selective incentives." . . .

SOCIAL INCENTIVES AND RATIONAL BEHAVIOR

Economic incentives are not, to be sure, the only incentives; people are sometimes also motivated by a desire to win prestige, respect, friendship, and other social and psychological objectives. Though the phrase "socio-economic status" often used in discussions of status suggests that there may be a correlation between economic position and social position, there is no doubt that the two are sometimes different. The possibility that, in a case where there was no economic incentive for an individual to contribute to the achievement of a group interest, there might nonetheless be a social incentive for him to make such a contribution, must therefore be considered. And it is obvious that this is a possibility. If a small group of people who had an interest in a collective good happened also to be personal friends, or belonged to the same social club, and some of the group left the burden of providing that collective good on others, they might, even if they gained economically by this course of action, lose socially by it, and the social loss might outweigh the economic gain. Their friends might use "social pressure" to encourage them to do their part toward achieving the group goal, or the social club might exclude them, and such steps might be effective, for everyday observation reveals that most people value the fellowship of their friends and associates, and value social status, personal prestige, and self-esteem.

The existence of these social incentives to group-oriented action does not, however, contradict or weaken the analysis of this study. If anything, it strengthens it, *for social status and social acceptance are individual, noncollective goods*. Social sanctions and social rewards are "selective incentives"; that is, they are among the kinds of incentives that may be used to mobilize a latent group. It is in the nature of social incentives that they can distinguish among individuals: the recalcitrant individual can be ostracized, and the cooperative individual can be invited into the center of the charmed circle. . . .

THE "BY-PRODUCT" THEORY OF LARGE PRESSURE GROUPS

If the individuals in a large group have no incentive to organize a lobby to obtain a collective benefit, how can the fact that some large groups are organized be explained? Though many groups with common interests, like the consumers, the white-collar workers, and the migrant agricultural workers, are not organized, other large groups, like the union laborers, the farmers, and the doctors have at least some degree of organization. The fact that there are many groups which, despite their needs, are not organized would seem to contradict the "group theory" of the analytical pluralists; but on the other hand the fact that other large groups have been organized would seem to contradict the theory of "latent groups" offered in this study.

But the large economic groups that are organized do have one common characteristic which distinguishes them from those large economic groups that are not, and which at the same time tends to support the theory of latent groups offered in this work. This common characteristic will, however, require an elaboration or addition to the theory of groups developed in this study.

The common characteristic which distinguishes all of the large economic groups with significant lobbying organizations is that these groups are also organized for some *other* purpose. The large and powerful economic lobbies are in fact the by-products of organizations that obtain their strength and support because they perform some function in addition to lobbying for collective goods.

The lobbies of the large economic groups are the by-products of organizations that have the capacity to "mobilize" a latent group with "selective incentives." The only organizations that have the "selective incentives" available are those that (1) have the authority and capacity to be coercive, or (2) have a source of positive inducements that they can offer the individuals in a latent group.

322

*Chapter 17
Social
Movements and
Collective
Behavior*

A purely political organization—an organization that has no function apart from its lobbying function—obviously cannot legally coerce individuals into becoming members. A political party, or any purely political organization, with a captive or compulsory membership would be quite unusual in a democratic political system. But if for some nonpolitical reason, if because of some other function it performs, an organization has a justification for having a compulsory membership, or if through this other function it has obtained the power needed to make membership in it compulsory, that organization may then be able to get the resources needed to support a lobby. The lobby is then a by-product of whatever function this organization performs that enables it to have a captive membership.

An organization that did nothing except lobby to obtain a collective good for some large group would not have a source of rewards or positive selective incentives it could offer potential members. Only an organization that also sold private or noncollective products, or provided social or recreational benefits to individual members, would have a source of these positive inducements. Only such an organization could make a joint offering or "tied sale" of a collective and a noncollective good that could stimulate a rational individual in a large group to bear part of the cost of obtaining a collective good. There are for this reason many organizations that have both lobbying functions and economic functions, or lobbying functions and social functions, or even all three of these types of functions at once. Therefore, in addition to the large group lobbies that depend on coercion, there are those that are associated with organizations that provide noncollective or private benefits which can be offered to any potential supporter who will bear his share of the cost of the lobbying for the collective good. . . .

THE "SPECIAL INTEREST" THEORY AND BUSINESS LOBBIES

The segment of society that has the largest number of lobbies working on its behalf is the business community. The *Lobby Index*, an index of organizations and individuals filing reports under the Lobbying Act of 1946 and 1949, reveals that (when Indian tribes are excluded), 825 out of a total of 1,247 organizations represented business. Similarly, a glance at the table of contents of the *Encyclopedia of Associations* shows that the "Trade, Business, and Commercial Organizations" and the "Chambers of Commerce" together take up more than ten times as many pages as the "Social Welfare Organizations," for example. Most of the books on the subject agree on this point. "The business character of the pressure system," according to [political scientist E. E.] Schattschneider, "is shown by almost every list available." This high degree of organization among businessmen, Schattschneider thinks, is particularly important in view of the fact that most other groups are so poorly organized: "only a chemical trace" of the nation's Negroes are members of the National Association for the Advancement of Colored People; "only one sixteen hundredths of 1 per cent of the consumers" have joined the National Consumers' League; "only 6 per cent of

American automobile drivers" are members of the American Automobile Association, and only "about 15 per cent of the veterans" belong to the American Legion. Another scholarly observer believes that "of the many organized groups maintaining offices in the capital, there are no interests more fully, more comprehensively, and more efficiently represented than those of American industry." [James MacGregor] Burns and [Jack Walter] Peltason say in their text that "businessmen's 'unions' are the most varied and numerous of all." V. O. Key points out that "almost every line of industrial and commercial activity has its association." Key also expresses surprise at the extent of the power of organized business in American democracy: "The power wielded by business in American politics may puzzle the person of democratic predilections: a comparatively small minority exercises enormous power."

The number and power of the lobbying organizations representing American business is indeed surprising in a democracy operating according to the majority rule. The power that the various segments of the business community wield in this democratic system, despite the smallness of their numbers, has not been adequately explained. There have been many rather vague, and even mystical, generalizations about the power of the business and propertied interests, but these generalizations normally do not *explain why* business groups have the influence that they have in democracies; they merely assert that they always have such an influence, as though it were self-evident that this should be so. "In the absence of military force," said Charles A. Beard, paraphrasing Daniel Webster, "political power naturally and necessarily goes into the hands which hold the property." But why? Why is it "natural" and "necessary," in democracies based on the rule of the majority, that the political power should fall into the hands of those who hold the property? Bold statements of this kind may tell us something about the ideological bias of the writer, but they do not help us understand reality.

The high degree of organization of business interests, and the power of these business interests, must be due in large part to the fact that the business community is divided into a series of (generally oligopolistic) "industries," each of which contains only a fairly small number of firms. Because the number of firms in each industry is often no more than would comprise a "privileged" group, and seldom more than would comprise an "intermediate" group, it follows that these industries will normally be small enough to organize voluntarily to provide themselves with an active lobby—with the political power that "naturally and necessarily" flows to those that control the business and property of the country. Whereas almost every occupational group involves thousands of workers, and whereas almost any subdivision of agriculture also involves thousands of people, the business interests of the country normally are congregated in oligopoly-sized groups or industries. It follows that the laboring, professional, and agricultural interests of the country make up large, latent groups that can organize and act effectively only when their latent power is crystallized by some organization which can provide political power as a by-product; and by contrast the business interests generally can voluntarily and directly organize and act to further their common interests without any such adventitious assistance. The multitude of workers, consumers, white-collar workers, farmers, and so on are organized only in special circumstances, but business interests are organized as a general rule.

Violence and Political Power: The Meek Don't Make It

As members of a pluralist democratic society, Americans can legally change the political system and enact new policies. Most of us are taught that such action should come about in a civilized, peaceful manner through socially acceptable channels, such as petitioning, lobbying, writing letters, telephoning, and organizing.

But according to William A. Gamson, the author of the following excerpt, many of those who engage in violence, boycotts, and other high-pressure tactics against an opponent are quite successful in achieving their goals. In a study of groups that engaged in extensive protest actions that challenged the existing powers, Gamson found that the groups that engaged in violence were generally more successful than those that were peaceful. The analogous idea in sports is "nice guys finish last," which is a troubling thought to any idealist. Gamson then examines the specific characteristics of the challenging groups to determine *why* some succeeded and some failed.

Gamson (b. 1934) is a political sociologist and a professor of sociology at Boston College in Chestnut Hill, Massachusetts, where he has been teaching since 1982. He is also the chairman of the editorial board for the *Journal of Conflict and Resolution*. Among his publications is *Power and Discontent* (Dorsey Press, 1968), which won the 1969 Sorokin Award presented by the American Sociological Association.

Key Concept: successful protest groups

Most political scientists view the American system as a pluralist democracy. The image is of a contest, carried out under orderly rules. "You scratch my back and I'll scratch yours"; "If you want to get along, go along"; "Don't make permanent enemies because today's adversary may be your ally next time around."

It's a contest for power and recognition that any number can play. If you've got a problem, get organized, play the game, and work for change. Don't expect to win every time or to win the whole pot; compromise is the lifeblood of pluralist politics. More likely than not you'll find some allies who are willing to help you because they think you can help them, now or in the future.

Of course, some people won't play by the rules. Instead of bargaining for advantages, forming coalitions with the powerful, writing peaceful propaganda, and petitioning, some groups get nasty. Contestants who misbehave, who resort to violence and, perish the thought, try to eliminate other contestants, must be excluded from the game.

In such a calculus, the Tobacco Night Riders should have failed. They began as a secret fraternal order, officially called the "Silent Brigade," whose purpose was to force tobacco growers to join the Planters Protective Association, hold tobacco off the market, and bargain collectively with the huge tobacco companies.

WHEN VIOLENCE PAID

The Night Riders didn't play by the rules of pluralist politics. On December 1, 1906, 250 masked and armed men swarmed into Princeton, Kentucky, and took control. They disarmed the police, shut off the water supply, and captured the courthouse and telephone offices. They patrolled the streets, ordered citizens to keep out of sight, and shot at those who disobeyed. Then they dynamited and burned two large tobacco factories and rode off singing "the fire shines bright in my old Kentucky home."

A year later, they struck again, at Hopkinsville, Kentucky. They occupied strategic posts and dragged a buyer from the Imperial Tobacco Company from his home to pistol-whip him. As usual, they marched out singing, but this time the sheriff organized a posse to pursue the raiders and attacked their rear. The pursuers killed one man and wounded another before the raiders drove the posse back into Hopkinsville.

Violence, we are told, doesn't pay, but the Night Riders enjoyed a considerable measure of success. By 1908, the Planters Protective Association was handling nine-tenths of the crop produced in its area. The power of the big tobacco companies was broken and they were buying their tobacco through the association at substantially increased prices. From the depressed conditions of a few years earlier, the black patch area of Kentucky and Tennessee prospered. Mortgages were paid off and new homes, new buggies, and new barns appeared everywhere. The state of Kentucky even passed a law providing a penalty of "triple damages" for any association member who sold his tobacco "outside."

FLAWS IN THE PLURALIST HEAVEN

In recent years the body of criticism about the assumptions of pluralist theory has grown. Critics such as C. Wright Mills, whose *The Power Elite* was one of the earliest and most vocal attacks on the theory, deny the pluralist premise that America has no single center of power. "The flaw in the pluralist heaven,"

326

*Chapter 17
Social
Movements and
Collective
Behavior*

writes political scientist E.E. Schattschneider, "is that the heavenly chorus sings with a strong upper-class accent. Probably about 90 percent of the people cannot get into the pressure system."

To know who gets into the system, and how, is to understand the central issue of American politics. In the last 200 years, hundreds of previously unorganized groups here challenged the existing powers. Many of them collapsed quickly and left no trace; some died and rose again from the ashes. Some were preempted by competitors, some won the trappings of influence without its substance. Some shoved their way into the political arena yelling and screaming, some walked in on the arm of powerful sponsors, some wandered in unnoticed. The fate of these challenging groups reveals just how permeable the American system is.

To see which groups make it, and what factors contribute to their success, I picked a random sample from the hundreds of challenging groups that surfaced in America between 1800 and 1945. I drew the line after World War II because the outcomes for current protest groups are still unclear. I defined a challenging group by its relationship to two targets: its *antagonist*, the object of actual or planned attempts at influence; and its *constituency*, the individuals or organizations whose resources and energy the group seeks to organize and mobilize.

A challenging group must meet two problems at the same time. Unlike an established interest group such as the American Medical Association, its membership is not already organized. A challenging group cannot send out a call to action and expect that most of its loyal members will follow it into battle; it must create this loyalty from scratch. Of course, many of today's established groups went through a period of challenge and we studied some of them during their early years.

Second, a challenging group must demand some change that its own membership cannot provide. A messianic group that offered salvation to members would not qualify unless the group wanted changes in laws or social institutions as well.

A challenge ends when one of three events occurs: the group disbands; the group stops trying to win friends and influence people, even though it continues to exist; or the group's major antagonists accept it as a legitimate spokesman for its constituency.

I drew my sample from an exhaustive list of social movements and formal organizations. After eliminating those that did not fit the definition of a challenging group, we were left with 64 valid groups, and of these we were able to get sufficient information on 53.

CHALLENGES FROM BICYCLES TO BIRTH CONTROL

The 53 groups are a representative sample of challenging groups in American history. . . . Some failed, some won. Some had quite humble goals; the League of American Wheelmen formed in 1880 to get the right to bicycle on public highways. Others sought nothing less than revolution. Some groups, such as the American Birth Control League, started radical and became establishment. Others, like the Night Riders, appear more disreputable today than they probably seemed then.

Twenty of the groups were occupationally based, such as the American Federation of Teachers; 17 were reform oriented, such as the Federal Suffrage Association; ten were socialist, such as the International Workingmen's Association (the First International); and six were some brand of right-wing or nativist group, such as the Christian Front Against Communism or the German-American Bund.

Definitions of success are complicated. We tried many and settled on two summary measures. The first focuses on whether other power holders came to accept the group as a valid representative of legitimate interests. The second measure focuses on whether the group gained new advantages for its constituents and beneficiaries and accomplished its goals.

The combination of these two definitions of success means that a group's efforts may have four possible outcomes. It may win many new advantages and full acceptance from its antagonists (complete success); no advantages but acceptance (cooptation); many advantages but no acceptance (preemption); or neither advantages nor acceptance (failure). More than half of the groups, 58 percent, were successful on one measure or the other; only 38 percent were successful in both meanings.

Next, I explored the strategies and characteristics of the groups to see why some succeeded and others failed. I began with the touchiest issue of all, violence.

Most of the groups had no violence at all in their history but 15 of them participated in some kind of violent exchange. It is misleading, however, to assume that these groups used violence as a tactic. In some cases, they were attacked by the police or by mobs with little or no provocation; in other cases, pitched battles took place but it is no easy matter to know who started in. Rather than trying to make that judgment, we divided the groups into two types—eight activist groups who, whether or not they initiated a fight, were willing to give and take if one started. The other seven were passive recipients; they were attacked and could not, or simply did not, fight back.

THE SUCCESS OF THE UNRULY

In the case of violence, it appears better to give than to receive if you want to succeed in American politics. The activist groups that fought back or, in some cases, initiated violence, had a higher-than-average success rate; six of the eight won new advantages and five of the six were eventually accepted as well. The nonviolent recipients of attack, however, lost out completely. None of them met their goals, although one, the Dairymen's League was coopted.

Violence is even more certain to reap benefits when the group's goals are limited and when the group does not aim to displace its antagonists but rather to coexist with them. When I eliminated revolutionary groups that aimed to

328

*Chapter 17
Social
Movements and
Collective
Behavior*

displace the opposition, I found that *every* violence user was successful in winning new advantages and every violence recipient was unsuccessful.

Several groups tried a strategy that we might call speaking loudly and carrying a small stick. They advocated violence but never actually used it. The Communist Labor Party, the Revolutionary Workers League, and the German-American Bund roared a good deal but they never bit. This is the least effective strategy of all, for such groups pay the cost of violence without gaining its benefits. They are threatening but they are weak, which makes them an easy target for repression.

Violence is not the only kind of high-pressure tactic that brings success. Ten groups used other unruly strategies on their opposition; such as strikes, boycotts, and efforts to humiliate or embarrass their antagonists. For example, A. Philip Randolph's March on Washington Committee threatened a mass march on the Capitol in the spring of 1941 to push President Franklin D. Roosevelt into a more active role in ending racial discrimination in employment. The government was then arousing the country for war with appeals that contrasted U.S. democracy with Nazi racism, so such a march would have been a considerable embarrassment to the administration. A week before the march was scheduled to happen, President Roosevelt promised a policy of non-discrimination in all federal hiring and, by executive order, created a Fair Employment Practices Committee to carry out this policy.

The League of Deliverance used the boycott against businesses that hired Chinese workers. They threatened worse. They notified "offenders" that after six days of non-compliance, their district would be declared "dangerous. . . . Should the Chinese remain within the proclaimed district after the expiration of . . . 30 days, the General Executive Committee will be required to abate the danger in whatever manner seems best to them." The league, however, never had call to go beyond the boycott tactic. By firing its Chinese employees, a business could buy peace with the league; many did just that.

Forceful tactics are associated with success, as violence is. Eight out of the ten groups that applied such pressures were accepted and won new advantages, a percentage that is twice as great as the percentage for groups that avoided such tactics.

VIOLENCE COMES FROM CONFIDENCE

These data undermine the pluralist argument that violence is the product of frustration, desperation, and weakness, that it is an act of last resort by those who are unable to attract a following and achieve their goals. Violence, pluralists assume, is unsuccessful as a tactic because it simply increases the hostility around it and invites the legitimate action of authorities against it.

My interpretation is nearly the opposite. Violence grows from an impatience born of confidence and a sense of rising power. It occurs when the challenging group senses that the surrounding community will condone it, when hostility toward the *victim* renders it a relatively safe strategy. In this sense, violence is as much a symptom of success as a cause.

Groups use violence to prevent being destroyed and to deter authorities from attack; less often, they use violence to gain a specific objective. Successful groups almost never used it as a primary tactic. Typically, the primary means of influence were strikes, bargaining, and propaganda. Violence, in short, is the spice of protest, not the meat and potatoes.

The size of the violent groups supports this interpretation. The active groups tend to be large; only one of the eight, the Night Riders, had fewer than 10,000 members, while five of the seven recipients of violence were this small. Such numbers seem more likely to breed confidence and impatience than desperation.

The successful group in American politics is not the polite petitioner who carefully observes all the rules. It is the rambunctious fighter, one with limited goals, that can elbow its way into the arena. But the willingness to fight is not enough. A group must be *able* to fight; it needs organization and discipline to focus its energies.

A challenging group faces antagonists that have control over their members, as established bureaucracies do. Challenging groups can overcome this disadvantage by adopting the structure of established organizations. They can deal on more equal terms if they are able to create their own apparatus of internal control—if they can turn *members* into *agents*.

Even when challenging groups have a committed membership, however, they may still lack unity of command. It is not enough to have agents if they have no direction, if some factions shout, "March!" and others cry, "Wait!"

THE READINESS IS ALL

One may convert members into soldiers, but soldiers fight civil wars as well as foreign ones. Thus a group needs a bureaucratic structure to help become ready for action, and centralized power to help it reach unified decisions.

I considered a group *bureaucratic* if it had three characteristics. It must have a constitution or charter that states the purpose of the group and rules for its operation; an ideological manifesto is not enough. It must keep a formal list of its members, which it distinguishes from mere sympathizers. And it must have at least three internal divisions; for example, executives, chapter heads, rank and file.

Twenty-four of the groups met all three criteria, and these were more likely than non-bureaucratic groups to win acceptance (71 percent to 28 percent) and new advantages (62 percent to 38 percent).

I defined a group as *centralized* if power resided in a single leader or central committee and local chapters had little autonomy. Slightly more than half of the groups, 28, had such a centralized structure; 19 of these had a single, dominant leader, and nine had some form of collective leadership such as a national board or an executive committee. The rest of the groups had no one center of power.

Centralization is unrelated to bureaucracy as defined above; half of the bureaucratic groups and half of the nonbureaucratic groups had centralized

330

*Chapter 17
Social
Movements and
Collective
Behavior*

power structures. Bureaucracy and centralization each contribute something to success but it is the combination that really does the trick. Groups that were both bureaucratic *and* centralized had the best chance of achieving their goals; 75 percent of them were successful. Groups that were neither bureaucratic nor centralized had very little chance of winning anything. Only one, Federal Suffrage Association, defied the odds and won both acceptance and advantages. The FSA was only one, and hardly the most important, of the groups that fought for women's suffrage. It achieved its objective, but it was neither alone nor always in the center of the struggle.

Thus modern protest groups that attempt to distribute authority among all their members and avoid hierarchy should take heed. If they are going to be involved with struggles with the authorities, they will have a difficult time avoiding factions in their ranks and reaching their goals.

JUNGLE LAWS VS. POLITE POLITICS

The pluralist image of orderly contest is a half-truth. It fits well enough the bargaining and give-and-take that goes on inside the political arena. But there is another kind of contest going on at the same time between those outside the arena and those already inside. This conflict is a great deal less orderly than what happens in the lobbies, the board rooms, and the other corridors of established power.

This second locus of conflict has its own rules too, but they are more like the laws of the jungle. Whatever differences the powerful may have among themselves, they are on the same team in the struggle between insiders and outsiders. Challengers who try to play by the rules that members observe among themselves should realize two things. Insiders won't apply their rules to outsiders; and outsiders, being poor in resources, have little to offer the powerful in an alliance.

Challengers do better when they realize that they are in a political combat situation. They don't need to look for a fight, but they had better be ready to participate in one if the occasion arises. They must therefore be organized like a combat group—with willing, committed people who know what to do, and a command structure that can keep its people out of the wrong fight at the wrong time.

But this advice really only applies to groups with limited goals. I included revolutionary groups in my sample but it should come as no surprise that none of them were successful. I can't say what makes for success among such groups since I had no successes to compare with the failures. A more complete picture of the successful group is one that is ready and willing to fight like hell for goals that can be met without overturning the system.

Perhaps it is disconcerting to discover that the meek do not inherit the earth—or at least that part of it presided over by the American political system. But those rambunctious groups that fight their way into the political arena escape misfortune because they are prepared to withstand counterattack, and to make it costly to those who would keep them out.

CHAPTER 18 Modernization and Social Change

18.1 IMMANUEL WALLERSTEIN

The Rise and Future Demise of the World Capitalist System

Immanuel Wallerstein (b. 1930), political sociologist, is the Distinguished Professor of Sociology and director of the Fernand Braudel Center for the Study of Economics, Historical Systems, and Civilizations at the State University of New York at Binghamton. He is the author of *The Capitalist World-Economy* (Cambridge University Press, 1979) and *Africa and the Modern World* (African World Press, 1986).

In the following excerpt, Wallerstein argues that macrosocial changes must be interpreted from a world-system perspective—as opposed to a developmental perspective—in which change is perceived as a process of organic development and progress. He points out that the economic structure of underdeveloped countries is not an earlier stage in the transition to development, but a reflection of a society's peripheral involvement in the world economy as simply a producer of raw material.

The essential feature of a capitalist world-economy is production for sale in a market to obtain maximum profit. Production is increased and innovations are implemented only if they increase profits. But, surprisingly, Wallerstein argues that communist countries can be part of the capitalist world-system.

Wallerstein sees the capitalist world-system as riddled with contradictions. Even the current consolidation of the capitalist world-economy does not ensure its survival. Although the demise of capitalism is not an immediate threat, it is a possibility, along with the creation of a new kind of world-system: a socialist world-government.

Wallerstein's world-systems theory has become the dominant paradigm in sociology for studying macro changes in developing countries. The recent events in Eastern Europe and the USSR will lead to revisions in the analysis of the role of these areas in the world system, but they also make Wallerstein's framework even more relevant than ever.

Key Concept: the capitalist world-economy

*I*f we are to talk of stages . . . and we should talk of stages, it must be stages of social systems, that is, of totalities. And the only totalities that exist or have historically existed are minisystems and world-systems, and in the nineteenth and twentieth centuries there has been only one world-system in existence, the capitalist world-economy.

We take the defining characteristic of a social system to be the existence within it of a division of labor, such that the various sectors or areas within are dependent upon economic exchange with others for the smooth and continuous provisioning of the needs of the area. Such economic exchange can clearly exist without a common political structure and even more obviously without sharing the same culture.

A minisystem is an entity that has within it a complete division of labor, and a single cultural framework. Such systems were found only in very simple agricultural or hunting and gathering societies. Such minisystems no longer exist in the world. Furthermore, there were fewer in the past than is often asserted, since any such system that became tied to an empire by the payment of tribute as "protection costs" ceased by that fact to be a "system," no longer having a self-contained division of labor. For such an area, the payment of tribute marked a shift, in Polanyi's language, from being a reciprocal economy to participating in a larger redistributive economy.[1]

Leaving aside the now defunct minisystems, the only kind of social system is a world-system, which we define quite simply as a unit with a single division of labor and multiple cultural systems. It follows logically that there can, however, be two varieties of such world-systems, one with a common political system and one without. We shall designate these respectively as world-empires and world-economies.

It turns out empirically that world-economies have historically been unstable structures leading either toward disintegration or conquest by one group and hence transformation into a world-empire. Examples of such world-empires emerging from world-economies are all the so-called great civilizations of premodern times, such as China, Egypt, Rome (each at appropriate periods of its history). On the other hand, the so-called nineteenth-century empires, such as Great Britain or France, were not world-empires at all, but nation-states with colonial appendages operating within the framework of a world-economy.

World-empires were basically redistributive in economic form. No doubt they bred clusters of merchants who engaged in economic exchange (primarily long-distance trade), but such clusters, however large, were a minor part of the total economy and not fundamentally determinative of its fate. Such long-distance trade tended to be, as Polanyi argues, "administered trade" and not market trade, utilizing "ports of trade."

It was only with the emergence of the modern world-economy in six-teenth-century Europe that we saw the full development and economic pre-dominance of market trade. This was the system called capitalism. Capitalism and a world-economy (that is, a single division of labor but multiple polities and cultures) are obverse sides of the same coin. One does not cause the other. We are merely defining the same indivisible phenomenon by different characteristics. . . .

We are, as you see, coming to the essential feature of a capitalist world-economy, which is production for sale in a market in which the object is to realize the maximum profit. In such a system production is constantly ex-panded as long as further production is profitable, and men constantly innovate new ways of producing things that will expand the profit margin. . . .

If capitalism is a mode of production, production for profit in a market, then we ought, I should have thought, to look to whether or not such production was or was not occurring. It turns out in fact that it was, and in a very substantial form. Most of this production, however, was not industrial production. What was happening in Europe from the sixteenth to the eigh-teenth centuries is that over a large geographical area going from Poland in the northeast westward and southward throughout Europe and including large parts of the Western Hemisphere as well, there grew up a world-economy with a single division of labor within which there was a world market, for which men produced largely agricultural products for sale and profit. I would think the simplest thing to do would be to call this agricultural capitalism. . . .

By a series of accidents—historical, ecological, geographic—northwest Europe was better situated in the sixteenth century to diversify its agricultural specialization and add to it certain industries (such as textiles, shipbuilding, and metal wares) than were other parts of Europe. Northwest Europe emerged as the core area of this world-economy, specializing in agricultural production of higher skill levels, which favored (again for reasons too complex to develop) tenancy and wage labor as the modes of labor control. Eastern Europe and the Western Hemisphere became peripheral areas specializing in export of grains, bullion, wood, cotton, sugar—all of which favored the use of slavery and coerced cash-crop labor as the modes of labor control. Mediterranean Europe emerged as the semiperipheral area of this world-economy specializing in high-cost industrial products (for example, silks) and credit and specie transactions, which had as a consequence in the agricultural arena sharecropping as the mode of labor control and little export to other areas.

The three structural positions in a world-economy—core, periphery, and semiperiphery—had become stabilized by about 1640. How certain areas be-came one and not the other is a long story.[2] The key fact is that given slightly different starting points, the interests of various local groups converged in northwest Europe, leading to the development of strong state mechanisms, and diverged sharply in the peripheral areas, leading to very weak ones. Once we get a difference in the strength of the state machineries, we get the operation of "unequal exchange,"[3] which is enforced by strong states on weak ones, by core states on peripheral areas. Thus capitalism involves not only appropriation of the surplus value by an owner from a laborer, but an appropriation of surplus of the whole world-economy by core areas. And this was as true in the stage of agricultural capitalism as it is in the stage of industrial capitalism. . . .

Capitalism was from the beginning an affair of the world-economy and not of nation-states. It is a misreading of the situation to claim that it is only in the twentieth century that capitalism has become "worldwide," although this claim is frequently made in various writings, particularly by Marxists. . . . Capital has never allowed its aspirations to be determined by national boundaries in a capitalist world-economy, and that the creation of "national" barriers—generically, mercantilism—has historically been a defensive mechanism of capitalists located in states which are one level below the high point of strength in the system. . . . In the process a large number of countries create national economic barriers whose consequences often last beyond their initial objectives. At this later point in the process the very same capitalists who pressed their national governments to impose the restrictions now find these restrictions constraining. This is not an "internationalization" of "national" capital. This is simply a new political demand by certain sectors of the capitalist classes who have at all points in time sought to maximize their profits within the real economic market, that of the world-economy.

If this is so, then what meaning does it have to talk of structural positions within this economy and identify states as being in one of these positions? And why talk of three positions, inserting that of "semiperiphery" in between the widely used concepts of core and periphery? The state machineries of the core states were strengthened to meet the needs of capitalist landowners and their merchant allies. . . .

The strengthening of the state machineries in core areas has as its direct counterpart the decline of the state machineries in peripheral areas. . . . In peripheral countries, the interests of the capitalist landowners lie in an opposite direction from those of the local commercial bourgeoisie. Their interests lie in maintaining an open economy to maximize their profit from world-market trade (no restrictions in exports and access to lower-cost industrial products from core countries) and in elimination of the commercial bourgeoisie in favor of outside merchants (who pose no local political threat). Thus, in terms of the state, the coalition which strengthened it in core countries was precisely absent.

The second reason, which has become ever more operative over the history of the modern world-system, is that the strength of the state machinery in core states is a function of the weakness of other state machineries. Hence intervention of outsiders via war, subversion, and diplomacy is the lot of peripheral states.

All this seems very obvious. I repeat it only in order to make clear two points. One cannot reasonably explain the strength of various state machineries at specific moments of the history of the modern world-system primarily in terms of a genetic-cultural line of argumentation, but rather in terms of the structural role a country plays in the world-economy at that moment in time. . . .

The second point we wish to make about the structural differences of core and periphery is that they are not comprehensible unless we realize that there is a third structural position: that of the semiperiphery. This is not the result merely of establishing arbitrary cutting-points on a continuum of characteristics. . . . The semiperiphery is needed to make a capitalist world-economy run smoothly. Both kinds of world-system, the world-empire with a redistributive economy and the world-economy with a capitalist market economy, involve markedly unequal distribution of rewards. Thus, logically, there is immediately posed the question of how it is possible politically for such a system to persist. Why do not the majority who are exploited simply overwhelm the minority who draw disproportionate benefits? . . .

There have been three major mechanisms that have enabled world-systems to retain relative political stability (not in terms of the particular groups who will play the leading roles in the system, but in terms of systemic survival itself). One obviously is the concentration of military strength in the hands of the dominant forces. The moralities of this obviously vary with the technology, and there are, to be sure, political prerequisites for such a concentration, but nonetheless sheer force is no doubt a central consideration.

A second mechanism is the pervasiveness of an ideological commitment to the system as a whole. I do not mean what has often been termed the "legitimation" of a system, because that term has been used to imply that the lower strata of a system feel some affinity with or loyalty toward the rulers, and I doubt that this has ever been a significant factor in the survival of world-systems. I mean rather the degree to which the staff or cadres of the system (and I leave this term deliberately vague) feel that their own well-being is wrapped up in the survival of the system as such and the competence of its leaders. It is this staff which not only propagates the myths; it is they who believe them.

But neither force nor the ideological commitment of the staff would suffice were it not for the division of the majority into a larger lower stratum and a smaller middle stratum. Both the revolutionary call for polarization as a strategy of change and the liberal encomium to consensus as the basis of the liberal polity reflect this proposition. The import is far wider than its use in the analysis of contemporary political problems suggests. It is the normal condition of either kind of world-system to have a three-layered structure. When and if this ceases to be the case, the world-system disintegrates.

In a world-empire, the middle stratum is in fact accorded the role of maintaining the marginally desirable long-distance luxury trade, while the upper stratum concentrates its resources on controlling the military machinery which can collect the tribute, the crucial mode of redistributing surplus. By providing, however, for an access to a limited portion of the surplus to urbanized elements who alone, in premodern societies, could contribute political cohesiveness to isolated clusters of primary producers, the upper stratum effectively buys off the potential leadership of coordinated revolt. And by denying access to political rights for this commercial-urban middle stratum, it makes them constantly vulnerable to confiscatory measures whenever their economic profits become sufficiently swollen so that they might begin to create for themselves military strength.

In a world-economy, such "cultural" stratification is not so simple, because the absence of a single political system means the concentration of economic roles vertically rather than horizontally throughout the system. The solution then is to have three *kinds* of states, with pressures for cultural homogenization within each of them—thus, besides the upper stratum of core states and the lower stratum of peripheral states, there is a middle stratum of semiperipheral ones.

This semiperiphery is then assigned as it were a specific economic role, but the reason is less economic than political. That is to say, one might make a good case that the world-economy as an economy would function every bit as well without a semiperiphery. But it would be far less *politically* stable, for it would mean a polarized world-system. The existence of the third category means precisely that the upper stratum is not faced with the *unified* opposition of all the others because the *middle* stratum is both exploited and exploiter. It follows that the specific economic role is not all that important and has thus changed through the various historical stages of the modern world-system. . . .

The functioning then of a capitalist world-economy requires that groups pursue their economic interests within a single world market while seeking to distort this market for their benefit by organizing to exert influence on states, some of which are far more powerful than others but none of which controls the world market in its entirety. Of course, we shall find on closer inspection that there are periods where one state is relatively quite powerful and other periods where power is more diffuse and contested, permitting weaker states broader ranges of action. We can talk then of the relative tightness or looseness of the world-system as an important variable and seek to analyze why this dimension tends to be cyclical in nature, as it seems to have been for several hundred years.

We are now in a position to look at the historical evolution of this capitalist world-economy itself and analyze the degree to which it is fruitful to talk of distinct stages in its evolution as a system. The emergence of the European world-economy in the "long" sixteenth century (1450–1640) was made possible by an historical conjuncture: on those long-term trends which were the culmination of what has been sometimes described as the "crisis of feudalism" was superimposed a more immediate cyclical crisis plus climatic changes, all of which created a dilemma that could only be resolved by a geographic expansion of the division of labor. Furthermore, the balance of intersystem forces was such as to make this realizable. Thus a geographic expansion did take place in conjunction with a demographic expansion and an upward price rise. . . .

Each of the states or potential states within the European world-economy was quickly in the race to bureaucratize, to raise a standing army, to homogenize its culture, to diversify its economic activities. By 1640, those in northwest Europe had succeeded in establishing themselves as the core states: Spain and the northern Italian city-states declined into being semiperipheral; northeastern Europe and Iberian America had become the periphery. At this point, those in semiperipheral status had reached it by virtue of decline from a former more pre-eminent status.

It was the system-wide recession of 1650–1730 that consolidated the European world-economy and opened stage two of the modern world-economy. For the recession forced retrenchment, and the decline in relative surplus allowed room for only one core state to survive. The mode of struggle was mercantilism. . . . In this struggle England first ousted the Netherlands from its commercial primacy and then resisted successfully France's attempt to catch up. As England began to speed up the process of industrialization after 1760, there was one last attempt of those capitalist forces located in France to break the imminent British hegemony. This attempt was expressed first in the French Revolution's replacement of the cadres of the regime and then in Napoleon's continental blockade. But it failed.

Stage three of the capitalist world-economy begins, then, a stage of industrial rather than of agricultural capitalism. Henceforth, industrial production is no longer a minor aspect of the world market but comprises an ever larger percentage of world gross production—and even more important, of world gross surplus. This involves a whole series of consequences for the world-system.

First of all, it led to the further geographic expansion of the European world-economy to include now the whole of the globe. This was in part the result of its technological feasibility both in terms of improved military firepower and improved shipping facilities which made regular trade sufficiently inexpensive to be viable. But, in addition, industrial production *required* access to raw materials of a nature and in a quantity such that the needs could not be supplied within the former boundaries. At first, however, the search for new markets was not a primary consideration in the geographic expansion since the new markets were more readily available within the old boundaries, as we shall see.

The geographic expansion of the European world-economy meant the elimination of other world-systems as well as the absorption of the remaining minisystems. The most important world-system up to then outside of the European world-economy, Russia, entered in semiperipheral status, the consequence of the strength of its state machinery (including its army) and the degree of industrialization already achieved in the eighteenth century. The independences in the Latin American countries did nothing to change their peripheral status. They merely eliminated the last vestiges of Spain's semiperipheral role and ended pockets of noninvolvement in the world-economy in the interior of Latin America. Asia and Africa were absorbed into the periphery in the nineteenth century, although Japan, because of the combination of the strength of its state machinery, the poverty of its resource base (which led to a certain disinterest on the part of world capitalist forces), and its geographic remoteness from the core areas, was able quickly to graduate into semiperipheral status. . . .

The creation of vast new areas as the periphery of the expanded world-economy made possible a shift in the role of some other areas. Specifically, both the United States and Germany (as it came into being) combined formerly peripheral and semiperipheral regions. The manufacturing sector in each was able to gain political ascendancy, as the peripheral subregions became less economically crucial to the world-economy. Mercantilism now became the major tool of semiperipheral countries seeking to become core countries, thus still performing a function analogous to that of the mercantilist drives of the late seventeenth and eighteenth centuries in England and France. To be sure, the struggle of semiperipheral countries to "industrialize" varied in the degree to which it succeeded in the period before World War I: all the way in the United States, only partially in Germany, not at all in Russia.

The internal structure of core states also changed fundamentally under industrial capitalism. For a core area, industrialism involved divesting itself of substantially all agricultural activities (except that in the twentieth century further mechanization was to create a new form of working the land that was so highly mechanized as to warrant the appellation industrial). Thus whereas, in the period 1700–1740, England not only was Europe's leading industrial exporter but was also Europe's leading agricultural exporter—this was at a high point in the economy-wide recession—by 1900, less than 10 percent of England's population was engaged in agricultural pursuits.

At first under industrial capitalism, the core exchanged manufactured products against the periphery's agricultural products—hence, Britain from 1815 to 1873 was the "workshop of the world." Even to those semiperipheral countries that had some manufacture (France, Germany, Belgium, the United States, Britain) in this period supplied about half their needs in manufactured goods. As, however, the mercantilist practices of this latter group both cut Britain off from outlets and even created competition for Britain in sales to peripheral areas, a competition which led to the late nineteenth-century "scramble for Africa," the world division of labor was reallocated to ensure a new special role for the core: less the provision of the manufactures, more the provision of the machines to make the manufactures as well as the provision of infrastructure (especially, in this period, railroads).

The rise of manufacturing created for the first time under capitalism a large-scale urban proletariat. And in the consequence for the first time there arose what Michels has called the "anticapitalist mass spirit,"[4] which was translated into concrete organizational forms (trade unions, socialist parties). This development intruded a new factor as threatening to the stability of the states and of the capitalist forces now so securely in control of them as the earlier centrifugal thrusts of regional anticapitalist landed elements had been in the seventeenth century.

At the same time that the bourgeoisies of the core countries were faced by this threat to the internal stability of their state structures, they were simultaneously faced with the economic crisis of the latter third of the nineteenth century resulting from the more rapid increase of agricultural production (and indeed of light manufactures) than the expansion of a potential market for these goods. Some of the surplus would have to be redistributed to someone to allow these goods to be bought and the economic machinery to return to smooth operation. By expanding the purchasing power of the industrial proletariat of the core countries, the world-economy was unburdened simultaneously of two problems: the bottleneck of demand, and the unsettling "class conflict" of the core states—hence, the social liberalism or welfare-state ideology that arose just at that point in time.

World War I was, as men of the time observed, the end of an era; and the Russian Revolution of October 1917 the beginning of a new one—our stage four. This stage was, to be sure, a stage of revolutionary turmoil but it also was, in a seeming paradox, the stage of the *consolidation* of the industrial capitalist world-economy. The Russian Revolution was essentially that of a semiperipheral country whose internal balance of forces had been just such that as of the late nineteenth century it began on a decline toward a peripheral status. . . . The Revolution brought to power a group of state managers who reversed each one of these trends by using the classic technique of mercantilist semiwithdrawal from the world-economy. In the process of doing this, the now USSR mobilized considerable popular support, especially in the urban sector. At the end of World War II, Russia was reinstated as a very strong member of the semiperiphery and could begin to seek full core status. . . .

It was World War II that enabled the United States for a brief period (1945–1965) to attain the same level of primacy as Britain had in the first part of the nineteenth century. United States growth in this period was spectacular and created a great need for expanded market outlets. The cold war closure denied not only the USSR but Eastern Europe to U.S. exports. And the Chinese Revolution meant that this region, which had been destined for much exploitative activity, was also cut off. Three alternative areas were available and each was pursued with assiduity. First, Western Europe had to be rapidly "reconstructed," and it was the Marshall Plan which thus allowed this area to play a primary role in the expansion of world productivity. Secondly, Latin America became the reserve of U.S. investment from which now Britain and Germany were completely cut off. Thirdly, Southern Asia, the Middle East, and Africa had to be decolonized. On the one hand, this was necessary in order to reduce the share of the surplus taken by the Western European intermediaries, as Canning covertly supported the Latin American revolutionaries against Spain in the 1820s.[5] But also, these countries had to be decolonized in order to mobilize productive potential in a way that had never been achieved in the colonial era. Colonial rule after all had been an *inferior* mode of relationship of core and periphery, one occasioned by the strenuous late-nineteenth-century conflict among industrial states but one no longer desirable from the point of view of the new hegemonic power.[6]

But a world capitalist economy does not permit true imperium. Charles V could not succeed in his dream of world-empire. The Pax Britannica stimulated its own demise. So too did the Pax Americana. . . .

Such a decline in U.S. state hegemony has actually *increased* the freedom of action of capitalist enterprises, the larger of which have now taken the form of multinational corporations which are able to maneuver against state bureaucracies whenever the national politicians become too responsive to internal worker pressures. Whether some effective links can be established between multinational corporations, presently limited to operating in certain areas, and the USSR remains to be seen, but it is by no means impossible. . . .

Are we not seeing the emergence of a political structure for *semiperipheral* nations adapted to stage four of the capitalist world-system? The fact that all enterprises are nationalized in these countries does not make the participation of these enterprises in the world-economy one that does not conform to the mode of operation of a capitalist market system: seeking increased efficiency of production in order to realize a maximum price on sales, thus achieving a more favorable allocation of the surplus of the world-economy. . . .

What then have been the consequences for the world-system of the emergence of many states in which there is no private ownership of the basic means of production? To some extent, this has meant an internal reallocation of consumption. It has certainly undermined the ideological justification in world capitalism, both by showing the political vulnerability of capitalist entrepreneurs and by demonstrating that private ownership is irrelevant to the rapid expansion of industrial productivity. But to the extent that it has raised the ability of the new semiperipheral areas to enjoy a larger share of the world surplus, it has once again depolarized the world, recreating the triad of strata that has been a fundamental element in the survival of the world-system.

Finally, in the peripheral areas of the world-economy, both the continued economic expansion of the core (even though the core is seeing some reallocation of surplus internal to it) and the new strength of the semiperiphery has led to a weakening of the political and hence economic position of the peripheral areas. The pundits note that "the gap is getting wider," but thus far no one has succeeded in doing much about it, and it is not clear that there are very many in whose interests it would be to do so. Far from a strengthening of state authority, in many parts of the world we are witnessing the same kind of deterioration Poland knew in the sixteenth century, a deterioration of which the frequency of military coups is only one of many signposts. And all of this leads us to conclude that stage four has been the stage of the *consolidation* of the capitalist world-economy.

Consolidation, however, does not mean the absence of contradictions and does not mean the likelihood of long-term survival. . . .

There are two fundamental contradictions, it seems to me, involved in the workings of the capitalist world-system. In the first place, there is the contradiction to which the nineteenth-century Marxian corpus pointed, which I would phrase as follows: whereas in the short run the maximization of profit requires maximizing the withdrawal of surplus from immediate consumption of the majority, in the long run the continued production of surplus requires a mass demand which can only be created by redistributing the surplus withdrawn. Since these two considerations move in opposite directions (a "contradiction"), the system has constant crises which in the long run both weaken it and make the game for those with privilege less worth playing.

The second fundamental contradiction, to which Mao's concept of socialism as process points, is the following: whenever the tenants of privilege seek to coopt an oppositional movement by including them in a minor share of the privilege, they may no doubt eliminate opponents in the short run; but they also up the ante for the next oppositional movement created in the next crisis of the world-economy. Thus the cost of "co-optation" rises ever higher and the advantages of co-option seem ever less worthwhile.

There are today no socialist systems in the world-economy any more than there are feudal systems because there is only *one* world-system. It is a world-economy and it is by definition capitalist in form. Socialism involves the creation of a new kind of *world*-system, neither a redistributive world-empire nor a capitalist world-economy but a socialist world-government. I don't see this projection as being in the least utopian but I also don't feel its institution is imminent. It will be the outcome of a long struggle in forms that may be familiar and perhaps in very few forms, that will take place in *all* the areas of the world-economy (Mao's continual "class struggle"). Governments may be in the hands of persons, groups, or movements sympathetic to this transformation but *states* as such are neither progressive nor reactionary. It is movements and forces that deserve such evaluative judgments.

NOTES

1. See Karl Polanyi, "The Economy as Instituted Process," in Karl Polanyi, Conrad M. Arsenberg, and Harry W. Pearson, eds., *Trade and Market in Early Empire* (Glencoe: Free Press, 1957), pp. 243–70.
2. I give a brief account of this in "Three Paths of National Development in the Sixteenth Century," *Studies in Comparative International Development*, 7:2 (Summer 1972): 95–101.
3. See Arghiri Emmanual, *Unequal Exchange* (New York: Monthly Review Press, 1972).
4. Robert Michels, "The Origins of the Anti-Capitalist Mass Spirit," *Man in Contemporary Society* (New York: Columbia University Press, 1955), vol. 1, pp. 740–65.
5. See William W. Kaufman, *British Policy and the Independence of Latin America, 1804–28* (New Haven: Yale University Press, 1951).
6. Cf. Catherine Coquery-Vidrovitch, "De l'impérialisme britannique à l'impérialisme contemporaine—l'avatar colonial," *L'Homme et la sociéte* 18 (October–December 1970): 61–90.

The Soviet Union's Quiet Revolution

Theorists of social change have widely debated on the importance of ideas and belief systems in causing basic structural transformations in society. In the following excerpt, Blair A. Ruble discusses social change in the Soviet Union from the perspective that beliefs play a major role in societal change. He argues that the changes instituted by Mikhail Gorbachev when he became general secretary of the Communist party in 1985 began a generation ago with a "revolution of the mind" that was associated with numerous changes in Soviet society.

Ruble describes the Soviet working class of the 1920s as a homogeneous group of illiterate peasants with a conservative and authoritarian mind-set that, over several decades, became an educated and highly differentiated labor force. Simultaneously, changes were taking place among the white-collar and professional groups as well. As a result, the educational achievements, employment patterns, and cultural tastes of the Soviet population came to resemble the non-Soviet industrial world. According to Ruble, the similarities between the Soviet Union and other societies in transition from authoritarian to democratic regimes became evident *before* Gorbachev rose to power.

Ruble (b. 1949) is the director of the Kennan Institute for Advanced Russian Studies at the Woodrow Wilson International Center for Scholars in Washington, D.C. A scholar of the former USSR and Russia, he has published extensively on the ethnic, political, and social organization of the former USSR. His 1981 work *Soviet Trade Unions: Their Development in the 1970's* (Cambridge University Press) is considered to be the best extant study in the United States. And his 1989 book *Leningrad: Shaping a Soviet City* (University of California Press) is a major work on urban policy and a profound lesson on the impact of socioeconomic and political forces on the functioning of the city of Leningrad.

Key Concept: revolution of the mind

I would like to argue that the perestroika launched by Mikhail Gorbachev when he emerged as the Communist Party's General Secretary in 1985, like Quebec's Quiet Revolution, began a generation or more before with a "revolution of the mind" that accompanied the Soviet Union's transition from a rural to an urban society. Consequently, we can not begin to appreciate the depth of change that has taken place in the USSR without looking back to the 1950s, 1960s, and 1970s. . . .

BREZHNEV'S QUIET REVOLUTION

The Soviet Union has witnessed a prolonged process of social differentiation and fragmentation during the past several decades. This coming apart of traditional society may be seen in such extensive social changes as increasingly specialized employment patterns, reduced opportunities for social mobility across group boundaries, rising levels of education for all social groups, urbanization (meaning not only rural-to-urban migration but also the formation of social strata that have been urbanized across one or more generations), complex ethnic relations and interactions among nationality groups, a shift in population growth to the south and the east, and the professionalization of the female labor force. Many of these processes find their origins in the immediate postwar period. They merged during the period when Leonid Brezhnev served as the Communist Party's General Secretary in a manner that emphasized the ever more diverse nature of Soviet society. These developments were masked by Brezhnev's complacent style and rhetoric.

Change in and of itself does not become politically significant until and unless the political system proves incapable of controlling and coordinating emerging patterns of social interaction. This was precisely what happened during Brezhnev's tenure as General Secretary. By the late 1970s, the evolution of economic and political institutions had failed to keep pace with a process of social change that was creating entire new social groups—the working middle class, young urban professionals, specialized nationality elites, and the like. This lag led to unprecedented social tensions and conflicts.

Individual space consequently expanded. New room for personal action was evidenced in the robust second economy of the period, the flowering second cultural life, and even a nascent second political system (as evidenced by dissent). When viewed as the outgrowth of the Soviet Union's Quiet Revolution that took place while Brezhnev was in power, perestroika becomes an at times frantic effort on the part of the leadership of the Communist Party to capture for the regime those energies released by deep-seated social differentiation that had already taken place *before* Gorbachev came to power. To illustrate this point, it might be helpful to explore briefly some of the changes that had been taking place within the Soviet working class, white-collar strata, and ethnic groups.

THE NEW WORKING MIDDLE CLASS

During the 1950s, the Soviet working class had become remarkably homogeneous. Fresh from the countryside, or just one generation removed, Soviet workers remained under-educated and under-skilled. Indeed, with very few exceptions, workers had little more than a primary education. Those workers who attained a higher level of educational achievement were often promoted into the ranks of the white-collar labor force.

As the Soviet Union moved towards the 1980s, not only did the quantity and quality of education increase for the Soviet population as a whole, but the level of educational achievement among workers became more differentiated. On the one hand, many workers from the 1950s who had only a primary education were still employed in the industrial work force. On the other, a new generation of workers had grown up during a period in which two-thirds of the general and nearly three-quarters of the urban populations had at least some secondary education. The spread in working class educational achievement expanded during the Soviet Union's Quiet Revolution of the 1950s, 1960s, and 1970s, from an educational profile encompassing almost solely primary education, to one reaching from incomplete primary school through some form of post-secondary training. The percentage of Soviet blue-collar workers who may be considered to be low or unskilled declined markedly during the same period, while the percentage of highly skilled industrial workers increased significantly.

By the 1980s, income, consumption levels, education, and prestige had become distributed among workers. When skill, sectoral, and geographic variables are taken into consideration, some groups of workers received greater compensation than did white-collar employees. The blue-collar/white-collar divide, once so pronounced in the Soviet social structure, became blurred by the emergence of a new working middle class.

The political significance of such broad social tendencies is considerable within a system that bases its legitimacy on its ability to represent the interests of the working class. During the 1950s, working class interests could be thought of as relatively homogenous, like the working class itself. Nikita Khrushchev's efforts to reduce wage differentials were seen as essentially "pro-worker" as well as "pro-peasant," in that blue-collar employees and collective farmers were concentrated almost exclusively in lower income brackets. Once workers became spread out along a continuum of income levels, greater wage equality need not benefit all workers. Soviet politicians of the 1980s, unlike their counterparts in the 1950s, must select from among a range of labor policy options having a differentiated impact on the industrial working class. Choosing to link wages to productivity, as Gorbachev has done, has ensured that contemporary wage policies differentiate among industrial workers every bit as much as they separate blue-collar from white-collar workers.

To the extent that Gorbachev appeals to the working middle class for support, he must turn his back on the needs of less-skilled and [less]-educated workers. With greater political liberalization, tensions can explode as social unrest and industrial disorder increase. The rash of wildcat strikes throughout the spring of 1989, as well as the better-publicized job actions by Siberian and Ukrainian coal miners and Leningrad rail workers in July, demonstrate the volatility of a labor regime under which traditionally favored elements of the industrial labor force now find themselves being left behind by other groups of workers for the first time. Both miners and rail workers, once glorified as heros, languish in a cycle of deteriorating living standards.

Recent strike actions in the Soviet Union amplify the problems confronting the Soviet trade union and Communist Party agencies as a consequence of a four-decade trend towards greater heterogeneity within the Soviet working class. The problem of the moment before the Soviet political leadership is not merely that Soviet workers—or any other social group—"want more." Rather, it is that the social organization of the Soviet working class has become sufficiently fragmented that choices must be made among social substrata that did not exist as recently as a generation ago. The Soviet Union's Quiet Revolution had already transformed labor relations before Mikhail Gorbachev came to power in April 1985.

WHITE-COLLAR PROFESSIONALS

The diversification that had been taking place in the Soviet white-collar world was every bit as complex as that which had occurred among industrial workers. Throughout the four decades between 1940 and 1980, the proportion of the Soviet work force employed in agriculture dropped steadily from roughly one-in-two employees to one-in-five, a work force ratio between agricultural and non-agricultural sectors roughly equivalent to that found in Italy in 1971. Concomitantly, the Soviet Union's non-agricultural work force grew, with industrial and construction sectors dominating employment by the early 1960s. Since 1965, however, the process of redistribution of the non-agricultural labor force among economic sectors has slackened, although service sector employment surpassed agricultural employment in the 1970s. The Soviet Union has come to resemble other advanced industrial societies in its degree of urbanization (66% in 1987) and, to only a slightly lesser degree, in its level of educational achievement. It has only begun to make the transformation to a service-oriented economy.

This dramatic restructuring of the Soviet economy has been accompanied by a rapid expansion in the number of white-collar professionals based largely in leading metropolitan areas. Between 1960 and 1980, employment in trade, health, education, culture and the arts, science, finance and state agencies more or less doubled. In science alone, the number of employees increased nine fold between 1950 and 1985, with the number of holders of all advanced degrees multiplying ten times during the same period. This growth took place at a time when the Soviet educational system discriminated against the children of working class origin, thereby inhibiting upward mobility and encouraging elite regeneration.

The structure of Soviet society began to solidify during the Brezhnev period around new groupings. As a result, society began to resemble a mature industrial social structure with relatively stable, multi-generational substrata. Social arrangements incorporating significant numbers of white-collar professionals and semi-professionals, clusters that had not existed in a stable form in Soviet society for well over a half-century, were fashioned throughout the 1960s and 1970s. Given their elite status, white-collar professionals based in the country's leading urban centers offered important social and cultural role models for other social groups. Many of these white-collar groups could be expected to respond in a distinctive manner to various elements of any package of political or economic reform put forward by the Communist Party's leadership.

The emergence of a reasonably well educated general population recast a multitude of social, political, military, and economic relationships. Higher levels of educational achievement usually are accompanied by skills that are readily transferable to a variety of institutional environments. In general, the more highly educated the person, the more independent he or she will be from the traditional paternalistic institutional ties. Authority based on long-standing personal and institutional relationships becomes more fluid and open-ended as employees become less dependent on employers. Societies experiencing the kind of broad social change reflected in increasing levels of education and urbanization frequently undergo a dramatic reorientation in authority relations, a quiet revolution of the mind. That revolution accompanied the emergence during the 1960s and 1970s of a developed industrial economy in the Soviet Union. . . .

QUIET REVOLUTIONS AND TRANSITIONS FROM AUTHORITARIANISM

For more than a generation before Mikhail Gorbachev emerged as the Soviet Union's supreme political leader, Soviet society had been coming apart, as the social groupings forged by the press of Stalinism became ever more fragmented. This historic social transformation took place quietly. Few Western specialists on Soviet affairs seemed to be aware, for example, that a greater percentage of the Soviet population had moved from the countryside to the city during the Khrushchev and Brezhnev years than during the massive industrialization drive of Stalin's initial prewar five year plans. Entire new social strata were formed during Leonid Brezhnev's "period of stagnation," some for the first time in Russian history. This process of social differentiation released pent-up social energies, expanded the personal space of Soviet citizens, and generally undercut the legitimacy of institutional structures inherited with remarkably few modifications from the period of High Stalinism. The Soviet population increasingly came to resemble the industrialized world in terms of educational achievement, employment patterns, and cultural taste. . . .

Throughout most of its history, the Soviet Union has lacked both the institutional arrangements and the leadership skills required to manage conflicts among diverse groups without resorting to repression. The Soviet state's claims to legitimacy were long based on an assumed harmony of interests among the "non-antagonistic" groups that constituted Soviet society. Faced with the growing differentiation of Soviet society during the 1960s and 1970s, Soviet political leaders of the 1980s have come to consider new economic and political arrangements intended to dissipate the growing tensions between new and old within Soviet society.

Political leaders frequently look to their own pasts for possible solutions to current pressing problems. We might expect Soviet politicians to view the period of Lenin's New Economic Policy, or NEP (1921–1928) with heightened interest. Many observers discerned just such a rise in the attention paid to the 1920s by Soviet political thinkers and activists throughout the 1970s and 1980s.

The NEP, with its mix of public and private economic institutions, its balance of working class political power and peasant economic power, and its limited cultural pluralism, provided a set of mechanisms through which the new Bolshevik leadership of the 1920s could seek a truce with several of the competing elements of a divided and contentious society. As Gorbachev and his colleagues fumbled for constructive responses to the malaise of the late 1970s, a malaise created at least in part by the increased social fragmentation of the post-Stalin era, Soviet political discourse naturally adopted NEP vocabulary and concepts. The NEP offered a uniquely legitimate model for Gorbachev, or any other Soviet leader, to begin to seek an accommodation among the diverse and differentiated political, economic, and social relationships that had emerged during the seemingly stagnant Brezhnev period.

We are now at a point at which our analysis can benefit from the introduction of comparative perspectives on social and political change. A number of specialists came together during 1979 and 1980 at an ongoing conference series convened at Washington, D.C.'s Woodrow Wilson International Center for Scholars to examine and monitor the processes by which a number of Latin American and Southern European authoritarian regimes were beginning to assume more democratic characteristics. Guillermo O'Donnell and Philippe C. Schmitter sought to draw together what had been learned by the conferees in a summary volume, *Transitions from Authoritarian Rule: Tentative Conclusions about Uncertain Democracies.* . . .

O'Donnell and Schmitter point out in their concluding overview that transitions from authoritarian rule often involve two distinct processes. Liberalization redefines and extends the individual and institutional rights. Democratization involves the more complex process of establishing both the right of citizens to be treated as equal in collective decision-making, and the obligation of those implementing such choices to be equally accountable and accessible to the citizens. In other words, democratization entails extending the rules and procedures of citizenship to political institutions previously governed by other principles (e.g., coercive control, social tradition, expert judgment, or administrative practice). It also means expanding the rights of citizens to embrace previously excluded groups of individuals (e.g., non-taxpayers, illiterates, women, youth, ethnic minorities, foreign residents). Finally it includes enlarging the range of issues and institutions subjected to citizen participation (e.g., state agencies, military establishments, partisan organizations, interest associations, productive enterprises, educational institutions). Both processes have been evident in the Soviet case. The glasnost of Gorbachev's initial years in power liberalized the enforcement of individual and institutional rights. Simultaneously, the perestroika of legislative institutions during 1988 and 1989 democratized the political process by expanding the range of issues and institutions subjected to citizen review (witness the new Supreme Soviet review of ministerial appointments and the unprecedented, in the Soviet context, establishment of Supreme Soviet oversight bodies in the areas of internal security and military affairs).

They are careful to observe that there is a great deal of variation among the countries examined by their colleagues, and that neither liberalization nor democratization proceed without setbacks, reversals, and difficulties. Nonetheless, they are able to identify a sequence of events shared in the broadest sense by the examined authoritarian regimes that were undergoing liberalization and/ or democratization.

Unlike the past, when periods of thaw were followed by renewed repression, a transition to a qualitatively different regime occurred when social mobilization in support of change extended beyond the capacities of the regimes in power to control it. The old regimes did not simply turn themselves into democracies overnight. Rather, a complex sequence of piecemeal reforms gradually extended citizen involvement in the political process. The cumulative effect of a number of steps towards liberalization and democratization brought about qualitative changes in the political life of the regimes.

O'Donnell and Schmitter note that the case studies on which they base their review reveal initial interest in change among intellectuals. Members of the "privileged sectors" in society—industrialists, merchants, bankers in Latin America, perhaps managers and some regional party elites in the Soviet Union—begin to see how they might benefit from variation in the existing rules of the game. Next, society's "middle sector" becomes involved in the process of change through the activities of human rights activists outside the regime, and legal reformers within the existing system. Finally, a popular upsurge of interest in dismantling authoritarian institutions surfaces. In an effort to manage escalating disenchantment, regimes frequently call tightly controlled elections to reduce tensions. Unexpectedly, the staunchest guardians of the older order are defeated, even if they are not actually removed from their offices. The old cycle of thaw and retrenchment that, in some cases, had continued unabated for years thus comes to an end, bringing into existence a qualitatively different regime.

They caution that there is nothing inevitable about this cycle, and it need not ultimately lead to democratization in any event. A desire by many to settle old scores is balanced by fear of a backlash from supporters of the old order, including the military and the security police. Yet, extreme backlash in the form of coups d'etat has not materialized in Southern Europe and Latin America, in part, O'Donnell and Schmitter speculate, because so many of the participants in the reform process are mindful of that possibility and moderate their behavior accordingly. . . .

A PERESTROIKA OF THE MIND

Interpretations predicated on the Soviet Union's *muzhik* culture tend to emphasize sources of resistance to change, especially during the recent past. A number of Soviet and non-Soviet academic, political, and journalistic commentators have spoken of cultural factors that inhibit and may ultimately destroy Gorbachevian perestroika, such as quiescent and deferential attitudes toward authority, innate distrust of entrepreneurship, tendencies toward envy rather than jealousy (i.e., a desire to level living standards by "bringing down" those with more, rather than a desire to raise oneself to a higher standard). Evidence of deep-seated resistance to change remains visible and powerful. Robust countervailing tendencies exist within Soviet society as well. Western specialists need to develop an analytic vocabulary that encompasses the social fragmentation that emerged in the Soviet Union during the seeming stagnation of the 1970s.

There can be no doubt that the Soviet economy is not performing well. Half-hearted attempts to stimulate growth of a private cooperative sector have not brought about miraculous changes in the quality of consumer life in the Soviet Union. Deep resentments have been building up across a wide spectrum of society about allegedly lavish and ill-gotten profits obtained by many cooperative managers. Muscovites regale visitors with tales of a "mafia" that has seized control of the city's fledgling cooperative sector. Cooperatives nevertheless remain in business and are making their presence felt. According to a guide published by a cooperative information service, for example, there were some 150 cooperative cafés and restaurants operating in the capital in October 1988. Acknowledging that such a number is modest indeed for a city of nearly 9 million inhabitants, it represents rather vigorous growth, given the overtly hostile climate within which Soviet entrepreneurs must function.

Less visible cooperatives in the service and scientific sectors are perhaps of greater importance for long-term economic growth. Cooperative enterprises have mushroomed in computer programming, office services, applied social science research, consultancy, and the like. White-collar entrepreneurs work hidden from public view under contracts with foreign companies, state agencies, and each other. Such co-ops provide a congenial refuge for younger professionals disenchanted with the constraints of official bureaucratic work environments. The risk-taking involved in establishing professional cooperatives stands in sharp contrast to the behavior of past generations of Soviet professionals who seemingly craved bureaucratic security. Behavioral variation runs deeper than variations in generational preferences and points to a quiet revolution of the mind that accompanied the formation of a permanent professional class during the half-century following the Second World War.

Manifestations of a quiet revolution of the mind have been particularly pronounced in the political sphere. 1989 will be remembered as a remarkable year in Soviet political history. The year's events consistently challenged previous notions of the unthinkable in Soviet political life. Such was the case with: rowdy local caucuses to nominate candidates for the new Congress of People's Deputies, unpredictable elections to that Congress in March (at which time a score of established Communist Party officials were defeated—frequently even without opposition candidates running against them); blanket live national television coverage of the most open and contentious official gathering in three-quarters of a century; the convening of a new national legislative body that immediately established its prerogative of review of all state agencies, including those responsible for state security; and the creation of a proto-opposition party within the Supreme Soviet, the "Inter-Regional Group." At each stage, and despite significant variations in the pace of political change across regional and ethnic boundaries, Soviet citizens pursued demonstrations, strikes, protest actions, and electoral politics, to push the political system to new frontiers of liberalization and democratization.

Social historians have demonstrated that the Soviet population has never been as compliant as was once imagined. Recent attempts by Soviet citizens to seize control of their own destinies nevertheless remain breathtakingly unprecedented. They suggest that a "quiet revolution of the mind" has indeed accompanied the social and economic metamorphosis of the post-Stalin era.

If the Soviet Union's Quiet Revolution has fostered entire new social strata with unique interests and behavior patterns, older social and economic groups continue to live side by side with the new. The political task of the moment is to structure conflict and competition among old and new in a manner that destroys neither. Otherwise, the regime will fail both to retain the loyalty of its long-standing beneficiaries and to mobilize on its own behalf the creativity and vitality of the very working middle class and professional groups on which the regime must depend in an ever more competitive international arena. The ability of the Communist Party's leadership to master social forces unleashed by the emergence of an urban society remains unknown at the moment. The present is a period of transition, while the future is unfamiliar. After all, even such seemingly successful transitions from authoritarian rule as those which transpired in Spain and Portugal remain incomplete, as they retain strong undercurrents of a fascistic political culture. Writing in the popular journal *Twentieth Century and Peace*, Aleksandr Smagin and Igor Zalygin urge Soviet leaders to consider the experience of Western European nations—especially West Germany and Italy—in their fight against political extremism and terrorism during the 1960s and 1970s.

According to Smagin and Zalygin, terrorism emerges during periods of radical change that follow a totalitarian past. They caution against the impulse to blame extremism on openness, countering that a sustained commitment to democratic institutions has proven itself to be the only reliable means for defusing political extremism. Their analysis reflects a quiet revolution of the mind that has prompted the dramatic political reforms taking place since Mikhail Gorbachev came to power in 1985. Simultaneously, their work accents the as yet unresolved confrontation between reform and a long-standing yearning to revert to more authoritarian methods of political control. The future of Soviet political and economic reform will be determined by the extent to which the quiet revolution of the mind already underway can continue to outrace longer-standing authoritarian predilections among both governors and governed in the Soviet Union.

18.3 DANIEL BELL

The Third Technological Revolution: And Its Possible Socioeconomic Consequences

Sociologist and futurist Daniel Bell (b. 1919) is a leading analyst of the current and future societal transformations associated with the emergence of the postindustrial society. Bell is the Henry Ford II Professor of Social Sciences at Harvard University and a member of the President's Commission on Technical Automation and Economic Progress. He is also the author of several books on politics, government, and sociology, including *The Deficits: How Big? How Long? How Dangerous?* (New York University Press, 1985). He has achieved notoriety as the first futurist to extensively chart the course of the postindustrial society from the early 1970s to the end of this century.

In the article that follows, Bell presents his recent thinking on America's course in the postindustrial future. He introduces his future scenario by reviewing the two major earlier technological revolutions of the industrial era: (1) the introduction of steam power and (2) the innovations of electricity and chemistry. These have led to major social changes in the past two centuries. He posits that a third technological revolution based on computers and telecommunication is currently revolutionizing the social structure of the postindustrial society. Bell's analysis reveals that there has been a shift from a predominantly industrial labor force to a professional, technical, and managerial work force in the United States.

Key Concept: technological revolution

We are today on the rising slope of a third technological revolution. It is a rising slope, for we have passed from the plus-minus stage of invention and innovation into the crucial period of diffusion. The rates of diffusion will vary, depending upon the economic conditions and political stabilities of societies.

351

Yet the phenomenon cannot be reversed, and its consequences may be even greater than the previous two technological revolutions that reshaped the West and now, with the spread of industrialization, other parts of the world as well. . . .

THREE TECHNOLOGICAL REVOLUTIONS

Any dating or numbering is somewhat arbitrary, yet if we look at the nature of the technological changes and their consequences, we are justified, I believe, in speaking of three major technological revolutions in the Western world in modern times.

The first is the introduction of steam power, more than two hundred years ago, an innovation identified largely with the name of James Watt. . . .

With steam power we could achieve a variety of technological feats impossible before. One was to have steam pumps. England was an island bedded on coal, but one could not dig down very far because of the large pools of underground water, which hand pumps could not extract. With steam pumps, the water could be expelled and coal dug out to create an iron and steel industry. With steam, we could create railroads that could go faster (and longer) than any known animal, steamships that could sail faster, and more steadily, than any wind-driven sails, machines that could card and spin and thus create cloth faster than the nimble fingers of a trained woman. More important than these, the first technological revolution introduced, and made possible, a vast new conception in the creation of wealth: the idea of productivity, the simple proposition of greater output with less effort, as a result of investment. . . .

The second technological revolution, only a hundred years or so ago, can be identified with two innovations: electricity and chemistry. Electricity gives us a new, enhanced form of power that can be transmitted hundreds of miles, as steam cannot, thus permitting new kinds of decentralization that the bunching of machines in a factory, to minimize the loss of steam heat, could not. Electricity gives us a new source of light, which changes our rhythms of night and day. Electricity allows us to code messages on wires or to transform voice electric signals, so as to create telephone and radio. Chemistry, for the first time, allows us to create synthetics, from dyes to plastics, from fibers to vinyls, that are unknown in nature.

And now, the third technological revolution. If we think of the changes that are beginning to occur, we think, inevitably of things and the ways we seek to use them: computers, telecommunications, and the like. But to think in these terms is to confuse applications or instruments with some underlying processes that are the crucial understandings for this revolution, and only by identifying the relevant underlying processes can we begin to "track" the vast number of changes in socioeconomic and political structures that may take place. Four technological innovations underlie this new technological revolution, and I shall describe each briefly:

(1) *The change of all mechanical and electric and electromechanical systems to electronics.* The machines of industrial society were mechanical instruments, powered first by steam and later by electricity. Increasingly, electronic systems have taken over and replaced mechanical parts. A telephone system was basically a set of mechanical parts (e.g. a dial system) in which signals were converted into electricity. Today, the telephone is entirely electronic. Printing was a system in which mechanical type was applied, with inked surfaces, to paper; today, printing is electronic. So is television, with solid-state circuits. The changes mean a reduction in the large number of parts, and an incredible increase in the speed of transmission. . . .

(2) *Miniaturization.* One of the most remarkable changes is the "shrinkage" of units that conduct electricity or switch electrical impulses. Our previous modes were vacuum tubes, each, as in the old-fashioned radios, about two or three inches high. The invention of the transistor is akin to the invention of steam power, for it represented a quantum change in the ability to manufacture microelectronic devices for the hundreds of different functions of control, regulation, direction, and memory that microprocessors perform. . . .

(3) *Digitalization.* In the new technology information is represented by digits. Digits are numbers, discrete in their relation to one another, rather than continuous variables. A telephone, for example, was an analogue system, for sound is a wave. Through digital switching a telephone becomes converted to the use of binary systems. One sees this in sound recordings, as on musical discs. The third technological revolution involves the conversion of all previous systems into digital form.

(4) *Software.* Older computers had the instructions or operating systems wired into the machine, and one had to learn a programming language, such as Cobol or Fortran, or the more specialized languages such as Pascal or Lisp, to use the machine. Software, an independent program, frees the user to do various tasks quickly. . . .

The most crucial fact about the new technology is that it is not a separate domain (such as the label "high-tech" implies), but a set of changes that pervade all aspects of society and reorganize all older relationships. . . .

We can already see the shape of the manifold changes. The old distinctions in communication between telephone (voice), television (image), computer (data), and text (facsimile) have broken down, physically interconnected by digital switching, and made compatible as a single unified set of teletransmissions. . . .

The intellectual task is how to "order" these changes in comprehensible ways, rather than just describing the multitude of changes, and thus to provide some basis of analysis rooted in sociological theory. What I intend to do, in the following sections, is to present a number of "social frameworks," or matrices, which may allow us to see how existing social structures come under pressure for change, and the ways in which such changes may occur. I repeat one caveat stated earlier: Technology does not determine social change; technology provides instrumentalities and potentialities. The ways that these are used are social choices. The frameworks that I sketch below, therefore, indicate the "areas" within which relevant changes may occur.

THE POSTINDUSTRIAL SOCIETY

The postindustrial society is not a projection or extrapolation of existing trends in Western society; it is a new principle of social-technical organization and ways of life, just as the industrial system (e.g., factories) replaced an agrarian way of life. It is, first, a shift in the centrality of industrial production, as it was organized on the basis of standardization and mass production. . . .

One can think of the world as divided into three kinds of social organization. One is preindustrial. These are primarily extractive industries: farming, mining, fishing, timber. This is still the lot of most of Africa, Latin America, and Southeast Asia, where 60 percent or more of the labor force is engaged in these activities. These are largely what I call "games against nature," subject to the vicissitudes of the weather, the exhaustion of the soils, the thinning out of forests, or the higher costs of the recovery of minerals and metals.

Similar sections of the world have been industrial, engaged in fabrication, the application of energy to machines for the mass production of goods. These have been the countries around the Atlantic littoral: those of Western Europe and the United States, and then the Soviet Union and Japan. Work, here, is a game against fabricated nature: the hitching of men to machines, the organized rhythmic pacing of work in a highly coordinated fashion.

The third type is postindustrial. These are activities that are primarily processing, control, and information. It is a social way of life that is, increasingly, a "game between persons." More important, there is a new principle of innovation, especially of knowledge and its relation to technology.

Let me describe some of the lineaments of the postindustrial society. It is, first, a society of services. In the United States today, more than 70 percent of the labor force is engaged in services. Yet "services" is inherently an ambiguous term and, in economic analysis, one without shape because it has been used primarily as a "residual" term. . . .

In a postindustrial society there is an expansion of new kinds of service. These are human services—education, health, social work, social services—and professional services—analysis and planning, design, programming, and the like. In the older conceptions of classical economics (including Marxism), services were thought of as inherently unproductive, since wealth was identified with goods, and lawyers and priests or barbers or waiters did not contribute to the national wealth. Yet surely education and health services contribute to the increased skills and strengths of a population, while professional services (such as linear programming in the organization of production, or new modes of layout of work and social interaction) contribute to the productivity of an enterprise and society. And the important fact is that the expansion of a postindustrial sector of a society requires the expansion of higher education and the education of many more in the population in abstract conceptual, technical, and alphanumeric skills.

In the United States today more than 30 percent of the labor force (of more than one hundred million persons) is professional, technical, and managerial, an amazing figure in social history. About 17 percent of the labor force does factory work (the industrial proletariat, in the older Marxian sense of the term), and it is likely that this will shrink to about 10 percent within a decade. If one thinks this is small, consider the fact that fewer than 4 percent of the labor force are farmers, producing a glut of food for the United States—as against 50 percent in 1900. . . .

The decisive change—what I call the axial principle of organization—is a change in the character of knowledge. . . .

What is radically new today is the codification of theoretical knowledge and its centrality for innovation, both of new knowledge and for economic goods and services. . . .

Let us take the relation of technological invention to science in the major sectors of industrial society. If we look at the major industries that were developed then and that still carry over today—steel, electricity, telephone, radio, aviation—we can see that they are all "nineteenth-century" industries (though steel was begun in the eighteenth century by Darby with the invention of the coking process and aviation in the twentieth century by the Wright brothers) created by "talented tinkerers," men who were adroit with the nature of equipment, but who knew little about, or were indifferent to, the developments of science, and in particular the theoretical aspects taking place at the time. . . .

But all of that has now changed radically. Let me take three instances for dramatic effect. . . .

Einstein's [1905] paper on the photoelectric effect flouted the concepts of classical physics, which held that light (like sound) was a wave. The paper postulated, hypothetically, that light was a *quanta*, or a stream of discontinuous particles. This paper met with extraordinary resistance among experimental physicists, was not vindicated experimentally until a decade later, and was finally resolved theoretically by the complementary principle of wave-particle dualism. Yet the crucial point is that Einstein's paper was the starting point for much twentieth-century work in optics, from such simple things as we now see in the application of photoelectric effects, in breaking light beams, to the work of Charles Townes in creating lasers (an acronym for "light amplification stimulated by the emission of radiation"), Dennis Gabor on holography, and the development of photonics as the new frontier for telecommunications.

The second illustration is the revolution in solid-state physics. The contemporary conceptions of solid-state physics play no role, and to some extent are unthinkable, within the purview of classical physics. Our shifts in the conception of matter go back to the model of the hydrogen atom that Niels Bohr constructed in 1912, with the idea of the nucleus and the orbits of electrons around the nucleus. The basic step forward was taken in 1927 with the picture of the lattice structure of matter, by Felix Bloch, in which one could show how electrons, in their spins, "jumped" from orbit to orbit as energy is given off. These "pictures" of the structures of matter led to the discovery of the transistor at Bell Labs by Bardeen, Brittain, and Shockley in the late 1940s and to the revolution in solid-state technology that is the basis of modern-day electronics and the computer.

And, finally, an innovation of an entirely different sort, Alan Turing's mathematical paper in 1937, "On Computable Numbers," which is the fundamental basis for programming, storage, and the creation of the digital computer. In 1928, the great German mathematician David Hilbert, at the World Congress of Mathematics, had laid down three questions in order to see whether a complete formulization of mathematics was possible. He asked whether mathematics could be complete, consistent, and decidable. Two years later, in 1930, the Czech mathematician Kurt Gödel had produced his theorems, which showed that, given the problems of providing a complete and consistent set of axioms, if mathematics was complete it could not be consistent, and if consistent it could not be complete.

When Alan Turing wrote his paper, which showed that there could be a principle of decidability (whether in principle a problem was solvable or not) if the numbers were computable, he invented a tape that would be a "table of behavior" that could through binary rules compute any possible configuration of finite numbers. The idea of a computer goes back to the work of an earlier Cambridge mathematician, Charles Babbage who in 1837 conceived of a "difference engine" that could mechanize any mechanical operation. What Turing's innovation did was utilize binary numbers (Boolean algebra) with internal program storage, to allow for the development of an automatic electronic digital computer. Thus, theory preceded artifice.

One consequence of this is that invention, or the "talent tinkerer," disappears from the horizon. There will always be innovations and changes in "things" that will create new products. But the basic point remains that fundamental innovations in theoretical knowledge—not just in physics, as in the illustrations above, but in biology (going back to the discovery of the double helix of the DNA molecule by Crick and Watson, and to the branching structure of molecular biology by Monod, Jacobs, and Lwoff) or in cognitive psychology (as the basis for expert inference systems)—become the new principle of innovation in society.

I said before that one has to distinguish technological changes (even when they are now not only in machine technology but in intellectual technology) from the more valuable changes in social structure. Changes in technology, as I have insisted, do not determine social changes; they pose problems that the political controllers of society have to deal with. . . . Let me briefly, however, with the more delimited framework of a postindustrial hypothesis, pose a number of questions.

1. The shrinkage of the traditional manufacturing sectors—augmented, in these instances, by the rising competition from Asia and the ease whereby the routinized, low-value-added production can be taken up by some of the Third

World societies—raises the question whether Western societies (all or some) can reorganize their production to move toward the new "high-tech, high-value-added" kinds of specialized production, or whether they will be "headquarter economies" providing investment and financial services to the rest of the world.

2. The costs of transition. Can these be managed? And if so, by the "market," or by some kind of "industrial policy"?

3. The reorganization of an educational system to provide a greater degree of "alphanumeric" fluency in larger portions of the population who would be employed in these postindustrial sectors.

4. The character of "work." If character is defined by work, then we shall see a society where "nature" is largely excluded and "things" are largely excluded within the experience of persons. If more and more individuals are in work situations that involve a "game between persons," clearly more and more questions of equity and "comparable worth" will arise. The nature of hierarchy in work may be increasingly questioned, and new modes of participation may be called for. All of these portend huge changes in the structures of organization from those we have seen in the older models of the army and the church, or the industrial factory organization, which have been the structures of organization (if not domination) until now.

SOCIETAL GEOGRAPHY AND INFRASTRUCTURES

Historically every society has been tied together by three kinds of infrastructure: These have been the nodes and highways of trade and transactions, of the location of cities and the connections between peoples. The first has been transportation: rivers, roads, canals, and, in modern times, railroads, highways, and airplanes. The second is energy systems: Hydropower, electricity grids, oil pipelines, gas pipelines, and the like. And the third has been communications: postal systems (which moved along highways), then telegraph (the first break in that linkage), telephone, radio, and now the entire panoply of new technological means from microwave to satellites.

The oldest system has been transportation. The breakdown between isolated segments of a society comes when roads are built to connect these, so that trade can commence. The location of human habitats has come with the crossing of roads or the merging of rivers and arms of lakes: traders stop with their wares, farmers bring their food, artisans settle down to provide services, and towns and cities develop.

Within the system of transport, the most important has been water routes. They are the easiest means for carrying bulk items; waterways weave around natural obstacles; tides and currents provide means of additional motion. It is striking to realize that almost every major city in the world, in the last millennia (leaving aside the fortified hill towns that arose during the breakdown of commerce and provided a means of protection against marauders) is located on water: Rome on the Tiber, Paris on the Seine, London on the Thames, not to mention the great cities located on the oceans, seas, and great lakes.

If one looks at industrial societies, the location of cities and the hubs of production come from the interplay of water and resources. . . .

Now all this is changing, as industrial society begins to give way. Communication begins to replace transportation as the major node of connection between people and as the mode of transaction.

Water and natural resources become less important as locational factors for cities, particularly as, with the newer technology, the size of manufacturing plants begins to shrink. Proximity to universities and culture becomes more important as a locational factor. If we look at the major development of high-tech in the United States, we see that the four major concentrations respond to these elements: Silicon Valley, in relation to Stanford University and San Francisco; the circumferential Route 128 around Boston, in relation to M.I.T. and Harvard; Route 1 in New Jersey, from New Brunswick to Trenton, with Princeton University at its hub; and Minneapolis-St. Paul in Minnesota, clustering around the large state university and the Twin City metropolis.

What we see, equally, with communication networks becoming so cheap, is a great pull toward decentralization. . . . Today, with the increasing cheapness of communication and the high cost of land, density and the external economies become less critical. So we find that dozens of major U.S. corporations, in the last decade or so, have moved their basic headquarters from New York to the suburban areas where land is cheaper, and transport to and from work easier: northeast to Fairfield County in Connecticut; north to Westchester County in New York; and west and southwest to Mercer County in New Jersey.

In Japan we see a major effort now under way, the Technopolis project, to create large, far-flung regional centers for the new computer and telecommunications industries. For status reasons, many corporations maintain a display building in New York or Tokyo; but the major managerial activities are now decentralized.

As geography is no longer the controller of costs, distance becomes a function not of space but of time; and the costs of time and rapidity of communication become the decisive variables. And, with the spread of mini- and microcomputers, the ability to "down-load" databases and memories, and to place these in the small computers (as well as give them access to the large mainframes) means there is less of a necessary relation to fixed sites in the location of work.

As with habitats, so with markets. What is a market? Again, it is a place where roads crossed and rivers merged and individuals settled down to buy and sell their wares. Markets were places. Perhaps no longer. . . .

What we have here, clearly, are the nerves, nodes and ganglia of a genuine international economy tied together in ways the world has never seen before. What this means—and I shall return to the question at the close of this article— is a widening of the arenas, the multiplication of the numbers of actors, and an increase in the velocity and volatility of transactions and exchanges. The crucial question is whether the older institutional structures are able to deal with this extraordinary volume of interactions.

359

Daniel Bell

THE SOCIAL ORGANIZATION OF PRODUCTION

The modern corporation—I take the United States as the model—is less than a hundred years old. Business, the exchange of goods and services, is as old as human civilization itself. But the modern corporation, as a social form to coordinate men, materials and markets for the mass production and mass consumption of goods, is an institution that has taken shape only in the past century.

There are three kinds of innovators who conjoined to create the modern industrial system. The greatest attention has been paid to those who have been the organizers of the production system itself: Eli Whitney, who created standardized forms and interchangeable parts in production; Frederick Taylor, who designed the measurement of work; and Henry Ford, who created the assembly line and mass production. (There were of course other forebears, and there were European counterparts: Siemens, Bedeaux, Renault, etc.)

Those who achieved the greatest notoriety were the capitalists, the men who by ruthless means put together the great enterprises: the Carnegies, the Rockefellers, Harriman, the men who initiated the large quasi-monopoly organizations, and the financiers, such as J.P. Morgan, who assembled the monies for the formation of such great corporations as U.S. Steel, General Electric, and the like.

But there was also a different social role, often unnoticed even in the history of business, played by men who, curiously, were probably just as important, and perhaps more so: the organizers of the corporate form, those who rationalized the system and gave it an ongoing structural continuity. I will discuss three individuals who symbolize the three crucial structural changes: one was Walter Teagle, of Standard Oil of New Jersey, who created vertical integration; another was Theodore N. Vail, who fashioned the American Telephone and Telegraph Co. and imposed the idea of a single uniform system; and the third was Alfred P. Sloan, of General Motors, who created the system of financial controls and budgetary accounting that still rules the corporate world today.

These three men created modern industrial capitalism. It is my thesis, implicit in this article and which can be stated only schematically here, that this system, marvelously adaptive to a mass-production society, is increasingly dysfunctional in today's postindustrial world.

Vertical integration, the control of all aspects of a product—in the case of Teagle, from oil in the ground, to shipping, refining, and distribution to industrial customers and retail outlets—was created for the clear reasons of economies of scale, reduction of transaction costs, the utilization of information within the entire process, and the control of prices, from raw materials to finished goods. What vertical integration did, as Alfred Chandler has pointed out in his book *The Visible Hand,* was to destroy "producer markets" within the chain of production and impose uniform controls. In the previous system, one of merchant capitalism, production was in the hands of independent artisans or small-business companies, and all of this was funneled through the matrix of the merchant capitalist, who ordered the goods he needed, or contracted production to the small workshop, and sold finished products to the customers. But the creation of large-scale, mass-produced, identical goods made vertical integration a functional necessity.

The idea of a single system arose when Vail, seeking to build a telephone utility, beheld the railroad system in the United States, where railroad systems grew "higgledy-piggledy," without plan, and often for financial reasons, to sell inflated stock. Franchises were obtained from corrupt legislatures or from congressional land grants, and the roads were built in sprawling ways. Before the advent of coast-to-coast air flight, if a traveler wanted to go from New York to the West Coast by train, he could not do so on a single system. He could take one of two competitive railroads from New York to Chicago, where he changed trains and then took one of three competitive systems to the Coast. (If one wished to ship a hog, or freight, it was not necessary to change trains. Animals or freight goods, unlike human beings, could not pick themselves up and move to another freight car; it was cheaper to shuttle the freight car onto different lines.) Even today there is no unified rational rail system in the United States.

Vail, in building a telephone network, decided that if there was to be efficient service between a person calling from any point in the United States to any other point, there would have to be a single set of "long lines" connecting all the local telephones to one another. Until the recent federal court decision which broke up the American Telephone and Telegraph Co., it was a unified, single system.

Alfred P. Sloan's innovations came about when he took over the sprawling General Motors from William C. Durant, a Wall Street speculator who had put together the different automobile companies (named for their early founders: Chevrolet, Olds, Cadillac, and the like) into a single firm, General Motors. But Durant had little talent for creating a rational structure. Alfred P. Sloan, the MIT-trained engineer who was installed as head of the company by the Du Pont interests (the largest block of stockholders until the courts forced them to divest their holdings about twenty-five years ago), installed unit cost accounting and financial controls with a single aim: to obtain a clear return on investment for the monies given to the different divisions. Durant never knew which of the companies was making money, and which was not; he did not know whether it was cheaper to make his own steel or buy outside, make his own parts or buy outside. Sloan rationalized the company. His key innovation was a pricing system for the different lines of automobiles that would provide a 20 percent return on investment based on a stipulated capacity, a break-even point based on overhead and fixed costs, and a market share for the particular line of car.

Together, these innovations were the corporate principles of modern industrial capitalism. Why are they now dysfunctional?

In the case of production, the older standardized, routinized, low-value-added forms of production are being increasingly taken over by the newly industrializing societies, where cheap wages provide the crucial cost differential in competition. More than that, the newer technologies—particularly computer-aided design (CAD), numerical-control machine tools (NC), and computer-aided manufacturing (CAM)—now make possible *flexible*, shorter-run, batch productions that can be easily adapted to different kinds of markets, and which can be responsive to specialized products and customized demands.

One of the great success stories in this respect is Italy, in such an "old-fashioned" industry as textiles. The textile district of Prato—the group of towns in Central Italy in the provinces of Florence and Pistoia—was able to survive and flourish because it could adapt. As two MIT scholars have pointed out (relying, of course, on Italian studies), "Prato's success rests on two factors: a long-term shift from standard to fashionable fabrics and a corresponding reorganization of production from large integrated mills to technologically sophisticated shops specializing in various phases of production—a modern *systeme* Motte."

But what holds true for textiles is true for a wide variety of industries as well. In steel, integrated production is now cumbersome and costly, and it is the minimills, with their specialized, flexible production, and the specialty steels that have become the basis for survival in the Western world. It is not, thus, deindustrialization, but a new form of industrialization, which is taking place.

In the case of telecommunications—to be brief— the breakdown of the old distinctions between telephone, computer, television, and facsimile (Xerox) means that new, highly differentiated systems—private branch exchanges, local area networks, "internal" communication networks between firms, international satellite communication—all emphasize diversity rather than uniformity, with many specialized systems rather than a single product such as the telephone.

In the case of Sloan's system of a return on investment through budgetary controls, the assumptions he made were those of a quasi-monopoly or oligopoly in a "steady-state" market, and that kind of financial planning can scarcely adapt to a changing world where old product lines are breaking down (one need simply consider the old distinctions between banks, insurance companies, brokerage houses, credit firms, real estate investment, all of which become to some extent interchangeable under the rubric of financial-asset management), where substitutions of products provide price challenges, where market share and cash flow may be more important momentarily, and a long-term commitment necessary technologically, than the simple unit-cost accounting that Alfred Sloan introduced.

In effect, the world of the postindustrial society requires new modes of social organization, and these are only now being fashioned by the new entrepreneurs of the new technology.

THE QUESTION OF SCALE

The crucial question, as I have indicated, is how new social structures will be created in response to the different values of societies, to the new technological instruments of a postindustrial world. Beyond the structural frameworks I have tried to identify, there is one crucial variable that must be taken into account—the change in scale.

It is a cliché of our time that ours is an era of acceleration in the pace of change. I must confess that I do not understand what this actually means. If we seek to use this concept analytically, we find a lack of boundary and meaning. To speak of "change" is in itself meaningless, for the question remains: change of what? To say that "everything" changes is hardly illuminating. And if one speaks of a pace, or of an acceleration in pace, the words imply a metric—a unit of measurement. But what is being measured?

However, one can gain a certain perspective about what is happening by thinking of the concept of scale. A change in the scale of an institution is a change of form. Metaphorically this goes back to Galileo's square-cube law: If you double the size of an object, you triple its volume. There is consequently a question of shape and proportion. A university with fifty thousand students may still be called by the same name it had thirty years before, with five thousand students, but the increase in numbers calls for a change in the institutional structure. And this is true of all social organizations.

What the revolutions in communication are doing is changing the scale of human activities. Given the nature of "real time" communication, we are for the first time forging an interdependent international economy with more and more characteristics of an unstable system in which changes in the magnitudes of some variables, or shocks and disturbances in some of the units, have immediate repercussions in all the others.

The management of scale has been one of the oldest problems in social institutions, whether it be the church, the army, or economic enterprise, let alone the political order. Societies have tended to function reasonably well when there is a congruence of scale between economic activities, social units and organization, and political and administrative control. But increasingly what is happening is a mismatch of scale. As I stated in an essay several years ago, the national state has become too small for the big problems of life, and too big for the small problems. The national state, with its political policies, is increasingly ineffective in dealing with the tidal waves of the international economy (coordination through economic summitry is only a charade) and too big, when political decisions are concentrated in a bureaucratic center, for the diversity and initiative of the varied local regional units under its control. To that extent, if there is a single overriding sociological problem in the post-industrial society—particularly in the management of transition—it is the management of scale.

2.3. From Colin M. Turnbull, *The Mountain People* (Simon & Schuster, 1972). Copyright © 1972 by Colin M. Turnbull. Reprinted by permission of Simon & Schuster, Inc.

3.1. From George Herbert Mead, *Mind, Self and Society* (University of Chicago Press, 1934). Copyright © 1934 by the University of Chicago Press. Reprinted by permission. Notes omitted.

3.2. From David Elkind, "Erik Erikson's Eight Ages of Man: One Man in His Time Plays Many Psychosocial Parts," *The New York Times Magazine* (April 5, 1970). Copyright © 1970 by The New York Times Company. Reprinted by permission.

3.3. From Lenore J. Weitzman, Deborah Eifler, Elizabeth Hokada, and Catherine Ross, "Sex-Role Socialization in Picture Books for Preschool Children," *American Journal of Sociology*, vol. 77, no. 6 (May 1972). Copyright © 1972 by the University of Chicago Press. Reprinted by permission. Notes omitted.

3.4. From J. Allen Williams, Jr., JoEtta A. Vernon, Martha C. Williams, and Karen Malecha, "Sex Role Socialization in Picture Books: An Update," *Social Science Quarterly*, vol. 68, no. 1 (March 1987). Copyright © 1987 by the University of Texas Press. Reprinted by permission. Notes and references omitted.

4.1. From Peter L. Berger, *Invitation to Sociology: A Humanistic Perspective* (Anchor Books, 1963). Copyright © 1963 by Peter L. Berger. Reprinted by permission of Doubleday, a division of Bantam Doubleday Dell Publishing Group, Inc.

4.2. From Erving Goffman, *The Presentation of Self in Everyday Life* (Anchor Books, 1959). Copyright © 1959 by Erving Goffman. Reprinted by permission of Doubleday, a division of Bantam Doubleday Dell Publishing Group, Inc. Some notes omitted.

5.1. From Robert K. Merton, *Social Theory and Social Structure* (Free Press, 1957). Copyright © 1957 by The Free Press; copyright renewed 1985 by Robert K. Merton. Reprinted by permission of The Free Press, a division of Macmillan, Inc. Notes omitted.

5.2. From Edwin H. Sutherland and Donald R. Cressey, *Principles of Criminology*, 7th ed. (J. B. Lippincott, 1966). Copyright © 1966 by Edwin H. Sutherland and Donald R. Cressey. Reprinted by permission.

5.3. From Stanley Milgram, "Some Conditions of Obedience and Disobedience to Authority," *Human Relations*, vol. 18, no. 1 (1965). Copyright © 1965 by Stanley Milgram. Reprinted by permission of Alexandra Milgram, literary executor. Notes omitted.

5.4. From James Q. Wilson, *Thinking About Crime* (Basic Books, 1975). Copyright © 1975 by Basic Books, Inc. Reprinted by permission of Basic Books, a division of HarperCollins Publishers.

6.1. From Charles Horton Cooley, *Social Organization* (Charles Scribner's Sons, 1909). Copyright © 1909 by Charles Scribner's Sons; copyright renewed 1937 by Elsie Jones Cooley.

6.2. From Robert K. Merton, *Social Theory and Social Structure* (Free Press, 1957). Copyright © 1957 by The Free Press; copyright renewed 1985 by Robert K. Merton. Reprinted by permission of The Free Press, a division of Macmillan, Inc. Some notes omitted.

7.1. From Karl Marx and Friedrich Engels, *The Communist Manifesto* (1848). Reprint. International Publishers, 1983. Reprinted by permission of International Publishers Company, Inc. Some notes omitted.

7.2. From Kingsley Davis and Wilbert E. Moore, "Some Principles of Stratification," *American Sociological Review*, vol. 10, no. 2 (1945). References omitted.

14.3. From D. L. Rosenhan, "On Being Sane in Insane Places," *Science*, vol. 179 (January 19, 1973), pp. 250–258. Copyright © 1973 by the American Association for the Advancement of Science. Reprinted by permission. Some notes omitted.

15.1. From Paul R. Ehrlich and Anne H. Ehrlich, "World Population Crisis," *Bulletin of the Atomic Scientists* (April 1986). Copyright © 1986 by the Educational Foundation for Nuclear Science, 6042 South Kimbark, Chicago, IL 60637, USA. Reprinted by permission. A one-year subscription is $30.00.

15.2. From Lester R. Brown, Christopher Flavin, and Edward C. Wolf, "Earth's Vital Signs," *The Futurist* (July/August 1988). Adapted from Lester R. Brown et al., *State of the World 1988* (W. W. Norton, 1988). Copyright © 1988 by the Worldwatch Institute. Reprinted by permission.

16.1. From Robert Redfield, "Antecedents of Urban Life: The Folk Society," *American Journal of Sociology*, vol. 52, no. 4 (January 1947). Copyright © 1947 by the University of Chicago Press. Reprinted by permission. Some notes omitted.

16.2. From Louis Wirth, "Urbanism as a Way of Life," *American Journal of Sociology*, vol. 44, no. 7 (July 1938). Copyright © 1938 by the University of Chicago Press. Reprinted by permission. Notes omitted.

17.1. From Mancur Olson, Jr., *The Logic of Collective Action: Public Goods and the Theory of Groups* (Harvard University Press, 1971). Copyright © 1965, 1971 by the President and Fellows of Harvard College. Reprinted by permission of Harvard University Press. Notes omitted.

17.2. From William A. Gamson, "Violence and Political Power: The Meek Don't Make It," *Psychology Today*, vol. 8 (July 1974). Copyright © 1974 by Sussex Publishers, Inc. Reprinted by permission of *Psychology Today*.

18.1. From Immanuel Wallerstein, "The Rise and Future Demise of the World Capitalist System: Concepts for Comparative Analysis," *Comparative Studies in Society and History* (1974). Copyright © 1974 by Immanuel Wallerstein. Reprinted by permission.

18.2. From Blair A. Ruble, "The Soviet Union's Quiet Revolution," in George W. Breslaver, ed., *Can Gorbechev's Reforms Succeed?* (Center for Slavic and European Languages, 1990). Copyright © 1990 by the Center for Slavic and European Languages, University of California at Berkeley. Reprinted by permission. Notes omitted.

18.3. From Daniel Bell, "The Third Technological Revolution: And Its Possible Socioeconomic Consequences," *Dissent* (Spring 1989). Copyright © 1989 by Daniel Bell. Excerpted and reprinted by permission. Notes omitted.

Index